MODELING AND IDENTIFICATION OF DYNAMIC SYSTEMS

MODELING AND IDENTIFICATION OF DYNAMIC SYSTEMS

N. K. SINHA and B. KUSZTA

Van Nostrand Reinhold Electrical/Computer Science and Engineering Series

 VAN NOSTRAND REINHOLD COMPANY
New York Cincinnati Toronto London Melbourne

Manufactured in the United States of America

Published by Van Nostrand Reinhold Company Inc.
135 West 50th Street, New York, N.Y. 10020

Van Nostrand Reinhold Publishing
1410 Birchmount Road
Scarborough, Ontario MIP 2E7, Canada

Van Nostrand Reinhold
480 Latrobe Street
Melbourne, Victoria 3000, Australia

Van Nostrand Reinhold Company Limited
Molly Millars Lane
Wokingham, Berkshire, England

15 14 13 12 11 10 9 8 7 6 5 4 3 2 1

Library of Congress Cataloging in Publication Data

Sinha, N. K. (Naresh Kumar), 1927–
  Modeling and identification of dynamic systems.

  (Van Nostrand Reinhold electrical computer science
and engineering series)
  Includes index.
  1. System identification. I. Kuszta, B. II. Title.
III. Series.
QA402.S54   1983   003   82-16123
ISBN 0-442-28162-5

Van Nostrand Reinhold
Electrical/Computer Science and Engineering Series
Sanjit Mitra, Series Editor

HANDBOOK OF ELECTRONIC DESIGN AND ANALYSIS PROCEDURES USING PROGRAMMABLE CALCULATORS, by Bruce K. Murdock

COMPILER DESIGN AND CONSTRUCTION, by Arthur B. Pyster

SINUSOIDAL ANALYSIS AND MODELING OF WEAKLY NONLINEAR CIRCUITS, by Donald D. Weiner and John F. Spina

APPLIED MULTIDIMENSIONAL SYSTEMS THEORY, by N. K. Bose

MICROWAVE SEMICONDUCTOR ENGINEERING, by Joseph F. White

INTRODUCTION TO QUARTZ CRYSTAL UNIT DESIGN, by Virgil E. Bottom

DIGITAL IMAGE PROCESSING, by William B. Green

SOFTWARE TESTING TECHNIQUES, by Boris Beizer

LIGHT TRANSMISSION OPTICS, Second edition, by Dietrich Marcuse

REAL TIME COMPUTING, edited by Duncan Mellichamp

HARDWARE AND SOFTWARE CONCEPTS IN VLSI, edited by Guy Rabbat

MODELING AND IDENTIFICATION OF DYNAMIC SYSTEMS, by N. K. Sinha and B. Kuszta

COMPUTER METHODS FOR CIRCUIT ANALYSIS AND DESIGN, by Jiri Vlach and Kishore Singhal

Preface

Although during the last twenty years a great deal of research has been done on the subject of system identification, and several very good books have been written on the subject, it has been felt that several topics of great importance to practicing engineers as well as control theorists have not appeared in a systematic form in a book. This book is an attempt to fill this gap.

Two basic types of models are discussed in this book: (i) models for control applications, and (ii) models of many physical, biological and socioeconomic phenomena. Both groups of models are studied by means of differential or difference equations. In the first group, although it may be possible to obtain a model by detailed analysis using the basic laws of physics and chemistry, it is usually preferable to determine the model from the observations of the input and the output. In the second group, it is not even possible to perform an analysis due to lack of complete knowledge; in such cases we may obtain stochastic models which are often very useful for understanding the phenomenon.

Even the systems belonging to the first group are generally of the distributed-parameter and nonlinear type. Although it may be possible to obtain suitable models using nonlinear partial differential equations, these are, generally, of little value for practical applications. On the other hand, a suitable linear lumped-parameter model, can be quite useful within certain limitation of operating ranges which can be estimated by proper examination. Hence, for such systems, it is necessary not only to be able to determine a suitable linear lumped-parameter model, but also to fully understand the conditions under which it is valid. We try to answer both of these basic questions.

The popular approach of investigating nonlinear systems by means of the Taylor series expansion of nonlinear operators (for example, Volterra series) or the describing function method will not be included in this book because of its limited practical application. Our approach is to determine suitable linear models, along with the regions over which they are valid.

The organization of the text will now be discussed. In Chapters 2 to 6, linear models are presented, including multivariable systems as well as stochastic models. In Chapter 7, the problem of identification of closed-loop linear systems is discussed. This is followed, in Chapter 8, by techniques for obtaining low-order models of high-order systems because of their usefulness in the understanding of such systems, as well as for the preliminary design of controllers. In Chapter 9, we consider the problem of combined state and parameter estimation because of its importance in the adaptive control of complex processes. Identification of distributed-parameter systems is discussed in Chapter 10. In Chapter 11 we consider nonlinear lumped-parameter systems, with emphasis on the determination of regions of bifurcation. Chapter 12 presents the design of optimal input signals for system identification with special consideration given to practical limitations. In Chapter 13, we describe methods for determining the order and the structure of linear models. Diagnostic tests for linear as well as nonlinear models are presented in Chapter 14. Concluding remarks along with a list of unsolved problems in the area are given in Chapter 15. A number of appendices are included to describe some of the theoretical background, as required.

It may be pointed out that the most of the material in Chapters 5 (multivariable systems), 8 (model reduction techniques), 9 (combined state and parameter estimation), 10 (distributed-parameter systems), 11 (nonlinear systems), and 12 (design of optimal inputs) appears for the first time in the form of a book in English in the control literature.

This book will be of value to both practicing engineers as well as students of control theory. The material has been arranged in such an order that it can be followed without difficulty by a person who has taken a first course on control theory and has the usual mathematical background in transform calculus and the theory of state equations. Most of this material has been used as a graduate course on system identification at McMaster University and at Tianjin University in China. The authors are grateful to the former students for finding several typographical errors.

This work owes a lot to the efforts of many former students. The authors are indebted to Drs. A. Sen, J. D. Hickin and H. El-Sherief for permission to reproduce some portions of their Ph.D. theses. The support of the research by the Natural Sciences and Engineering Research Council of Canada is gratefully acknowledged. Discussions with many colleagues were very helpful, and in particular, the authors would like to thank Dr. B. Beliczynski of the Technical University of Warsaw, and Drs. J. F. McGregor and J. D. Wright of McMaster University. The authors are very grateful for the encouragement received from the late Professor N. S. Rajbman of the Institute of Control Sciences, Moscow.

Thanks are due to Pat Dillon, Nancy Sine and Amy Stott of the Word Processing Centre, McMaster University, for their very cheerful and untiring efforts in typing the manuscript and making innumerable corrections. Finally, this work would have proved impossible without the support and understanding of our wives, Meena Sinha and Krystyna Kuszta.

N. K. SINHA
B. KUSZTA

Contents

MODELING AND IDENTIFICATION OF DYNAMIC SYSTEMS

1
Introduction

The problem of system modeling and identification has attracted considerable attention during the past twenty years mostly because of a large number of applications in diverse fields like chemical processes, biomedical systems, socio-economic systems, transportation, ecology, electric power systems, hydrology, aeronautics, and astronautics. In each of these cases, a model consists basically of mathematical equations which can be used for understanding the behavior of the system, and wherever possible, for prediction and control.

Two basic types of modeling problems arise. In the first type one can associate with each physical phenomenon, a small number of measurable causes (inputs) and a small number of measurable effects (outputs). The outputs and the inputs can generally be related through a set of mathematical equations, in most cases nonlinear partial differential equations. The determination of these equations is the problem of modeling in such cases. These can be obtained either by writing a set of equilibrium equations based on mass and energy balance and other physical laws, or one may use the "black-box" approach which consists of determining the equations from the past records of the inputs and the outputs. Modeling problems of this type appear quite often in engineering practice. Some typical problems are modeling of (i) a stirred-tank chemical reactor, (ii) a multimachine electrical power system, (iii) a synchronous-orbit communications satellite, and (iv) the control mechanism of a nuclear power reactor. In each of these examples one can easily identify certain input and output quantities, and then obtain the mathematical model relating them. Some of these will be discussed in the book in the later chapters.

Another type of modeling problem arises in those situations where although we can identify a certain quantity as a definite measureable output or effect, the causes are not so well defined. Some typical examples are (1) the annual population of the United States, (2) the annual rainfall in a certain country, (3) the average annual flow in a river, and (4) the daily value of a certain stock in the stock market. In all these cases, we have available a sequence of outputs, which will be called a time series, but the inputs or causes are numerous and not quite known in addition to often being unobservable. Nevertheless, it is important to develop a model in order that one may have some understanding of the process which may be used for planning. The models in such cases are called stochastic models, due to a certain amount of uncertainty which is unavoidable.

In this book we shall be studying both of these types of modeling problems. The first will be referred to as the problem of system identification, whereas the second will be called the problem of stochastic modeling. It must be clearly understood that the two problems are related closely. Moreover in both cases, we must be able to choose the best from a set of rival models. This requires development of methods for testing such models as well as suitable criteria for deciding on the optimum.

In system identification, we are concerned with the determination of system models from records of system operation. The problem can be represented diagrammatically as below

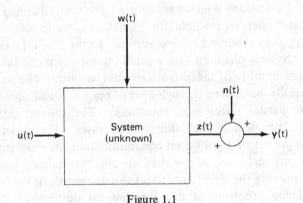

Figure 1.1

where

$\underset{\sim}{u}(t)$ is the known input vector of dimension m

$\underset{\sim}{z}(t)$ is the output vector of dimension p

$\underset{\sim}{w}(t)$ is the input disturbance vector

$\underset{\sim}{n}(t)$ is the observation noise vector

$\underset{\sim}{y}(t)$ is the measured output vector of dimension p

Thus, the problem of system identification is the determination of the system model from records of u(t) and y(t).

At this point it is important to distinguish between the system and its model. A system is defined as "a collection of objects arranged in an ordered form, which is, in some sense, purpose or goal directed." What constitutes a 'system' depends upon the viewpoint of the analyst or designer. For instance, an electronic amplifier consisting of a large number of components may be regarded as a system by the electronic engineer. On the other hand, the same amplifier may be one of the many parts of a "feedback control system." Furthermore, this feedback control system may be a part of a chemical process (or system) containing many loops of this type. Finally, we may have a plant containing many such units.

A model may be defined as "a representation of the essential aspects of a system which presents knowledge of that system in a usable form." A model, to be useful, must not be so complicated that it cannot be understood and thereby be unsuitable for predicting the behavior of the system; at the same time it must not be trivial to the extent that predictions of the behavior of the system based on the model are grossly inaccurate.

A fundamental problem in system identification is the choice of the nature of the model which should be used for the system. The model may be one of the following types:

(a) linear time-invariant (lumped-parameter)—ordinary linear differential equations
(b) linear time-varying (lumped parameter)—ordinary linear differential equations
(c) linear but with distributed parameters—partial differential equations
(d) nonlinear—nonlinear differential equations

Although, in practice, most systems are nonlinear with distributed parameters, linear models for such systems are often used because of their simplicity. In a large number of cases, "incremental," or "piecewise" linear models can be conveniently used for approximate understanding of the system. In using such models, one must be careful and should have an idea of the limits of their validity. Nevertheless, a great deal of work has been done on obtaining linear models for systems; so much that often by system identification one understands the determination of the parameters of "suitable" linear model for the system.

Some of the problems in system identification are:

(a) determining the order of the linear model
(b) selection of a suitable criterion for determining the "accuracy" of the model
(c) designing an input signal which will maximize the accuracy of the estimates of the parameters of the model.

Although most systems are of the "continuous-time" type, the application of the digital computer for identification makes it desirable to use "discrete-time" models. Often the determination of the parameters of a discrete-time model is more straightforward. Furthermore, provided that the sampling interval satisfies certain conditions, the determination of the continuous-time model from the discrete-time model is fairly straightforward.

Many applications require "on-line" identification instead of "off-line." An identification method is said to be of the "off-line" type when one collects a large amount of input and output data for the system which may be stored in a computer or recorded in some manner. These data are then processed in a batch to estimate the parameters of the model and obtain the best fit according to a prescribed cost function. In off-line identification, one may often select the type of input most suitable. Also, there is a greater flexibility in selecting computational methods without any restriction on computing time. As a result the accuracy of the estimates can be made fairly high, approaching the Cramer-Rao bound.

In a number of control applications, especially adaptive control, it is necessary to identify the system in a fairly short time. An identification scheme is said to be of the "on-line" type if it satisfies the following conditions:

(a) it does not require a special input
(b) all the data need not be stored
(c) a recursive algorithm is used for adjusting the estimates of the parameter after each sampling instant
(d) the amount of computation required for "model adjustment" is a fraction of the sampling period.

It may be added that, in general, on-line methods will not lead to as accurate models as possible with off-line methods which can use a much larger amount of data. But in many practical situations one cannot afford to wait for the time required to collect all the data. As a matter of fact, it will be recognized that life is the art of reaching sufficient conclusions from insufficient data. Some typical examples of situations where one must make an important decision on the basis of insufficient information are: (i) getting married, (ii) accepting a job, (iii) hiring a new employee, and (iv) investing in the stock market.

An important application of on-line identification is the development of the self-tuning regulator, proposed recently by Professor K. Aström and his colleagues.

A large variety of methods have been applied to system identification, both off-line and on-line. The methods can be classified in many ways; one scheme for classification is given below.

I. Classical Methods: (mostly off-line)
   (a) Frequency Reponse Identification
   (b) Impulse response identification by deconvolution
   (c) Step response identification
   (d) Identification from correlation functions
II. Equation-error Approach: (batch-processing)
   (a) Least-squares
   (b) Generalized least squares
   (c) Maximum likelihood
   (d) Minimum variance
   (e) Gradient Methods
III. Model Adjustment Techniques:
   (a) Least-squares (recursive)
   (b) Generalized least squares (recursive)
   (c) Instrumental variables
   (d) Bootstrap
   (e) Maximum likelihood (recursive)
   (f) Correlation (recursive)
   (g) Stochastic approximation

In Chapter 2 we shall be discussing the classical methods for system identification, which have been known for more than fifteen years.

REFERENCES

Aström, K. J. and Eykhoff, P. (1971), "System Identification—A Survey," *Automatica*, vol. 7, pp. 123–162.

Aström, K. J. and Wittenmark, B. (1973), "On Self Tuning Regulators," *Automatica*, vol. 9, pp. 185–199.

Eykhoff, P. (1974), *System Identification, Parameter and State Estimation*, Wiley, London.

Graupe, D. (1975), *Identification of Systems*, Robert E. Kreiger Publishing Co., Inc., New York (2nd edition).

Hsia, T. C. (1977), *System Identification*, Lexington Books, Lexington, Mass.

Mendel, J. M. (1973), *Discrete Techniques of Parameter Estimation*, Marcel Dekker, Inc., New York.

2
Classical Methods of System Identification

We shall now consider a number of methods of system identification that are called classical in the sense that they have been around for a longer time than the so-called modern methods. The first such method is based on the frequency response of the system.

2.1 FREQUENCY RESPONSE METHOD

The frequency response method for identification of linear systems is based upon the familiar Bode diagrams of frequency response.

In this method, sine-wave inputs are applied to the system and the steady-state output is observed; both the magnitude ratio and the phase shift between the output and input are measured. These measurements are made over the entire range of frequencies of interest. If the transfer function of the system (Figure 2.1) is G(s), then the frequency response is obtained by replacing s by $j\omega$, i.e.,

$$G(j\omega) = M(\omega) \cdot e^{j\phi(\omega)} = \frac{Y(j\omega)}{X(j\omega)} \qquad (2.01)$$

where M is the ratio of the magnitudes, and ϕ is the phase shift between the output and the input.

The plot of $M(\omega)$ in decibels against ω (log scale), as well as the plot of $\phi(\omega)$ against ω (log scale), can then be used for estimating the various break-frequencies (poles and zeros) of the transfer function.

In practical application of this method, one must be able to generate the sine-wave inputs of various frequencies, and also be able to measure the magnitude ratios and phase-shifts accurately at these frequencies. The method is applicable

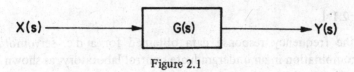

Figure 2.1

only to linear stationary processes and assumes off-line identification. Moreover, the method is applicable only to stable systems, since the frequency-response of an unstable system cannot be measured in practice.

The estimation of the transfer function is based on approximating the magnitude response curves with straight lines of slopes 6n db/octave, where n is an integer. These give the break frequencies and hence the transfer function, which is then verified from the phase shift curve. Although the case of real poles or zeros is quite straightforward, the case of complex poles requires estimating the damping ratios as well. The following figures illustrate the variation of M and ϕ with the damping ratio.

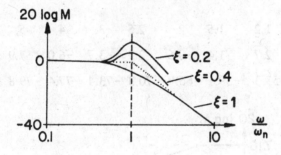

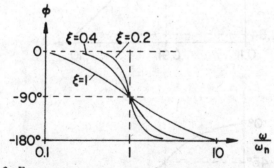

Figure 2.2. Frequency response curves for a second-order system given by

$$G(s) = \frac{1}{1 + 2\xi s/\omega_n + (s/\omega_n)^2}$$

EXAMPLE 2.1.1

Consider the frequency response data obtained for a d.c. servomotor/servo-amplifier combination in an undergraduate control laboratory, as shown below

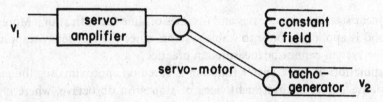

Figure 2.3. Identification of a servomotor/servoamplifier combination.

Frequency (Hz)	0.1	0.2	0.3	0.4	0.5	0.6	0.7	0.8	0.9
$20 \log |v_2/v_1|$	7.1	7.0	6.7	6.4	6.0	5.6	5.1	4.6	4.1
$\sphericalangle v_2/v_1$		-6.35	-12.6	-18.5	-24.1	-29.2	-33.8	-38.0	-41.8	-45.1

1.0	1.2	1.5	2.	2.5	3.	4.	5.	7.	10.
3.7	2.7	1.4	-0.6	-2.3	-3.7	-6.0	-7.9	-10.8	-13.8
-48.1	-53.3	-59.1	-65.9	-70.3	-73.4	-77.4	-79.8	-82.7	-84.9

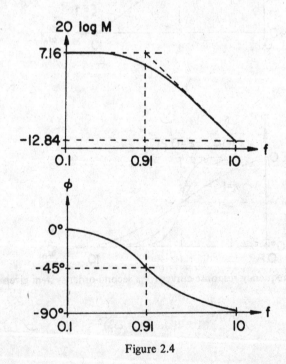

Figure 2.4

The frequency response plots are shown in Figure 2.4. By drawing straight-line asymptotes to the magnitude ratio curve, the break frequency is estimated as 0.9 Hz. This is confirmed by the phase-shift plot giving phase shift equal to 45° at this frequency. Estimating the d.c. gain as 7.2 decibels the transfer function is estimated as

$$G(s) = \frac{10^{7.2/20}}{1 + s/(2\pi \times 0.9)} = \frac{2.28}{1 + s/1.8\pi} = \frac{12.89}{s + 5.65} \qquad (2.02)$$

In this case it is rather straightforward to obtain the transfer function because the model was of the first order. For a system of higher order, it is not so easy to estimate the transfer function accurately from the frequency response plots; specially if the poles and zeros are not far apart. The following example will illustrate the difficulty.

EXAMPLE 2.1.2

Consider the transfer function

$$G(s) = \frac{200(s + 2)}{(s + 4)(s^2 + 10s + 100)} \qquad (2.03)$$

This represents the overall transfer function of a position control servo with a lead compensator. Samples of the frequency response are given in the following table

ω	0.1	0.2	0.3	0.4	0.5	0.7	1.0
$20 \log |G|$	0.32	1.10	2.04	2.93	3.72	4.96	6.15
$\angle G$ (deg)	4.90	7.43	7.01	4.33	0.16	-10.77	-31.25

	1.5	2.0	2.5	3	4	5	7
	5.95	2.89	-0.83	-4.15	-9.45	-13.50	-19.52
	-72.22	-106.13	-126.02	-137.64	-150.21	-156.88	-163.92

	10	15	20	30	40	50	100
	-25.81	-32.91	-37.92	-44.98	-49.98	-53.86	-65.9
	-168.51	-172.66	-174.51	-176.35	-177.26	-177.81	-178.9

The frequency response curves are shown in Figure 2.5.

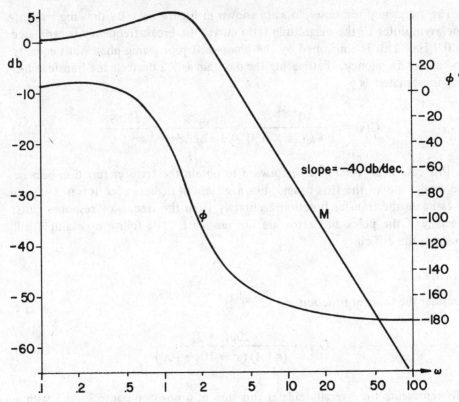

Figure 2.5. Frequency response curves for Example 2.12.

From these curves, we can deduce that the d.c. gain is 0 decibels and there are two more poles than zeros since at high frequencies the gain approaches $-\infty$ and the phase shift approaches $-180°$. The -40 db/decade slope of the gain curve, and the rapid change in phase indicates a pair of complex poles with undamped natural frequency close to 1.5 rad/sec. The small increase in phase shift at low frequencies is indicative of the lead compensator. It is not obvious how one can determine the pole-zero locations and the damping ratio accurately in this case, except by solving for the four unknowns from four (or more) points in the frequency response curves. It should be noted that we would have to solve non-linear equations.

2.2   IDENTIFICATION FROM STEP RESPONSE

The simplest input which can be applied to a system for identification is a step input, accomplished by a sudden switching off (or on) of an input voltage (or current), or by a sudden opening (or closing) of an input valve, etc. Although an ideal step is physically impossible to realize, the approximation is fairly close if the rise-time of the step input is much shorter than the period of the highest frequency of interest in the identification.

Although this is essentially an "off-line" method, there are many processes where step disturbances may often be applied during normal operation. In such cases, therefore, the method may also be used for on-line identification.

Since the impulse response of a system is the derivative of the step response, the identification problem in this case may be regarded as the determination of the transfer function from the impulse response. This corresponds to the time-domain approximation problem in circuit and systems theory, which is the determination of a proper rational function of s which is the Laplace transform of a given function of time (either step or impulse response). It must be added, however, that since the observations are usually contaminated with noise, it will be assumed that adequate filtering of the noise has been carried out before attempting the time-domain approximation.

There are a number of methods of time-domain approximation described in the literature on network synthesis. Basically, these amount to finding a set of exponentials (either real or in conjugate pairs) the sum of which approximates the given response as closely as possible. A digital method for time-domain approximation, using gradient techniques, was presented in a recent paper (Sinha, Sen, and To, 1973; see also Ishak and Sinha, 1976). Some of the basic principles will now be discussed briefly.

If the system model is of the first-order, one may need only obtain two pieces of information: (i) the steady-state response to the step input and (ii) the time constant. The latter can be obtained either from the initial slope of the step response or from the 10% to 90% rise time.

For a second-order system model (with two poles and no zero), there are two possible situations: (1) when the two poles are real and (2) when the poles are a complex conjugate pair. Formulas for finding these from measurements of (a) steady-state response, (b) maximum overshoot, (c) time required to reach the first-peak, and (d) time required to reach 50% of the steady-state value (for overdamped systems) can be easily derived. (For example, see Sinha and Wismath, 1971).

For the general case of high-order systems, reference may be made to the books by Guillemin (*Passive Network Synthesis*) and Yengst (*Network Synthesis*), where a number of methods have been discussed. For practical applications, it is perhaps best to use a gradient method to find the parameters of the model of a given order such that the integral of the square of the error is minimized (see Sinha, Sen, and To, 1973).

EXAMPLE 2.2.1

The samples of step response of the system described in Example 2.1.1 are given below

t	0	0.05	0.1	0.15	0.20	0.25	0.3	0.4	0.5
y(t)	0	0.561	0.984	1.303	1.543	1.725	1.861	2.042	2.145

	0.7	1.0	1.5	2
	2.236	2.272	2.280	2.280

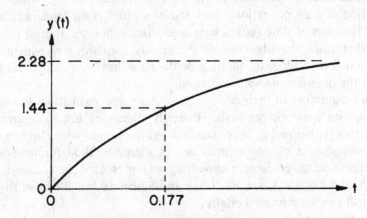

Figure 2.6. Plot of the step-response of a first-order system.

The plot of the response is shown in Figure 2.6. First we note that the steady-state response is 2.28. Now we determine the value of the time constant τ, as that value of t for which $y(t) = (1 - e^{-1}) 2.28 = 1.441$. This gives $\tau = 0.177$. Hence,

$$G(s) = \frac{2.28}{1 + 0.177s} = \frac{12.89}{s + 5.65} \qquad (2.04)$$

EXAMPLE 2.2.2

Consider the underdamped second-order system described by the transfer function

$$G(s) = \frac{\omega_n^2}{s^2 + 2\xi\omega_n s + \omega_n^2} \qquad \text{for } \xi < 1 \qquad (2.05)$$

The response of this system to a unit step is given by

$$y(t) = 1 - \frac{1}{B} e^{-\xi\omega_n t} \cos(\omega_n B t - \phi) \qquad (2.06)$$

where

$$B = \sqrt{1 - \xi^2} \qquad \text{and} \qquad \phi = \tan^{-1} \frac{\xi}{B}$$

It can easily be shown that the maximum response is given by

$$M_t = 1 + e^{-\xi\pi/B} \qquad (2.07)$$

and it occurs at

$$t_p = \frac{\pi}{B\omega_n} \qquad (2.08)$$

Hence, by measuring M_t, the value of the damping ratio, ξ, can be calculated from equation (2.07). Finally equation (2.08) can be used to determine the undamped natural frequency, ω_n.

2.3 DECONVOLUTION

If the input is different from the simple step function, one may relate the input and output of the system through the convolution integral

$$y(t) = \int_0^t x(\tau) \, w(t - \tau) \, d\tau \qquad (2.09)$$

where $w(\tau)$ is the impulse response of the system.

The determination of the impulse response from the input and the output is called deconvolution. Once $w(\tau)$ is determined, the system transfer function may be evaluated following the methods described in the previous section. Hence, we shall now consider a method for deconvolution.

Let us approximate the input and the output by assuming that they are held constant between sampling instants at a value at the beginning of the sampling interval, i.e.,

$$x(t) = x(nT) \qquad \text{for } nT < t < (n+1)T$$
$$y(t) = y(nT) \qquad n = 0, 1, 2, \ldots \tag{2.10}$$

Then, from the convolution integral, we have

$$\left.\begin{aligned}
y(T) &= x(0)\, w(0) \cdot T \\
y(2T) &= [x(0)\, w(T) + x(T)\, w(0)]\, T \\
&\;\;\vdots \\
y(NT) &= T \sum_{i=0}^{N-1} x(iT)\, w(NT - iT - T)
\end{aligned}\right\} \tag{2.11}$$

These equations may be written as

$$\underline{y} = T \cdot X \cdot \underline{w} \tag{2.12}$$

where

$$\underline{y} = \begin{bmatrix} y(T) \\ \vdots \\ y(NT) \end{bmatrix}, \qquad \underline{w} = \begin{bmatrix} w(0) \\ w(T) \\ \vdots \\ w(NT - T) \end{bmatrix} \tag{2.13}$$

and the matrix X is given by

$$X = \begin{bmatrix}
x(0) & 0 & 0 & \cdots & 0 \\
x(T) & x(0) & 0 & \cdots & 0 \\
x(2T) & x(T) & x(0) & \cdots & 0 \\
\vdots & & & & \vdots \\
x(NT - T) & & \cdots & & x(0)
\end{bmatrix} \tag{2.14}$$

Due to the lower triangular nature of X, the above equations can be easily solved if and only if $x(0) \neq 0$. The solution can be written in the following recursive form

$$w(nT) = \frac{1}{x(0)} \left[\frac{1}{T} y(nT + T) - \sum_{i=1}^{n} x(iT) w(nT - iT) \right] \qquad (2.15)$$

Note that for the method to be reasonably accurate T must be sufficiently small. One way to determine if T is sufficiently small is to let $T' = \frac{1}{2} T$ and repeat the computations. If no appreciable change is noted then T is sufficiently small; otherwise, we may let $T'' = \frac{1}{2} T'$, and repeat.

One problem with this method is that an ever increasing amount of data must be processed in the summation. Hence, this method can be usefully employed in on-line algorithms only if the impulse response approaches zero very fast. However, the process is considerably simplified when the input is a step, i.e., $x(iT) = 1$ for all i. In that case,

$$w(nT) = \frac{1}{T} y(nT + T) - \sum_{i=0}^{n-1} w(iT) \qquad (2.16)$$

Defining

$$h_n = \sum_{i=0}^{n-1} w(nT) \qquad (2.17)$$

we now have the simple recursive algorithm

$$\left. \begin{array}{l} w(nT) = \dfrac{1}{T} y(nT + T) - h_n; \\[2ex] h_n = h_{n-1} + w(nT - T) \end{array} \right\} \qquad (2.18)$$

Equations (2.18) may also be written as

$$w(nT) = \frac{1}{T} [y(nT + T) - y(nT)] \qquad (2.19)$$

which is an approximation to the derivative of $y(t)$ at $t = nT$. This approximation is rather crude unless the value of T is sufficiently small.

EXAMPLE 2.3.1

Consider the transfer function given in equation (2.03), the values of the impulse response and the response to a unit step at intervals of 0.05 second are given in the following table.

t	0	0.05	0.10	0.15	0.20	0.25	0.30	0.35	0.40
w(t)	0	7.157	9.491	8.564	5.931	2.846	0.145	-1.753	2.755
y(t)	0	0.202	0.635	1.097	1.463	1.682	1.754	1.710	1.594

0.45	0.50	0.55	0.60	0.65	0.70	0.75	0.80
-2.987	-2.679	-2.079	-1.400	-0.788	-0.322	-0.024	0.123
1.448	1.305	1.185	1.098	1.044	1.017	1.009	1.012

0.85	0.90	0.95	1.00	1.05	1.10
0.158	0.123	0.057	-0.011	-0.065	-0.096
1.019	1.026	1.031	1.032	1.030	1.026

If we attempt to obtain samples of the impulse response from the step response using equation (2.19) from the above table, we shall get very inaccurate results. For example, we get for nT = 0.20,

$$w'(0.20) = \frac{1}{0.05} [1.682 - 1.463] = 4.380 \qquad (2.20)$$

whereas the correct value is 5.931.
    However, if we use T = 0.0001, we get

$$w'(0.20) = \frac{1}{0.0001} [y(0.2001) - y(0.2000)] = \frac{1.463790 - 1.463197}{0.0001}$$

$$= 5.930 \qquad (2.21)$$

which is much closer to the actual value of 5.931.

2.4   CORRELATION METHOD

This method is based on applying a random input to the process, and takes a simpler form if the input is, in particular, a white noise input. Although it is not possible in practice to obtain an ideal white noise input, it can be approximated by noise with power spectral density constant over the frequency range of interest for identification.

$$x(t) \longrightarrow \boxed{w(\tau)} \longrightarrow y(t)$$

Figure 2.7

The input-output relationship for a linear time invariant system may be written as

$$y(t) = \int_0^\infty w(t - \tau)\, x(\tau)\, d\tau = \int_0^\infty w(\tau)\, x(t - \tau)\, d\tau \qquad (2.22)$$

The cross-correlation between the input and the output is obtained as

$$\phi_{yx}(\theta) = E[y(t) \cdot x(t - \theta)], \text{ assuming stationariness}$$

$$= E\left[\int_0^\infty w(\tau)\, x(t - \tau)\, d\tau \cdot x(t - \theta)\right]$$

$$= \int_0^\infty w(\tau) \cdot E[x(t - \tau)\, x(t - \theta)]\, d\tau$$

$$= \int_0^\infty w(\tau)\, \phi_{xx}(\theta - \tau)\, d\tau \qquad (2.23)$$

For the particular case when the input $x(t)$ is white noise, we have

$$\phi_{xx}(\theta - \tau) = \delta(\theta - \tau), \qquad (2.24)$$

where $\delta(t - k)$ represents the unit impulse or delta function occurring at $t = k$.
Hence, for this case,

$$\phi_{yx}(\theta) = \int_0^\infty w(\tau) \cdot \delta(\theta - \tau)\, d\tau$$

$$= w(\theta) \qquad (2.25)$$

Thus $\phi_{yx}(\theta)$ is the same as the impulse response of the system at $t = \theta$.

With white noise input approximated by a pseudorandom input (whose auto-correlation approximates a delta function), it is possible to implement on-line identification by superimposing this input on the normal input to the system. As the system is assumed linear, the output is the sum of the two outputs (1) due to the normal input and (2) due to white noise input. Since there is no correlation between the output due to the white noise and the normal input, as well as between the white noise input and normal input or output, the cross-correlation yields the impulse response. The implementation is shown in the following block diagram

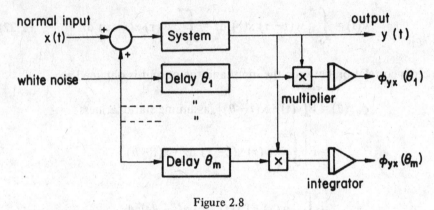

Figure 2.8

It may be noted that in the above, the ergodic hypothesis leads to

$$\phi_{yx}(\theta) = \lim_{T \to \infty} \frac{1}{2T} \left[\int_{-T}^{T} y(t)\, x(t - \theta)\, dt \right] \qquad (2.26)$$

The advantages of the correlation method are given below:

(i) Identification is not critically dependent upon normal operating records.
(ii) By correlating over a long period of time, the level of the white noise disturbance can be made so small that it does not appreciably affect the normal operation.
(iii) No a priori knowledge of the system model (order or other information) is required.

The disadvantages are the following:

(i) Nonstationarity of the noise or the system will affect the identification, since the correlation is based on stationarity and ergodicity. While these may hold true for the pseudorandom noise, they may not be true for the system parameters.

(ii) Since the cross-correlation is done in the time domain, the time for identification is quite long, especially if high accuracy is desired.

(iii) Additional system hardware (or software) are required for generating the white noise and computing the cross-correlation.

2.5   ESTIMATION OF THE TRANSFER FUNCTION OF CONTINUOUS TIME SYSTEM FROM THE SAMPLES OF THE IMPULSE RESPONSE

In the last two sections we considered methods for determining the samples of the impulse response of the system. We shall now discuss how we can estimate the transfer function of the corresponding continuous-time system from the impulse response sequence. This is done in two steps. The first step consists of determining the pulse transfer function, H(z), of a discrete-time system which gives exactly the same impulse response sequence. The second step is the derivation of the corresponding continuous-time transfer function. The procedure described in this section is based on two important assumptions. The first is that the samples of the impulse response are known exactly, and are not contaminated with noise. The second assumption is that the order of the system model is known a priori. In practical situations, none of these conditions is satisfied. In such cases, we can use the samples of the impulse response to determine the pulse transfer function that provides the least-squares fit if the order is known. The procedure for estimating the order of the model from noise-contaminated samples of the impulse response is discussed in Chapter 13. Closely related to this problem is the choice of the sampling interval. It can be shown (Haykin 1972) that if all the modes of the continuous-time system G(s) are to be retained in the discrete-time transfer function H(z) the sampling interval T must satisfy the following inequality

$$p_k T < 0.5 \qquad (2.27)$$

where p_k is the magnitude of the pole of G(s) farthest from the origin.

2.5.1   Determination of the Discrete-Time Transfer Function H(z) from the Samples of the Impulse Response

Consider a discrete-time transfer function H(z) of order n described by the following equation

$$H(z) = \frac{a_0 + a_1 z^{-1} + a_2 z^{-2} + \cdots + a_n z^{-n}}{1 + b_1 z^{-1} + b_2 z^{-2} + \cdots + b_n z^{-n}} \qquad (2.28)$$

From the definition of the pulse transfer function, it also follows that

$$H(z) = w_0 + w_1 z^{-1} + w_2 z^{-2} + \cdots \qquad (2.29)$$

where

$$w_i \triangleq w(iT) \qquad (2.30)$$

and T is the sampling interval.

Multiplying equation (2.28) and (2.29) by the denominator of equation (2.28), we have

$$a_0 + a_1 z^{-1} + \cdots + a_n z^{-n} = w_0 + (w_1 + b_1 w_0) z^{-1} + \cdots + \left(w_n + \sum_{i=1}^{n} b_i w_{n-i} \right) z^{-n}$$

$$+ \left(w_m + \sum_{i=1}^{n} b_i w_{m-i} \right) z^{-m} + \cdots \qquad (m > n) \quad (2.31)$$

Equating the coefficients of like powers of z^{-1} from both sides, we get $(n + 1)$ equations containing the numerator coefficients, which can be arranged as follows

$$
\begin{bmatrix} a_0 \\ a_1 \\ a_2 \\ \vdots \\ a_n \end{bmatrix}
=
\begin{bmatrix}
1 & 0 & 0 & \cdots & 0 & 0 \\
b_1 & 1 & 0 & \cdots & 0 & 0 \\
b_2 & b_1 & 1 & & & \vdots \\
\vdots & \vdots & \vdots & \ddots & & \vdots \\
b_n & b_{n-1} & b_{n-2} & \cdots & b_1 & 1
\end{bmatrix}
\begin{bmatrix} w_0 \\ w_1 \\ w_2 \\ \vdots \\ w_n \end{bmatrix}
\qquad (2.32)
$$

Due to the lower triangular nature of the matrix in equation (2.32), it is evident that the calculation of the numerator coefficients is straightforward, provided that the denominator coefficients, b_i, are known.

To determine b_i, we consider the terms containing $z^{-(n+1)}$ to z^{-2n}. Since there are no such terms on the left-hand side of equation (2.31), these equations do not contain a_i, and can be rearranged in the following form

$$
\begin{bmatrix}
w_1 & w_2 & \cdots & w_n \\
w_2 & w_3 & \cdots & w_{n+1} \\
\vdots & \vdots & & \vdots \\
w_n & w_{n+1} & & w_{2n-1}
\end{bmatrix}
\begin{bmatrix} b_n \\ b_{n-1} \\ \vdots \\ b_1 \end{bmatrix}
=
\begin{bmatrix} -w_{n+1} \\ -w_{n+2} \\ \vdots \\ -w_{2n} \end{bmatrix}
\qquad (2.33)
$$

A solution to equation (2.33) will always exist since the rank of the Hankel matrix consisting of the impulse response sequence is equal to the order of the system, n. Hence, equation (2.33) can be solved for the denominator coefficients which can then be substituted into equation (2.32) to solve for the numerator coefficients.

In case there is some uncertainty about the values of the impulse response sequence, one may add more rows to equation (2.33) and obtain a least-squares estimate for the denominator parameters. The procedure for obtaining such an estimate is described in Chapter 3.

2.5.2 Determination of the Continuous-Time Transfer Function G(s) Having the Same Impulse Response at the Sampling Instants as H(z)

We shall now consider the problem of determining the continuous-time transfer function $G(s)$ which has the same impulse response as $H(z)$ at the sampling instants. This can be done by selecting $G(s)$ in such a manner that its inverse Laplace transform $g(t)$ satisfies the following relationship

$$g(iT) = w_i, \qquad i = 0, 1, 2, \ldots \qquad (2.34)$$

To do this we shall first require that the poles of $G(s)$ correspond to the poles of $H(z)$ through the transformation

$$z = e^{st} \qquad (2.35)$$

or

$$s = \frac{1}{T} \ln z \qquad (2.36)$$

In addition, the residues of $G(s)$ at its poles, must be equal to the residues of $1/z \, H(z)$ at its poles.

Hence our procedure will consist of the following steps:

(i) Determine the poles of $H(z)$.

(ii) Corresponding to each pole of $H(z)$, determine a pole of $G(s)$ according to equation (2.36). It may be noted that for complex conjugate poles of $H(z)$, we get correspondingly complex conjugate poles in the s-plane.

(iii) Evaluate the residues of $1/z \, H(z)$ at its poles.

(iv) Using the same residues at the corresponding poles of $G(s)$, obtain the transfer function $G(s)$.

It may be noted that although the impulse response of G(s) is equal to that of H(z) at the sampling instants, there is no guarantee that the responses of G(s) and H(z) to other inputs will be equal at the sampling instants. All we can guarantee is that if we apply a sequence of impulses to the continuous-time system G(s), its response at the sampling instants will be identical to that of H(z) for the same sequence of impulses. For other inputs, the response of G(s) will be determined largely by how the input is varying between sampling instants.

Given any continuous time transfer function G(s), it is possible to determine a discrete time function, H(z) so that the responses of the two, for a given continuous time input, will be identical (Sinha 1972, Franklin and Powell 1980). For further details, the reader is advised to study the references cited. Problem 7 at the end of this chapter describes the determination of the transfer function from the step response.

EXAMPLE 2.5.1

For the third-order transfer function

$$G(s) = \frac{200(s + 2)}{(s + 4)(s^2 + 10s + 100)} \tag{2.37}$$

which was considered in example 2.3.1, the values of the impulse response, at intervals of 0.05 second, are given below

t	0	0.05	0.10	0.15	0.20	0.25	0.30
w(t)	0	7.157039	9.491077	8.563889	5.930506	2.845972	0.144611

The discrete transfer function will be of the form

$$H(z) = \frac{a_0 + a_1 z^{-1} + a_2 z^{-2} + a_3 z^{-3}}{1 + b_1 z^{-1} + b_2 z^{-2} + b_3 z^{-3}} = \frac{a_0 z^3 + a_1 z^2 + a_2 z + a_3}{z^3 + b_1 z^2 + b_2 z + b_3} \tag{2.38}$$

From equation (2.33), the coefficients of the denominator satisfy the following equation

$$\begin{bmatrix} 7.157039 & 9.491077 & 8.563889 \\ 9.491077 & 8.563889 & 5.930506 \\ 8.563889 & 5.930506 & 2.845972 \end{bmatrix} \begin{bmatrix} b_3 \\ b_2 \\ b_1 \end{bmatrix} = \begin{bmatrix} -5.930506 \\ -2.845972 \\ -0.144611 \end{bmatrix} \tag{2.39}$$

Solving these equations, we have $b_1 = -2.232575$, $b_2 = 1.764088$, and $b_3 = -0.496585$.

Substituting these values in equation (2.32), we obtain the numerator parameters directly. The resulting discrete-time transfer function is shown below

$$H(z) = \frac{7.157309z^2 - 6.487547z}{z^3 - 2.232575z^2 + 1.764088z - 0.496585} \qquad (2.40)$$

The poles of $H(z)$ are obtained as 0.818731 and $0.706923 \pm j0.32679$. Using equation (2.36), the corresponding s-plane poles are found to be -4 and $-5 \pm j\sqrt{75}$.

Next, we perform the partial fraction expansion of $1/z\, H(z)$. This is obtained as

$$\frac{1}{z}\,H(z) = \frac{-5.263158}{z - 0.818731} + \frac{5.263158z + 4.024965}{z^2 - 1.413844z + 0.660531}$$

$$= \frac{-5.263158}{z - e^{-4T}}$$

$$+ \frac{5.261358\,(z - e^{-5T}\cos\sqrt{75}\,T) + 23.701748\,e^{-5T}\sin\sqrt{75}\,T}{z^2 - 2\,e^{-5T}\,z\cos\sqrt{75}\,T + e^{-10T}}$$

$$(2.41)$$

Hence,

$$G(s) = \frac{-5.263158}{s + 4} + \frac{5.261358(s + 5) + 205.263158}{(s + 5)^2 + 75}$$

$$= \frac{200s + 400}{(s + 4)(s^2 + 10s + 100)} \qquad (2.42)$$

which is seen as the correct transfer function.

2.6   MODEL ADJUSTMENT TECHNIQUES

All the identification methods discussed so far are of the "open-loop" type in the sense that identification is based on records of input-output data (or tests). A conceptually simpler approach, which is of the "closed-loop" type, is based on using a model subject to the same input as the system, and then adjusting the parameters of the model so that the error between the output of the system and that of the model is minimized according to a given criterion. Such a scheme has also been called a "learning model approach" by some authors.

The basic idea of this approach is shown in the block diagram of Figure 2.9.

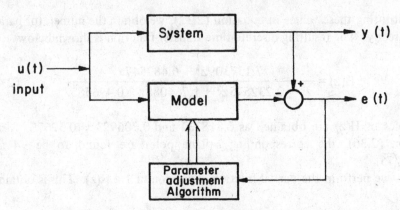

Figure 2.9. Block diagram of model adjustment identification.

This procedure can be used for on-line identification if the input and output are sampled, and the computation for model adjustment carried out recursively during each sampling interval.

Some important practical problems in the implementation of such a procedure are listed below:

(i)   selection of the structure and order of the model
(ii) error criterion to be used
(iii) time-scaling (with hybrid computation)
(iv) initial conditions
(v)   method for computing the desired adjustment of the model.

Each of these problems will be discussed in detail in the following chapters.

2.7   REFERENCES

Guillemin, E. A. (1957), *Synthesis of Passive Networks*, John Wiley & Sons, Inc., New York.

Ishak, W. and Sinha, N. K. (1976), "Time domain approximation and system modelling using a damped least-squares algorithm," *Int. J. of Systems Science*, vol. 7, pp. 635–640.

Franklin, G. F. and Powell, J. D. (1980), *Digital Control of Dynamic Systems*, Addison-Wesley Publishing Company, Reading, Mass.

Haykin, S. S. (1972), "A unified treatment of recursive digital filtering," *IEEE Trans. on Automatic Control*, vol. AC-17, pp. 113–116.

Sinha, N. K. (1972), "Estimation of transfer function of continuous system from sampled data," *Proceedings IEE*, vol. 119, pp. 612–614.

Sinha, N. K., Sen, A., and To, R. (1974), "Time domain approximation using digital methods," *Int. J. of Systems Science*, vol. 5, pp. 373–382.

Sinha, N. K. and Wismath, J. C. (1971), "Reduction of high-order linear dynamic systems," *Trans. of the Engineering Institute of Canada*, EIC-71-CE2A2, vol. 15, No. C-5.

Yengst, W. C. (1964), *Procedures of Modern Network Synthesis*, Macmillan, New York.

2.8   PROBLEMS

1. Show that for the second-order transfer function with complex poles and no zeros, described by

$$G(s) = \frac{\omega_n^2}{s^2 + 2\zeta\omega_n s + \omega_n^2}$$

   (a) The phase shift for $\omega = \omega_n$ is 90°
   (b) For $\zeta < 0.707$, the resonant frequency is given by

$$\omega_r = \omega_n \sqrt{1 - 2\zeta^2}$$

   and the maximum magnitude of $|G(j\omega)|$ is

$$M_m = \frac{1}{2\zeta \sqrt{1 - \zeta^2}}$$

   How would you use these relationships to determine the transfer function of such a system from its frequency response?

2. A position control system is underdamped, so that the closed-loop transfer function has exactly the same form as in the previous problem. Determine the transfer function from the experimentally obtained frequency response data given below.

f(Hz)	0.1	0.2	0.4	0.6	0.8	1.0	1.2
M(db)	0.02	0.09	0.35	0.77	1.28	1.73	1.89
ϕ(degree)	-3.4	-6.9	-14.4	-23.0	-33.5	-46.6	-62.6

	1.5	2.0	3.0	4.0	6.0
	0.98	-2.97	-10.72	-16.2	-23.6
	-89.0	-122.2	-148.7	-158.4	-166.4

3. When a unit step input was applied to a second-order system, the steady-state response was measured as 2.85. The maximum overshoot was found to be 20%, and occurred at 25 msec after the application of the step. Identify the transfer function of the system.

4. The samples of the impulse response of a second-order system are given below. Determine the equivalent continuous-time transfer function.

t	0	0.05	0.10	0.15	0.20	0.25
w(t)	0	0.683227	1.072520	1.269229	1.341902	1.336673

	0.30	0.35	0.40
	1.284386	1.205478	1.113323

5. The samples of the impulse response of a third-order system are given below. Determine the equivalent continuous-time transfer function.

t	0	0.1	0.2	0.3	0.4	0.5
w(t)	10	6.988715	4.711109	3.135561	2.137192	1.558995

	0.6	0.7	0.8	0.9	1.0
	1.25203	1.096492	1.008595	0.937857	0.859576

6. Repeat for the samples of the impulse response of the following third-order system

t	0	0.1	0.2	0.3	0.4	0.5
w(t)	4	0.450714	-1.578017	-2.693167	-3.262210	-3.507414

	0.6	0.7	0.8
	-3.563025	-3.509949	-3.396782

7. The method for obtaining the transfer function from the samples of the impulse response, discussed in section 2.5 can be extended to the case where the samples of the step response are available. Since the step response sequence is the z-transform of $(1/s)\,G(s)$, one must follow the procedure of section 2.5 to obtain $(1/s)\,G(s)$ and them multiply by s to get $G(s)$. Note that the order of $(1/s)\,G(s)$ is one more than that of $G(s)$.

Use this procedure to identify a third-order continuous-time system from the following samples of its response to a unit step

t	0	0.1	0.2	0.3	0.4	0.5
y(t)	0	0.357280	0.781155	1.208115	1.588302	1.887082

	0.6	0.7	0.8	0.9
	2.085035	2.176652	2.168066	2.074195

8. Write a computer program for calculating the transfer function of a continuous-time system of a given order (from 2 to 10) from the samples of its response to a unit step.

3
Off-Line Methods for System Identification

In this chapter we shall discuss several off-line (nonsequential) methods for estimating the parameters of a linear model from the input-output data of a single-input single-output system. It will be assumed that the order of the model is known a priori, and that equispaced samples of the input-output data are available. We shall, therefore, first consider various methods for estimating the parameters of a linear discrete-time model. The problem of estimating the parameters of the corresponding continuous-time model will then be discussed.

3.1 ESTIMATION OF THE PARAMETERS OF A DISCRETE-TIME MODEL FROM NOISE-FREE INPUT-OUTPUT DATA

Consider the single-input single-output system shown in Fig. 3.1. Using z-transforms, the input-output relationship is given by

$$\frac{X(z)}{U(z)} = H(z) = \frac{a_0 + a_1 z^{-1} + \cdots + a_m z^{-m}}{1 + b_1 z^{-1} + \cdots + b_n z^{-n}} \qquad (3.01)$$

where $z = e^{st}$ and T is the sampling interval.

Equation (3.01) may also be written in the form of a difference equation, as below,

$$x_k = \sum_{i=0}^{m} a_i u_{k-i} - \sum_{i=1}^{n} b_i x_{k-i} \qquad (3.02)$$

where

$$x_i \triangleq x(iT)$$

$$u_i \triangleq u(iT) \qquad i = 1, 2, \ldots$$

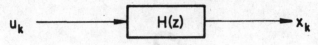

Figure 3.1

Thus, our problem is the determination of the parameters $a_0, a_1, \ldots, a_m$, $b_1, \ldots, b_n$ from the input-output data.

Collecting the various sets of x_i and u_i, equation (3.02) may be concatenated (Mendel 1972) to give the following matrix equation

$$
\begin{bmatrix}
u_k & u_{k-1} & \cdots u_{k-m} & -x_{k-1} & -x_{k-2} & \cdots & -x_{k-n} \\
u_{k+1} & u_k & \cdots u_{k-m+1} & -x_k & -x_{k-1} & \cdots & -x_{k-n+1} \\
\vdots & \vdots & \vdots & \vdots & \vdots & & \vdots \\
u_{k+p-1} & u_{k+p-2} & \cdots u_{k+p-m-1} & -x_{k+p-2} & -x_{k+p-3} & \cdots & -x_{k+p-n-1}
\end{bmatrix}
\cdot
\begin{bmatrix}
a_0 \\
a_1 \\
\vdots \\
a_m \\
b_1 \\
b_2 \\
\vdots \\
b_n
\end{bmatrix}
=
\begin{bmatrix}
x_k \\
x_{k+1} \\
\vdots \\
x_{k+p-1}
\end{bmatrix}
\qquad (3.03)
$$

or

$$
A_k' \underline{\theta} = \underline{x}_k \qquad (3.04)
$$

where

$$
A_k' =
\begin{bmatrix}
u_k & u_{k-1} & \cdots u_{k-m} & -x_{k-1} & -x_{k-2} & \cdots & -x_{k-n} \\
u_{k+1} & u_k & \cdots u_{k-m+1} & -x_k & -x_{k-1} & \cdots & -x_{k-n+1} \\
\vdots & \vdots & \vdots & \vdots & \vdots & & \vdots \\
u_{k+p-1} & u_{k+p-2} & \cdots u_{k+p-m-1} & -x_{k+p-2} & -x_{k+p-3} & \cdots & -x_{k+p-1}
\end{bmatrix}
$$

$$
(3.05)
$$

$$\theta = \begin{bmatrix} a_0 \\ a_1 \\ \vdots \\ a_m \\ b_1 \\ b_2 \\ \vdots \\ b_n \end{bmatrix} \triangleq \text{parameter vector} \tag{3.06}$$

and

$$\underline{x}_k = \begin{bmatrix} x_k \\ x_{k+1} \\ \vdots \\ x_{k+p-1} \end{bmatrix} \triangleq \text{concatenated output vector} \tag{3.07}$$

It may be noted that if A_k' is a square nonsingular matrix (i.e., $p = m + n + 1$ and $\det A_k' \neq 0$), then one may obtain the parameter vector simply as

$$\theta = (A_k')^{-1} \underline{x}_k \tag{3.08}$$

3.2 WEIGHTED LEAST-SQUARES ESTIMATES OF PARAMETERS FROM NOISE-CONTAMINATED DATA

The result derived in the previous section is of theoretical interest only, since the measurements are always contaminated with noise. In such practical situations, one may model the system as shown in Figure 3.2, where the measured output is shown as

$$y_i = x_i + n_i \tag{3.09}$$

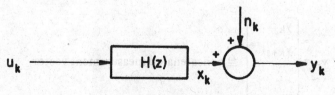

Figure 3.2

It may be noted that the term n_i represents the measurements noise at the output as well as the effect of input and internal disturbance.

We may or may not know much about the noise sequence $\{n_i\}$. In the absence of any information, we may assume that $\{n_i\}$ is a white Gaussian noise sequence. If the measurement noise is not white, we may often consider it as the output of a linear filter with a unit-variance white Gaussian noise input.

Substituting equation (3.09) into (3.02), we obtain

$$y_k = \sum_{i=0}^{m} a_i u_{k-i} - \sum_{i=1}^{n} b_i y_{k-i} + v_k = \underline{\phi}_k^T \underline{\theta} + v_k \tag{3.10}$$

where

$$\underline{\phi}_k^T = [u_k \quad u_{k-1} \cdots u_{k-m} \quad -y_{k-1} \quad -y_{k-2} \cdots -y_{k-n}] \tag{3.10a}$$

and

$$v_k = n_k + \sum_{i=1}^{n} b_i n_{k-i} \tag{3.11}$$

are called the output or equation errors.

Equation (3.10) may be concatenated (Mendel 1972), as before, to give

$$A_p \underline{\theta} = \underline{y}_p - \underline{v}_p \tag{3.12}$$

where

$$A_p = \begin{bmatrix} u_k & u_{k-1} & \cdots u_{k-m} & -y_{k-1} & -y_{k-2} & \cdots -y_{k-n} \\ u_{k+1} & u_k & \cdots u_{k-m+1} & -y_k & -y_{k-1} & \cdots -y_{k-n+1} \\ \vdots & \vdots & \vdots & \vdots & \vdots & \vdots \\ u_{k+p-1} & u_{k+p-2} & \cdots u_{k+p-m-1} & -y_{k+p-2} & -y_{k+p-3} & \cdots -y_{k+p-n-1} \end{bmatrix}$$

$$\triangleq \text{concatenated observation matrix} \tag{3.13}$$

and

$$\underline{y}_p = \begin{bmatrix} y_k \\ y_{k+1} \\ \vdots \\ y_{k+p-1} \end{bmatrix} \triangleq \text{concatenated measurement vector} \tag{3.14}$$

Because of the presence of noise, we shall now need more than $(m + n + 1)$ equations to estimate the parameter vector from equation (3.12); i.e., now we must have

$$p > m + n + 1 \tag{3.15}$$

Let us denote the estimate of $\underline{\theta}$, based on the p sets of input-output data as $\underline{\hat{\theta}}_p$. If we assume that $\underline{\hat{\theta}}_p$ is the optimal estimate of the parameter vector in some sense, then the optimal estimate of the output vector, $\underline{\hat{y}}_p$, would be denoted by

$$\underline{\hat{y}}_p = A_p \underline{\hat{\theta}}_p \tag{3.16}$$

Define the parameter estimation error vector as

$$\underline{\tilde{\theta}}_p = \underline{\theta} - \underline{\hat{\theta}}_p \tag{3.17}$$

and the output error vector as

$$\underline{\tilde{y}}_p = \underline{y}_p - \underline{\hat{y}}_p \tag{3.18}$$

Substituting equations (3.12) and (3.16) into (3.18), we get

$$\underline{\tilde{y}}_p = A_p \underline{\tilde{\theta}}_p + \underline{v}_p \tag{3.19}$$

Here $\underline{\tilde{y}}_p$ is called the vector equation error.

We shall now consider obtaining $\underline{\hat{\theta}}_p$ such that a given measure of the vector equation error $\underline{\tilde{y}}_p$ is minimized.

The simplest case occurs when we minimize the norm-squared of $\underline{\tilde{y}}_p$, i.e.,

$$J = \underline{\tilde{y}}_p^T \underline{\tilde{y}}_p \tag{3.20}$$

Recall that

$$\underline{\tilde{y}}_p = \underline{y}_p - \underline{\hat{y}}_p = \underline{y}_p - A_p \underline{\hat{\theta}}_p \tag{3.21}$$

Hence

$$J = \underline{y}_p^T \underline{y}_p - \underline{y}_p^T A_p \underline{\hat{\theta}} - \underline{\hat{\theta}}^T A_p^T \underline{y}_p + \underline{\hat{\theta}}^T A_p^T A_p \underline{\hat{\theta}}_p \tag{3.22}$$

To select $\hat{\underline{\theta}}_p$ which will minimize J, let us differentiate J with respect to $\hat{\underline{\theta}}_p$ and equate to zero. Hence, we have*

$$\hat{\underline{\theta}}_p = (A_p^T A_p)^{-1} A_p^T \underline{y}_p \qquad (3.23)$$

or

$$\hat{\underline{\theta}}_p = A_p^+ \cdot \underline{y}_p \qquad (3.24)$$

where $A_p^+ \triangleq (A_p^T A_p)^{-1} A_p$ is the pseudoinverse of A_p, provided that A_p has more rows than columns, and is unique if A_p is of full rank, i.e., the columns of A_p are linearly independent.

The estimate given by equation (3.23) is called the least-squares estimate as it minimizes the sum of the squares of the components of the equation error vector, $\tilde{\underline{y}}_p$.

A more general error criterion is obtained when a weighted sum of the squares of the components of $\tilde{\underline{y}}_p$ is minimized, i.e.,

$$J = \tilde{\underline{y}}_p^T W \tilde{\underline{y}}_p \qquad (3.25)$$

where W is a positive definite symmetric matrix, and in the simplest case it is a diagonal matrix, i.e.,

$$W = \text{diag}(w_1, w_2, \ldots, w_p) \qquad (3.26)$$

---

*Equation (3.23) may be derived as follows. Differentiating (3.22) with respect to $\hat{\theta}_p$, we have

$$\frac{dJ}{d\hat{\underline{\theta}}_p} = 0 - \underline{y}_p^T A_p - [A_p^T \underline{y}_p]^T + 2\hat{\underline{\theta}}^T A_p^T A_p = 0$$

or

$$2A_p^T \underline{y}_p = 2A_p^T A \hat{\underline{\theta}}$$

giving

$$\hat{\underline{\theta}} = (A_p^T A_p)^{-1} A_p^T y_p$$

Also,

$$\frac{d^2J}{d\hat{\theta}_p^2} = 2A_p^T A_p$$

which is symmetric and positive definite if A_p is of full rank.

In this case, it is easily shown that

$$J = \underline{y}_p^T W \underline{y}_p - \underline{y}_p^T W A_p \hat{\underline{\theta}} - \hat{\underline{\theta}}^T A_p^T W \underline{y}_p + \hat{\underline{\theta}}_p^T A^T W A_p \hat{\underline{\theta}} \qquad (3.27)$$

and, as before for minimum J,

$$\hat{\underline{\theta}}_p = (A_p^T W A_p)^{-1} A_p^T W \underline{y}_p \qquad (3.28)$$

Since W is assumed to be positive definite (and symmetric), the solution will exist if A_p is of full rank.

Note that making W = I, changes equation (3.28) into equation (3.24). Thus, the least squares solution is a special case of the present solution, which is called the weighted least-squares solution. We shall now consider a number of important questions about equation (3.28).

3.3 CONDITIONS FOR THE EXISTENCE OF THE WEIGHTED LEAST-SQUARES SOLUTION

First of all, we must know when a solution to this equation exists, as it requires the inversion of the matrix $A_p^T W A_p$. Since in most practical situations W is a diagonal matrix, and always positive definite, we need only check the rank of $A_p^T A_p$. Recalling that the elements of A_p are the observed values of the input and output sequences gives us some insight into the problem. For the various columns of $A_p^T A_p$ to be linearly independent, the input sequence must be such that it excites all the modes of the system to be identified. Furthermore, since we like to use all of the input-output data to obtain the best estimate of the parameters in the weighted least-squares sense, the input sequence must keep on exciting the system persistently. As pointed out by Aström and Bohlin (1966), this latter condition will be satisfied if the upper left (m X m) matrix component of $A_p^T A_p$ is nonsingular. In general, the matrix $A_p^T A_p$ will be nonsingular if the input sequence satisfies one of the following conditions:

(i) $\{u_i\}$ is a random sequence
(ii) $\{u_i\}$ is a pseudorandom binary sequence
(iii) $\{u_i\}$ has been obtained from the samples of a periodic function containing at least n sinusoids the frequencies of which are not integrally related and the period of the function is greater than the total time over which the input-output data have been observed. Also, all natural modes are present in the output sequence.

It may be added that if the system has one or more unobservable modes, these cannot be identified using any method, since these modes do not affect the output in any manner.

3.4   BIAS AND CONSISTENCY OF THE ESTIMATES

The next important question arises about the nature of the estimates. The estimate $\hat{\underline{\theta}}_p$ of the parameter vector $\underline{\theta}$ is said to be consistent if, in the long run, the difference between $\hat{\underline{\theta}}$ and $\underline{\theta}$ approaches zero, i.e.,

$$\lim_{p \to \infty} E[(\hat{\underline{\theta}}_p - \underline{\theta})] = 0 \tag{3.29}$$

Alternatively, one may use the mean-square criterion,

$$\lim_{p \to \infty} \operatorname{tr} E[\tilde{\underline{\theta}}_p \tilde{\underline{\theta}}_p^T] = 0 \tag{3.30}$$

The estimate $\hat{\underline{\theta}}_p$ of $\underline{\theta}$ is said to be unbiased if the expected value of the left-hand side of equation (3.29) is zero for all p, i.e.,

$$E[\tilde{\underline{\theta}}_p] = 0 \qquad \text{for all} \quad p > m + n + 1. \tag{3.31}$$

We shall now examine the bias and consistency of the weighted least-squares solution. From equations (3.28) and (3.12), we have

$$\hat{\underline{\theta}}_p = (A_p^T W A_p)^{-1} A_p^T W (A_p \underline{\theta} + \underline{v}_p) \tag{3.32}$$

Hence,

$$\hat{\underline{\theta}}_p = \underline{\theta} + (A_p^T W A_p)^{-1} A_p^T W \underline{v}_p \tag{3.33}$$

Taking expectations, we obtain

$$E[\hat{\underline{\theta}}_p] = \underline{\theta} + E[(A_p^T W A_p)^{-1} A_p^T W \underline{v}_p] \tag{3.34}$$

Let us consider first the case when A_p is deterministic. In this case, we have

$$E[\hat{\underline{\theta}}_p] = \underline{\theta} + [(A_p^T W A_p)^{-1} A_p^T W \cdot E[\underline{v}_p] \tag{3.35}$$

Hence, the estimates will be consistent and unbiased if

$$E[\underline{v}_p] = 0 \tag{3.36}$$

For stochastic A_p, if we assume that A_p is statistically independent of $\underline{v}_p$, we may write

$$E[\hat{\underline{\theta}}_p] = \underline{\theta} + E[(A_p^TWA_p)^{-1}A_p^T]\,W \cdot E[\underline{v}_p] \qquad (3.37)$$

Hence, for the general stochastic case, it follows that the weighted least squares estimate is consistent and unbiased for any W if

(i) A_p and $\underline{v}_p$ are statistically independent and
(ii) the expected value $E[\underline{v}_p]$ of the residual errors is zero.

It may be pointed out that the above are sufficient but not necessary conditions for the unbiasedness of the weighted least-squares estimate. The necessary condition is that

$$E[(A_p^TWA_p)^{-1}A_p^TW\underline{v}_p] = 0 \qquad (3.38)$$

which is a vector orthogonality condition. Since this is a weaker condition than the earlier ones (although more difficult to verify), this provides us with an approach to obtaining unbiased estimates even when $E[\underline{v}_p] \neq 0$. This is to select a positive definite matrix W such that the orthogonality condition is satisfied. As will be shown later, it leads to the method of instrumental variables, where A_p is replaced by A_p^* so chosen that A_p^* is uncorrelated with $\underline{v}_p$. This method will be discussed in section 3.8.

3.5 COVARIANCE OF THE ERROR

We shall now compute the covariance of the error in parameter estimation. By definition

$$\text{cov}[\tilde{\underline{\theta}}_p] = E[\tilde{\underline{\theta}}_p \tilde{\underline{\theta}}_p^T] \qquad (3.39)$$

Recalling that $\tilde{\underline{\theta}}_p = \underline{\theta} - \hat{\underline{\theta}}_p$, and substituting from equation (3.33), we have

$$\text{cov}[\tilde{\underline{\theta}}_p] = E[(A_p^TWA_p)^{-1}A_p^TW\underline{v}_p\underline{v}_p^TWA_p(A_p^TWA_p)^{-1}] \qquad (3.40)$$

For the particular case when A_p is deterministic, equation (3.40) takes the following form

$$\text{cov}[\tilde{\underline{\theta}}_p] = E[(A_p^TWA_p)^{-1}A_p^TWRWA_p(A_p^TWA_p)^{-1}] \qquad (3.41)$$

where

$$R = E[\underline{v}_p\underline{v}_p^T] \qquad (3.42)$$

It is interesting to note that in the special case when $W = R^{-1}$, equation (3.41) takes the simple form

$$\text{cov}\,[\tilde{\theta}_p] = (A_p^T R^{-1} A_p)^{-1} \tag{3.43}$$

It can be shown (Deutsch 1965) that the minimum value of the error covariance matrix is obtained when $W = R^{-1}$, as in equation (3.43), and any other value of W gives a larger error covariance.

It follows that if the residual errors have the property

$$R = E[\underline{v}_p \underline{v}_p^T] = \sigma^2 I \tag{3.44}$$

then the ordinary least squares estimate is also the minimum-variance estimate. Moreover, in this case, the error covariance matrix is obtained as

$$\text{cov}\,[\tilde{\underline{\theta}}_p \tilde{\underline{\theta}}_p^T] = \sigma^2 (A_p^T A_p)^{-1} = \frac{\sigma^2}{p} \left(\frac{1}{p} A_p^T A_p \right)^{-1} \tag{3.45}$$

As p is increased, we obtain

$$\lim_{p \to \infty} \text{cov}\,[\tilde{\underline{\theta}}_p \tilde{\underline{\theta}}_p^T] = \lim_{p \to \infty} \frac{\sigma^2}{p} \cdot \left(\frac{1}{p} A_p^T A \right)^{-1} = 0 \tag{3.46}$$

This indicates that as p approaches infinity, $\hat{\underline{\theta}}$ approaches $\underline{\theta}$, and we have a consistent estimator.

As seen from equations (3.11), in general, $\underline{v}_p$ will not be independent of A_p, because v_i is related to the noise in the previous observations. Hence, if $E[\underline{v}_p] \neq 0$, the ordinary least squares method will not give unbiased or consistent estimates. The weighted least squares method can give such estimates, provided that we use a suitable weighting matrix W.

3.6 MAXIMUM LIKELIHOOD ESTIMATION

This is one of the most successful approaches to obtaining unbiased estimates. The basic principle is very straightforward and will be explained first before applying it to the problem of system identification.

Let $\{v_k\}$ be a discrete random process depending on an unknown parameter θ. We shall assume that we know the probability density function $f(v; \theta)$. Suppose we have available n independent observations $v_1, v_2, \ldots, v_n$, and from these we want to determine the best estimate of θ on the basis of these samples. We choose θ in such a way that the observations v_i are most likely to occur. To do this, we define a likelihood function and then determine the value of θ which will maximize this likelihood function.

The likelihood function is usually defined as the joint probability density function of v_i. Since we have assumed that $\{v_i\}$ are uncorrelated, we may write

$$L(v_1, v_2, \ldots, v_n; \theta) = f(v_1; \theta) \cdot f(v_2; \theta) \cdots f(v_n; \theta) \tag{3.47}$$

Since the right-hand side of equation (3.47) is the product of a number of density functions, and because log L is a monotonic function of L, attaining its maximum when L is maximum, it is simpler to maximize log L rather than L. Hence, the maximum likelihood estimate of θ is given by $\hat{\theta}_{ML}$, satisfying the following equation

$$\left. \frac{\partial}{\partial \theta} \log L \right|_{\vartheta = \hat{\theta}_{ML}} = 0 \tag{3.48}$$

Let us now apply the principle of maximum likelihood to the problem of system identification. Starting with equations (3.10) and (3.12), and assuming that $\{v_i\}$ is a zero-mean white Gaussian noise sequence uncorrelated with $\{u_i\}$, we can express the likelihood function as

$$L[\underline{y}_p; \underline{\theta}] = (2\pi\sigma^2)^{-p/2} \exp\left[-\frac{1}{2} \frac{(\underline{y}_p - A_p\underline{\theta})^T (\underline{y}_p - A_p\underline{\theta})}{\sigma^2}\right] \tag{3.49}$$

Taking the logarithms of both sides, we get the logarithmic likelihood function

$$\log L[\underline{y}_p; \underline{\theta}] = -\frac{p}{2} \log 2\pi - \frac{p}{2} \log \sigma^2 - \frac{1}{2} \frac{(\underline{y}_p - A_p\underline{\theta})^T (\underline{y}_p - A_p\underline{\theta})}{\sigma^2} \tag{3.50}$$

Setting to zero the partial derivatives with respect to the unknown quantities $\underline{\theta}$ and σ, we have the following expressions for the maximum likelihood estimates

$$\frac{1}{\hat{\sigma}_{ML}^2} (A_p^T A_p \hat{\underline{\theta}}_{ML} - A_p^T \underline{y}_p) = 0 \tag{3.51}$$

$$-\frac{p}{2\hat{\sigma}_{ML}^2} + \frac{Q}{2\hat{\sigma}_{ML}^4} = 0 \tag{3.52}$$

where

$$Q = (\underline{y}_p - A_p \hat{\underline{\theta}}_{ML})^T (\underline{y}_p - A_p \hat{\underline{\theta}}_{ML}) = \tilde{\underline{y}}_p^T \tilde{\underline{y}}_p \tag{3.53}$$

Note that equations (3.51) and (3.52) are uncoupled. We can solve equation (3.51) to get the maximum likelihood estimate for the parameter vector

$$\underline{\hat{\theta}}_{ML} = (A_p^T A_p)^{-1} A_p^T \underline{y}_p \qquad (3.54)$$

It is thus seen that for this special case (zero-mean white Gaussian observation noise), the maximum likelihood estimate is identical with the ordinary least-squares estimate obtained in equation (3.23). In addition, the maximum likelihood estimate for the variance of the observation noise is given by

$$\hat{\sigma}_{ML}^2 = \frac{Q}{p} = \frac{1}{p} \sum_{k=1}^{p} e_k^2 \qquad (3.55)$$

where

$$e_k = y_k - \underline{\phi}_k^T \underline{\hat{\phi}}_{ML} \qquad (3.56)$$

We shall now consider the more realistic situation when the observation noise is nonwhite. In this case we can model it as the output of a linear system subject to white noise input, i.e.,

$$v_k = \sum_{i=1}^{r} c_i z_{k-1} + z_k \qquad (3.57)$$

where $\{z_i\}$ is a zero-mean normally distributed white noise sequence uncorrelated with $\{u_i\}$. It may be noted that although $\{v_i\}$ is no longer a white noise sequence, it is still normally distributed as it is a linear combination of several normally distributed random variables $\{z_i\}$. Our input-output relationship, equation (3.12) still applies, but now we need the covariance matrix for $\{v_i\}$. Define

$$R = E[\underline{v}_p \underline{v}_p^T] \qquad (3.58)$$

Then, our logarithmic likelihood function is obtained as

$$\log L[\underline{y}_p; \underline{\theta}] = -\frac{p}{2} \log 2\pi - \frac{1}{2} \log (\det R) + \frac{1}{2} (\underline{y}_p - A_p \underline{\theta})^T R^{-1} (\underline{y}_p - A_p \underline{\theta}) \qquad (3.59)$$

Although equation (3.59) is very similar to (3.50), we shall not be able to obtain an explicit solution this time because of the dependence of the likelihood function on the parameter c_i through R^{-1} and det R. Hence, an iterative scheme for numerical solution must be followed. This is summarized below (Aström and Eykhoff 1971).

(i) Obtain an initial estimate for the parameters, based on classical methods of identification and/or the ordinary least-squares method. Also, assume an initial estimate of the parameters c_i, and include these with a_i and b_i to obtain $\underline{\hat{\theta}}_o$.

(ii) Calculate the sequence of residuals e_k, defined as the difference between the observed output y_k and the predicted output $\hat{y}_k$.

(iii) From the sequence of residuals, calculate the following partial derivatives

$$\frac{\partial e_k}{\partial a_i} = -u_{k-i} - \sum_{j=1}^{r} c_j \frac{\partial e_{k-j}}{\partial a_i} \qquad (3.60)$$

$$\frac{\partial e_k}{\partial b_i} = -y_{k-i} - \sum_{j=1}^{r} c_j \frac{\partial e_{k-j}}{\partial b_i} \qquad (3.61)$$

$$\frac{\partial e_k}{\partial c_i} = -e_{k-i} - \sum_{j=1}^{r} c_j \frac{\partial e_{k-j}}{\partial c_i} \qquad (3.62)$$

(iv) Calculate

$$\hat{\sigma}_k^2 = \frac{1}{p} \sum_{k=1}^{p} e_k^2, \qquad (3.63)$$

$$\sum_{k=1}^{p} e_k \cdot \frac{\partial e_k}{\partial \underline{\theta}} \qquad (3.64)$$

and

$$\sum_{k=1}^{p} \left(\frac{\partial e_k}{\partial \underline{\theta}}\right)^T \frac{\partial e_k}{\partial \underline{\theta}} \qquad (3.65)$$

(v) Calulate the change in the parameter vector, $\delta\underline{\theta}$, given by

$$\delta\underline{\theta} = -\sum_{k=1}^{p} \left(\frac{\partial e_k}{\partial \underline{\theta}}\right)^T \frac{\partial e_k}{\partial \underline{\theta}} + \sum_{k=1}^{p} e_k \left(\frac{\partial^2 e_k}{\partial \underline{\theta} \partial \underline{\theta}}\right)^{-1} \sum_{k=1}^{p} e_k \cdot \frac{\partial e_k}{\partial \underline{\theta}} \qquad (3.66)$$

(vi) Determine the new estimate of the parameter vector

$$\hat{\underline{\theta}}_{k+1} = \hat{\underline{\theta}}_k + \delta\underline{\theta} \tag{3.67}$$

(vii) If $(\hat{\sigma}_{k+1}^2 - \hat{\sigma}_k^2/\hat{\sigma}_k^2) < 10^{-4}$, stop. Otherwise go back to step 2.

Note that step (vii) in this algorithm suggests that when the sum of the squares of the residual errors fails to reduce by more than 0.01 percent, we should stop. This is based on a statistical test of the significance of the reduction (Aström and Eykhoff 1971).

3.7 THE GENERALIZED LEAST-SQUARES METHOD

The method described in the previous section is based on the assumption that the probability density function is known. Furthermore, it appears to be rather complex computationally. We shall, therefore, discuss another approach which gives unbiased estimates of the parameters. This too is an iterative procedure in which we estimate the parameters of the process and noise models to minimize the mean square error. Define the auxiliary parameter vector

$$\underline{\psi} = [c_1 \quad c_2 \cdots c_r]^T \tag{3.68}$$

which defines an autoregressive model for the noise (see Chapter 6 for AR models) and let

$$B_p = \begin{bmatrix} v_{k-1} & v_{k-2} & \cdots & v_{k-r} \\ v_k & v_{k-1} & \cdots & v_{k+1-r} \\ \vdots & \vdots & & \vdots \\ v_{k+p-2} & v_{k+p-3} & \cdots & v_{k+p-r-1} \end{bmatrix}$$

We shall discuss a computationally efficient algorithm developed by Hsia (1976). From the system and noise models, we get the following equations

$$\left. \begin{array}{l} \underline{y}_p = A_p\underline{\theta} + \underline{v}_p \\ \underline{v}_p = B_p\underline{\psi} + \underline{z}_p \end{array} \right\} \tag{3.69}$$

These may be combined to obtain

$$\underline{y}_p = [A_p B_p] \begin{bmatrix} \underline{\theta} \\ \overline{\underline{\psi}} \end{bmatrix} + \underline{z}_p \tag{3.70}$$

Hence, a least-squares estimate is obtained as below

$$
\begin{bmatrix} \hat{\theta}_p \\ \hat{\psi}_p \end{bmatrix} = \begin{bmatrix} A_p^T A_p & A_p^T B_p \\ B_p^T A_p & B_p^T B_p \end{bmatrix}^{-1} \begin{bmatrix} A_p^T \\ B_p^T \end{bmatrix} y_p \tag{3.71}
$$

Solving for $\hat{\theta}_p$ and $\hat{\psi}_p$, we obtain

$$
\hat{\theta}_p = (A_p^T A_p)^{-1} A_p^T y_p - (A_p^T A_p)^{-1} A_p^T B_p \hat{\psi}_p \tag{3.72}
$$

and

$$
\hat{\psi}_p = D^{-1} B_p^T M y_p \tag{3.73}
$$

where

$$
M = I - A_p (A_p^T A_p)^{-1} A_p^T \tag{3.74}
$$

$$
D = B_p^T M B_p \tag{3.75}
$$

It may be noted that the first term in the expression for $\hat{\theta}_p$ is the ordinary least-squares estimate and the second term is the correction required for the bias.

The algorithm requires the following steps:

(i) Calculate the least-squares estimate using equation (3.24)

$$
\hat{\theta}_{LS} = A_p^+ y_p
$$

and set

$$
\hat{\theta}_i = \hat{\theta}_{LS} \tag{3.76}
$$

(ii) Generate the residuals using

$$
v_p = y_p - A_p \hat{\theta}_i \tag{3.77}
$$

Hence, obtain B_p and calculate D using equation (3.75).

(iii) Calculate $\hat{\psi}$ using equation (3.73) and hence update the estimate for θ using the relationship

$$
\hat{\theta}_{i+1} = \hat{\theta}_i - A_p^+ B_p \hat{\psi} \tag{3.78}
$$

(iv) Return to step (ii) and repeat until convergence is obtained.

It may be noted that the main idea behind the method is to keep on updating the estimate of the auxiliary parameter vector $\underline{\psi}$ and making the corresponding correction in the estimate for the process parameter $\underline{\theta}$ until no further improvement is obtained. Thus, the generalized least-squares algorithm is essentially an iterative procedure for solving a highly nonlinear minimization problem. It may not converge to the optimal solution in some cases (Soderstrom 1974), since the presence of local minima is possible, specially if the signal-to-noise ratio is low.

3.8 THE INSTRUMENTAL VARIABLE METHOD

The algorithm described in the previous section requires a considerable amount of iterative computation. We shall now consider another method of obtaining consistent estimates which is nearly as simple as the ordinary least-squares method (Wong and Polak 1967, Young 1970). Consider again equation (3.12)

$$\underline{y}_p = A_p \underline{\theta} + \underline{v}_p \tag{3.79}$$

Let us assume that there exists a matrix Z of the same dimensions as A_p such that

$$E[Z^T \underline{v}_p] = 0 \tag{3.80}$$

$$E[Z^T A_p] = Q, \tag{3.81}$$

where Q is a nonsingular matrix.

Then, premultiplying both sides of (3.79) by Z^T, we have

$$Z^T \underline{y}_p = Z^T A_p \underline{\theta} + Z^T \underline{v}_p \tag{3.82}$$

Thus, an unbiased and consistent estimate of $\underline{\theta}$ is obtained as

$$\hat{\underline{\theta}}_{IV} = (Z^T A_p)^{-1} Z^T \underline{y}_p \tag{3.83}$$

in view of equation (3.80).

A comparison of equation (3.83) with the weighted least-squares estimate (3.28) indicates that the two are identical if

$$Z = W A_p \tag{3.84}$$

The matrix Z is called the instrumental variable matrix, and its elements the instrumental variables. The important question is how to construct the matrix Z such that equations (3.80) and (3.81) are satisfied. Note that equa-

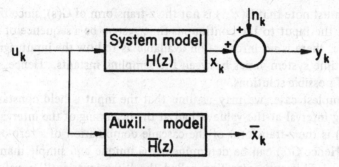

Figure 3.3.   Generation of instrumental variables.

tion (3.80) implies that the instrumental variables are uncorrelated with the sequence $\{v_i\}$, whereas equation (3.81) implies that they are strongly correlated with $\{u_i\}$ and $\{y_i\}$ in A_p. Hence, one obvious choice for Z is given below

$$
Z = \begin{bmatrix}
u_k & u_{k-1} & \cdots & u_{k-m} & -x_{k-1} & -x_{k-2} & \cdots & -x_{k-n} \\
u_{k+1} & u_k & \cdots & u_{k-m+1} & -x_k & -x_{k-1} & \cdots & -x_{k-n+1} \\
\vdots & \vdots & & \vdots & \vdots & \vdots & & \vdots \\
u_{k+p-1} & u_{k+p-2} & \cdots & u_{k+p-m-1} & -x_{k+p-2} & -x_{k+p-3} & \cdots & -x_{k+p-n-1}
\end{bmatrix}
$$

$$(3.85)$$

which consists of the actual (noise-free) inputs and outputs of the system. However, the actual output sequence is not available. One simple approximation is to use the output of any auxiliary model whose transfer function is an estimate of the system transfer function, although any stable auxiliary model of the same order as the system will be acceptable (Finigan and Rowe 1974). This scheme is shown in the block diagram in Figure 3.3.

The main advantage of the instrumental variable method is that it is less complicated to use. In general, however, it is a less efficient estimator than the generalized least-squares method.

3.9   ESTIMATION OF THE CONTINUOUS-TIME SYSTEM MODEL FROM SAMPLED DATA

Having considered various methods for estimating the parameters of a discrete-time model, $H(z^{-1})$, from the samples of input-output data, we now need to discuss the estimation of the transfer function, $G(s)$, of the equivalent continuous-time model.

First we must note that $H(z^{-1})$ is not the z-transform of $G(s)$, since this would require that the input to the continuous-time system be a sequence of impulses. Furthermore, there is no information available as to how the input signal to the continuous-time system varies between the sampling instants. Hence, there are a number of possible solutions.

In the simplest case, we may assume that the input is held constant during the sampling interval at the value it had at the beginning of the interval. In this case, $H(z^{-1})$ is the z-transform of the cascade combination of a zero-order hold and $G(s)$. Hence $G(s)$ can be determined in a unique and simple manner for a given $H(z^{-1})$. This approximation called the "step-invariant" transformation, is exact when the input is actually a step function, or a sequence of steps, with changes occurring only at the sampling instants. For other inputs, the approximation may not be good.

A better approximation, in many cases, may be to assume that during a given sampling interval $nT \leqslant t < (n+1)T$, the input $u(t)$ varies linearly from $u(nT)$ to $u(nT + T)$. This leads to the so-called "ramp-invariant" transformation (Haykin 1972).

For both of these approximations, the poles of $H(z^{-1})$ and $G(s)$ are related through the simple transformation $z = e^{sT}$, where T is the sampling interval, and can be easily evaluated. The residues at the poles are different for the two cases. To be more specific, consider the case when

$$G(s) = \sum_{k=1}^{n} \frac{A_k}{s + p_k} \tag{3.86}$$

Then the poles of $H(z)$ are obtained as

$$z_k = e^{-p_k T} \tag{3.87}$$

For the step invariant transformation, the discrete-time transfer function is given by (Haykin 1972)

$$H(z) = \sum_{k=1}^{n} \frac{A_k(1 - e^{-p_k T})}{p_k(z - e^{-p_k T})} = \sum_{k=1}^{n} \frac{B_k}{z - e^{-p_k T}} \tag{3.88}$$

Hence,

$$A_k = \frac{B_k p_k}{1 - e^{-p_k T}} \tag{3.89}$$

Hence, in this case, we may calculate B_k given A_k, or vice-versa, fairly easily.

For the ramp-invariant transformation (Haykin 1972),

$$H(z) = \frac{1}{T} \sum_{k=1}^{n} \frac{A_k}{p_k^2} \frac{(Tp_k - 1 + e^{-p_kT})z + (1 - e^{-p_kT} - Tp_k e^{-p_kT})}{z - e^{-p_kT}}$$

$$= \sum_{k=1}^{n} \frac{C_k z + D_k}{z - e^{-p_kT}} \tag{3.90}$$

where

$$C_k = \frac{A_k}{Tp_k^2}(Tp_k - 1 + e^{-p_kT})$$

$$D_k = \frac{A_k}{Tp_k^2}(1 - e^{-p_kT} - Tp_k e^{-p_kT}) \tag{3.91}$$

For both of these transformations, a large amount of computation is required. First one must determine the poles of $H(z)$, and then evaluate the residues at the poles. Then the residues of $G(s)$ must be evaluated at the corresponding poles before $G(s)$ is obtained. Although, in general, the ramp-invariant transformation will provide a better approximation, there is no guarantee that it will be good for all inputs.

Another important consideration is the rate of sampling. In particular, if $|p_k T| \leq 0.5$ for all poles of $G(s)$, or equivalently, if $|z_k| \leq 0.6$, one may use the so called "bilinear z transformation," given by

$$s = \frac{2}{T} \frac{1 - z^{-1}}{1 + z^{-1}}$$

$$\text{or} \quad z^{-1} = \frac{2 - sT}{2 + sT} \tag{3.92}$$

to obtain $G(s)$, given $H(z)$. This method requires much less computation, and usually gives a better approximation than the step-invariant and ramp-invariant transformations for a more general input (Sinha 1972).

3.10   REFERENCES

Aström, K. J. and Bohlin T. (1966), "Numerical identification of linear dynamical systems from normal operating records," in: *Theory of Self-Adaptive Control Systems*, P. Hammond, ed., Plenum Press, New York.

Aström, K. J. and Eykhoff, P. E. (1971), "System identification—a survey," *Automatica*, vol. 7, pp. 123–162.

Deutsch, R. (1965), *Estimation Theory*, Prentice-Hall, Englewood Cliffs, N.J.

Finigan, B. M. and Rowe, J. H. (1974), "Strongly consistent parameter estimation by the introduction of strong instrumental variables," *IEEE Transactions. Automatic Control*, vol. AC-19, pp. 825–830.

Haykin, S. S. (1972), "A unified treatment of recursive digital filtering," *IEEE Transactions. Automatic Control*, vol. AC-17, pp. 113–116.

Hsia, T. C. (1976), "On least squares algorithm for system parameter identification," *IEEE Transactions. Automatic Control*, vol. AC-21, pp. 104–108.

Mendel, J. M. (1973), *Discrete Techniques of Parameter Estimation*, Marcel Dekker, New York.

Sinha, N. K. (1972), "Estimation of transfer function of continuous systems from sampled data," *Proc. IEE*, vol. 119, pp. 612–614.

Söderström, T. (1974), "Convergence properties of the generalized least squares method," *Automatica*, vol. 10, pp. 617–626.

Wong, K. Y. and Polak, E. (1967), "Identification of linear discrete time systems using the instrumental variable approach," *IEEE Transactions. Automatic Control*, vol. AC-12, pp. 707–718.

Young, P. C. (1970), "An instrumental variable method for real-time identification of noisy processes," *Automatica*, vol. 6, pp. 271–287.

3.11   PROBLEMS

1. 200 samples of the input-output data obtained from a second-order system are given in Table 3.1. Obtain the least-squares estimates of the parameter of the system. Hence, determine the sequence of residual errors and the generalized least squares estimate. (Hint: assume a noise model of order 2.)

2. Using the ordinary least-squares estimates, obtained in the previous problem, for the auxiliary model, apply the instrumental variable method for estimating the parameter vector.

3. Apply the correlation method, described in Chapter 2, to estimate the discrete-time system the input-output data for which are given in Table 3.1.

4. Determine an equivalent continuous-time transfer function G(s) for the discrete-time system

$$H(z) = \frac{4z - 2}{(z - 0.2)(z^2 - 0.6z + 0.25)}$$

if the sampling interval is 0.1 second, using (a) the step-invariant transformation, (b) the ramp-invariant transformation and (c) the bilinear z transformation.

For each case, compare the responses of G(s) and H(z) to the input $u(t) = 2 \sin t + 3 \cos 1.2t$.

5. 200 samples of input-output data obtained from a second-order system are given in Table 3.2, where the noise level is fairly high. Use (a) the maximum likelihood method, (b) the correlation method, and (c) the generalized least-squares method to obtain the best estimates of the parameters. Make a critical comparison of the methods.

Table 3.1.

k	1	2	3	4	5	6	7	8
u_k	1.147	0.201	-0.787	-1.589	-1.052	0.866	1.152	1.573
y_k	0.086	2.210	0.486	-1.862	-3.705	-2.688	1.577	2.883

k	9	10	11	12	13	14	15	16
u_k	0.626	0.433	-0.958	0.810	-0.044	0.947	-1.474	-0.719
y_k	3.705	1.642	0.805	-2.088	0.946	-0.039	1.984	-2.545

k	17	18	19	20	21	22	23	24
u_k	-0.086	1.099	1.450	1.151	0.485	1.633	0.043	1.326
y_k	-1.737	-0.231	2.440	3.583	2.915	1.443	3.598	0.702

k	25	26	27	28	29	30	31	32
u_k	1.706	-0.304	0.890	0.144	1.177	-0.390	-0.982	1.435
y_k	2.638	3.611	-0.168	1.732	0.666	2.377	-0.554	-2.088

k	33	34	35	36	37	38	39	40
u_k	-0.119	-0.769	-0.899	0.882	-1.008	-0.844	0.628	-0.679
y_k	2.698	0.189	-1.633	-2.010	1.716	-1.641	-1.885	1.061

k	41	42	43	44	45	46	47	48
u_k	1.541	1.375	-0.984	-0.582	1.609	0.090	-0.813	-0.428
y_k	-0.968	2.911	3.088	-1.629	-1.533	3.030	0.614	-1.483

k	49	50	51	52	53	54	55	56
u_k	-0.848	-0.410	0.048	-1.099	-1.108	0.259	-1.627	-0.538
y_k	-1.029	-1.947	-1.066	-0.113	-2.144	-2.626	0.134	-3.043

k	57	58	59	60	61	62	63	64
u_k	0.203	1.204	1.691	-1.235	-1.228	-1.267	1.675	0.309
y_k	-1.341	0.338	2.702	3.813	-1.924	-2.813	-2.795	3.002

k	65	66	67	68	69	70	71	72
u_k	0.043	1.461	1.585	0.552	-0.601	-0.319	0.744	0.829
y_k	1.027	0.053	2.755	3.584	1.737	-0.837	-0.617	1.703

k	73	74	75	76	77	78	79	80
u_k	-1.626	-0.127	-1.578	-0.822	1.469	-0.379	-0.212	0.178
y_k	2.045	-2.886	-0.542	-2.991	-1.859	3.045	0.068	-0.375

k	81	82	83	84	85	86	87	88
u_k	0.493	-0.056	-0.294	1.228	-1.606	-0.382	-0.229	0.313
y_k	0.451	1.036	0.153	-0.474	2.512	-2.681	-0.954	-0.307

k	89	90	91	92	93	94	95	96
u_k	-0.161	-0.810	-0.277	0.983	-0.288	0.846	1.325	0.723
y_k	0.628	-0.270	-1.719	-0.981	-1.613	-0.432	1.613	2.902

k	97	98	99	100	101	102	103	104
u_k	0.713	0.643	0.463	0.786	1.161	0.850	-1.349	-0.596
y_k	1.750	1.401	1.340	0.916	1.396	2.446	2.103	-2.432

Table 3.1.   (*Continued*)

k	105	106	107	108	109	110	111	112
u_k	1.512	0.795	−0.713	−0.453	−1.604	0.889	−0.938	0.056
y_k	−1.486	3.031	2.373	−0.763	−0.752	−3.207	1.385	−1.642

k	113	114	115	116	117	118	119	120
u_k	0.829	−0.981	−1.232	1.327	−0.681	0.114	−1.135	1.284
y_k	−0.118	1.756	−1.613	−2.690	2.136	−1.136	−0.005	−2.210

k	121	122	123	124	125	126	127	128
u_k	−1.302	0.758	0.590	−1.007	0.390	0.836	−1.252	−1.053
y_k	2.331	−2.204	0.983	1.347	−1.691	0.595	1.809	−2.204

k	129	130	131	132	133	134	135	136
u_k	−0.083	0.619	0.840	−1.258	−0.354	0.629	−0.242	1.680
y_k	−2.330	−0.454	1.290	2.080	−1.990	−0.770	1.240	−0.252

k	137	138	139	140	141	142	143	144
u_k	−1.326	0.803	0.537	−1.100	1.417	−1.024	0.671	0.688
y_k	3.137	−2.379	1.206	1.221	−1.977	2.471	−1.680	1.148

k	145	146	147	148	149	150	151	152
u_k	−0.123	−0.952	0.232	−0.793	−1.138	1.154	0.206	1.196
y_k	1.816	0.055	−1.865	0.269	−1.323	−2.486	1.958	0.823

k	153	154	155	156	157	158	159	160
u_k	1.013	1.518	−0.553	−0.987	0.167	−1.445	0.630	1.255
y_k	2.481	2.209	3.617	−0.762	−2.225	−0.123	−2.786	1.026

k	161	162	163	164	165	166	167	168
u_k	0.311	−1.726	0.975	1.718	1.360	1.667	−1.111	1.018
y_k	2.843	1.071	−3.317	1.514	3.807	3.388	3.683	−1.935

k	169	170	171	172	173	174	175	176
u_k	0.078	−1.665	−0.760	1.184	−0.614	0.994	−0.089	0.947
y_k	−1.423	0.309	−3.390	−2.124	2.192	−0.855	1.656	0.016

k	177	178	179	180	181	182	183	184
u_k	1.706	−0.395	1.222	−1.351	0.231	1.425	0.114	−0.689
y_k	1.804	3.774	−0.059	2.371	−2.322	−0.032	2.632	0.565

k	185	186	187	188	189	190	191	192
u_k	−0.704	1.070	0.262	1.610	1.489	−1.602	0.020	−0.601
y_k	−1.460	−1.839	1.917	0.865	3.180	3.261	−2.755	−0.536

k	193	194	195	196	197	198	199	200
u_k	−0.384	−1.637	−0.235	1.245	1.226	−0.204	0.926	−1.297
y_k	−1.171	−0.905	−3.303	−0.834	2.490	3.039	0.134	1.901

Table 3.2

k	1	2	3	4	5	6	7	8
u_k	1.147	0.201	-0.787	-1.589	-1.052	0.866	1.152	1.575
y_k	1.381	3.794	2.481	-0.280	-2.742	-1.554	2.129	2.691

k	9	10	11	12	13	14	15	16
u_k	0.626	0.433	-0.958	0.810	-0.044	0.947	-1.474	-0.719
y_k	3.427	2.199	1.679	-1.249	1.371	0.637	3.131	-0.819

k	17	18	19	20	21	22	23	24
u_k	-0.086	1.099	1.450	1.151	0.485	1.633	0.043	1.326
y_k	0.235	1.262	2.849	3.374	2.346	0.664	3.015	0.561

k	25	26	27	28	29	30	31	32
u_k	1.706	-0.340	0.890	0.144	1.177	-0.390	-0.982	1.435
y_k	2.271	3.650	0.625	2.305	0.364	1.857	-0.912	-2.547

k	33	34	35	36	37	38	39	40
u_k	-0.119	-0.769	-0.899	0.882	-1.008	-0.844	0.628	-0.679
y_k	1.940	0.262	-0.379	-0.176	3.720	0.058	-0.752	1.983

k	41	42	43	44	45	46	47	48
u_k	1.541	1.375	-0.984	-0.582	1.609	0.090	-0.813	-0.428
y_k	-0.923	3.361	4.240	-0.074	-0.481	3.780	2.137	0.086

k	49	50	51	52	53	54	55	56
u_k	-0.848	-0.410	0.048	-1.099	-1.108	0.259	-1.627	-0.538
y_k	0.638	-0.971	-0.929	0.679	-0.664	-0.433	1.570	-2.785

k	57	58	59	60	61	62	63	64
u_k	0.203	1.204	1.691	-1.235	-1.228	-1.267	1.675	0.309
y_k	-1.153	0.819	3.484	4.091	-2.375	-2.561	-2.778	2.911

k	65	66	67	68	69	70	71	72
u_k	0.043	1.461	1.585	0.552	-0.601	-0.319	0.744	0.829
y_k	1.362	0.735	3.118	3.770	2.381	-0.812	-1.635	0.589

k	73	74	75	76	77	78	79	80
u_k	-1.626	-0.127	-1.578	-0.822	1.469	-0.379	-0.212	0.178
y_k	1.550	-3.410	-1.249	-3.692	-2.358	2.552	-0.228	0.554

k	81	82	83	84	85	86	87	88
u_k	0.493	-0.056	-0.294	1.228	-1.606	-0.382	-0.229	0.313
y_k	2.178	2.471	0.743	-0.004	2.504	-3.204	-1.800	-1.284

k	89	90	91	92	93	94	95	96
u_k	-0.161	-0.810	-0.277	0.983	-0.288	0.846	1.325	0.723
y_k	0.159	0.426	0.059	0.395	2.371	-0.157	2.248	3.297

k	97	98	99	100	101	102	103	104
u_k	0.713	0.643	0.463	0.786	1.161	0.850	-1.349	-0.596
y_k	2.329	2.780	2.375	1.873	2.411	3.928	2.846	-2.215

Table 3.2.   (*Continued*)

k	105	106	107	108	109	110	111	112
u_k	1.512	0.795	-0.713	-0.453	-1.604	0.889	-0.938	0.056
y_k	-1.104	3.460	2.883	0.245	-0.231	-2.963	2.072	-0.845

k	113	114	115	116	117	118	119	120
u_k	0.829	-0.981	-1.232	1.327	-0.681	0.114	-1.135	1.284
y_k	-0.074	1.037	-2.468	-3.679	2.149	-0.081	1.639	-1.291

k	121	122	123	124	125	126	127	128
u_k	-1.302	0.758	0.590	-1.007	0.390	0.836	-1.252	-1.053
y_k	2.548	-1.681	2.307	2.227	-1.558	0.008	2.055	-1.102

k	129	130	131	132	133	134	135	136
u_k	-0.083	0.619	0.840	-1.258	-0.354	0.629	-0.242	1.680
y_k	-1.427	0.350	2.736	2.965	-2.346	-1.510	0.809	-0.592

k	137	138	139	140	141	142	143	144
u_k	-1.326	0.803	0.537	-1.100	1.417	-1.024	0.671	0.688
y_k	2.706	-1.941	2.275	2.802	-1.337	2.091	-2.585	0.013

k	145	146	147	148	149	150	151	152
u_k	-0.123	-0.952	0.232	-0.793	-1.138	1.154	0.206	1.196
y_k	1.217	0.691	-0.491	2.114	0.333	-0.482	3.388	2.082

k	153	154	155	156	157	158	159	160
u_k	1.013	1.518	-0.553	-0.987	0.162	-1.445	0.630	1.255
y_k	3.797	4.079	5.036	1.250	-1.019	-0.160	-3.201	1.161

k	161	162	163	164	165	166	167	168
u_k	0.311	-1.726	0.975	1.718	1.360	1.667	-1.111	1.018
y_k	3.926	1.789	-2.703	2.125	5.054	4.678	5.236	-0.241

k	169	170	171	172	173	174	175	176
u_k	0.078	-1.665	-0.760	1.184	-0.614	0.994	-0.089	0.947
y_k	2.152	0.356	-3.519	-2.213	1.527	-1.206	2.151	0.264

k	177	178	179	180	181	182	183	184
u_k	1.706	-0.395	1.222	-1.351	0.231	1.425	0.114	-0.689
y_k	1.595	2.864	-0.539	1.982	-3.104	-0.264	2.433	0.009

k	185	186	187	188	189	190	191	192
u_k	-0.704	1.070	0.262	1.610	1.489	-1.602	0.020	-0.601
y_k	-1.360	-0.521	3.319	1.445	3.105	3.783	-1.973	-0.138

k	193	194	195	196	197	198	199	200
u_k	-0.384	-1.637	-0.235	1.245	1.226	-0.204	0.926	-1.297
y_k	-0.452	-0.586	-4.045	-1.743	2.577	3.849	0.367	1.324

4

On-Line Identification of Discrete-Time Systems

4.1 INTRODUCTION

An identification method may be classified as an "on-line" method if it satisfies the following criteria:

(i) it must not require the application of a special input to the process in order that it can be used with the process under operation,

(ii) it does not require the storage of all the data,

(iii) it uses a recursive algorithm so that one does not have to wait for the accumulation of large amounts of data to make the identification possible, but may start with an initial estimate of the parameters even after the first set of data has been obtained, and then keep on updating the estimate as more data arrive, and

(iv) the amount of computation required for each iteration of the recursive algorithm must be such that it can be carried out within one sampling interval.

Furthermore, a realistic method for identification must take into account the fact that in practice all measurements are contaminated with noise.

During the past fifteen years, several methods have been proposed for on-line system identification. Comparisons of these methods have been made in some recent papers (Isermann et al. 1974, Saridis 1974, Sinha and Sen 1975) both for simulated systems, as well as for systems under operation.

We shall first consider the derivation of a recursive algorithm for weighted least-squares estimation that requires no matrix inversion and is, therefore, suitable for on-line applications. The derivation will be started from the first principles.

4.2 DERIVATION OF THE SEQUENTIAL WLS ALGORITHM

Consider the process model shown in Fig. 4.1.

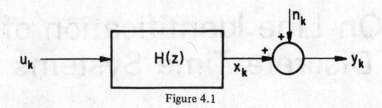

Figure 4.1

If we recall from Chapter 3 our original expression relating the input and the output of a discrete-time system, we have

$$y_k = \sum_{i=0}^{m} a_i u_{k-i} - \sum_{i=1}^{n} b_i y_{k-i} + v_k \tag{4.01}$$

where

$$v_k \triangleq n_k + \sum_{i=1}^{n} b_i n_{k-i} \tag{4.02}$$

Equation (4.01) may be rewritten as

$$y_k = \underline{\phi}_k^T \underline{\theta} + v_k \tag{4.03}$$

where

$$\underline{\phi}_k^T = [u_k \quad u_{k-1} \cdots u_{k-m} \quad -y_{k-1} \quad -y_{k-2} \cdots -y_{k-n}] \tag{4.04}$$

and

$$\underline{\theta} = [a_0 \quad a_1 \cdots a_m \quad b_1 \quad b_2 \cdots b_n]^T \tag{4.05}$$

Concatenation of p sets of measurements indicated by equation (4.03) gives

$$\underline{y}_p = A_p \underline{\theta} + \underline{v}_p \tag{4.06}$$

where

$$
\underline{y}_p = \begin{bmatrix} y_k \\ y_{k+1} \\ \vdots \\ y_{k+p-1} \end{bmatrix} \in R_p \tag{4.07}
$$

$$
A_p = \begin{bmatrix} \underline{\phi}_k^T \\ \underline{\phi}_{k+1}^T \\ \vdots \\ \underline{\phi}_{k+p-1}^T \end{bmatrix} \in R_{p \times (m+n+1)} \tag{4.08}
$$

$$
\underline{v}_p = \begin{bmatrix} v_k \\ v_{k+1} \\ \vdots \\ v_{k+p-1} \end{bmatrix} \in R_p \tag{4.09}
$$

From equation (4.06), the weighted least-squares estimate of $\underline{\theta}$ is given as

$$
\hat{\underline{\theta}}_p = (A_p^T W_p A_p)^{-1} A_p^T W_p \underline{y}_p \tag{4.10}
$$

where

$$
W = \text{diag.} \ [w_1, w_2, \ldots, w_p] \tag{4.11}
$$

Let us now consider addition of one more set of data. Define

$$
A_{p+1} \triangleq \begin{bmatrix} A_p \\ \underline{\phi}_{k+p}^T \end{bmatrix} \in R_{(p+1) \times (m+n+1)} \tag{4.12}
$$

$$
\underline{y}_{p+1} \triangleq \begin{bmatrix} \underline{y}_p \\ y_{k+p} \end{bmatrix} \in R_{p+1} \tag{4.13}
$$

$$
W_{p+1} \triangleq \left[\begin{array}{c|c} W_p & 0 \\ \hline \underline{0}^T & w_{p+1} \end{array} \right] = \text{diag} \ [w_1, w_2, \ldots, w_p, w_{p+1}] \tag{4.14}
$$

Then, corresponding to equation (4.10), we may write

$$\hat{\underline{\theta}}_{p+1} = (A_{p+1}^T W_{p+1} A_{p+1})^{-1} A_{p+1}^T W_{p+1} \underline{y}_{p+1} \tag{4.15}$$

We shall now derive a relationship between $\hat{\underline{\theta}}_{p+1}$ and $\hat{\underline{\theta}}_p$. Substituting for A_{p+1}, W_{p+1} and $\underline{y}_{p+1}$ from equations (4.12)–(4.14), we may rewrite equation (4.15) as

$$\hat{\underline{\theta}}_{p+1} = [A_p^T W_p A_p + \underline{\phi}_{k+p} w_{p+1} \underline{\phi}_{k+p}^T]^{-1} [A_p^T W_p \underline{y}_p + \underline{\phi}_{k+p} w_{p+1} y_{k+p}] \tag{4.16}$$

Define

$$P_p \triangleq (A_p^T W_p A_p)^{-1} \tag{4.17}$$

Hence, equation (4.10) may be written as

$$\hat{\underline{\theta}}_p = P_p A_p^T W_p \underline{y}_p \tag{4.18}$$

From equations (4.15) and (4.16), we may write

$$P_{p+1}^{-1} = P_p^{-1} + \underline{\phi}_{k+p} w_{p+1} \underline{\phi}_{k+p}^T \tag{4.19}$$

and

$$\hat{\underline{\theta}}_{p+1} = P_{p+1}(A_p^T W_p \underline{y}_p + \underline{\phi}_{k+p} w_{p+1} y_{k+p}) \tag{4.20}$$

$$= P_{p+1}(P_p^{-1} \hat{\underline{\theta}}_p + \underline{\phi}_{k+p} w_{p+1} y_{k+p}) \tag{4.21}$$

In the last equation, use has been made of equation (4.18), solved for $A_p^T W_p \underline{y}_p$. Substituting for P_p^{-1} in equation (4.21) from equation (4.19), we have

$$\hat{\underline{\theta}}_{p+1} = P_{p+1}[(P_{p+1}^{-1} - \underline{\phi}_{k+p} w_{p+1} \underline{\phi}_{k+p}^T) \hat{\underline{\theta}}_p + \underline{\phi}_{k+p} w_{p+1} y_{k+p}] \tag{4.22}$$

Equation (4.22) may now be simplified to give

$$\hat{\underline{\theta}}_{p+1} = \hat{\underline{\theta}}_p + P_{p+1} \underline{\phi}_{k+p} w_{p+1}(y_{k+p} - \underline{\phi}_{k+p}^T \hat{\underline{\theta}}_p) \tag{4.23}$$

Note that equation (4.23) may also be written as

$$\hat{\underline{\theta}}_{p+1} = \hat{\underline{\theta}}_p + K_{p+1} \tilde{y}_{k+p} \tag{4.24}$$

where

$$K_{p+1} = P_{p+1} \underline{\phi}_{k+p} \cdot w_{p+1} \qquad (4.25)$$

$$\triangleq \text{weighted least-squares gain matrix}$$
$$\text{(corresponding to Kalman gain matrix)}$$

and

$$\tilde{y}_{k+p} = y_{k+p} - \underline{\phi}^T_{k+p} \hat{\underline{\theta}}_p \qquad (4.26)$$

$$\triangleq \text{error between actual measured}$$
$$\text{output and predicted output}$$
$$\text{(corresponding to the innovations}$$
$$\text{sequence) called the residual error.}$$

Equation (4.24) provides a good recursive algorithm for obtaining $\hat{\underline{\theta}}_{p+1}$ from $\hat{\underline{\theta}}_p$. The only problem is the computation of K_{p+1} which requires P_{p+1}, defined as the inverse of the matrix product $(A^T_{p+1} W_{p+1} A_{p+1})$. This matrix inversion is undesirable for a recursive algorithm, and can be avoided by making use of the following matrix inversion lemma.

Matrix Inversion Lemma

If

$$P_2^{-1} = P_1^{-1} + H^T R^{-1} H \qquad (4.27)$$

then

$$P_2 = P_1 - P_1 H^T (H P_1 H^T + R)^{-1} H P_1 \qquad (4.28)$$

Proof. Premultiplying equation (4.27) by P_2, and then postmultiplying by $P_1 H^T$, we have

$$P_1 H^T = P_2 H^T + P_2 H^T R^{-1} H P_1 H^T$$
$$= P_2 H^T R^{-1} (R + H P_1 H^T) \qquad (4.29)$$

Postmultiplying equation (4.29) by $(R + H P_1 H^T)^{-1} H P_1$, we have

$$P_1 H^T (H P_1 H^T + R)^{-1} H P_1 = P_2 H^T R^{-1} H P_1 \qquad (4.30)$$

Subtracting equation (4.30) from P_1, we have

$$P_1 - P_1 H^T (HP_1 H^T + R)^{-1} HP_1 = P_1 - P_2 H^T R^{-1} HP_1$$
$$= P_1 - P_2 (P_2^{-1} - P_1^{-1}) P_1$$
$$\text{(substitution from (4.27))}$$
$$= P_1 - P_2 P_2^{-1} P_1 + P_2 P_1^{-1} P_1$$
$$= P_2$$

This proves equation (4.28).

Application of this lemma to equation (4.19), gives us

$$P_{p+1} = P_p - P_p \underline{\phi}_{k+p} (\underline{\phi}_{k+p}^T P_p \underline{\phi}_{k+p} + w_{p+1}^{-1})^{-1} \underline{\phi}_{k+p}^T P_p \qquad (4.31)$$

Finally, noting that the expression under the inversion sign is a scalar, we may write

$$P_{p+1} = P_p - \frac{(P_p \underline{\phi}_{k+p}) \, \underline{\phi}_{k+p}^T \cdot P_p}{\underline{\phi}_{k+p}^T P_p \underline{\phi}_{k+p} + w_{p+1}^{-1}} \qquad (4.32)$$

Furthermore, since P_p is a symmetric matrix, one may write

$$P_{p+1} = P_p - \frac{(P_p \underline{\phi}_{k+p}) \cdot (P_p \underline{\phi}_{k+p})^T}{\underline{\phi}_{k+p}^T (P_p \underline{\phi}_{k+p}) + w_{p+1}^{-1}} \qquad (4.33)$$

Combining equation (4.33) with equation (4.24) and (4.25) gives us a recursive algorithm, which does not require matrix inversion.

Further simplification of K_{p+1} is possible if an equation (4.24), P_{p+1} is replaced by equation (4.33). This leads to

$$K_{p+1} = \frac{P_p \underline{\phi}_{k+p}}{\underline{\phi}_{k+p}^T P_p \underline{\phi}_{k+p} + w_{p+1}^{-1}} \qquad (4.34)$$

To summarize, the equations forming the recursive algorithm will be collected as below:

$$\hat{\underline{\theta}}_{p+1} = \hat{\underline{\theta}}_p + \frac{P_p \underline{\phi}_{k+p}}{\underline{\phi}_{k+p}^T P_p \underline{\phi}_{k+p} + w_{p+1}^{-1}} (y_{k+p} - \underline{\phi}_{k+p}^T \hat{\underline{\theta}}_p)$$

$$\qquad (4.35)$$

$$P_{p+1} = P_p - \frac{(P_p \underline{\phi}_{k+p}) (P_p \underline{\phi}_{k+p})^T}{\underline{\phi}_{k+p}^T P_p \underline{\phi}_{k+p} + w_{p+1}^{-1}}$$

To start the algorithm, we must know an initial value of $\hat{\theta}_p$ and P_p, which we shall denote by $\hat{\theta}_\alpha$ and P_α. Such an initial estimate may be obtained by making A_p in equation (4.10) a square matrix, with $p = m + n + 1 = \alpha$. Thus, one matrix inversion is required of an $(m + n + 1) \times (m + n + 1)$ matrix.

It is possible to eliminate matrix inversion completely for the ordinary least-squares case if one recalls that the pseudoinverse of a matrix with fewer rows than columns provides a minimum-norm solution. The details of the algorithm (Sinha and Pille 1971) are described in the appendix. The main equations will be given here. These are

For $p < m + n + 1$ (minimum-norm solutions)

$$\hat{\theta}_{p+1} = \hat{\theta}_p + \frac{Q_p \underline{\phi}_p}{\underline{\phi}_p^T Q_p \underline{\phi}_p} (y - \underline{\mu}^T \hat{\theta}_p)$$

$$Q_{p+1} = Q_p - \frac{(Q_p \underline{\phi}_p)(Q_p \underline{\phi}_p)^T}{\underline{\phi}_p^T Q_p \underline{\phi}_p}$$

and (4.36)

$$P_{p+1} = Q_p - \frac{(p_p \underline{\phi}_p)(Q_p \underline{\phi}_p)^T + (Q_p \underline{\phi}_p)(P_p \underline{\phi}_p)^T}{\underline{\phi}_p^T Q_p \underline{\phi}_p}$$

$$+ \frac{(Q_p \underline{\phi}_p)(Q_p \underline{\phi}_p)^T + (1 + \underline{\phi}_p^T P_p \underline{\phi}_p)}{(\underline{\phi}_p^T Q_p \underline{\phi}_p)^2}$$

with initial conditions

$$\left. \begin{array}{r} Q_0 = I \\ P_0 = \underline{0} \\ \hat{\theta}_0 = \underline{0} \end{array} \right\} \qquad (4.37)$$

For $p > m + n + 1$, the algorithm is identical with equations (4.35), with $W = I$, $w_{p+1} = 1$, and $k = 0$

$$\hat{\theta}_{p+1} = \hat{\theta}_p + \frac{P_p \underline{\phi}_p}{\underline{\phi}_p^T Q_p \underline{\phi}_p} (y_p - \underline{\phi}_p^T \hat{\theta}_p)$$

$$P_{p+1} = P_p - \frac{(P_p \underline{\phi}_p)(P_p \underline{\phi}_p)^T}{1 + \underline{\phi}_p^T P_p \underline{\phi}_p}$$

(4.38)

Furthermore, it is shown that the matrix P_p is positive definite if the matrix A_p is of full rank.

A comparison between equations (4.35) and (4.38) shows that the recursive least algorithm can be obtained from the recursive weighted least squares algorithm by setting all the weights $w_p = 1$. Another special case arises when the weights w_p are set equal to a constant λ, which lies between 0 and 1. This is called the exponentially weighted least-squares algorithm, and implies that the present observations are given a heavier weighting than the past ones. The constant, λ, can be regarded as a "forgetting factor." As λ approaches 1, the memory becomes perfect, and all the past observations are weighted equally. A suitable choice of λ can often lead to faster convergence of the recursive algorithm in the presence of noise.

4.3 THE GENERALIZED LEAST-SQUARES ALGORITHM FOR UNBIASED PARAMETER ESTIMATION

As shown in Chapter 3, the least squares estimates are generally biased. A sufficient condition for the estimates to be unbiased is that the residual sequence, $\{\hat{e}_k\}$, defined as

$$\hat{e}_k = y_k - \sum_{j=0}^{m} \hat{a}_j u_{k-j} - \sum_{j=0}^{n} \hat{b}_j y_{k-j}$$

$$= y_k - \underline{\phi}_T^k \hat{\theta}_k \tag{4.39}$$

forms an uncorrelated (white-noise) random sequence with zero mean.

Although it is possible to find a weighting matrix W such that this condition is satisfied, the determination of W is possible only if a priori statistical information about the noise sequence $\{n_k\}$ and thus about $\{\hat{e}_k\}$ is available. Following Clarke (1967), one may model the residuals using the following equation, and then filter the input-output data so that the resulting residuals are uncorrelated

$$\hat{e}_k = -f_1 \hat{e}_{k-1} - f_2 \hat{e}_{k-2} - \cdots - f_s \hat{e}_{k-s} + w_k \tag{4.40}$$

where w_k is an uncorrelated random sequence.

It may be noted that equation (4.31) models the "colored" sequence $\{\hat{e}_k\}$ as a linear transformation of the "white" sequence $\{w_k\}$ through an autoregressive model

$$\frac{E_1(z)}{W_k(z)} = \frac{1}{1 + f_1 z^{-1} + f_2 z^{-2} + \cdots + f_s z^{-s}} \tag{4.41}$$

Concatentation of equation (4.40) leads to the matrix equation

$$\hat{\underline{e}}_k = G_k \underline{\psi} + \underline{w}_k \qquad (4.42)$$

where

$$\hat{\underline{e}}_k = \begin{bmatrix} \hat{e}_1 \\ \hat{e}_2 \\ \cdot \\ \cdot \\ \hat{e}_k \end{bmatrix} \qquad (4.43)$$

$$\underline{\psi} = \begin{bmatrix} f_1 \\ f_2 \\ \cdot \\ \cdot \\ f_3 \end{bmatrix} \triangleq \text{auxiliary parameter vector} \qquad (4.44)$$

$$G_k = \begin{bmatrix} -\hat{e}_0 & -\hat{e}_{-1} & \cdots & -\hat{e}_{1-s} \\ -\hat{e}_1 & -\hat{e}_0 & \cdots & -\hat{e}_{2-s} \\ \cdot & \cdot & & \cdot \\ \cdot & \cdot & & \cdot \\ -\hat{e}_{k-1} & -\hat{e}_{k-2} & \cdots & -\hat{e}_{k-s} \end{bmatrix} \qquad (4.45)$$

and

$$\underline{w}_k = \begin{bmatrix} w_1 \\ w_2 \\ \cdot \\ \cdot \\ w_k \end{bmatrix} \qquad (4.46)$$

From equation (4.33), one may obtain the least-squares estimate of the parameter vector $\underline{\psi}$ as (provided $k > s$),

$$\hat{\underline{\psi}}_k = G_k^+ \cdot \underline{e}_k \qquad (4.47)$$

where G_k^+ is the pseudoinverse of G_k, as before.

Utilizing this estimate, $\hat{\underline{\psi}}_k$, the noisy input and output sequences, u_k and y_k, are filtered to obtain

$$u_k^* = u_k + \sum_{j=1}^{s} \hat{f}_j u_{k-j} \tag{4.48}$$

$$y_k^* = y_k + \sum_{j=1}^{s} \hat{f}_j y_{k-j} \tag{4.49}$$

From these filtered sequences, a corrected matrix, A_k^*, is obtained instead of A_k, for use in the sequential least-squares algorithm, resulting in an unbiased estimate of the parameter vector.

One may derive the following recursive algorithm (Sen and Sinha 1975a) combining both steps.

$$\hat{\underline{\theta}}_{k+1} = \hat{\underline{\theta}}_k + \frac{P_k \underline{\phi}_{k+1}^* (y_{k+1} - \underline{\phi}_{k+1}^{*T} \hat{\underline{\theta}}_k)}{1 + \underline{\phi}_{k+1}^{*T} P_k \underline{\phi}_{k+1}^*} \tag{4.50}$$

$$P_{k+1} = P_k - \frac{(P_k \underline{\phi}_{k+1}^*)(P_k \underline{\phi}_{k+1}^*)^T}{1 + \underline{\phi}_{k+1}^{*T} P_k \underline{\phi}_{k+1}^*} \tag{4.51}$$

$$\hat{\underline{\psi}}_{k+1} = \hat{\underline{\psi}}_k + \frac{R_k \underline{g}_{k+1} (\hat{e}_{k+1} - \underline{g}_{k+1}^T \hat{\underline{\psi}}_k)}{1 + \underline{g}_{k+1}^T R_k \underline{g}_{k+1}} \tag{4.52}$$

and

$$R_{k+1} = R_k - \frac{(R_k \underline{g}_{k+1})(R_k \underline{g}_{k+1})^T}{1 + \underline{g}_{k+1}^T R_k \underline{g}_{k+1}} \tag{4.53}$$

where

$$A_{k+1}^* = \begin{bmatrix} A_k^* \\ \underline{\phi}_{k+1}^{*T} \end{bmatrix} \tag{4.54}$$

$$G_{k+1} = \begin{bmatrix} G_k \\ \underline{g}_{k+1}^T \end{bmatrix} \tag{4.55}$$

$$\underline{\phi}_k^{*T} = [u_k^* \quad u_{k-1}^* \cdots u_{k-m}^* \quad -y_{k-1}^* \quad -y_{k-2}^* \cdots -y_{k-n}^*] \tag{4.56}$$

$$\underline{g}_k^T = [-\hat{e}_k \quad -\hat{e}_{k-1} \cdots -\hat{e}_{k+1-s}] \tag{4.57}$$

$$u_k^* = u_k + \sum_{j=1}^{s} \hat{f}_j u_{k-j} \tag{4.58}$$

$$y_k^* = y_k + \sum_{j=1}^{s} \hat{f}_j y_{k-j} \tag{4.59}$$

To start the algorithm, one may either invert a matrix of size $(m+n+1) \times (m+n+1)$ for the main parameters and $s \times s$ for the auxiliary parameters, or start with a minimum-norm estimate.

4.4   THE INSTRUMENTAL VARIABLE METHOD

This method has already been described in Chapter 3. Here we shall discuss a recursive algorithm utilizing this approach. Let us reconsider our concatenated matrix equation

$$\underline{y}_k = A_k \underline{\theta} + \underline{v}_k \tag{4.60}$$

We have already seen that estimates will be unbiased with the least-squares method only if $E[\underline{v}_k] = 0$. To obtain this condition, let us premultiply both sides of equation (4.60) by a matrix W_k^T to obtain

$$W_k^T \underline{y}_k = W_k^T A_k \underline{\theta} + W_k^T \underline{v}_k \tag{4.61}$$

where

and
$$\left. \begin{array}{l} E[W_k^T \underline{v}_k] = 0 \\ E[W_k^T A_k] \text{ is nonsingular} \end{array} \right\} \tag{4.62}$$

If the conditions of equation (4.62) are satisfied then

$$\hat{\underline{\theta}}_k = (W_k^T A_k)^{-1} W_k^T \underline{y}_k \tag{4.63}$$

gives an unbiased estimate of the parameter vector $\underline{\theta}$.

The matrix W_k represents the so-called "instrumental variables," and the main problem is that of finding this matrix. The method proposed by Wong and Polak and by Young is illustrated in Figure 4.2.

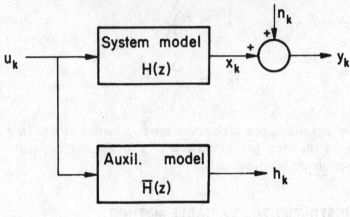

Figure 4.2

It consists of taking the instrumental variables as the undisturbed output, h_k, of an auxiliary model to which the same input, u_k, is applied. This $\{h_k\}$ will be correlated with $\{u_k\}$ but uncorrelated with $\{n_k\}$ and, therefore, with $\{v_k\}$. The matrix W_k, then takes the form

$$W_k = \begin{bmatrix} u_0 & u_{-1} & \cdots u_{1-m} & -h_0 & -h_1 & \cdots -h_{1-n} \\ u_1 & u_0 & u_{2-m} & -h_1 & -h_0 & \cdots -h_{2-n} \\ \vdots & \vdots & \vdots & \vdots & \vdots & \vdots \\ u_{k-1} & u_{k-2} & u_{k-m} & -h_{k-1} & -h_{k-2} & \cdots -h_{k-n} \end{bmatrix} \qquad (4.64)$$

A recursive algorithm for estimation can now be obtained following the procedure described in section 4.2, and is given below

$$\hat{\underline{\theta}}_{k+1} = \hat{\underline{\theta}}_k + \frac{P_k \underline{w}_{k+1}(y_{k+1} - \underline{\phi}_{k+1}^T \hat{\underline{\theta}}_k)}{1 + \underline{\phi}_{k+1}^T P_k \underline{w}_{k+1}} \qquad (4.65)$$

$$P_{k+1} = P_k - \frac{P_k \underline{w}_{k+1}(P_k \phi_{k+1})^T}{1 + \underline{\phi}_{k+1}^T P_k \underline{w}_{k+1}} \qquad (4.66)$$

where

$$\underline{w}_{k+1} = [u_k \quad u_{k-1} \cdots u_{k+1-m} \quad -h_k \quad -h_{k-1} \cdots -h_{k+1-n}]^T \qquad (4.67)$$

To start the algorithm, one must invert one matrix when $k = m + n + 1 = \alpha$. For this case,

$$\hat{\underline{\theta}}_\alpha = (W_\alpha^T A_\alpha)^{-1} W_\alpha^T y_\alpha \qquad (4.68)$$

$$P_0 = (W_\alpha^T A_\alpha)^{-1} \qquad (4.69)$$

Young (1971) introduced a low-pass filter and time delay before updating the auxiliary model, so that the auxiliary model parameters are uncorrelated with e_k at the same instant. This low-pass filter may be of the form

$$\hat{\underline{\phi}}_{aux}(k) = (1 - \nu)\, \hat{\underline{\phi}}_{aux}(k-1) + \nu\hat{\underline{\theta}}(k) \qquad (4.70)$$

where $\nu = 0.03$ to 0.05, has to be chosen to prevent instability in estimation.

The difficulty of checking that the chosen W_k is uncorrelated with $\underline{v}_k$ makes the method somewhat unattractive.

4.5 THE BOOTSTRAP METHOD

The bootstrap estimator basically consists of two recursive estimators, one for structural parameters, and the other for incidental parameters, with continuous exchange of information between the two. It is characterized by the fact that the structural parameters are estimated recursively in such a way that the latest estimates of the structural parameters are used in estimating the incidental parameters, and vice versa.

The recursive algorithm for the bootstrap estimator, as proposed by Pandya (1972), has the following form

$$\hat{\underline{\theta}}_{k+1} = \hat{\underline{\theta}}_k + \frac{P_k \underline{z}_{k+1}(y_{k+1} - \underline{m}_{k+1}^T \hat{\underline{\theta}}_k)}{1 + \underline{m}_{k+1}^T P_k \underline{z}_{k+1}} \qquad (4.71)$$

$$P_{k+1} = P_k - \frac{P_k \underline{z}_{k+1}(P_k \underline{m}_{k+1})^T}{1 + \underline{m}_{k+1}^T P_k \underline{z}_{k+1}} \qquad (4.72)$$

$$\underline{m}_{k+1}^T = [u_{k+1} \quad u_k \cdots u_{k+m+1} \quad -y_k \cdots -y_{k-n+1}] \qquad (4.73)$$

$$\underline{z}_{k+1}^T = [u_{k+1} \quad u_k \cdots u_{k-m+1} \quad -\hat{x}_k \cdots -\hat{x}_{k-n+1}] \qquad (4.74)$$

$$\hat{x}_k = \underline{z}_k^T \underline{\theta}_k + \nu(k)[y_k - \underline{z}_k^T \underline{\theta}_k] \qquad (4.75)$$

where

$$0 < \nu(k) < 1 \qquad (4.76)$$

4.6   THE SEQUENTIAL CORRELATION METHOD

If the input sequence $\{u_k\}$ is a stationary random process, its autocorrelation (assuming ergodicity) is given by

$$\phi_{uu}(\tau) = \lim_{N \to \infty} \frac{1}{N+1} \sum_{k=0}^{N} u(k)\, u(k - \tau) \qquad (4.77)$$

and the cross-correlation between the input and the output signals is

$$\phi_{uy}(\tau) = \lim_{N \to \infty} \frac{1}{N+1} \sum_{k=0}^{N} u(k - \tau)\, y(k) \qquad (4.78)$$

Noting that $y(k) = x(k) + n(k)$ and assuming that the input sequence and the noise sequence are uncorrelated, it may be assumed that

$$\phi_{uy}(\tau) = \phi_{ux}(\tau) \qquad (4.79)$$

This is the key fact to the use of the correlation method. The convolution equation

$$\phi_{uy}(\tau) = \sum_{\nu=0}^{\infty} g(\nu)\, \phi_{uu}(\tau - \nu) \qquad (4.80)$$

relates the two correlation sequences to the impulse response sequence of the process, $g(\nu)$. Hence, we obtain the following matrix equation by concatenation

$$\begin{bmatrix} \phi_{uu}(-M) & \cdots & \phi_{uu}(-M - \ell) \\ \phi_{uu}(1 - M) & \cdots & \phi_{uu}(1 - M - \ell) \\ \vdots & & \vdots \\ \vdots & & \vdots \\ \phi_{uu}(M) & \cdots & \phi_{uu}(M - \ell) \end{bmatrix} \begin{bmatrix} g(0) \\ g(1) \\ \vdots \\ g(\ell) \end{bmatrix} = \begin{bmatrix} \phi_{uy}(-M) \\ \phi_{uy}(1 - M) \\ \vdots \\ \phi_{uy}(M) \end{bmatrix} \qquad (4.81)$$

Equation (4.81) can be solved using the pseudoinverse algorithm presented earlier to obtain a recursive procedure for estimating the impulse response ordinates $g(0), g(1), \ldots, g(\ell)$, of the system.

One weakness of this method is that the impulse response sequence has to be truncated at some value ℓ although it is an infinite sequence. This will affect the accuracy of the method. The truncation can usually be justified for a stable system provided that ℓ is sufficiently large; this increases the amount of computation.

Another difficulty is caused by the error in estimating the correlation-ordinates when N is not infinite (or not very large). This difficulty can be partly overcome by using the following relationship to improve the estimates of the correlation ordinates recursively as more data arrive

$$\phi_{uy}(\tau, k) = \phi_{uy}(\tau, k - 1) + \frac{1}{k + 1} [u(k - \tau) y(k) - \phi_{uy}(\tau, k - 1)] \quad (4.82)$$

where k is the number of samples being used and it is assumed that $\{u(k)\}$ and $\{y(k)\}$ have zero mean values.

The problem of determining the z-transfer function (or difference equation) model of the system from the impulse response estimates is now a purely deterministic problem of time-domain approximation, and can be solved using the standard techniques discussed in Chapter 2.

In spite of these problems, the correlation method is attractive as it is relatively easy to implement and gives unbiased estimates. The computation and computer storage requirements are small, and of the same order as for the bootstrap method or the instrumental variable method. Moreover, there is no problem of stability which might arise in the other methods.

4.7   MAXIMUM LIKELIHOOD ESTIMATION

The maximum likelihood method described in Chapter 3 (Aström and Bohlin 1965) gives good estimates even when the noise level is quite high, but is inconvenient for on-line identification. We shall discuss in this section the algorithm of Gertler and Bányász (1974) which is recursive and suitable for on-line application.

In this algorithm, the process model is assumed to have the same form as in Figure 4.1, with the following input-output relationship

$$y_k = \frac{G(z^{-1})}{1 + H(z^{-1})} u_k + \frac{1}{[1 + H(z^{-1})][1 + D(z^{-1})]} w_k \quad (4.83)$$

where G, H and D are polynomials in z^{-1}.

The parameter vector is now

$$\underline{\theta} = \begin{bmatrix} \underline{g} \\ \underline{h} \\ \underline{d} \end{bmatrix} \quad (4.84)$$

where the vector $\underline{g}$, $\underline{h}$ and $\underline{d}$ are the coefficients of the corresponding polynomials.

From equation (4.83), the noise sequence w_k may be expressed as

$$w_k = [1 + D(z^{-1})] \{[1 + H(z^{-1})] y_k - G(z^{-1}) u_k\} \qquad (4.85)$$

The partial derivatives of w_k with respect to the various parameters are obtained as

$$\frac{\partial w_k}{\partial g_j} = -[1 + D(z^{-1})] z^{-j} u_k = -u_{k-j}^F \qquad (4.86)$$

$$\frac{\partial w_k}{\partial h_j} = [1 + D(z^{-1})] z^{-j} y_k = y_{k-j}^F \qquad (4.87)$$

$$\frac{\partial w_k}{\partial d_j} = z^{-j} \{[1 + H(z^{-1})] y_k - G(z^{-1}) u_k\} = \mu_{k-j} \qquad (4.88)$$

where

$$u_k^F \triangleq [1 + D(z^{-1})] u_k \qquad (4.89)$$

$$y_k^F \triangleq [1 + D(z^{-1})] y_k \qquad (4.90)$$

and

$$\mu_k \triangleq G(z^{-1}) u_k - [1 + H(z^{-1})] y_k \qquad (4.91)$$

These derivatives are generated by moving average filtering and shifting. The vector of the first derivative of noise is built up as

$$\underline{v}_k = \begin{bmatrix} -\underline{u}_{n+1}^F \\ \underline{y}_n^F \\ -\underline{u}_n \end{bmatrix} \qquad (4.92)$$

where

$$\underline{u}_{n+1}^F = \begin{bmatrix} u_k^F \\ u_{k-1}^F \\ \vdots \\ u_{k-n}^F \end{bmatrix}, \quad \underline{y}_n^F = \begin{bmatrix} y_{k-1}^F \\ \vdots \\ y_{k-n}^F \end{bmatrix}, \quad \underline{u}_n = \begin{bmatrix} u_{k-1} \\ u_{k-2} \\ \vdots \\ u_{k-n} \end{bmatrix}$$

The nonzero second derivatives are

$$\frac{\partial^2 w_k}{\partial g_j \partial d_m} = -z^{-(j+m)} u_k = -u_{k-j-m} \qquad (4.93)$$

$$\frac{\partial^2 w_k}{\partial h_j \partial d_m} = z^{-(j+m)} y_k = -y_{k-j-m} \qquad (4.94)$$

Thus, the second derivatives are generated simply by double shifting. The matrix of the second derivatives is

$$W_k = \begin{bmatrix} 0 & X_k \\ X_k^T & 0 \end{bmatrix} \qquad (4.95)$$

where

$$X_k \triangleq \begin{bmatrix} -U_{(k-1)n,\, n+1} \\ Y_{(k-2)n,\, n} \end{bmatrix} \qquad (4.96)$$

and the double subscripts indicate the respective number of previous consecutive values in the columns and rows of the matrix.

The recursive equivalent of equation (3.66) is

$$\hat{\underline{\theta}}_k = \hat{\underline{\theta}}_{k-1} - R^{-1}(k, N, \hat{\underline{\theta}}_{k-1})\, \underline{q}(k, n, \hat{\underline{\theta}}_{k-1}) \qquad (4.97)$$

where

$$\underline{q}(k, n, \hat{\underline{\theta}}_{k-1}) \triangleq \left[\frac{\partial}{\partial \underline{\theta}} (\underline{w}_n^T \underline{w}_n) \right]_{\underline{\theta} = \hat{\underline{\theta}}_{k-1}}^T \qquad (4.98)$$

Introducing conditional arguments for the sake of brevity,

$$\hat{\underline{\theta}}_k = \hat{\underline{\theta}}_{k-1} - R^{-1}(k; k-1, N)\, \underline{q}(k; k-1, N) \qquad (4.99)$$

$$\underline{q}(k; k-1, N) = \underline{q}(k-1; k-2, N-1) + \underline{v}(k)\, w(k) \qquad (4.100)$$

$$R(k; h-1, N) = R(k-1; k-2, N-1) + \underline{v}(k)\, \underline{v}(k) + W_k w_k \qquad (4.101)$$

Introducing a filtering factor $\lambda \in [0, 1]$ to suppress exponentially the effects of previous measurements, we have

$$\underline{q}(k; k-1, N) = \lambda \underline{q}(k-1; k-2, N-1) + \underline{v}(k)\, w(k)$$
$$R(k; k-1, N) = \lambda R(k-1; k-2, N-1) + \underline{v}^T(k)\, \underline{v}(h) + W_k w_k \qquad (4.102)$$

Since the algorithm in equation (4.90) requires the inverse of R, we may use the matrix inversion lemma to obtain recursively

$$R^{-1}(k; k-1, N) = R_I^{-1}(k; k-1, N) \ [I - W_k w_k R_I^{-1}(k; k-1, N] \qquad (4.103)$$

where

$$R_I^{-1}(k; k-1, N) \triangleq \frac{1}{\lambda} R^{-1}(k-1; k-2, N-1)$$

$$- \frac{R^{-1}(k-1; k-2, N-1) \underline{v}_k \ v_k^T R^{-1}(k-1; k-2, N-1)}{\lambda + \underline{v}_k^T R^{-1}(k-1; k-2, N-1) \underline{v}_k} \qquad (4.104)$$

Equations (4.99), (4.102), (4.103), and (4.104) form a recursive algorithm for maximum likelihood estimation.

4.8   STOCHASTIC APPROXIMATION

The subject of stochastic approximation is of recent origin, and may be regarded as the application of gradient methods to stochastic problems. It may be defined as a scheme for successive approximation of a sought quantity when the observations involve random errors due to the stochastic nature of the problem. It can be applied to any problem which can be formulated as some form of regression in which repeated observations are made. An important advantage of the method is that a priori knowledge of the noise statistics is not necessary. Its main characteristic is the enormous simplicity of its implementation which makes it more appealing than some of the faster but more complex sequential estimation methods.

Important contributions to the area of stochastic approximation have been made by Robbins and Monro (1951), Kiefer and Wolfowitz (1952), and Dvoretzky (1956). Robbins and Monro, who first introduced the method, developed an algorithm which is the statistical analogue of the simple gradient method for finding the unique root of the equation

$$h(x) = 0 \qquad (4.105)$$

which is

$$x_{i+1} = x_i - K_i h(x_i) \qquad (4.106)$$

where K_i is a sequence of real numbers which must satisfy certain conditions to ensure that the algorithm will converge. When there is uncertainty such that instead of $h(x_i)$ one obtained

$$z(x_i) = h(x_i) + v_i \qquad (4.107)$$

where v_i is a zero-mean random noise sequence, then $h(x)$ is called the regression function of z on x, since for independent x and z we have

$$E[z|x] = \int_{-\infty}^{\infty} zp(z|x) \; dx = h(x) \tag{4.108}$$

Note that equation (4.106) cannot be used in the noisy situation since $h(x)$ is not available. However, since the expectation of (4.107) is just $h(x)$, we see that a stochastic algorithm to find the root is

$$x_{i+1} = x_i - K_i z(x_i) \tag{4.109}$$

The x_i determined from the solution of equation (4.109) are a sequence of random variables which, hopefully, converge to the solution of equation (4.106). The main contribution of Robbins and Monro was to show that this convergence occurs if the following three requirements are met:

$$\left. \begin{array}{c} \lim\limits_{i \to \infty} K_i = 0 \\[2em] \sum\limits_{i=1}^{\infty} K_i = \infty \\[2em] \sum\limits_{i=1}^{\infty} K_i^2 < \infty \end{array} \right\} \tag{4.110}$$

A simple sequence which meets this requirement is

$$K_i = \frac{\alpha}{\beta + i} \tag{4.111}$$

where α and β are constants with $\alpha > 0$ and $\beta \geqslant 0$. Also, it is required that the regression function $h(x)$ be bounded on either side of a true solution by straight lines, such that it is not possible to overshoot the solution x which cannot be corrected by K_i satisfying equations (4.110). Thus, for the scalar case

$$|h(x_i)| < a|x - \hat{x}| + b; \quad a, b > 0. \tag{4.112}$$

As will be evident, this latter requirement is not very severe.

Kiefer and Wolfowitz extended the method to include finding the extremum of an unknown unimodel regression function $\theta(u)$. Their approach is the exact analogue of the deterministic gradient procedure, which yields an optimization algorithm

$$u_{i+1} = u_i - K_i \frac{d\theta(u_i)}{du_i} \tag{4.113}$$

In the noisy case, we cannot observe θ, but we observe

$$\phi = \theta(u) + \zeta \tag{4.114}$$

so that we replace the deterministic algorithm by its stochastic counterpart

$$u_{i+1} = u_i - K_i \frac{d\phi(u_i)}{du_i} \tag{4.115}$$

which corresponds to equation (4.113) in the sense that the conditional expectation of equation (4.115) yields equation (4.113). In some instances direct differentiation of ϕ to obtain $(d\phi(u_i))/(du_i)$ may not be possible. In such cases one may use the approximation

$$\frac{d\phi(u_i)}{du_i} \simeq \frac{\phi(u_{i+\Delta} - u_i) - \phi(u_{i-\Delta} - u_i)}{2\Delta u_i} \tag{4.116}$$

as well as a requirement corresponding to equation (4.112).

Dvoretzky formulated a generalized theorem applicable to a class of stochastic approximation algorithms. It can be shown that the Robbins–Monro and the Kiefer–Wolfowitz algorithms are special cases which follow from Dvoretzky's theorem. A general Dvoretzky-type algorithm is of the form

$$x_{n+1} = x_n + \gamma_{n+1} \{f(r_1, r_2, \ldots, r_{n+1}) - x_n\} \tag{4.117}$$

where

$x_n = n^{th}$ estimate of x
$\gamma_{n+1} =$ gain sequence corresponding to K_i in (4.109) and (4.115), and satisfying equation (4.110)
$r_n = n^{th}$ observation
$f(r_1, r_2, \ldots, r_n) =$ scalar functional of the observations $r_1, r_2, \ldots, r_n$

Fu et al. (1966) have proposed two stochastic approximation algorithms of the Dvoretzky type, and another such algorithm has been proposed by Sinha and Griscik (1971).

An algorithm for system identification using stochastic approximation was proposed by Saridis and Stein (1968). Recently, Kwatny (1972) has proposed another algorithm which works very well. A survey of stochastic approximation methods has been presented by Saridis (1974).

The algorithm proposed by Saridis and Stein is of the form

$$\hat{\underline{g}}_{k+1} = \hat{\underline{g}}_k + \gamma_{k+1} \underline{u}_{k+1} [y_{k+1} - \underline{u}_{k+1}^T \hat{\underline{g}}_k] \tag{4.118}$$

where

$$\underline{g} = [g_1 \quad g_2 \cdots g_\ell]^T$$

$$g_i = g(iT), \text{ samples of the impulse response}$$

$$\hat{\underline{g}}_k = k^{th} \text{ estimate of } \underline{g}$$

$$\underline{u}_k = [u_{k-1} \quad u_{k-2} \cdots u_{k-\ell}]^T$$

and

$$\gamma_{k+1} = \frac{1}{k+1}, \quad k = 1, 2, \ldots$$

If the transfer function of the system model contains $m + n + 1$ parameters then $\ell = m + n + 1$ samples of the impulse response are estimated using equation (4.118). The parameters of the model are then calculated from these estimates of g_i.

The algorithm of Kwatny may be described by

$$\hat{\underline{\theta}}_{k+1} = \hat{\underline{\theta}}_k - \frac{\gamma}{k+1} \frac{(\phi_{k+1}^T \hat{\underline{\theta}}_k - y_{k+1}) \hat{\underline{\phi}}_k}{\|\hat{\underline{\phi}}_k\|^2} \tag{4.119}$$

where the notation is similar to that used in the development of the generalized pseudoinverse algorithm, and γ is a positive constant.

The algorithm of equation (4.118) gives biased estimates, although the bias is small even in the presence of large noise. Sen and Sinha (1975b) have presented an algorithm of the generalized least-squares type in which the stochastic approximation algorithm of equation (4.119) is used for estimating the noise model and the recursive pseudoinverse algorithm is used for estimating the system model. The combined algorithm converges in fewer iterations than other algorithms even in the presence of large noise.

4.9 COMPARISON OF THE DIFFERENT METHODS FOR ON-LINE IDENTIFICATION

In this chapter we have considered several methods for on-line identification of single-input single-output discrete-time linear models from the input-output data. In this section we shall compare the application of seven of these methods to the identification of a two-stage heat exchanger process (Sinha and Sen 1975). Following Wright, Bacon, and Hoffman (1972), the process may be modeled as

$$y_k = by_{k-1} + a_1 u_{k-1} + a_2 u_{k-2} \qquad (4.120)$$

where, the parameters were estimated using the off-line time-series approach as $b = 0.825$, $a_1 = 0.0148$ and $a_2 = 0.022$ within 95% confidence limits.

For this comparison, 300 samples of the input-output data, obtained at intervals of 5 seconds, were used for recursive estimation of the three parameters of the model. The following methods were considered

(a) Recursive least-squares
(b) Generalized least-squares
(c) Instrumental variables
(d) Bootstrap
(e) Correlation
(f) Stochastic approximation
(g) Algorithm combining stochastic approximation (for the noise model) with ordinary least-squares

The final estimates of the parameters of the process model using each of these methods are given in the following table.

Method	a_1	a_2	b
Least-squares	0.0153	0.0238	0.8582
Generalized least-squares	0.0148	0.0228	0.8202
Instrumental variables	0.0125	0.024	0.860
Bootstrap	0.0157	0.0243	0.8296
Correlation	0.00915	0.0211	0.8716
Stochastic approximation	0.0167	0.0143	0.849
Algorithm combining stochastic approximation with least-squares	0.0148	0.0225	0.826
Time-series (off-line)	0.0148	0.022	0.829

The results indicate considerable bias in the estimates using the least-squares method. Good results are obtained with the other algorithms, which take into account a noise model. The following table makes a comparison of the computational time and effort required for the different methods.

Method	Total Computation Time for 300 Iterations on a CDC 6400 (in seconds)	Number of Arithmetic Operations per Iteration
Least-squares	1.7	66
Generalized least-squares	7	146
Instrumental variable	2.5	81
Bootstrap	2.4	75
Correlation	2.5	82
Stochastic approximation	1.2	16
Algorithm combining stochastic approximation with least-squares	5.8	95

Sinha and Sen (1975) have made further comparisons with simulated systems with additive measurement noise and different noise-to-signal ratios. In all of these cases, the results were similar to the above. For a noise-to-signal ratio of about 100% only three of these methods gave good results; these were the correlation method, the instrumental variable method, and the algorithm combining stochastic approximation with least square. The maximum likelihood method was not tried in these comparisons as it was felt that it would require much more computation.

4.10 CONCLUSIONS

On the basis of several comparative studies of various methods the following conclusions can be made (Saridis 1974, Isermann et al. 1976, Sinha and Sen 1975).

(a) The least-squares algorithm is the most efficient approach for parameter estimation for low noise levels. The estimates converge to their correct values very fast, and the amount of computation is smaller than that required in other algorithms with the exception of stochastic approximation.

(b) The stochastic approximation algorithm of Kwatny (1972) requires the least amount of computation per iteration and gives good estimates of the parameters. The only difficulty is the slow rate of convergence of this algorithm.

(c) The correlation method gives good results even for high noise, but one must wait for a sufficient amount of data to get a reasonable initial estimate of the correlation ordinates. There is the additional problem of estimating the transfer function from the impulse response sequence, and the error caused by truncation of the latter.

(d) The generalized least-squares method gives quite good results but requires a large amount of computation. Problems of convergence may also arise. Using the stochastic approximation method for the noise model and the least squares for the process model gives a better version of the generalized least-squares method, with less computational requirements.

(e) The maximum likelihood method gives very good estimates when used off-line. Its on-line version requires more computation than generalized least-squares, but will converge to the correct value provided that the assumptions about the probability distribution are correct.

4.11 REFERENCES

Aström, K. J. and Bohlin, T. (1966), "Numerical identification of linear dynamical systems from normal operating records," in: *Theory of Self-adaptive Control Systems*, P. Hammond, ed., Plenum Press, New York.

Clarke, D. W. (1967), "Generalized least squares estimation of the parameters of a dynamic model," *Preprints of the First IFAC Symposium on Identification* (Prague, Czechoslovakia).

Dvoretzky, A. (1956), "On stochastic approximation," *Proc. 3rd Berkeley Symp. on Mathematical Statistics and Probability*, vol. 1, University of California Press.

Fu, K. S., Nicolic, Z. Z., Chien, T. Y. and Wu, W. G. (1966), "On the stochastic approximation and related learning techniques," Purdue University, Lafayette, IN, Rep. TR-EE66.

Gertler, J. and Bányász, C. (1974), "A recursive (on-line) maximum likelihood identification method," *IEEE Transactions. Automatic Control*, vol. AC-19, pp. 816–820.

Isermann, R., Baur, U., Bamberger, W., Kneppo, P. and Siebert, H. (1974), "Comparison of six on-line identification and parameter estimation methods," *Automatica*, vol. 10, pp. 81–103.

Kiefer, J. and Wolfowitz, J. (1952), "Stochastic estimation of the maximum of regression problems," *Annals of Math. Stat.*, vol. 23.

Kwatny, H. G. (1972), "A note on stochastic approximation algorithms in system identification," *IEEE Transactions. Automatic Control*, vol. AC-17, pp. 570–572.

Pandya, R. N. (1972), "A class of bootstrap estimators for linear system identification," *International Journal of Control*, vol. 14, pp. 1091–1104.

Robbins, H. and Monro, S. (1951), "A stochastic approximation method," *Annals of Math. Stat.*, vol. 22.

Saridis, G. N. and Stein, G. (1968), "Stochastic approximation algorithms for linear system identification," *IEEE Transactions. Automatic Control*, vol. AC-13, pp. 515–523.

Saridis, G. N. (1974), "Comparison of six on-line identification algorithms," *Automatica*, vol. 10, pp. 69–80.

Sen, A. and Sinha, N. K. (1975a), "A generalized pseudoinverse algorithm for unbiased parameter estimation," *International Journal of Systems Science*, vol. 6, pp. 1103–1109.

Sen, A. and Sinha, N. K. (1975b), "On-line system identification algorithm combining stochastic approximation and pseudoinverse," *Automatica*, vol. 11, pp. 425–429.

Sinha, N. K. and Griscik, M. P. (1971), "A stochastic approximation method," *IEEE Transactions Systems, Man and Cybernetics*, vol. SMC-1, pp. 338–344.

Sinha, N. K. and Pille, W. (1971), "On-line parameter estimation using the matrix pseudoinverse," *Proc. IEE*, vol. 118, pp. 1041–1046.

Sinha, N. K. and Sen, A. (1975), "Critical evaluation of on-line identification methods," *Proc. IEE*, vol. 122, pp. 1153–1158.

Wright, J. D., Bacon, D. W. and Hoffman, T. W. (1972), "Analysis of a heat exchanger network using statistical time-series analysis methods," *Proc. Eastern Simulation Conference Fall meeting* (University of Waterloo, Waterloo, ON).

Young, P. C. (1970), "An instrumental variable method for real-time identification of a noisy process," *Automatica*, vol. 6, pp. 271–287.

4.12   PROBLEMS

1. Corresponding to the recursive algorithm for least squares estimation derived in section 4.2, derive another algorithm where the successive observations are weighted by $w_k = \lambda^1$, $k = 1, 2, \ldots$ and $0 < \lambda < 1$.

2. Use each of the algorithms discussed in Chapter 4 to estimate recursively the parameters of the second-order model for which 200 samples of the input-output data are given in Table 2 at the end of Chapter 3. For each case, plot the rate of convergence of the normalized error in the process parameter vector $[\|\hat{\underline{\theta}}_k - \underline{\theta}\|/\|\underline{\theta}\|]$ against the number of iterations.

[Hints: (i)   The starting point for each of the methods may be taken as the least-squares estimates based on 10 samples only.

(ii) For the maximum likelihood method assume that the observation error is distributed normally.]

5
Linear Multivariable Systems

A multivariable system is defined as one with several inputs and outputs, as indicated by the following block diagram.

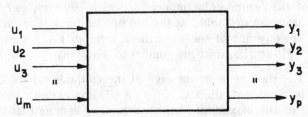

Figure 5.1.   Linear multivariable system.

As in the previous chapters, we shall consider the discrete-time case, where the samples of the input and the output are available for identification. Define

$$\underline{u}(t) = \begin{bmatrix} u_1(t) \\ u_2(t) \\ \cdot \\ \cdot \\ u_m(t) \end{bmatrix} = \text{m-dimensional input vector} \qquad (5.01)$$

$$\underline{y}(t) = \begin{bmatrix} y_1(t) \\ y_2(t) \\ \cdot \\ \cdot \\ y_p(t) \end{bmatrix} = \text{p-dimensional output vector} \qquad (5.02)$$

For the discrete-time case, we shall consider that the samples of u(t) and y(t), at t = kT, k = 1, 2, 3, ..., are available, and that the outputs y(kT) may be contaminated with noise.

The first important question for the multivariable case is the choice of the type of model to represent the system. In general there are four types of system models which have been studied and used for identification of linear discrete-time multivariable systems. These models are (i) the transfer function matrix, (ii) the impulse response matrix, (iii) the input-output difference equation model, and (iv) the state space formulation. Although these four models are equivalent and transformations between them are possible, each model has some special properties affecting the number of parameters to be estimated and the unbiasedness of the estimates when the ordinary least-squares algorithm is used.

The second important question is the structure of the model. Each of the four types of models has its own structural parameters which must be known before an attempt is made to estimate the parameters of the model. This problem of determination of the structure will be considered in Chapter 13.

In this chapter we shall discuss in detail each of the four types of models (El-Sherief and Sinha 1979a) for multivariable systems and the main algorithms proposed for estimating the parameters of the model if the structure is already known. For all these cases, it will be assumed that the measurement noise can be modeled as shown below

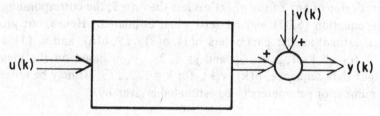

Figure 5.2.   Multivariable system with output noise.

5.1.   TRANSFER FUNCTION MATRIX REPRESENTATION

The system can be modeled as

$$\underline{y}(k) = G(z)\,\underline{u}(k) + \underline{v}(k) \qquad (5.03)$$

where

$$\underline{v}(k) = N(z)\,\underline{e}(k) \qquad (5.04)$$

In the above, z is the unit advance operator, $G(z)$ is a $p \times m$ matrix and $N(z)$ is a $p \times r$ matrix. Each element of the matrices $G(z)$ and $N(z)$, represented by $g_{ij}(z)$ and $n_{ij}(z)$, respectively, is a rational function of z. The structural parameters required to characterize the transfer function matrix of the system are the degrees of the denominator and the numerator polynomials of each element, $g_{ij}(z)$, of the transfer function matrix.

The transfer function matrix $G(z)$ may also be written as

$$G(z) = \frac{1}{C(z)} \begin{bmatrix} g_{11}^*(z) & g_{12}^*(z) \cdots g_{1m}^*(z) \\ g_{21}^*(z) & g_{22}^*(z) \cdots g_{2m}^*(z) \\ \vdots & \vdots & \vdots \\ g_{p1}^*(z) & g_{p2}^*(z) \cdots g_{pm}^*(z) \end{bmatrix} \tag{5.05}$$

where $C(z)$ is the characteristic polynomial of the system, defined as the least common monic denominator of all minors of $G(z)$. It will be assumed that $C(z)$ is a polynomial of degree n, the order of the system, and $g_{ij}^*(z)$ are polynomials of degree n - 1. Hence, one may write

$$C(z) = z^n + b(1) z^{n-1} + \cdots + b(n-1) z + b(n) \tag{5.06}$$

$$g_{ij}^*(z) = a_{ij}(1) z^{n-1} + a_{ij}(2) z^{n-2} + \cdots + a_{ij}(n-1) z + a_{ij}(n) \tag{5.07}$$

If the true degree of any of the $g_{ij}^*(z)$'s is less than n - 1, the corresponding coefficients in equation (5.07) will be zero when estimated. Hence, our problem consists of estimating the parameters $b(1), b(2), \ldots, b(n)$, and $a_{ij}(1), a_{ij}(2), \ldots, a_{ij}(n)$ for all $i = 1, 2, \ldots, p$ and $j = 1, 2, \ldots, m$ based on the measured input-output data sequence, $\underline{u}(k), \underline{y}(k)$, for $k = 1, 2, \ldots$. It may be noted that the total number of parameters to be estimated is given by

$$N_1 = n(pm + 1) \tag{5.08}$$

If we neglect the noise model, an ordinary recursive least-squares algorithm can be derived by decomposing the system into p subsystems, each corresponding to one row of the matrix $G(z)$ and regarded as a single-output multiple-input system. From equation (5.03), ignoring $v(k)$, we may write, utilizing (5.05), (El-Sherief and Sinha, 1979b)

$$C(z) y_i(k) = \sum_{j=1}^{m} g_{ij}^*(z) u_j(k), \qquad i = 1, 2, \ldots, p \tag{5.09}$$

Substituting for $C(z)$ and $g_{ij}^*(z)$ from equations (5.06) and (5.07), equation (5.09) can be written more explicitly in the following form

$$y_i(k) = \sum_{j=1}^{m} \sum_{\ell=1}^{n} a_{ij}(\ell) u_j(k - \ell) - \sum_{\ell=1}^{n} b(\ell) y_i(k - \ell), \qquad i = 1, 2, \ldots, p \tag{5.10}$$

Following the procedure in Chapter 4, one may develop, for each subsystem, a recursive algorithm for estimating the parameters. For example, the jth subsystem may be expressed as

$$\underline{Y}_j(k) = H_j(k) \, \underline{\phi}_j \qquad (5.11)$$

where

$$H_j(k) = \begin{bmatrix} u_1(0) & u_1(-1) & \cdots u_1(1-n) & u_2(0) & \cdots u_m(1-n) & -y_j(0) & \cdots -y_j(1-n) \\ u_1(1) & u_1(0) & \cdots u_1(2-n) & u_2(1) & \cdots u_m(2-n) & -y_j(1) & \cdots -y_j(2-n) \\ \vdots & \vdots & \vdots & \vdots & \vdots & \vdots & \vdots \\ u_1(k-1) & u_1(k-2) & \cdots u_1(k-n-1) & u_2(k-1) & \cdots u_m(k-n-1) & -y_j(k-1) & \cdots -y_j(k-n-1) \end{bmatrix}$$

$$(5.12)$$

$$\underline{Y}_j(k) = [y_j(1) \quad y_j(2) \cdots y_j(k)]^T \qquad (5.13)$$

and $\underline{\phi}_j$ is the parameter vector of the subsystem defined as

$$\underline{\phi}_j = [a_{j1}(1) \quad a_{j1}(2) \cdots a_{j1}(n) \quad a_{j2}(1) \cdots a_{jm}(n) \quad b(1) \quad b(2) \cdots b(n)]^T$$

$$(5.14)$$

For large values of k, the least-squares estimate of $\underline{\phi}_j$ is given by

$$\hat{\underline{\phi}}_j(k) = [H_j^T(k) \, H_j(k)]^{-1} \, H_j(k) \, \underline{Y}_j(k) \qquad (5.15)$$

where $\hat{\underline{\phi}}_j(k)$ is the estimate of the parameter ϕ_j from k observations.

A recursive version of equation (5.15) is given by the following equations:

$$\hat{\underline{\phi}}_j(k+1) = \hat{\underline{\phi}}_j(k) + \frac{P_j(k) \, \underline{h}_j(k+1) \, [y_j(k+1) - \underline{h}_j(k+1) \, \hat{\underline{\phi}}_j(k)]}{1 + \underline{h}_j^T(k+1) \, P_j(k) \, \underline{h}_j(k+1)} \qquad (5.16)$$

and

$$P_j(k+1) = P_j(k) - \frac{P_j(k) \, \underline{h}_j(k+1) \, [P_j(k) \, \underline{h}_j(k+1)]^T}{1 + \underline{h}_j^T(k+1) \, P_j(k) \, \underline{h}_j(k+1)} \qquad (5.17)$$

where

$$\underline{h}_j(k+1) = [u_1(k) \quad u_1(k-1) \cdots u_1(k-n) \quad u_2(k) \cdots u_m(k-n)$$
$$-y_j(k) \cdots -y_j(k-n)]^T \qquad (5.18)$$

From equations (5.10) and (5.15), it may be noted that the parameters of the characteristic polynomial, $C(z)$, are estimated for each subsystem, and thus, p times during each iteration. To reduce the amount of computation, one may determine $C(z)$ from the first output alone, and then use the following transformation

$$\hat{\bar{y}}_i(k) = y_i(k) + \sum_{\ell=1}^{n} \hat{b}(\ell)\, y_i(k - \ell) \qquad (5.19)$$

where $\hat{b}(\ell)$ is an estimate of the parameter $b(\ell)$ and $\hat{\bar{y}}_i$ is an estimate of $\bar{y}_i$, defined as

$$\bar{y}_i(k) = y_i(k) + \sum_{\ell=1}^{n} b(\ell)\, y_i(k - \ell) \qquad (5.20)$$

By using equation (5.19), the output equations (5.10) for $i = 1, 2, 3, \ldots, p$ can be modified to

$$\hat{\bar{y}}_i(k) = \sum_{j=1}^{m} \sum_{\ell=1}^{n} a_{ij}(\ell)\, u_j(k - \ell) \qquad (5.21)$$

In the above equation, we have eliminated the parameters of the polynomial $C(z)$ for the outputs $\bar{y}_i(k)$, $i = 2, 3, \ldots, p$. Hence the only parameters that need be estimated for these outputs are the $a_{ij}(\ell)$'s, which can be estimated using the recursive least-squares algorithm with the dimension of the parameter vector reduced to $n(m + 1)$. The resulting numbers of arithmetic operations required per iteration are given below:

Total number of additions and subtractions

$$= 2n[(m + 1)(nm + n + 1) + m(p - 1)(nm + 1)] \quad (5.22)$$

Total number of multiplications and divisions

$$= 2n^2(m + 1)^2 + 4npm + 2n^2 m^2 (p - 1) + 4n + p \quad (5.23)$$

Whereas the method proposed above is good for the case when the outputs are contaminated with very little noise, for the general case they give biased estimates of the parameters which may also be inconsistent. In such cases, one may use the generalized least squares algorithm for each subsystem on the same lines as described in Chapter 4. Alternatively, one may use a multivariable version of the adaptive least-squares algorithm proposed by Panuska (1969). Following El-Sherief (1979), for each subsystem we may write the following equation

$$y_i(k) = \sum_{j=1}^{m} \sum_{\ell=1}^{n_i} a_{ij}(\ell) u_j(k - \ell) - \sum_{\ell=1}^{n_i} d_i(\ell) [y_i(k - \ell) + v_i(k - \ell)] + v_i(k)$$

$$i = 1, 2, \ldots, p \qquad\qquad (5.24)$$

In the above equation, $v_i(k)$ is the additive noise sequence contaminating the ith output, and it is assumed the lowest common denominator of the ith row of $G(z)$ is given by

$$D_i(z) = z^{n_i} + d_i(1) z^{n_i - 1} + \cdots + d_i(n_i - 1) z + d_i(n_i) \qquad (5.25)$$

Equation (5.24) can be written in a vector form as follows

$$y_i(k) = \underline{h}_i^{*T}(k) \, \underline{\phi}_i^* + v_i(k); \qquad i = 1, 2, \ldots, p \qquad (5.26)$$

where

$$\underline{h}_i^*(k + 1) = [u_1(k) \quad u_1(k - 1) \cdots u_1(k - n_i) \cdots u_p(k - n_i) \quad -z_i(k)$$
$$\cdots -z_i(k - n_i) \quad v_i(k) \cdots v_i(k - n_i)]^T \qquad (5.27)$$

and

$$\underline{\phi}_i^* = [a_{i1}(1) \quad a_{i1}(2) \cdots a_{i1}(n) \cdots a_{im}(n) \quad d_i(1)$$
$$\cdots d_i(n_i) \quad d_i(1) \cdots d_i(n_i)]^T \qquad (5.28)$$

The extended parameter vector ϕ_i^* for each subsystem can be estimated using the recursive least-squares algorithm, but the residuals, $v_i(k)$ are not known. However, a reasonable estimate of the residuals can be obtained as follows

$$\hat{v}_i(k) = y_i(k) - \underline{\hat{h}}_i^{*T} \underline{\hat{\phi}}_i^*(k), \qquad i = 1, 2, \ldots, p \qquad (5.29)$$

where $\underline{\hat{\phi}}_i^*(k)$ is the estimate of ϕ_i^* at the kth iteration which is obtained using the recursive least-squares algorithm, and the vector $\underline{\hat{h}}_i^*$ is constructed as in equation (5.27) but with the values of $v_i(k)$ substituted by their current estimates from equation (5.29). Assuming that the predictor of equation (5.29) is stable, the convergence of the identification algorithm can be shown in the same way as Panuska (1969).

It may be noted that it has been assumed that the orders n_i are known. These are the structural parameters for this case, and the method for determining them will be discussed in Chapter 13.

5.2 THE IMPULSE RESPONSE MATRIX REPRESENTATION

The transfer function matrix, $G(z)$, can be expanded in the following infinite series

$$G(z) = J_0 z^{-1} + j_1 z^{-2} + J_2 z^{-3} + \cdots \qquad (5.30)$$

where $J_0, J_1, \ldots$ are constant matrices called the Markov parameters of the system. If $G(z)$ represents a stable system, it is possible to truncate the series after ℓ terms, and obtain a good approximation. Hence, the output of the system at the kth sampling instant may be written as

$$\underline{y}(k) = (J_0 z^{-1} + J_1 z^{-2} + \cdots + J_{\ell-1} z^{-\ell}) \underline{u}(k) + \underline{v}(k) \qquad (5.31)$$

This particular model has been considered for identification by Mehra (1971), Sinha et al. (1978) and El-Sherief and Sinha (1979a), and others. The structural parameter required to characterize the system in this model is the value ℓ, the minimum number of Markov parameters required to describe the system completely. The number of parameters of the model required to be estimated is given by

$$N_2 = \ell m p \qquad (5.32)$$

An important property of this model is that the ordinary least squares estimation method leads to unbiased estimates.

We shall now consider a normalized stochastic approximation algorithm proposed by El-Sherief and Sinha (1979a) for estimating the Markov parameters. Define the (ℓm)-dimensional vectors.

$$\underline{\theta}_i = [J_{0,i} \quad J_{1,i} \cdots J_{\ell-1,i}]^T \qquad (5.33)$$

and

$$\underline{u}(k + \ell - 1) = [\underline{u}^T(k + \ell - 1) \quad \underline{u}^T(k + \ell - 2) \cdots \underline{u}^T(k)]^T \qquad (5.34)$$

where $J_s, s = 0, 1, \ldots, \ell$ has been partitioned as

$$J_s = [\underline{J}_{s,1}^T \quad \underline{J}_{s,2}^T \cdots \underline{J}_{s,m}^T]^T \qquad (5.35)$$

Then the ith output in equation (5.31) may be written as

$$y_i(k + \ell) = \underline{u}^T(k + \ell - 1) \underline{\theta}_i + v_i(k + \ell), \qquad i = 1, 2, \ldots, p \qquad (5.36)$$

The parameter vectors $\underline{\theta}_i$, $i = 1, 2, \ldots, p$ can be estimated recursively by means of the following set of normalized stochastic approximation algorithms

$$\underline{\hat{\theta}}_i(k + 1) = \underline{\hat{\theta}}_i(k) + \nu(k) \frac{\underline{u}(k + \ell - 1)}{\| \underline{u}(k + \ell - 1) \|^2} [y_i(k + \ell) - \underline{u}^T(k + \ell - 1) \underline{\hat{\theta}}_i(k - 1)]$$

$$i = 1, 2, \ldots, p; \quad k = 1, 2, \ldots \qquad (5.37)$$

where the sequence $\nu(k)$ satisfies the following conditions

$$\lim_{i \to \infty} \nu(i) = 0, \quad \sum_{i=1}^{\infty} \nu(i) = \infty \quad \text{and} \quad \sum_{i=1}^{\infty} \nu^2(i) < \infty \qquad (5.38)$$

An on-line algorithm for estimating the Markov parameters based on cross-correlation between the outputs and a white noise input sequence will now be described (Sinha, Mahalanabis, and El-Sherief (1978).

Postmultiplying both sides of equation (5.31) by $u^T(j)$ and taking expectations, we get

$$E[\underline{y}(k) \underline{u}^T(j)] = \sum_{i=0}^{\ell-1} J_i E[\underline{u}(k - i - 1) \underline{u}^T(j)] + E[\underline{v}(k) \underline{u}^T(j)] \qquad (5.39)$$

Since the noise sequence $\underline{v}(k)$ is a zero-mean sequence uncorrelated with $u(k)$, equation (5.38) can be reduced to

$$E[\underline{y}(k) \underline{u}^T(j)] = \sum_{i=0}^{\ell-1} J_i E[\underline{u}(k - i - 1) \underline{u}^T(j)] \qquad (5.40)$$

Furthermore, if the input sequence $\{\underline{u}(k)\}$ is a white noise sequence, i.e.,

$$E[\underline{u}(i) \underline{u}^T(j)] = I\delta_{ij} \qquad (5.41)$$

where δ_{ij} is the Kronecker delta, we get

$$J_{k-j-1} = E[\underline{y}(k) \underline{u}^T(j)] \qquad (5.42)$$

Equation (5.41) indicates that the Markov parameters can be obtained from the cross-correlation between the input and the output if the input is a white noise sequence of unit variance, and is uncorrelated with the measurement noise. This expression is not very convenient, however, since it implies an ensemble average. Assuming ergodicity, one may use the time average to obtain

$$J_{k-1} = \lim_{N \to \infty} \frac{1}{N} \sum_{j=0}^{N-1} \underline{y}(k+j) \, u^T(j) \tag{5.43}$$

For a good approximation, it is necessary that N, the number of samples, be very large. This would require storing a large amount of data. The following recursive algorithm may be used for improving the estimates as more data arrive, and may, therefore, be used for on-line estimation

$$J_{k-1}(N+1) = J_{k-1}(N) - \frac{1}{N+1} \left[J_{k-1}(N) - \underline{y}(k-N+1) \, \underline{u}^T(N+1) \right] \tag{5.44}$$

where $J_k(N)$ is the estimate of J_k obtained from N samples of the input-output data.

It may be pointed out that although the proposed algorithm requires that the input sequence be white noise, this does not present any difficulty for those cases where it is necessary to identify the system under actual operation with some other inputs. In such cases, it is usually permissible to add a white noise dither signal from a pseudo-random noise generator to the actual input. The cross-correlation between this signal and the observed output can be utilized as before, provided that this dither signal is uncorrelated with the other input signal and the observation noise. It may also be added that this method does not require the prior knowledge of any structural parameter and also it does not suffer from the effect of the truncation in the sequence of Markov parameters, but a sufficient number of these must be estimated in order that a closed-form representation in the state space may be obtained. An efficient algorithm for the transformation to the state-space form, using the block Hankel matrix made up from the Markov parameters, has been proposed by Rozsa and Sinha (1974), and is described in detail in Appendix II.

5.3   THE STATE-SPACE MODEL

The linear multivariable system shown in Fig. 5.2 can be represented by the equations

$$x(k+1) = A\underline{x}(k) + B\underline{u}(k) \tag{5.45}$$

$$\underline{y}(k) = C\underline{x}(k) + \underline{v}(k) \tag{5.46}$$

where $x(k)$ is the n-dimensional state vector and A, B, and C are $n \times n$, $n \times m$ and $p \times n$ constant matrices, respectively.

The identification problem consists of estimating the parameters of the matrices A, B, and C. In addition, the order, n, of the system is the structural parameter which must also be determined. If n is known, the total number of parameters to be estimated is given by

$$N_3' = n(n + m + p) \tag{5.47}$$

It may also be noted that for a given input-output description, the matrices A, B, and C are not unique, and any nonsingular linear transformation of the state will give another set of these matrices. This has led to the development of several canonical forms of the state-space formulation that reduce the number of parameters to be estimated, as well as make the problem of identification simpler (Weinert and Anton 1972, Mayne 1972, Irwin and Roberts 1976, Guidorzi 1975). However, each canonical form introduces some additional structural parameters which must also be determined before the model parameters are estimated.

We shall now discuss a canonical form which has been much used for identification (Lobbia and Saridis 1973, Beghelli and Guidorzi 1976, Sinha and Kwong 1979). The A and C matrices in this canonical form have the following structures

$$A = \begin{bmatrix} A_{11} & A_{12} & \cdots & A_{1p} \\ A_{21} & A_{22} & \cdots & A_{2p} \\ \vdots & \vdots & & \vdots \\ A_{p1} & A_{p2} & \cdots & A_{pp} \end{bmatrix} \tag{5.48}$$

$$A_{ii} = \begin{bmatrix} 0 & & & \\ \vdots & & I_{n_i - 1} & \\ a_{ii}(1) & a_{ii}(2) & \cdots & a_{ii}(n) \end{bmatrix} \tag{5.49}$$

$$A_{ij}_{i \neq j} = \begin{bmatrix} 0 & 0 & \cdots & 0 & 0 \cdots 0 \\ \vdots & \vdots & & \vdots & \vdots \\ 0 & 0 & \cdots & 0 & 0 \cdots 0 \\ a_{ij}(1) & a_{ij}(2) & \cdots & a_{ij}(n_{ij}) & 0 \cdots 0 \end{bmatrix} \tag{5.50}$$

$$C = \begin{bmatrix} \underline{e}^1 \\ \underline{e}^{n_1+1} \\ \underline{e}^{n_2+1} \\ \vdots \\ \underline{e}^{n_1+n_2+\cdots+n_m-1} \end{bmatrix} \qquad (5.51)$$

In the above equations e^i is the ith unit row vector of dimension n_i, the structural parameters n_i are the observability subindices* of the system, and n_{ij} is the number of nonzero elements in the last row of A_{ij}. As shown by Guidorzi (1975)

$$\begin{aligned} n_{ij} &\leqslant n_i + 1 \qquad \text{if} \quad i > j \\ n_{ij} &\leqslant n_i \qquad\quad \text{if} \quad i < j \end{aligned} \qquad (5.52)$$

It will be seen that with this canonical form the total number of unknown parameters is given by

$$N_3 \leqslant n(p + m), \qquad (5.53)$$

these being the elements of p rows of the A matrix and the elements of the B matrix. In addition, one must also determine the p structural parameters n_i.

Due to the importance of state space representation in many applications of control theory several papers have been published on the identification of multivariable systems in this form. Most of this work can be put into two classes; the first is identification from noise-free input-output data and the second is identification from noisy data. The pioneering work in the first category was done by Ho and Kalman (1966), Gopinath (1969) and Budin (1971). Budin's approach is similar to that of Gopinath but requires less computation. We shall, therefore, discuss this briefly.

A selector matrix S is defined as a $k \times \ell$ matrix ($k \leqslant \ell$) with the property that when premultiplying an $\ell \times m$ matrix F, the resulting $k \times m$ matrix SF consists of k of the rows of F as they are ordered in F. From this definition it follows that:

---

*The observability subindices of the system are obtained from the observability matrix of the system in the following manner. Let the ith row of the matrix C be denoted by c^i. Then, we select n rows of the observability matrix, starting from the top, that are linearly independent. The observability subindex n_i is equal to the number of rows containing c^i in this matrix, i.e., $\underline{c}^i, \underline{c}^i A, \underline{c}^i A^2, \ldots, \underline{c}^i A^{n_i-1}$ will be the total number of rows containing c^i. It also follows that $\sum_{i=1}^{p} n_i = n$.

(i)   the elements s_{ij} of S are either 1 or 0
(ii) for all i there is one and only one value of j, called j_i such that $s_{ij} = 1$
(iii) $j_1 < j_2 < \cdots < j_k$.

It also follows that if a p $\times$ q matrix R has rank r then there are two selector matrices S_1 (an r $\times$ p matrix) and S_2 (an r $\times$ q matrix) such that $S_1 RS_2^T$ is nonsingular. Also, if r = q then $S_2 = I$, and if r = p then $S_1 = I$.

The notation $S(i_1, i_2, \ldots, i_m)$ is used to specify the selector matrix which deletes the rows $i_1, i_2, \ldots, i_m$ from the matrix it multiplies.

Budin has shown that for a completely observable system there exists an n $\times$ n*p selector matrix, S, where

$$n^* = n + 1 - \text{rank of C}, \qquad (5.54)$$

such that

$$SV = T \qquad (5.55)$$

is nonsingular, where V is the observability matrix of the system. Furthermore, without any loss of generality, it can be assumed that T = I, since a linear transformation of the state vector will not affect the input-output description.

Using any selector matrix that satisfies equation (5.55), the following direct input-output relation for a completely observable system is obtained.

$$S\bar{y}_{n*}(k + 1) = [A, R] \begin{bmatrix} S\bar{y}_{n*}(k) \\ \bar{u}_{n*}(k) \end{bmatrix} \qquad (5.56)$$

where

$$\bar{y}_{n*}(k) \triangleq [y^Y(k) \quad \underline{y}^T(k + 1) \cdots \underline{y}^T(k + n^* - 1)]^T \qquad (5.57)$$

$$\bar{u}_{n*}(k) \triangleq [\underline{u}^T(k) \quad \underline{u}^T(k + 1) \cdots \underline{u}^T(k + n^* - 1)]^T \qquad (5.58)$$

$$R \triangleq -ASS(pn^* + 1, pn^* + 2, \ldots, pn^* + p) R_{n*} \qquad (5.59)$$

and

$$R_{n*} \triangleq \begin{bmatrix} 0 & 0 & \cdots & 0 \\ CB & 0 & \cdots & 0 \\ CAB & CB & \cdots & 0 \\ \vdots & \vdots & & \vdots \\ CA^{n^*-1}B & CA^{n^*-2}B & \cdots & CB \end{bmatrix} \qquad (5.60)$$

Using equation (5.56), we have

$$S[\bar{y}_{n*}(k+1) \cdots \bar{y}_{n*}(k+n+mn^*)]$$

$$= [A \mid R] \begin{bmatrix} S & 0 & \bar{y}_{n*}(k) \cdots \bar{y}_{n*}(k+n+mn^*-1) \\ 0 & I_{mn*} & \bar{u}_{n*}(k) \cdots \bar{u}_{n*}(k+n+mn^*-1) \end{bmatrix} \quad (5.61)$$

which can be written more compactly as

$$SF_{n*}(k+1) = [A \mid R] \, \bar{S}G_{n*}(k) \quad (5.62)$$

where the correspondences are obvious. Note that $\bar{S}$ is an $(mn^* + n) \times (m + p) n^*$ selector matrix.

A unique solution for $[A \mid R]$ exists whenever $\bar{S}G_{n*}(k)$ is nonsingular. This requires that the rank of $G_{n*}(k)$ must be equal to $n + mn^*$.

Budin (1971) has proved that if the system is completely observable and controllable and the assumed system dimension n_a is greater than the actual minimal dimension n, then for almost all input sequences $\{u(i)\}$,

$$\text{rank } [G_{n*}(k)] = n + mn_a^* \quad (5.63)$$

In the above statement, the phrase "almost all input sequences" implies that the input sequences must not map into a subspace of dimension lower than the dimension of the space spanned by the general input sequence. For a randomly chosen input sequence, the probability of not satisfying this property may be taken as zero.

Based on the above theorem, Budin's procedure is carried out in the following steps:

(i) Construct the matrix $P_{N*}(k)$ where $N^* = N + 1 -$ rank of C, and N is the upper bound on the minimal dimension. If the rank of C is not known, but it is known that it is equal to or greater than q, use $N^* = N - q + 1$. The matrix $P_{N*}(k)$ is defined below

$$P_{N*}(k) = \begin{bmatrix} \underline{u}(k) & \cdots & \underline{u}(k+N+mN^*-1) \\ \underline{y}(k) & \cdots & \underline{y}(k+N+mN^*-1) \\ \vdots & & \vdots \\ \underline{u}(k+N^*-1) & \cdots & \underline{u}(k+N+mN^*+N^*-2) \\ \underline{y}(k+N^*-1) & \cdots & \underline{y}(k+N+mN^*+N^*-2) \end{bmatrix} \quad (5.64)$$

(ii) Obtain the first identifier matrix $_1[P_{N*}(k)]$. The mN^* rows of $P_{N*}(k)$ consisting of the input observations will be among the independent rows, and n of the first p_{n*} rows of $P_{N*}(k)$ consisting of the output observations will complete the set of independent rows.

(iii) Determine the order of the minimal realization given by

$$n = \text{number of independent rows of } _1[P_{N*}(k)] = mN^* \qquad (5.65)$$

(iv) Construct the $pn^* \times n$ submatrix $\overline{K}$ of $_1[P_{N*}(k)]$ consisting of the first pn^* output rows and the first n columns not containing 1's associated input rows. Then

$$S = \overline{K}^T \qquad (5.66)$$

(v) Construct the matrices $F_{n*}(k + 1)$, $G_{n*}(k)$ and S and obtain A from the equation

$$[A \mathbin{|} R] = SF_{n*}(k + 1) [SG_{n*}(k)]^{-1} \qquad (5.67)$$

(vi) Obtain B from the equation

$$B = \overline{R}_0 + A\overline{R}_1 + \cdots + A^{n^*-1}\overline{R}_{n*-1} \qquad (5.68)$$

where

$$R = [\overline{R}_0 \quad \overline{R}_1 \cdots \overline{R}_{n*-1}] \text{ with each } \overline{R}_i \text{ an } n \times m \text{ matrix}$$

Bingulac and Farias (1977) have proposed an algorithm based on an identification identity which enables the determination of the system matrices in another canonical form from the input-output data for the noise-free case.

Guidorzi (1975) has used the canonical form described by equations (5.48)–(5.51) for identification by first showing a one-to-one equivalence between this canonical form and a canonical set of input-output difference equations. His procedure will be discussed in the next section.

The identification of multivariable systems in the state space model from noisy data is much more complicated. Two main approaches have been considered. In the first, the algorithms for identification from noise-free data are suitably modified, whereas in the second, identification is carried out directly from the noisy data. Guidorzi (1975) has extended his algorithm, discussed above, to obtain least-squares estimates in a manner similar to the instrumental variable approach. Sinha and Kwong (1977) have developed a recursive version of Guidorzi's algorithm and proposed the use of the generalized least-squares algorithm for estimation of the parameters. El-Sherief and Sinha (1978) have proposed combining stochastic approximation and pseudoinverse for estimating the parameters of the input-output difference equations. This method will also be discussed in the next section.

5.4   THE INPUT-OUTPUT DIFFERENCE EQUATION MODEL

Another way to represent the multivariable system is through the equation

$$P(z) [y(k) + \underline{v}(k)] = Q(z) \underline{u}(k) \tag{5.69}$$

where the elements of the $p \times p$ matrix $P(z)$ and the $p \times m$ matrix $Q(z)$ are polynomials in z. It will be seen immediately that this representation is not unique since both sides of the equation may be premultiplied by a nonsingular $p \times p$ polynomial matrix $R(z)$ without altering the basic form. The representation is said to be minimal when the degree of the polynomial matrix $P(z)$, defined as the degree of its determinant is as small as possible, and in this case, equal to the degree of the characteristic polynomial of the system. By a suitable choice of $R(z)$, it is possible to obtain $P(z)$ in a canonical form. In particular, it is fairly straightforward to obtain a canonical form of equation (5.69) which may be related directly to the state-space canonical form equations (5.48) to (5.51). As shown by Guidorizi (1975) the elements of $P(z)$ are obtained as

$$p_{ii}(z) = z^{n_i} - a_{ii}(n_i) z^{n_i - 1} - \cdots - a_{ii}(2) z - a_{ii}(1) \tag{5.70}$$

$$p_{ij}(z) = -a_{ij}(n_{ij}) z^{n_{ij} - 1} - \cdots - a_{ij}(2) z - a_{ij}(1) \tag{5.71}$$

A comparison with equations (5.49) and (5.50) shows that one set of equations can be obtained from the other directly by inspection.

The elements of $Q(z)$ are obtained as

$$q_{ij}(z) = \beta_{(n_1 + \cdots + n_i), j} z^{n_i - 1} + \cdots + \beta_{(n_1 + \cdots + n_{i-1} + 2), j} z$$
$$+ \beta_{(n_1 + \cdots n_{i-1} + 1), j} \tag{5.72}$$

where the coefficients of β_{ij} are the entries of the matrix

$$\bar{B} = \begin{bmatrix} \beta_{11} & \cdots & \beta_{1m} \\ \vdots & & \vdots \\ \beta_{n1} & \cdots & \beta_{nm} \end{bmatrix} = MB \tag{5.73}$$

and the matrix M is given by

$$
M = \begin{bmatrix}
-a_{11}(2) & -a_{11}(3) \cdots -a_{11}(n_1) & 1 \cdots -a_{1p}(2) & \cdots -a_{11}(n_1 p) & 0 \\
-a_{11}(3) & -a_{11}(4) \cdots \quad 1 & 0 \cdots -a_{1p}(3) & & \\
\vdots & & \vdots \quad \vdots & & \\
-a_{11}(n_1) & & -a_{1p}(n_{1p}) & & \\
& & \vdots & & \\
1 & 0 & 0 \cdots \quad 0 & & 0 \\
\vdots & \vdots \quad \vdots & \cdots & & \\
-a_{p1}(2) & & \cdots -a_{pp}(2) & \cdots -a_{pp}(n_p) & 1 \\
-a_{p1}(3) & & \cdots -a_{pp}(3) & & 0 \\
\vdots & & & & \\
-a_{p1}(n_{p1}) & & \cdots \quad \vdots & & \vdots \\
0 & & & & \\
\vdots & & -a_{pp}(n_p) & & \\
0 & & 1 & 0 \quad \cdots & 0
\end{bmatrix}
$$

$$(5.74)$$

It may be noted that the matrix M is always nonsingular and its determinant is equal to -1. Hence, the matrix B can always be determined from the knowledge of $P(z)$ and $Q(z)$. Similarly, knowing A and B, we can always determine both $P(z)$ and $Q(z)$ uniquely in this canonical form.

Assuming that the structural parameters, n_i, are known, we shall now discuss the estimation of the parameters in the matrices $P(z)$ and $Q(z)$. Evidently, this method also leads directly to the canonical state-space representation of equations (5.48) to (5.50). If the system is completely observable it can be decomposed into p observable subsystems. Each of these subsystems corresponds to one row of the matrices $P(z)$ and $Q(z)$. The jth subsystem can be written as

$$
\sum_{i=1}^{p} p_{ji}(z) y_i(k) = \sum_{i=1}^{m} q_{ji}(z) u_i(k) - \sum_{i=1}^{p} p_{ji}(z) v_i(k) \qquad (5.75)
$$

Equation (5.75) may be written more explicitly in the following form

$$y_j(k + n_j) = \sum_{i=1}^{p} \sum_{\ell=1}^{n_{ji}} a_{ji}(\ell)\, y_i(k + \ell - 1)$$

$$+ \sum_{i=1}^{m} \sum_{\ell=1}^{n_j} \beta_{(n_1 + \cdots + n_{j-1} + \ell),\, i}\, u_i(k + \ell - 1) + e_j(k + n_j) \quad (5.76)$$

where

$$e_j(k + n_j) = v_j(k + n_j) + \sum_{i=1}^{p} \sum_{\ell=1}^{n_{ji}} a_{ji}(\ell)\, v_i(k + \ell - 1) \quad (5.77)$$

To estimate the parameters $a_{ji}(\ell)$ and β_{ij} of the subsystem, we may first rewrite equation (5.76) in the form

$$y_j(k) = q_j^T(k)\, \phi_j + e_j(k) \quad (5.78)$$

where

$$q_j(k) = [y_1(k) \quad y_1(k + 1) \cdots y_1(k + n_{j1} - 1) \quad y_2(k) \cdots y_p(k + n_{jp} - 1)$$
$$u_1(k) \quad u_1(k + 1) \cdots u_p(k + n_p - 1)]^T \quad (5.79)$$

and

$$\phi_j = [a_{j1}(1) \quad a_{j1}(2) \cdots a_{j1}(n_{j1} - 1) \quad a_{j2}(1) \cdots a_{jp}(n_{jp})$$
$$\beta_{(n_1 + \cdots + n_{j-1} + 1),\, 1} \cdots \beta_{(n_1 + \cdots + n_{j-1} + n_j),\, r}]^T \quad (5.80)$$

A recursive pseudoinverse algorithm can be used for obtaining least-squares estimates of the parameter vector ϕ_j in exactly the same way as in Chapter 4. This is given below where $\hat{\phi}_j(k)$ is the estimate of ϕ_j at the kth iteration

$$\left.\begin{array}{l} \hat{\phi}_j(k + 1) = \hat{\phi}_j(k) + \dfrac{P_j(k)\, q_j(k + 1)\, [y_j(k + 1) - q_j^T(k + 1)\, \hat{\phi}_j(k)]}{1 + q_j^T(k + 1)\, P_j(k)\, q_j(k + 1)} \\[2em] P_j(k + 1) = P_j(k) - \dfrac{P_j(k)\, q_j(k + 1)\, [P_j(k)\, q_j(k + 1)]^T}{1 + q_j^T(k + 1)\, P_j(k)\, q_j(k + 1)} \end{array}\right\} \quad (5.81)$$

It is known that the least-squares method gives biased estimates if the residuals are correlated. One way of overcoming this difficulty is to filter the input-output sequence before using the algorithm of equation (5.81) such that the resulting residuals are uncorrelated. Proceeding as in Chapter 4, the correlated residuals are modeled as the output of a linear system with white noise input as below

$$e_j(k) = - \sum_{i=1}^{s} f_{ji} e_j(k - i) + \omega_j(k) \qquad (5.82)$$

where $\omega_j(k)$ is an uncorrelated zero-mean random sequence, and the parameters f_{ji} are to be estimated from the sequence $e_j(k)$ as defined in equation (5.78).

Equation (5.82) may be written as

$$e_j(k) = \underline{\psi}_j^T \underline{\epsilon}_j(k) + \omega_j(k) \qquad (5.83)$$

where

$$\underline{\psi}_j = [f_{j1} \quad f_{j2} \cdots f_{js}]^T \qquad (5.84)$$

and

$$\underline{\epsilon}_j = [-e_j(k-1) \quad -e_j(k-2) \cdots -e_j(k-s)]^T \qquad (5.85)$$

In Chapter 4, the auxiliary parameter vector $\underline{\psi}_j$ was estimated using the recursive least squares algorithm. Alternatively, we may use the normalized stochastic approximation algorithm

$$\hat{\underline{\psi}}_j(k+1) = \hat{\underline{\psi}}_j(k) + \frac{\nu}{k+1} \frac{e_j(k) - \hat{\underline{\psi}}_j^T(k) \underline{\epsilon}_j(k)}{\| \underline{\epsilon}_j(k) \|^2} \underline{\epsilon}_j(k) \qquad (5.86)$$

where ν is a positive gain constant.

Utilizing the estimate of $\underline{\psi}_j$, the input-output sequences can be filtered according to the equations

$$\left. \begin{array}{l} u_j^*(k) = u_j(k) - \sum_{i=1}^{s} f_{ji} u_j(k-1) \\[1em] y_j^*(k) = y_j(k) - \sum_{i=1}^{s} f_{ji} y_j(k-1) \end{array} \right\} \qquad (5.87)$$

In the algorithm of equations (5.81) the filtered sequences $u_j^*(k)$ and $y_j^*(k)$ are used in place of $u_j(k)$ and $y_j(k)$, respectively, resulting in uncorrelated residuals. This method, therefore, consists of using the normalized stochastic approximation algorithm to obtain the parameters of the auxiliary noise model and the recursive pseudoinverse algorithm to estimate the process model parameters after the input-output data are suitably corrected utilizing the noise model. Results of simulation for a 2-input 2-output system (El-Sherief and Sinha 1978) indicate that the method gives quite good parameter estimates with noise-to-signal ratios of 30% at each of the two outputs.

It may be pointed out here that although this method gives very good estimates of the parameters even in the presence of noise, a large amount of computation is required for estimating the parameters of the auxiliary noise model as well as the system model. This is much more than that necessary if the ordinary least-squares algorithm is used, but since it gives biased estimates for noisy estimates this is the price one must pay. This will be further discussed in the next section.

5.5 COMPARISON OF DIFFERENT TYPES OF MODELS USING THE LEAST-SQUARES ESTIMATION ALGORITHM

The least-squares estimation algorithm is often used because it does not require any prior statistical information. In particular, the recursive version of this algorithm (also called the recursive pseudoinverse algorithm) is attractive because it can be used for on-line parameter estimation. On the other hand, sometimes it gives biased estimates in the presence of noise.

Among the four different types of models for linear multivariable systems discussed in this chapter, it was pointed out that the impulse response matrix respresentation gives unbiased estimates. To verify this fact, and to compare with the other models, the results of a simulated example will be described (El-Sherief 1979).

The example considered is of a 4th-order system with two inputs and two outputs. The transfer function matrix of this system is given by

$$
G(z) = \begin{bmatrix} \dfrac{1}{z - 0.25} & \dfrac{2}{z - 0.4} \\[2ex] \dfrac{2}{z - 0.25} & \dfrac{4}{(z - 0.5)^2} \end{bmatrix}
\tag{5.88}
$$

which may also be written as

$$
G(z) = \begin{bmatrix} \dfrac{z - 0.4}{z^2 - 0.65z + 0.1} & \dfrac{2z - 0.5}{z^2 - 0.65z + 0.1} \\[2ex] \dfrac{2z^2 - 2z + 0.5}{z^3 - 1.25z^2 + 0.5z - 0.0625} & \dfrac{4z - 1}{z^3 - 1.25z^2 + 0.5z - 0.625} \end{bmatrix}
\tag{5.89}
$$

The first five Markov parameters of the system are easily obtained by long division of each element of G(z), and are given below

$$
J_0 = \begin{bmatrix} 1 & 2 \\ 2 & 0 \end{bmatrix}, \quad J_1 = \begin{bmatrix} 0.25 & 0.8 \\ 0.5 & 4 \end{bmatrix}, \quad J_2 = \begin{bmatrix} 0.0625 & 0.32 \\ 0.125 & 4 \end{bmatrix},
$$

$$
J_3 = \begin{bmatrix} 0.0156 & 0.128 \\ 0.031 & 3 \end{bmatrix}, \quad \text{and} \quad J_4 = \begin{bmatrix} 0.0039 & 0.0512 \\ 0.0078 & 2 \end{bmatrix}
$$

(5.90)

The canonical state space form is given by the following matrices following the method proposed by Hickin and Sinha (1977)

$$
A = \begin{bmatrix} 0 & 1 & 0 & 0 \\ -0.1 & 0.65 & 0 & 0 \\ 0 & 0 & 0 & 1 \\ \frac{1}{3} & \frac{5}{6} & -0.25 & 1 \end{bmatrix}, \quad B = \begin{bmatrix} 1 & 2 \\ 0.25 & 0.8 \\ 2 & 0 \\ 0.5 & 4 \end{bmatrix}, \quad C = \begin{bmatrix} 1 & 0 & 0 & 0 \\ 0 & 0 & 1 & 0 \end{bmatrix} \quad (5.91)
$$

The canonical input-output difference equation form is given below

$$
P(z) = \begin{bmatrix} z^2 - 0.65z + 0.1 & 0 \\ -\frac{5}{6}z - \frac{1}{3} & z^2 - z + 0.25 \end{bmatrix}, \quad Q(z) = \begin{bmatrix} z - 0.4 & 2z - 0.5 \\ 2z - \frac{2}{3} & \frac{7}{3} \end{bmatrix} \quad (5.92)
$$

The above system was simulated on a CDC-6400 computer using the state-space model representation of equation (5.90) with zeroinitial states and the two inputs were taken as uncorrelated zero-mean white noise sequences with standard deviation of value 1. To each output a zero-mean white noise sequence was added with standard deviation adjusted to vary the noise level at that output. The parameters of the above system in the four different model representations were estimated using the recursive least squares method for different noise levels. The final estimate of the parameters of each model after 500 iterations is shown in Tables 5.1–5.4.

We can see from Tables 5.1–5.4 that good estimates of the parameters of the system in each of the four models have been obtained for the noise free case. For the noisy case, the estimate of the parameters of the three models, transfer-function matrix, input-output difference equation, and state-space, is biased and inconsistent. On the other hand we can notice from Table 5.2 that good estimates of the parameters of the impulse response model have been obtained even for high noise level, $\sigma_1 = \sigma_2 = 0.1$.

Table 5.1. Estimate of the Parameters of the Transfer-Function Matrix Model

True Parameters	Noise Free Case	$\sigma_1 = .01$ $\sigma_2 = .01$	$\sigma_1 = .05$ $\sigma_2 = .05$	$\sigma_1 = .1$ $\sigma_2 = .1$
.65	.6500	.6454	.5432	.3791
.10	.1000	−0.982	−.0600	.0002
1.00	1.0000	.9994	.9972	.9970
−.40	−.4000	−.3954	−.2924	−.1277
2.00	2.0000	2.0001	2.0004	1.9996
−.50	−.5000	−.4912	−.2879	.0353
1.25	1.2500	1.2431	1.0223	.6903
−.50	−.5000	−.4932	−.2725	.0600
.0625	.0625	.0610	.0072	−.0742
2.00	2.0000	1.9997	1.9982	1.9983
−2.00	−2.0000	−1.9850	−1.5379	−.8688
.50	.50000	.4880	.1504	0.3551
.00	.0000	.0015	.0076	.0038
4.00	4.0000	3.9976	3.9880	3.9886
−1.00	−1.0000	0.9706	−0.818	1.2464
Error square of parameter estimates	.0000	.0407	1.3792	3.3167

Table 5.2. Estimate of the Parameters of the Impulse Response Model

True Parameters	Noise Free Case	$\sigma_1 = .01$ $\sigma_2 = .01$	$\sigma_1 = .05$ $\sigma_2 = .05$	$\sigma_1 = .1$ $\sigma_2 = .1$
1.00	1.0010	1.0014	1.0031	1.0052
2.00	1.9997	1.9993	1.9975	1.9953
.25	.2509	.2513	.2524	.2540
.80	.7989	.7985	.7969	.7950
.0625	.0619	.0619	.0619	.0619
.32	.3207	.3209	.3218	.3229
.0156	.0154	.0161	.0187	.0220
.128	.1282	.1279	.1270	.1258
.0039	.0043	.0044	.0049	.0056
.0512	.0509	.0514	.0531	.0552
2.00	2.0407	2.0473	2.0500	2.0534
.00	−0.423	−0.0414	−0.0378	−.0333
.50	.5632	.5648	.5709	.5785
4.00	3.9156	3.9145	3.9100	3.9045
.125	.1012	.1009	.0995	.0978
4.00	4.0180	4.0180	4.0183	4.0186
.0313	.0142	.0141	.0135	.0128
3.00	3.0096	3.0096	3.0098	3.0101
.0078	.0239	.0242	.0252	.0265
2.00	1.9821	1.9825	1.9843	1.9865
Error square of parameter estimates	.0614	.0174	.0191	.0214

Table 5.3.   Estimate of the Parameters of the Input-Output Difference Equation Model

True Parameters	Noise Free Case	$\sigma_1 = .01$ $\sigma_2 = .01$	$\sigma_1 = .05$ $\sigma_2 = .05$	$\sigma_1 = .1$ $\sigma_2 = .1$
.65	.6497	.0792	−.0029	−.0071
−.10	−.1000	.0644	.0877	.0884
.00	.0000	.0319	.0368	.0375
.00	.0000	−.0817	−.0213	−.0213
1.00	1.0000	1.0003	1.0022	1.0045
−.40	−.3997	.1072	.1801	.1835
2.00	2.0000	1.9995	1.9975	1.9951
−.50	−.4994	.6412	.8035	.8098
−.83	−.8316	.0708	.1784	.1815
.33	.3328	.0721	.0383	.0350
1.00	.9999	.9503	.9467	.9487
−.25	−.2499	−.2207	−.2188	−.2201
2.00	2.0000	1.9996	1.9974	1.9947
−.67	−.6682	−1.4705	−1.5672	−1.5695
.00	.0000	.0016	.0079	.0157
5.67	5.6633	3.8566	3.6334	3.6177
Error square of parameter estimates	.0001	6.7243	8.2693	8.5007

Table 5.4.   Estimate of the Parameters of the State-Space Model

True Parameters	Noise Free Case	$\sigma_1 = .01$ $\sigma_2 = .01$	$\sigma_1 = .05$ $\sigma_2 = .05$	$\sigma_1 = .1$ $\sigma_2 = .1$
−.10	−.1000	.0644	.0877	.0884
.65	.6497	.0792	−.0029	−.0071
.00	.0000	.0319	.0368	.0375
.00	.0000	−.0183	−.0213	−.0213
.33	.3328	.0721	.0383	.0350
−.83	−.8316	.0708	.1784	.1815
−.25	−.2499	−.2207	−.2188	−.2201
1.00	.9999	.9503	.9467	.9487
1.00	1.0000	1.0003	1.0022	1.0045
2.00	2.0000	1.9995	1.9975	1.9951
.25	.2500	.2502	.2507	.2512
.80	.8000	.7050	.7980	.7962
2.00	2.0000	1.9996	1.9974	1.9947
.00	.0000	.0165	.0079	.0157
.50	.5000	.5018	.3621	.3580
4.00	4.0001	4.0164	3.7174	3.7024
Error square of parameter estimates	.0000	1.3402	1.6681	1.6919

5.6 IDENTIFICATION OF CONTINUOUS-TIME MULTIVARIABLE SYSTEMS FROM SAMPLES OF INPUT-OUTPUT DATA

In the previous sections we have discussed the methods for estimating the parameters of a discrete-time multivariable system from the samples of input-output data. In many practical situations, we wish to identify a continuous-time system from these samples.

There are two approaches for solving this problem. In the so-called indirect approach we first obtain a discrete-time model from the samples, and then, determine an equivalent continuous-time model. In this case, for the first step, we can utilize the methods described in the previous sections. The other approach attempts to obtain the continuous-time model directly. In both the approaches, the results can only be approximate since there is no knowledge about the input between the sampling instants. It is also assumed that the sampling interval, T, has been selected carefully, so that $|\lambda_* T| \leq 0.5$, where λ_* is the eigenvalue of the continuous-time system farthest away from the origin of the complex plane. It may be added that, in practice, it is not very desirable to make the sampling interval very small as well, since this leads to ill-conditioning and numerical difficulties caused by the fact that all the eigenvalues of the discrete-time model are forced to lie in a very small region of the z-plane.

Consider a linear multivariable continuous-time system described by the equations

$$\left.\begin{array}{l} \dot{x} = Ax + Bu \\ y = Cx + w(t) \end{array}\right\} \tag{5.93}$$

where $w(t)$ is measurement noise.

Then our problem is the determination of A, B, and C (in a suitable canonical form) from the samples $u(kT)$ and $y(kT)$ of the measured input and output vectors, respectively. For convenience in notation, these will be denoted as $u(k)$ and $y(k)$, respectively.

5.6.1 The Indirect Method

If we assume that the input is held constant during the sampling interval, we get the following relationships

$$x(k + 1) = Fx(k) + Gu(k) \tag{5.94}$$

where

$$F = e^{AT} = I + AT + \frac{1}{2!} (AT)^2 + \frac{1}{3!} (AT)^3 + \cdots \tag{5.95}$$

$$G = \int_0^T e^{AT} B \, dt = \left(IT + \frac{1}{2!} AT^2 + \frac{1}{3!} A^2 T^3 + \cdots \right) B \qquad (5.96)$$

Thus, our problem reduces to determining A and B after we have estimated F and G using the methods discussed in the previous sections.

Since, in general, the input is not actually held constant between the sampling instants, as assumed above, it may be a better approximation to modify equation (5.94) as follows

$$x(k + 1) = Fx(k) + G\bar{u}(k) \qquad (5.97)$$

where

$$\bar{u}(k) = \tfrac{1}{2} [u(k) + u(k + 1)] \qquad (5.98)$$

and use $y(k)$ and $\bar{u}(k)$ for estimating F and G.

We shall now discuss the problem of determining A and B from F and G. One way of doing this is to first diagonalize F and obtain the natural logarithm of each diagonal element to obtain the corresponding diagonal form of A. This follows from the fact that A and F have the same eigenvectors (Strmcnik and Bremsak 1979). However, a difficulty is encountered when the eigenvalues of F are real and negative. The case when F cannot be diagonalized is more involved. Even when F can be diagonalized, calculating its eigenvalues and eigenvectors is computationally cumbersome. In view of these difficulties, we shall consider a computational algorithm (Sinha and Lastman 1981). It uses fixed-point iteration, and is given by

$$(AT)^{(k+1)} = (AT)^{(k)} + F^{-1}(F - F^{(k)})$$
$$= AT^{(k)} + I - F^{-1} F^{(k)} \qquad (5.99)$$

where $AT^{(k)}$ is the value of AT at the kth iteration and

$$F^{(k)} = e^{(AT)^{(k)}} \qquad (5.100)$$

which can be calculated using the power series similar to equation (5.95). Note that this method requires that the spectral radius of AT and F be less than one. Both of these conditions are satisfied if A represents a stable system and if the sampling interval is selected suitably so that the spectral radius of AT is less than or equal to 0.5.

For the initial guess we may use

$$AT^{(0)} = \tfrac{1}{2} (F - F^{-1}) \qquad (5.101)$$

which is obtained by truncating the Taylor series expansion of e^{AT} and e^{-AT} after the first three terms.

After AT has been obtained using the algorithm described in equation (5.99), the matrix B can be determined from the relationship

$$B = R^{-1}G \qquad (5.102)$$

where

$$R = \left[I + \frac{1}{2!}AT + \frac{1}{3!}(AT)^2 + \cdots\right]T \qquad (5.103)$$

It may be noted that if the series indicated by equations (5.95) and (5.96) are truncated after the first eleven terms, an error of less than 10^{-9} is obtained if the condition on the spectral radius of AT is satisfied.

The following example will illustrate the procedure. Let

$$A = \begin{bmatrix} 0 & 1 & 0 \\ 0 & 0 & 1 \\ -1 & -2 & -2 \end{bmatrix} \quad \text{and} \quad T = 0.5 \qquad (5.104)$$

It may be noted that the eigenvalues of AT are -0.5 and $-0.25 \pm j0.433$, i.e., they lie on a circle of radius 0.5. The matrix F is easily calculated, and is given below:

$$F = e^{AT} = \begin{bmatrix} 0.983876 & 0.465627 & 0.088281 \\ -0.088281 & 0.807313 & 0.289064 \\ -0.289064 & -0.666409 & 0.229185 \end{bmatrix} \qquad (5.105)$$

We shall now apply the proposed algorithm to calculate AT from F. First we calculate the inverse of F. This is given below:

$$F^{-1} = \begin{bmatrix} 1.026584 & -0.450002 & 0.172136 \\ -0.172136 & 0.682313 & -0.794273 \\ 0.794273 & 1.416410 & 2.270858 \end{bmatrix} \qquad (5.106)$$

The initial guess for AT is obtained from equation 5.101 as

$$(AT)^{(0)} = \tfrac{1}{2}(F - F^{-1}) = \begin{bmatrix} -0.02135 & 0.457814 & -0.041927 \\ 0.041927 & 0.062500 & 0.541668 \\ -0.541688 & -0.041409 & -1.020836 \end{bmatrix} \qquad (5.107)$$

The exponential of this matrix is calculated using the Taylor series expansion truncated after 12 terms to obtain

$$F^{(0)} = e^{(AT)^{(0)}} = \begin{bmatrix} 0.978921 & 0.449663 & 0.064611 \\ -0.064611 & 0.849700 & 0.320440 \\ 0.320440 & -0.705492 & 0.208818 \end{bmatrix} \quad (5.108)$$

Hence

$$(AT)^{(1)} = (AT)^{(0)} + I - F^{-1}F^{(0)}$$

$$= \begin{bmatrix} -0.000216 & 0.500003 & 0.000002 \\ 0.000002 & -0.000021 & 0.500008 \\ -0.500008 & -1.000013 & -1.000226 \end{bmatrix} \quad (5.109)$$

which is already very close to AT. Carrying on one more iteration gives

$$(AT)^{(2)} = \begin{bmatrix} 0 & 0.50002 & 0.000002 \\ 0.000004 & 0.00001 & 0.5 \\ -0.5 & -1 & -1.000001 \end{bmatrix} \quad (5.110)$$

with a maximum error of 4×10^{-6}.

5.6.2 The Direct Method

We shall discuss the direct algebraic approach proposed by Hung, Liu, and Chan (1980). Integrating equation (5.93) we get

$$x(k + 1) = x(k) + A \int_{kT}^{kT+T} x \, dt + B \int_{kT}^{kT+T} u \, dt \quad (5.111)$$

An approximation to these integrals may be obtained by using the trapezoidal rule. Hence,

$$x(k + 1) = x(k) + \tfrac{1}{2} AT[x(k + 1) + x(k)] + \tfrac{1}{2} BT[u(k + 1) + u(k)] \quad (5.112)$$

which may be rearranged as

$$x(k + 1) = \overline{F}x(k) + \overline{G} \cdot \overline{u}(k) \quad (5.113)$$

where

$$\overline{F} = (I - AT/2)^{-1}(I + AT/2) \tag{5.114}$$

$$\overline{G} = (I - AT/2)^{-1} BT \tag{5.115}$$

and $\overline{u}(k)$ was defined in equation (5.98).

The matrices $\overline{F}$ and $\overline{G}$ can be estimated from the samples of the input-output data. From these, A and B can be evaluated through the equations

$$\left.\begin{array}{l} AT = -2(I - \overline{F})(I + \overline{F})^{-1} \\ BT = (I - AT/2)\overline{G} \end{array}\right\} \tag{5.116}$$

Alternatively, one may estimate A and B directly by rearranging equation (5.112) as

$$A[x(k + 1) + x(k)] + B[u(k + 1) + u(k)] = \frac{2}{T}[x(k + 1) - x(h)] \tag{5.117}$$

The least-squares estimate of the parameters of A and B can now be obtained from the knowledge of the state $x(k)$ and the input $u(k)$.

Note that this latter method requires the measurement of the state, not the output. In practice, the states of a system are seldom available for observation. It may be possible to modify these equations to determine A, B, and C from the measurements of the samples of the input and the output when the system is observable. This requires further investigation.

5.7 CONCLUDING REMARKS

It has been shown that based on a given set of samples of input-output data different discrete-time models can be identified from this data to represent the system. In general, four different model representations have been used in the area of identification of linear multivariable systems and all these models are equivalent and transformations between them are possible. Each model has its own structural parameters which have to be determined in advance (before parameter estimation) from a record of the input-output data.

Out of the four models used for identification, the state-space model is used much because of the smaller number of parameters needed in the model when canonical forms are used, and also because of its practical use in control theory. In general, to identify the system in state-space form, a nonparametric model for the system has to be estimated first, then estimates of the parameters of the state-space model are obtained by a certain transformation.

When estimating the parameters of the system from noisy data using the ordinary least-squares method the parameter estimates are biased if the residual error is correlated with the forcing function. In general, most of the identification algorithms concentrate mainly on the problem of removing this bias in the estimated parameters (e.g., generalized least-squares stochastic approximation and maximum likelihood). It has been shown in section 5.2 that out of the four models, identifying the system in the impulse response form by the ordinary least-squares method results in unbiased estimate of the parameters of the system. This fact has been demonstrated by the simulation results of section 5.5.

In section 5.6, two approaches to obtaining the continuous-time model from discrete data have been discussed. In the indirect approach, one first estimates the state transition matrices from the data. The continuous-time model is then obtained. In the direct method, the trapezoidal rule is utilized to obtain an algebraic relationship between the parameters and the samples of the states and the inputs. This needs further investigation so that one may use the samples of the outputs instead of the states.

5.8 REFERENCES

Ackermann, J. E. and Bucy, R. S. (1971a), "Canonical minimal realization of a matrix of impulse response systems," *Information and Control, 19*, 224.

Ackermann, J. E. (1971b), "Die minimale Ein-Ausgangs-Beschreibung von Mehrgro ensystemen und ihre Bestimmung aus Ein-Ausgangs-Messungen." *Regelungstechnik*, vol. 19, pp. 203–206.

Beghelli, S. and Guidorzi, R. (1976), "A new input-output canonical form for multivariable systems," *IEEE Transactions. Automatic Control, AC-21*, pp. 692–696.

Bingulac, S. P. and Farias, M. A. C. (1977), "Identification and minimal realization of multivariable systems," *Proc. IFAC Symp. on Multivariable Tech. Syst.*, pp. 373–377.

Budin, M. A. (1971), "Minimal realization of discrete linear systems from input-output observations," *IEEE Transactions. Automatic Control*, vol. AC-16, pp. 395–401.

El-Sherief, H. and Sinha, N. K. (1978), "Algorithm for identification of the parameters of multivariable systems combining stochastic approximation and pseudo-inverse," *Automatic Control Theory and Applications*, vol. 6, pp. 37–40.

El-Sherief, H. and Sinha, N. K. (1979a), "Stochastic approximation for the identification of linear multivariable system," *IEEE Transactions. Automatic Control*, AC-24, pp. 331–333.

El-Sherief, H. and Sinha, N. K. (1979b), "Identification and modeling for linear multivariable discrete-time systems: a survey," *Journal of Cybernetics, 9*, pp. 43–71.

El-Sherief, H. and Sinha, N. K. (1979c), "Identification of multivariable systems in the transfer-function matrix form," *Journal of Cybernetics, 9*, pp. 113–125.

El-Sherief, H. (1979), "Identification of multivariable systems," Ph.D. Thesis, McMaster University.

Furuta, K. (1973), "An application of realization theory to identification of multivariable processes," *Proc. 3rd IFAC Symp. on Ident. and Syst. Parameter Estimation* (The Hague), pp. 939–941.

Gopinath, B. (1969), "On the identification of linear time-invariant systems from input-output data," *Bell System Technical Journal*, vol. 48, pp. 1101–1113.

Guidorzi, R. (1975), "Canonical structures in the identification of multivariable systems," *Automatica*, vol. 11, pp. 361–374.

Gupta, R. D. and Fairman, F. W. (1974), "Luenberger's canonical form revisted," *IEEE Transactions. Automatic Control*, vol. AC-19, pp. 440–441.

Ho, B. L. and Kalman, R. E. (1966), "Effective construction of linear state variable models from input–output functions," *Regelungstechnik*, vol. 14, pp. 545–558.

Hung, J. C., Liu, C. C. and Chou, P. Y. (1980), "An algebraic method for system parameter identification," *Proc. 14th Asilomar Conf. on Circuits, Systems, and Computers*, pp. 277–279.

Lobbia, R. N. and Saridis, G. N. (1973), "Identification and control of multivariable stochastic discrete systems," *J. of Cybernetics*, vol. 3, pp. 40–59.

Luenberger, D. G. (1967), "Canonical forms for linear multivariable systems," *IEEE Transactions. Automatic Control*, vol. AC-12, pp. 290–293.

Mayne, D. Q. (1972), "Parametrization and identification of linear multivariable systems," *Stability of Stochastic Dynamical Systems* (Lecture Notes in Mathematics: Vol. 294), Springer-Verlag, New York.

Mehra, R. K. (1971), "On-line identification of linear dynamic systems with applications to Kalman filtering," *IEEE Transactions. Automatic Control*, vol. AC-16, pp. 12–21.

Panuska, V. (1969), "An adaptive recursive least-squares identification algorithm," *Proc. 8th IEEE Symp. on Adaptive Processes*.

Rajbman, N. S. and Sinha, N. K. (1977), "Identification of multivariable systems: a critical review," *Int. J. Systems Science*, vol. 8, pp. 1415–1427.

Rózsa, P. and Sinha, N. K. (1974), "Efficient algorithm for realization of rational matrices," *Int. J. of Control*, 20, pp. 739–751.

Sen, A. and Sinha, N. K. (1976), "On-line estimation of the parameter of a multivariable system using matrix pseudoinverse," *Int. J. of Systems Science*, 7, pp. 461–471.

Sinha, N. K., Mahalanabis, A. K. and El-Sherief, H. (1978), "A nonparametric approach to the identification of linear multivariable systems," *Int. J. of Systems Science*, 8, pp. 425–430.

Sinha, N. K. and Kwong, Y. H. (1979), "Recursive identification of the parameters of linear multivariable systems," *Automatica*, 15, pp. 471–475.

Sinha, N. K. and Lastman, G. J. (1981), "Transformation algorithm for identification of continuous-time multivariable systems from discrete data," *Electronics Letters*, vol. 17, pp. 779–780.

Strmcnik, S., and Bremsak, F. (1979), "Some new transformation algorithms in the identification of continuous time multivariable systems using discrete identification methods," *Preprints 5th IFAC Symp. on Identification and System Parameter Estimation* (Darmstadt, W. Germany), pp. 397–405.

Weinert, H. and Anton, J. (1972), "Canonical forms for multivariable system identification," *Proc. IEEE Conf. on Decision and Control*, pp. 37–39.

6
Stochastic Modeling

6.1 INTRODUCTION

As pointed out in Chapter 1, in a large number of problems concerned with environmental, social and engineering systems, although the effect or the output is easily observed, it is not possible to observe or measure the causes or the inputs. In some of these cases there may be a large number of independent unobservable inputs, whereas in some other cases sufficient theoretical knowledge is not available to relate the output to the various possible inputs. Some examples are the annual flow of a river, the annual population of a particular country, the daily average temperature in a certain city, the per capita gross national product of a specified country, the hourly concentration of a particular chemical in a complex chemical plant, and the growth of the demand for electric power in a certain region. In all of these cases, one has available records of past values of the process under observation and it is desired to develop a model which may be used for forecasting, planning, and control. It is customary to refer to the sequence of the observations as a time series, and the model is said to be stochastic. It is always desirable to make the model have as few parameters as possible, consistent with a desired accuracy.

Two basic types of approaches can be used to obtain a stochastic model for a given time series, y_k, $k = 1, 2, \ldots, N$. In the first approach, one tries to determine the parameters of the model in the form

$$y_k = f(k) + w_k \tag{6.01}$$

where $f(k)$ is a given function, and w_k represents a random noise sequence. The objective is to select the parameters of the function $f(k)$ in such a manner that w_k is a zero-mean white noise sequence of minimum possible variance. The most common forms of $f(k)$ are when it is either a power series in k with a finite number of terms or a simple exponential. The parameters of the models are determined through regression analysis and the procedure will be discussed in the next section.

Another approach to stochastic modeling is to consider that the time series is a linear transformation of a zero-mean white noise sequence. In the simplest cases, this may be regarded as the output of a linear time-invariant discrete-time system subject to white noise input and the object of the modeling is to estimate the parameters of the transfer function or the difference equation of this system. These are generally called stationary time series models, and will be discussed in section 6.3. In other cases, such a model may not be adequate, and it may be necessary to fit a difference equation model to the nth successive differences (equivalent to derivatives for the continuous-time case) of the given time series. This is called a nonstationary time series model, and will be discussed in section 6.4.

6.2 MODELS OBTAINED USING REGRESSION METHODS

The main idea here is to assume a simple model and determine its parameters in such a manner that the mean square error is minimized. We shall first consider the case of linear regression.

6.2.1 Linear Regression

One may decide to fit a linear model to the time series, given by

$$y_k = a + bk + w_k, \qquad k = 1, 2, \ldots, N \tag{6.02}$$

Assuming that $\{w_k\}$ is a zero-mean white noise sequence, the model for estimation is given by

$$\hat{y}_k = a + bk \tag{6.03}$$

and the objective is to determine the values of a and b which will minimize the mean-square error

$$J = \frac{1}{N} \sum_{k=1}^{N} (y_k - \hat{y}_k)^2 = \frac{1}{N} \sum_{k=1}^{N} w_k^2 \tag{6.04}$$

It is easily shown that J will be minimized if

$$b = \frac{\displaystyle\sum_{k=1}^{N} k y_k - N \bar{k} \bar{y}}{\displaystyle\sum_{k=1}^{N} k^2 - N \cdot \bar{k}^2} \tag{6.05}$$

and

$$a = \bar{y} - b\bar{k} \tag{6.06}$$

where

$$\bar{y} = \frac{1}{N} \sum_{k=1}^{N} y_k \tag{6.07}$$

and

$$\bar{k} = \frac{1}{N} \sum_{k=1}^{N} k \tag{6.08}$$

With the values of a and b obtained from equations (6.05) and (6.06), the minimum value of the mean square error that can be obtained from a linear model is given by

$$J_{min} = \frac{1}{N} \sum_{k=1}^{N} y^2 - a^2 - (N+1)\,ab - \frac{1}{6}(N+1)(2N+1)\,b^2 \tag{6.09}$$

6.2.2   Exponential Regression

In this case, the model for estimation is given by

$$\hat{y}_k = \alpha\, e^{\beta k} \tag{6.10}$$

and the values of the constants α and β are determined so as to minimize the mean-square error given by equation (6.04). These values are given by

$$\beta = \frac{\sum\limits_{k=1}^{N} k \ln y_k - \bar{k} \sum\limits_{k=1}^{N} \ln y_k}{\sum\limits_{k=1}^{N} k^2 - N\bar{k}^2} \tag{6.11}$$

and

$$\alpha = \exp\left[\frac{1}{N} \sum_{k=1}^{N} \ln y_k - b\bar{k}\right] \tag{6.12}$$

with $\bar{k}$ as defined in equation (6.08).

For these values of α and β, the mean square value of the error is given by

$$J_{min} = \frac{1}{N} \sum_{k=1}^{N} y_k^2 - \frac{1}{N} \alpha^2 e^{2\beta} \frac{1 - e^{2(N-1)\beta}}{1 - e^{2\beta}} \qquad (6.13)$$

A model of this type is usually suitable when a phenomenon is expected to have an exponential growth (or decay).

6.2.3   Polynomial Models

For many time series, a much better fit is obtained using a polynomial model of the following type

$$\hat{y}_k = a_0 + a_1 k + a_2 k^2 + \cdots + a_m k^m \qquad (6.14)$$

It will be seen that linear regression is a special case of equation (6.14) with $m = 1$. The parameters a_i, which minimize the mean square error for a given value m, are obtained by solving the following set of linear simultaneous equations

$$\begin{bmatrix} 1 & \overline{k} & \overline{k^2} & \cdots \overline{k^m} \\ \overline{k} & \overline{k^2} & \overline{k^3} & \cdots \overline{k^{m+1}} \\ \overline{k^2} & \overline{k^3} & \overline{k^4} & \cdots \overline{k^{m+2}} \\ \vdots & \vdots & \vdots & \vdots \\ \overline{k^m} & \overline{k^{m+1}} & \overline{k^{m+2}} & \cdots \overline{k^{2m}} \end{bmatrix} \begin{bmatrix} a_0 \\ a_1 \\ a_2 \\ \vdots \\ a_m \end{bmatrix} = \begin{bmatrix} \overline{y_k} \\ \overline{ky_k} \\ \overline{k^2 y_k} \\ \vdots \\ \overline{k^m y_k} \end{bmatrix} \qquad (6.15)$$

where

$$\overline{k^j} = \frac{1}{N} \sum_{k=1}^{N} k^j \qquad (6.16)$$

and

$$\overline{k^j y_k} = \frac{1}{N} \sum_{k=1}^{N} (k^j y_k) \qquad (6.17)$$

For these values of a_i, the mean square error is obtained as

$$J_{min} = \frac{1}{N} \sum_{k=1}^{N} y_k^2 - \sum_{i=0}^{m} a_i \overline{k^i y_k} \qquad (6.18)$$

Values of m greater than 5 are seldom used in practical problems.

6.3   STATIONARY TIME SERIES MODELS

Consider a time series $\{y_k\}$ for which the mean value $\bar{y}_k$ is zero. In this case, it is often possible to represent it as the output of a linear time-invariant system as shown below where the input sequence $\{w_k\}$ is a zero-mean white noise sequence and

$$G(z) = \frac{1 - \theta_1 z^{-1} - \theta_2 z^{-2} - \cdots - \theta_n z^{-n}}{1 - \phi_1 z^{-1} - \phi_2 z^{-2} - \cdots - \phi_m z^{-m}} \qquad (6.19)$$

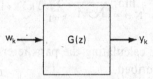

Figure 6.1.   A stationary stochastic process.

Equation (6.19) may also be expressed as the following difference equation

$$y_k = \phi_1 y_{k-1} + \phi_2 y_{k-2} + \cdots + \phi_m y_{k-m}$$
$$+ w_k - \theta_1 w_{k-1} - \theta_2 w_{k-2} - \cdots - \theta_n w_{k-n} \qquad (6.20)$$

Since the sequence $\{w_k\}$ is an uncorrelated white noise sequence, it cannot be predicted from its past values. Hence, the best estimate for y_k is given by $\hat{y}_k$ through the following equation

$$\hat{y}_k = \phi_1 y_{k-1} + \phi_2 y_{k-2} + \cdots + \phi_m y_{k-m}$$
$$- \theta_1 w_{k-1} - \theta_2 w_{k-2} - \cdots - \theta_n w_{k-n} \qquad (6.21)$$

where

$$w_i = y_i - \hat{y}_i, \qquad i = 1, 2, \ldots, k-1 \qquad (6.22)$$

Following Box and Jenkins (1970), this will be called a mixed autoregressive moving-average model of order (m, n), denoted by ARMA(m, n). The parameters ϕ_i are called the autoregressive parameters whereas θ_i are called the moving-average parameters.

If the time-series $\{y_k\}$ does not have a zero mean value, one may subtract the mean, $\bar{y}$, from each y_i to obtain the deviations from the mean. In such a case, equation (6.21) will take the following form

$$\hat{y}_k = \phi_1 y_{k-1} + \phi_2 y_{k-2} + \cdots + \phi_m y_{k-m} - \theta_1 w_{k-1} - \theta_2 w_{k-2} - \cdots - \theta_n w_{k-n}$$
$$+ (1 - \phi_1 - \phi_2 - \cdots - \phi_m)\, \bar{y} \qquad (6.23)$$

The calculation of the parameters ϕ_i and θ_i requires knowledge of the auto-correlation coefficients of the sequence $\{y_k\}$, defined as

$$\rho_i = \frac{\gamma_i}{\gamma_0} \tag{6.24}$$

where

$$\gamma_i = \lim_{N \to \infty} \frac{1}{N-i} \sum_{k=1}^{N-i} y_k y_{k+i} \tag{6.25}$$

The explicit formulas for calculating the parameters of the models for some special cases will now be described.

6.3.1   The First-Order Autoregressive Model (AR1)

This model is of the form

$$\hat{y}_k = \phi_1 y_{k-1} + (1 - \phi_1)\bar{y} \tag{6.26}$$

where

$$\phi_1 = \rho_1 \tag{6.27}$$

In this case, the expected mean-square error is given by

$$\sigma_w^2 = \sigma_y^2 (1 - \phi_1^2) \tag{6.28}$$

where σ_y^2 is the variance of y_k.

For stationarity it is necessary that the magnitude of ϕ_1 be less than 1. It also follows that for a process to satisfy the difference equation (6.26) exactly, we have

$$\rho_k = \phi_1 \rho_{k-1}, \qquad k > 0 \tag{6.29}$$

6.3.2   The Second-Order Autoregressive Model (AR2)

This model is of the form

$$\hat{y}_k = \phi_1 y_{k-1} + \phi_2 y_{k-2} + (1 - \phi_1 - \phi_2)\bar{y} \tag{6.30}$$

where

$$\phi_1 = \frac{\rho_1(1 - \rho_2)}{1 - \rho_1^2} \tag{6.31}$$

and

$$\phi_2 = \frac{\rho_2 - \rho_1^2}{1 - \rho_1^2} \tag{6.32}$$

For the model to be stationary, the roots of the equation

$$z^2 - \phi_1 z - \phi_2 = 0 \tag{6.33}$$

must lie inside the unit circle in the z-plane. As shown by Box and Jenkins (1970), this implies that the parameters ϕ_1 and ϕ_2 must lie within the triangular region denoted by

$$\left. \begin{array}{r} \phi_2 + \phi_1 < 1 \\ \phi_2 - \phi_1 < 1 \\ -1 < \phi_2 < 1 \end{array} \right\} \tag{6.34}$$

A process will satisfy the difference equation (6.30) if the autocorrelation function satisfies the second-order difference equation

$$\rho_k = \phi_1 \rho_{k-1} + \phi_2 \phi_{k-2}, \quad k > 0 \tag{6.35}$$

The expected mean square error is given by

$$\sigma_w^2 = (1 - \rho_1 \phi_1 - \rho_2 \phi_2) \sigma_y^2 \tag{6.36}$$

6.3.3   The nth-Order Autoregressive Model (ARn)

In the general case of the nth-order autoregressive model we have

$$\hat{y}_l = \sum_{i=1}^{n} \phi_i y_{k-i} + (1 - \phi_1 - \phi_2 - \cdots - \phi_n) \bar{y} \tag{6.37}$$

The autoregressive parameters are obtained by solving the following set of simultaneous equations

$$
\begin{bmatrix}
1 & \rho_1 & \rho_2 & \cdots & \rho_{n-1} \\
\rho_1 & 1 & \rho_1 & \cdots & \rho_{n-2} \\
\rho_2 & \rho_1 & 1 & \cdots & \rho_{n-3} \\
\vdots & \vdots & \vdots & & \vdots \\
\rho_{n-1} & \rho_{n-2} & \rho_{n-3} & \cdots & 1
\end{bmatrix}
\begin{bmatrix}
\phi_1 \\ \phi_2 \\ \phi_3 \\ \vdots \\ \phi_n
\end{bmatrix}
=
\begin{bmatrix}
\rho_1 \\ \rho_2 \\ \rho_3 \\ \vdots \\ \rho_n
\end{bmatrix}
\tag{6.38}
$$

and the expected mean square error is given by

$$
\sigma_w^2 = (1 - \rho_1 \phi_1 - \rho_2 \phi_2 - \cdots - \rho_n \phi_n)\, \sigma_y^2 \tag{6.39}
$$

Stationarity of the model requires that the roots of the equation

$$
z^n - \phi_1 z^{n-1} - \cdots - \phi_{n-1} z - \phi_n = 0 \tag{6.40}
$$

must lie inside the unit circle in the z-plane.

A process will satisfy equation (6.37) if its autocorrelation function satisfies the difference equation

$$
\rho_k = \phi_1 \rho_{k-1} + \phi_2 \rho_{k-2} + \cdots + \phi_n \rho_{k-n}; \quad k > 0 \tag{6.41}
$$

6.3.4 The First-Order Moving-Average Model (MA1)

This model is of the form

$$
\hat{y}_k = \bar{y} - \theta_1 w_{k-1}
$$
or
$$
\hat{y}_k = \bar{y} - \theta_1(y_{k-1} - \hat{y}_{k-1}) \tag{6.42}
$$

where θ_1 is a root of the quadratic equation

$$
\theta_1^2 + \frac{1}{\rho_1} \theta_1 + 1 = 0 \tag{6.43}
$$

It may be noted that equation (6.43) will have real roots only if $-0.5 \leqslant \rho_1 \leqslant 0.5$. If this condition is satisfied then the real root of magnitude less than unity must be used in order to satisfy the invertibility condition (Box and Jenkins, 1970).

The expected mean square error is given by

$$
\sigma_w^2 = \frac{\sigma_y^2}{1 + \theta_1^2} \tag{6.44}
$$

For a process to satisfy the model of equation (6.42) exactly it is necessary that

$$\rho_k = 0, \quad k > 1 \tag{6.45}$$

6.3.5 The Second-Order Moving-Average Model (MA2)

In this case the model is represented as

$$\hat{y}_k = \bar{y} - \theta_1(y_{k-1} - \hat{y}_{k-1}) - \theta_2(y_{k-2} - \hat{y}_{k-2}) \tag{6.46}$$

where the parameters θ_1 and θ_2 are obtained from the following equations

$$\theta_2^4 + \left(\frac{1}{\rho_2} - 2\right)\theta_2^3 + \left(2 - \frac{2}{\rho_2} + \frac{\rho_1^2}{\rho_2^2}\right)\theta_2^2 + \left(\frac{1}{\rho_2} - 2\right)\theta_2 + 1 = 0 \tag{6.47}$$

and

$$\theta_1 = \frac{\rho_1 \theta_2}{\rho_2(1 - \theta_2)} \tag{6.48}$$

The expected mean square error is given by

$$\sigma_w^2 = \frac{\sigma_y^2}{1 + \theta_1^2 + \theta_2^2} \tag{6.49}$$

The invertibility condition requires that the roots of

$$z^2 - \theta_1 z - \theta_2 = 0 \tag{6.50}$$

lie inside the unit circle in the z-plane.

It has been shown by Box and Jenkins (1970) that solutions for θ_1 and θ_2 satisfying equations (6.45) and (6.50) will exist if and only if the correlation coefficients ρ_1 and ρ_2 lie within the area bounded by segments of the curves

$$\left.\begin{array}{c} \rho_1 + \rho_2 = -0.5 \\ \rho_2 - \rho_1 = -0.5 \\ \rho_1^2 = 4\rho_2(1 - 2\rho_2) \end{array}\right\} \tag{6.51}$$

and

Furthermore, we must have $\rho_k = 0, k > 2$ for a process to satisfy this model.

6.3.6 The nth-Order Moving-Average Model (MAn)

In this case we have

$$\hat{y}_k = \bar{y} - \theta_1(y_{k-1} - \hat{y}_{k-1}) - \theta_2(y_{k-2} - \hat{y}_{k-2}) - \cdots - \theta_n(y_{k-n} - \hat{y}_{k-n}) \qquad (6.52)$$

The parameters of the model can be obtained by solving the following set of n nonlinear equations

$$\rho_i = \frac{-\theta_i + \theta_1\theta_i + \cdots + \theta_{n-i+1}\theta_n}{1 + \theta_1^2 + \theta_2^2 + \cdots + \theta_n^2}; \qquad i = 1, 2, \ldots, n \qquad (6.53)$$

subject to the invertibility condition that the roots of the polynomial

$$z^n - \theta_1 z^{n-1} - \theta_2 z^{n-2} - \cdots - \theta_{n-1}z - \theta_n = 0 \qquad (6.54)$$

lie inside the unit circle in the z-plane.

The variance of the smoothing error is given by

$$\sigma_w^2 = \frac{\sigma_y^2}{1 + \theta_1^2 + \theta_2^2 + \cdots + \theta_n^2} \qquad (6.55)$$

Due to the nonlinear nature of equation (6.53), it is not possible to obtain an explicit solution for θ_i.

For a process to satisfy the model of equation (6.52), it is necessary that the correlation coefficients ρ_i be zero for i greater than n.

6.3.7 The First-Order Autoregressive First-Order Moving-Average Model (ARMA1, 1)

This model is of the form

$$\hat{y}_k = \phi_1 y_{k-1} + (1 - \phi_1)\bar{y} - \theta_1(y_{k-1} - \hat{y}_{k-1}) \qquad (6.56)$$

where

$$\phi_1 = \frac{\rho_2}{\rho_1} \qquad (6.57)$$

and θ_1 is obtained as the real root, with magnitude less than unity, of the quadratic

$$\theta_1^2 + \frac{1 - 2\rho_2 + \phi_1^2}{\rho_1 - \phi_1}\theta_1 + 1 = 0 \qquad (6.58)$$

The variance of the smoothing error is given by

$$\sigma_w^2 = \frac{\sigma_y^2(1 - \phi_1^2)}{1 - 2\phi_1\theta_1 + \theta_1^2} \tag{6.59}$$

In order that real roots may exist for equation (6.48). The correlation coefficients ρ_1 and ρ_2 must lie in the region defined by the following equations

$$\left.\begin{array}{l} |\rho_2| < |\rho_1| \\[4pt] \rho_2 > \rho_1(2\rho_1 + 1) \quad \text{for} \quad \rho_1 < 0 \\[4pt] \rho_2 > \rho_1(2\rho_1 - 1) \quad \text{for} \quad \rho_1 > 0 \end{array}\right\} \tag{6.60}$$

It may be noted that equation (6.56) is exactly of the same form as the discrete Kalman filter of a first-order system provided that the mean value of y is zero, or, alternatively, one is considering only the deviations from the mean in the model.

6.4 NONSTATIONARY TIME SERIES MODELS

Many time series do not have stationary means. For such cases it may be assumed that some suitable difference of the series is stationary. The resulting model is called an autoregressive integrated moving average (ARIMA) model. For example, the ARIMA(1, 1, 1) model is given by

$$\hat{y}_k - \hat{y}_{k-1} = \phi_1(y_{k-1} - y_{k-2}) - \theta_1(y_{k-1} - \hat{y}_{k-1}) \tag{6.61}$$

which may be rearranged as

$$\hat{y}_k = (\phi_1 - \theta_1)\, y_{k-1} - \phi_1 y_{k-2} + (1 + \theta_1)\, \hat{y}_{k-1} \tag{6.62}$$

The calculations of the parameters ϕ_1 and θ_1 can be carried out as for the ARMA(1, 1) model after obtaining the time series resulting from the first differences $y_i - y_{i-1}$, $i = 2, 3, \ldots, N$ of the original time series. In this case, the original time series can be regarded as having been obtained by integrating a stationary process.

In the general case, a nonstationary time series may be obtained after p integrations of a stationary time series. From the resulting time series, the m autoregressive parameters and the n moving-average parameters can be obtained as described in section 6.3. The stationarity of the model can be verified by noting that the roots of the polynomial containing the autoregressive parameters, as in equation (6.40), must all lie within the unit circle in the z-plane. The resulting model is called the ARIMA(m, p, n) model.

Following the principle of parsimony (Box and Jenkins 1970) it has been suggested that a maximum of two to three integrations may be necessary for most cases.

6.5 EXAMPLES

We shall now consider two examples to illustrate the methods of stochastic modeling discussed in this chapter.

For the first example we shall consider modeling the annual flow of the Nile River at Aswan Dam using the data for the period 1903 to 1944, shown in Table 6.1, along with the one-step predicted values using the fourth-order autoregres-

**Table 6.1. Comparison of Actual and
Predicted Flows of the
Nile River**

Year	Actual Flow	Predicted Flow using AR(4)
1903	2950.904	–
1904	2247.875	–
1905	2628.277	–
1906	2491.124	–
1907	2792.827	2547.145
1908	3324.487	2833.017
1909	3058.081	2914.167
1910	2889.850	2680.220
1911	2495.270	2518.412
1912	1848.821	2287.923
1913	1981.981	2190.258
1914	2411.070	2483.055
1915	3035.200	2823.468
1916	3558.132	3141.767
1917	3281.957	3136.141
1918	2377.891	2712.190
1919	2394.982	2159.605
1920	2499.997	2269.967
1921	2610.239	2499.672
1922	2743.831	2751.894
1923	2744.114	2766.087
1924	2338.835	2695.585
1925	2694.981	2477.708
1926	2474.437	2597.808
1927	2448.371	2609.560

Table 6.1. *(Continued)*

Year	Actual Flow	Predicted Flow using AR(4)
1928	2983.055	2685.379
1929	2732.250	2880.554
1930	2205.147	2666.855
1931	2881.808	2432.781
1932	2580.533	2731.349
1933	2954.375	2591.472
1934	3025.941	2858.888
1935	2902.774	2675.871
1936	2642.455	2634.752
1937	2880.239	2446.217
1938	2885.499	2601.829
1939	2308.904	2618.794
1940	1848.087	2407.764
1941	2569.538	2276.384
1942	2503.951	2758.353
1943	2438.750	2782.822
1944	2211.127	2790.056

sive model. From the data, twelve different models were obtained using the methods described earlier. A summary of the results is given in Table 6.2, which also lists the average prediction error, the mean square error, and the standard deviation of the error for each model.

It will be seen that the fourth order autoregressive model (AR4) gave the best results. It may be added that the ARMA(1, 1) and the MA(2) models did not exist since the conditions specified in equations (6.60) and (6.51) were not satisfied.

As another example, it was desired to obtain a model for the population of the United States of America from annual data given over the period 1948 to 1971. These values are given in Table 6.3, along with the estimates obtained using linear regression as well as the one step ahead predictions given by the ARMA(1, 1) and the ARIMA(1, 1, 0) models. The predictions obtained from ARIMA(1, 1, 1) and ARIMA(2, 1, 0) are almost identical with those of ARIMA(1, 1, 0) up to four significant figures, and have not been shown separately.

The models obtained for the three cases are given in Table 6.4, along with the average error as well as the mean-square error for each case.

It will be seen that in this case the best results are obtained from the ARIMA(1, 1, 0) model since the population represents a nonstationary time series which can be approximated as the first integral of a stationary time series.

Table 6.2. Different Models for Annual Flow

No.	Type of Model	Equation	Average Error	Mean Square Error	Standard Deviation of Error
1.	Linear regression	$\hat{y}_k = 2735.142 - 4.649k$	-0.004	132251.286	363.664
2.	Exponential regression	$\hat{y}_k = 2701.331e^{-0.001617k}$	80.949	219799.647	461.789
3.	Second-order polynomial	$\hat{y}_k = 2627.023 + 10.09478k - 0.3428801k^2$	0.000	130224.348	360.866
4.	Third-order polynomial	$\hat{y}_k = 2809.831 - 38.11421k + 2.427237k^2 - 0.04298375k^3$	0.730	126750.158	356.019
5.	First-order autoregressive (AR1)	$\hat{y}_k = 0.433785y_{k-1} + 0.566215\overline{y}$	-12.187	110611.425	336.488
6.	Second-order autoregressive (AR2)	$\hat{y}_k = 0.57337y_{k-1} + 0.321785y_{k-2} + 0.748415\overline{y}$	5.135	94200.518	306.878
7.	Third-order autoregressive (AR3)	$\hat{y}_k = 0.563926y_{k-1} - 0.331229y_{k-2} - 0.185325y_{k-3} + 0.952689\overline{y}$	1.007	90056.561	300.093
8.	Fourth-order autoregresssve (AR4)	$\hat{y}_k = 0.423770y_{k-1} - 0.217247y_{k-2} - 0.134357y_{k-3} - 0.255087y_{k-4} + 1.182921\overline{y}$	1.051	84424.5040	290.557
9.	First-order moving-average (MA1)	$\hat{y}_k = \overline{y} - 0.579416(y_{k-1} - \hat{y}_{k-1})$	-8.364	99826.986	315.843
10.	ARMA(2, 1)	$\hat{y}_k = 1.29583y_{k-1} - 0.635178y_{k-2} - 0.1641014(y_{k-1} - \hat{y}_{k-1})$	11.083	128442.506	358.217
11.	ARIMA(1, 1, 0)	$\hat{y}_k = 0.9745y_{k-1} - 0.0255y_{k-2}$	-1.215	141050.701	375.565
12.	ARIMA(2, 1, 0)	$\hat{y}_k = 0.968721y_{k-1} - 0.193419y_{k-2} + 0.224698y_{k-3}$	-13.118	137526.837	370.614

Table 6.3. Comparison of Actual and Predicted Populations of the United States (in millions)

Year	Actual	Linear Regression	ARMA(1, 1)	ARIMA(1, 1, 0)
1948	147.2	147.5	—	—
1949	149.8	150.2	150.2	—
1950	152.3	152.9	152.5	152.4
1951	154.9	155.6	154.8	154.8
1952	157.6	158.2	157.1	157.5
1953	160.2	160.9	159.6	160.3
1954	163.0	163.6	162.0	162.8
1955	165.9	166.3	164.6	165.8
1956	168.9	169.0	167.2	168.8
1957	172.0	171.7	170.0	171.9
1958	174.9	174.4	172.8	175.1
1959	177.8	177.0	175.5	177.8
1960	180.7	179.7	178.1	180.7
1961	183.7	182.4	180.8	183.6
1962	186.5	185.1	183.5	186.7
1963	189.2	187.8	186.1	189.3
1964	191.9	190.5	188.5	191.9
1965	194.3	193.2	191.0	194.6
1966	196.6	195.9	193.1	196.7
1967	198.7	198.5	195.2	198.9
1968	200.7	201.2	197.1	200.8
1969	202.7	203.9	199.0	202.7
1970	204.9	206.6	200.8	204.7
1971	207.0	209.3	202.8	207.1

Table 6.4. Different Models for Population Growth

No.	Type of Model	Equation	Average Error	Mean Square Error
1.	Linear Regression	$\hat{x}_k = 144.813 + 2.687k$	0	0.985
2.	ARMA(1, 1)	$\hat{x}_k = 1.0125x_{k-1} - 0.1072\hat{x}_k + 0.0947\bar{x}$	2.17	6.55
3.	ARIMA(1, 1, 0)	$\hat{x}_k = 2.007153x_{k-1} - 1.007153x_{k-2}$	−0.038	0.020
4.	ARIMA(2, 1, 0)	$\hat{x}_k = 2.056214x_{k-1} - 1.104927x_{k-2} + 0.0487126x_{k-3}$	−0.038	0.020
5.	ARIMA(1, 1, 1)	$\hat{x}_k = 1.05623x_{k-1} - 1.00785x_{k-2} - 0.048482\hat{x}_{k-1}$	−0.038	0.020

6.6   CONCLUDING REMARKS

In this chapter, various methods of obtaining stochastic models have been described. It may be noted from the examples that in each case one particular model gives better results. In a large number of practical problems, one is required to choose from a number of rival models and also to decide to what extent a given model is "satisfactory" without requiring too many parameters. Some of these questions will be discussed in further detail in Chapter 14.

6.7   REFERENCES

Box, G. E. P. and Jenkins, G. M. (1970), *Time Series Analysis—Forecasting and Control*, Holden Day, San Francisco.

Kashyap, R. L. and Rao, A. Ramachandra (1976), *Dynamic Stochastic Models from Empirical Data*, Academic Press, London.

Kendall, M. G. (1973), *Time Series*, Hafner, New York.

Sinha, N. K. and Prasad, T. (1979), "Some stochastic modelling techniques and their applications," *Applied Mathematical Modelling*, vol. 3, pp. 2–6.

7

Identification of a Closed-Loop System

7.1 INTRODUCTION

In many cases it is not possible to remove the feedback during an identification experiment because this may lead to instability. The feedback may also be inherent in many dynamic systems (e.g., economical, biological). A regulator path can also be introduced to obtain a desirable condition of measurements and estimation. Irrespective of the reason for existence of the feedback path the process identification displays in all cases certain common features which will be briefly described in this chapter.

This chapter is organized as follows:

in section 2 the concept of feedback between stationary stochastic processes and a simple procedure of this feedback detection will be introduced,

in section 3 the classification of identification schemes based on signals-plant-regulator architecture and their identifiability will be carried out,

in section 4 the identifiability and accuracy of estimates for least-squares (maximum likelihood) procedure will be discussed, and

in section 5 a simple method of transfer function parameter identification (referring to the method of nonlinear system model verification discussed in Chapter 13) in a deliberately introduced closed-loop configuration will be outlined.

The references cited in this chapter do not pretend to cover a rapidly increasing literature on the problem. The survey paper by Gustavsson, et al. (1977) is suggested for further reading.

7.2 EXISTENCE OF FEEDBACK

One of the main assumptions in open loop experiments is the lack of feedback between input and output signals. Even in cases when there is no evident feedback path (in the sense of controller usage or operator intervention) a danger of inherent, hidden within the process, interaction can violate the experimental conditions.

Then one of the first steps in identification is the test of existence of possible feedback between two time series. This problem is closely connected to the notion of causality introduced by Wiener (1956). A time series is called causal to a second if knowledge of the first series reduces the mean-square prediction error of the second series. Feedback is said to be present when each of two series is causal to the other.

The absence of feedback may also be defined (Caines and Chan 1975) for the system of the form

$$y_t = \sum_{i=0}^{\infty} a_t u_{t-i} + \sum_{i=0}^{\infty} \ell_i v_{t-i}$$

$$u_t = \sum_{i=0}^{\infty} m_i y_{t-i} + \sum_{i=0}^{\infty} n_i w_{t-i} \tag{7.01}$$

as the independence of the processes u and y. This definition is not convenient for an immediate practical usage because the process v usually is unobserved. Wiener's definition of causality gives a clue for practical feedback estimation.

Consider two parts of a given time sequence: $x(t_1)$ and $x(t_2)$, $t_1 < t_2$. The subsequent $x(t_2)$ will influence the past $x(t_1)$ (i.e., the future signal will influence the present signal) if $x(t_2)$ is treated as the output of the noncausal filter excited by the input signal $x(t_1)$. Therefore the following statement is true (Caines and Chan 1975; Akaike 1967):

The ordered pair of stationary processes (y, u) is feedback-free if the causal filter for the linear least-squares estimation of y from observation of u is identical to the noncausal filter. For two given processes y and u, with autocorrelation function $R_u(i, j)$ and crosscorrelation function $R_{yu}(i, j)$ one may formulate the corresponding Wiener filtering problem, i.e., find the impulse response $h(i, j)$ of the linear system which, when driven by the process u, has output $\hat{y}$ which minimizes

$$\text{tr } E\{[y(t) - \hat{y}(t)] \; [y(t) - \hat{y}(t)]^T\} \tag{7.02}$$

for each t. The solution to this problem for the stationary case is the Wiener-Hopf equation

$$\sum_{r=-\infty}^{+\infty} h(r) R_u(r, s) = R_{uy}(s) \tag{7.03}$$

and

$$H(z) = \psi_{yu}(z) \, \psi_u^{-1}(z) \tag{7.04}$$

where $\psi_{yu}(z)$, $\psi_u(z)$ are the z-transforms of $R_{yu}(t)$ and $R_u(t)$, respectively. $H(z)$ is the z-transform of $h(t)$.

Let $[H(z)]_+$ denote $\sum_{i=0}^{\infty} A_i z^{-i}$, the causal truncation of

$$H(z) = \sum_{i=-\infty}^{+\infty} A_i z^{-i}$$

For the feedback-free case, the following factorization is valid

$$\left. \begin{aligned} \psi_{yu}(z) &= B(z) \, D^*(z) \\ \psi_u(z) &= D(z) \, D^*(z) \end{aligned} \right\} \tag{7.05}$$

where $D^*(z)$ denotes $D(z^{-1})$. The causal filter dynamics is given by

$$H_+(z) = [B(z) \, D^*(z) \, D^*(z)^{-1}]_+ \, D^{-1}(z) = B(z) \, D^{-1}(z) = H(z) \tag{7.06}$$

where $H(z)$ is noncausal. A practical procedure, suggested by Akaike (1967) is as follows:

(i)   from the given records of the two time series find an estimate of the frequency response function $H(j\omega)$
(ii) apply inverse Fourier transformation to get a time domain representation of the impulse response $h(t)$
(iii) check the impulse response in the negative side of the time axis.

Its significant value suggests that the system under observation has a feedback loop.

7.3   DIRECT IDENTIFICATION OF SYSTEMS WITH FEEDBACK

Let us consider the identification of the system with feedback. In the case when the feedback path is not available, this kind of identification is called direct identification (Ljung et al. 1974). In experiments of that kind the input-output data are treated as if they were obtained from an open-loop experiment. Box and MacGregor (1975) have derived the necessary conditions for estimability and the effect of adding a known dither signal.

In indirect identification, the knowledge of the controller is assumed and the open-loop process parameters can then be determined from the estimated closed-loop parameters. The validity of both approaches can be analyzed on the basis of the signal-noise-regulator architecture presented in Fig. 7.1.

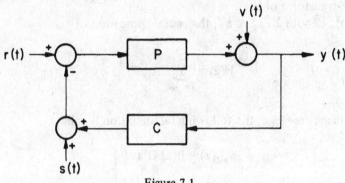

Figure 7.1.

In Figure 7.1 the following symbols are used:

    P—process (plant)
    C—controller
    v—forward path noise
    s—feedback path noise
    r—external input

Let us consider first the case, when

$r \equiv 0$
s, v—a pair of uncorrelated noise signals*

The estimate $\hat{P}(j\omega)$ of the forward path transfer function is given by equation (7.07)

$$E\{\hat{P}(j\omega)\} = \frac{E\{\hat{S}_{uy}(j\omega)\}}{E\{\hat{S}_{u}(j\omega)\}} \tag{7.07}$$

---

*The case when s and v are correlated has been considered by Vorchik (1975).

From Figure 7.1 one can obtain

$$S_{uy}(j\omega) = \overline{U^*(j\omega)\, Y(j\omega)}$$

$$= \frac{1}{\left|1 + P(j\omega)\, C(j\omega)\right|^2}\, [P(j\omega)\, S_s(j\omega) + C^*(j\omega)\, S_v(j\omega)] \qquad (7.08)$$

$$S_{uu}(\omega) = \overline{U^*(j\omega)\, U(j\omega)}$$

$$= \frac{1}{\left|1 + P(j\omega)\, C(j\omega)\right|^2}\, [S_s(\omega) + \left|C(j\omega)\right|^2\, S_v(\omega)] \qquad (7.09)$$

Dividing (7.08) by (7.09) one can obtain

$$\hat{P}(j\omega) = \frac{P(j\omega)\, S_s(\omega) + C^*(j\omega)\, S_v(\omega)}{S_s(\omega) + \left|C(j\omega)\right|^2\, S_v(\omega)} \qquad (7.10)$$

Thus, the estimate $\hat{P}(j\omega)$ of the forward path transfer function is systematically in error. Only in the case when $v(t) \equiv 0$, may the true estimate be obtained. At the other extreme, the following result is true when $s(t) \equiv 0$

$$\hat{P}(j\omega) = \frac{1}{C(j\omega)} \qquad (7.11)$$

When the external input $r(t)$ is applied $(r(t) \neq 0)$ one can use for identification purposes the following relation

$$S_{ry}(j\omega) = P(j\omega)\, S_{ru}(j\omega) + S_{rv}(j\omega) \qquad (7.12)$$

In the case, when the disturbance $v(t)$ is statistically orthogonal to the external input $r(t)$, finally one can get

$$\hat{P}(j\omega) = \frac{S_{ry}(j\omega)}{S_{ru}(j\omega)} \qquad (7.13)$$

It can be shown (Wellstead 1977), that the variance of the estimate $P(j\omega)$ is given by

$$\frac{\text{var}\,\{|\hat{P}(j\omega)|\}}{|P(j\omega)|^2} \simeq \frac{1}{2N}\left[\frac{S_v(\omega)}{S_r(\omega)\,|G(j\omega)|^2}\right] \qquad (7.14a)$$

$$\text{var}\,\{\arg \hat{P}(j\omega)\} \simeq \frac{1}{2N}\left[\frac{S_v(\omega)}{S_r(\omega)\,|G(j\omega)|^2}\right] \tag{7.14b}$$

where

$$G(j\omega) = \frac{P(j\omega)}{1 + P(j\omega)\,C(j\omega)}$$

$S_v(\omega)$ is the autospectrum of the disturbance $v(t)$,
$S_r(\omega)$ is the autospectrum of the reference signal, and
N is number of the spectra samples.

The following conclusions can be drawn from equation (7.14). The variance is:

(i)   inversely proportional to the spectral power density of the signal $r(t)$ and the number of sample spectra
(ii) independent of the disturbance $s(t)$ in the feedback
(iii) inversely proportional to the closed-loop gain.

In the case when external signal is used, unconditional identifiability during the experiment is guaranteed. During the passive experiment $(r(t) \equiv 0)$, the identifiability should be carefully checked out.

7.4 ESTIMATION OF THE TRANSFER FUNCTION OF THE FORWARD PATH

The possibility of the forward-path transfer function estimation via passive experiment can be investigated on the basis of equation (7.10). In this case the following assumptions should be satisfied:

(i)   knowledge of the order of the identified system,
(ii) knowledge of the controller (or the absence of the noise signal $v(t)$), and
(iii) presence of the feedback path noise.

Let us consider the least-squares identification when the assumptions (i), (ii), and (iii) are satisfied (Wellstead and Edmonds 1975). Let the forward-path transfer function be given by the linear difference equation

$$y(k) = -\sum_{i=1}^{\beta} b_i y(k-i) + \sum_{j=q}^{\alpha} a_j u(k-j) + v(k), \qquad k = 0, \pm 1, \pm 2, \ldots \tag{7.15}$$

where

u(k) is the control variable,
y(k) is the output signal, and
v(k) is the white noise sequence.

The control variable u(k) is generated by a feedback regulator described by

$$u(k) = -\sum_{i=1}^{\delta} d_i u(k-i) + \sum_{j=p}^{\gamma} c_j y_j(k-j) + s(k) \qquad (7.16)$$

where

s(k) is the white noise sequence orthogonal to v(t).

Using the vector notation, equation (7.15) can be rewritten in the form

$$y(k) = \underline{z}^T(k)\,\underline{\theta} + v(k) \qquad (7.17)$$

$$\underline{z}^T(k) = [y(k-1), \ldots, y(k-\beta), u(k-q), \ldots, u(k-\alpha)] \qquad (7.18)$$

$$\underline{\theta}^T = [-b_1, \ldots, -b_\beta, a_q, \ldots, a_\alpha] \qquad (7.19)$$

For least-squares estimation the following matrix expression is studied

$$\underline{Y} = Z\underline{\theta} + \underline{V} \qquad (7.20)$$

where

$$\underline{Y}^T = [y(k), y(k+1), \ldots, y(k+N-1)] \qquad (7.21)$$

$$\underline{V}^T = [v(k), v(k+1), \ldots, v(k+N-1)] \qquad (7.22)$$

and Z is an $N \times (\beta + \alpha - q + 1)$ matrix defined by

$$Z^T = [\underline{z}(k), \underline{z}(k+1), \ldots, \underline{z}(k+N-1)] \qquad (7.23)$$

In equations (7.21)–(7.23), N denotes the length of the observed time series. For $N > (\alpha + \beta - q)$ the least-squares solution to (7.20) is

$$\hat{\theta} = (Z^T Z)^{-1} Z^T Y \qquad (7.24)$$

under the assumption that $(Z^T Z)^{-1}$ exists.

The problem of uniqueness and consistency of (7.24) (i.e., asymptotic properties of the estimates) was treated by Wellstead and Edmonds (1975). It can be proved that the requirement of consistency is satisfied when*

$$\text{plim} \left[\frac{1}{N} Z^T V \right] = 0 \tag{7.25}$$

The requirement (7.25) is satisfied automatically when $v(t) = 0$ (cf. assumption (ii)).

It can be proved that the expectation and the variance of (7.25) vanish in the limit as N tends to infinity provided that $q > 0$ or $p > 0$, i.e., there is no instantaneous transmission path around the loop and the system is closed-loop stable.

If the assumption (iii) is violated (i.e., $s(k)$ is absent), the least-squares estimate $\hat{\theta}$ is unique when

$$\max (\delta - \alpha + q, \gamma - \beta + q) \geqslant 0 \tag{7.26}$$

Similar consideration can be carried out for the maximum likelihood method (Ljung et al. 1974). It has been proved that direct identification with a prediction error method gives asymptotically the same results as indirect identification.

7.5 IDENTIFICATION WITH THE LOOP CLOSED

In many cases, it is convenient to perform the identification with the loop closed due to the following reasons:

(a) The system is identified in actual operation with the input signals as occurring in practice, and

(b) the time of the experiment can be significantly shortened when the system has large and small time constants, as is usually the case with closed-loop systems having large loop gain.

Let us consider the identification of a closed-loop system with high-gain feedback. In such systems, the presence of small and large time constants permits simplification of the description of the complete system. In order to satisfy the identifiability condition for closed-loop systems, a reference signal should be applied.

Let us consider the single-input single-output system described by the transfer

---

*plim denotes limit in probability.

function

$$G(s) = \frac{k_o}{\prod\limits_{i=1}^{n-1} (1 + sT_i)(1 + \alpha s)} \qquad (7.27)$$

where T_i are the large time constants and α is a small time constant (Kuszta and Sinha 1980).

The time constant α will be considered as a substitute for "all" small time constants of the system. The value of α is very difficult to identify with the system in the open-loop configuration, and is often neglected. On the other hand, this value plays an important role in the adjustment of the controller in the closed-loop situation. For closed-loop systems with large forward gain, and with resulting small steady-state error, the need for the knowledge of the small time constant is also evident.

Consider the basic closed-loop system shown in Figure 7.2. The controller $H(s)$ is designed to satisfy certain performance criteria, for example to cancel the large time constant of the system evaluated by open-loop identification.

The characteristic equation of the system shown in Figure 7.2 may be written as

$$\sum_{i=0}^{n} a_i s^i + Kk_o \sum_{j=0}^{m} c_j s^j = 0 \qquad (7.28)$$

where for a physical system $m \leqslant n$.

In order to examine equation (7.28) in the high-frequency range, one may introduce the "fast" time τ (Kuszta and Sinha 1980)

$$\tau = \mu^{-1} t \qquad (7.29)$$

where μ is a sufficiently small real number.

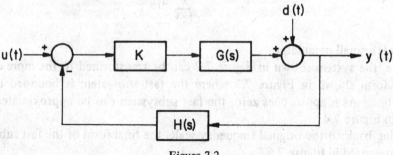

Figure 7.2.

From equation (7.29), one may define a new operator

$$q = \mu s \tag{7.30}$$

Substituting equation (7.30) into (7.28), we get

$$\sum_{i=0}^{n} a_i \mu^{n-i} q^i + K k_0 \sum_{j=0}^{m} c_j \mu^{n-j} q^j = 0 \tag{7.31}$$

Following Meerov (1965), we may choose

$$\mu = K^{-1/n-m} \tag{7.32}$$

Substituting equation (7.32) into (7.31), we get

$$\sum_{i=0}^{n} a_i K^{i-n/n-m} q^i + K k_0 \sum_{j=0}^{m} c_j K^{j-n/n-m} q^j = 0 \tag{7.33}$$

For very large K, we obtain from equation (7.28) as $K \to \infty$

$$a_n q^{n-m} + k_0 c_m = 0 \tag{7.34}$$

For the system to be stable we must have $n - m$ equal to either 0 or 1. In the sequel we shall consider $m = n - 1$.

For the controller to be physically realizable, the transfer function, H(s), should have the following form

$$H(s) = \frac{C(s)}{D(s)} = \frac{\displaystyle\sum_{i=0}^{m} c_i s^i}{\displaystyle\sum_{j=1}^{n} d_j \mu^j s^j} \tag{7.35}$$

where μ is a small parameter.

Hence, the system shown in Figure 7.2 can be transformed to the more convenient form shown in Figure 7.3 where the fast subsystem is bounded by a dotted line. As μ approaches zero, the fast subsystem can be approximated as shown in Figure 7.4.

Coming back to the original frequency scale, the final form of the fast subsystem is presented in Figure 7.5.

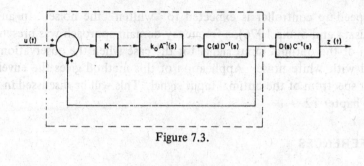

Figure 7.3.

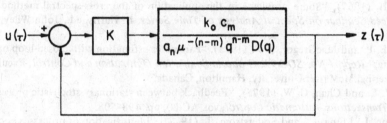

Figure 7.4.

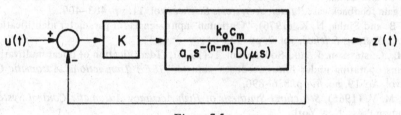

Figure 7.5.

In the case when the signal $y(t)$, shown in Figure 7.2 is observed, the total dynamics of the system will be equivalent to the dynamics of the fast subsystem, which in turn, depends on the gain constant K, the small time constants of the controller, and the coefficients c_m and a_n.

The main objective of the scheme for identification is estimation of the value of the parameter a_n from which the small time constant α can be deduced.

7.6 DESIGN OF THE OPTIMAL INPUT SIGNAL
FOR IDENTIFICATION

The identification of a closed-loop system with large forward gain is similar to the identification of an open-loop system in the noise-free situation. In the presence of noise, as indicated in the block diagram of Figure 7.3, the assumption that the signal $y(t)$ is contaminated with white noise is quite valid, since a suitable speed-up controller is expected to "whiten" the noise. In an earlier paper (Kuszta and Sinha 1976), a frequency-domain approach was presented for the design of the optimal input signal for the case when the observation is contaminated with white noise. Application of this method gives the envelope of the power spectrum of the optimal input signal. This will be discussed in further detail in Chapter 12.

7.7 REFERENCES

Akaike, H. (1967), "Some problems in the application of the cross-spectral method," in: *Advanced Seminar on Spectral Analysis of Time Series*, B. Harris, ed., John Wiley, New York.

Box, G. E. P. and MacGregor, J. F. (1975), "Parameter estimation with closed-loop operating data," *Report No. SOC-99, Group in Simulation Optimation and Control*, Faculty of Engineering, McMaster University, Hamilton, Canada.

Caines, P. E. and Chan, C. W. (1975), "Feedback between stationary stochastic processes," *IEEE Transactions. Automatic Control*, vol. AC-20, pp. 498–508.

Gustavsson, I., Ljung, L., and Soderstrom, T. (1977), "Identification of processes in closed loop–Identifiability and accuracy aspects," *Automatica*, 13, pp. 59–75.

Kuszta, B. and Sinha, N. K. (1980), "On identification of linear systems with feedback: High gain feedback case," *Inter. J. Systems Science*, vol. 11. pp. 403–409.

Kuszta, B. and Sinha, N. K. (1976), "Optimum input signals for parameter identification," *Inter. J. Systems Science*, vol. 7, pp. 935–941.

Ljung, L., Gustavsson, I., and Soderstrom, T. (1974), "Identification of linear multivariable systems operating under linear feedback control," *IEEE Transactions. Automatic Control*, vol. AC-19, no. 6, pp. 836–890.

Meerov, M. V. (1965), *Structural Synthesis of High-Accuracy Automatic Control Systems*, Pergamon Press, New York.

Wellstead, P. E. (1977), "Reference signals for closed-loop identification," *Int. J. Control*, 26, pp. 945–962.

Wellstead, P. E. and Edmonds, J. M. (1975), "Least-squares identification of closed-loop systems," *Int. J. Control*, vol. 21, no. 4, pp. 689–699.

Wiener, N. (1956), "Theory of Prediction," in: *Modern Mathematics for Engineers*. E. F. Beckenback, ed., McGraw-Hill, New York, Chap. 8.

Vorchik, B. G. (1975), "Plant identification in a stochastic closed model," *Automation and Remote Control*, no. 4, pp. 32–48.

8
Reduction of High-Order Systems

8.1 INTRODUCTION

So far in this book we have considered the problem of determining a "suitable" model for a system from input-output data. In practice, since most systems are nonlinear and of the distributed parameter type, it turns out to be the problem of fitting a model of the lowest possible order consistent with a specified accuracy. The problem of actually estimating this order will be discussed in Chapter 13.

In this chapter we shall consider another problem which is closely related. In many practical situations, one can obtain a fairly complex and high-order model for a system from analytical considerations. For example, consider a multimachine power system. The model for each synchronous generator including the prime-mover, the governor and the exciter can be obtained in this manner, but the order of the model turns out to be fairly high. This complexity often makes it difficult to obtain a good understanding of the behavior of the system. The preliminary design and optimization of such systems can often be accomplished with greater ease if a low-order linear model is derived which provides a good approximation to the system.

A great deal of work has been done during the last 15 years on the subject of obtaining low-order models for high-order systems, as will be evident from the comprehensive bibliography prepared by Genesio and Milanese (1976). Although many different approaches have been presented, these may be divided into three main groups. The first group of methods attempts to retain the dominant eigenvalues of the original system and then obtain the parameters of the low-order model in such a manner that its response to certain inputs approximates closely that of the high-order system. The methods proposed by Davison (1966), Marshall (1966), Mitra (1967), and Aoki (1968) belong to this category. It has been shown (Hickin 1978) that the first three may be regarded as special

133

cases of the aggregation method proposed by Aoki. Another method which preserves the dominant eigenvalues is the method of singular perturbations (Sannuti and Kokotovic 1969), which has certain special properties.

The second group of methods is based on obtaining a model of a specified order such that its impulse- or step-response (or, alternatively, its frequency response) matches that of the original system in an optimum manner, with no restriction on the location of the eigenvalues. Anderson (1967) used a geometric approach, based on orthogonal projection to obtain a low-order model minimizing the integral square error in the time domain. Sinha and Pille (1971) have proposed utilizing the matrix pseudoinverse for a least-squares fit. Other methods for obtaining optimum low-order models in the frequency domain have also been proposed (Langholz and Bistritz 1978, Elliott and Wolovich 1980).

The third group of methods is based on matching some other properties of the responses. Chen and Shieh (1968) showed that if a continued-fraction expansion of a transfer function was truncated, it led to a low-order model the step-response of which matched that of the original system closely. The main attraction of this approach was its computational simplicity, as compared with the methods described in the first two categories. The method of matching time moments, proposed by Gibarillo and Lees (1969) is another interesting approach to the problem. It was shown later by Shamash (1974) that these methods are equivalent, and can be classified as Padé approximation. Although initially these methods were developed for single-input single-output systems only, it has been shown by Hickin and Sinha (1976) that one may also match the time moments and obtain low-order models for multivariable systems using partial realization with the generalized Markov parameters. An important drawback of the methods using Padé approximation is that the low-order models obtained may sometimes turn out to be unstable even though the original system is stable. This has led to the development of the Routh approximation method (Hutton and Friedland 1975). Another solution is to combine aggregation with the matching of time moments to ensure stability (Hickin and Sinha 1978). Bistritz and Langholz (1979) have proposed a method for obtaining stable Chebyshev-Padé approximation.

In this chapter we shall be discussing in detail the basic ideas behind the three groups of methods. These will also be illustrated by means of examples. Finally, a comparison between the methods will be made, for a single-input single-output system, as well as for a multivariable system.

8.2 STATEMENT OF THE PROBLEM

Consider a linear time-invariant multivariable system described by the equations

$$\left.\begin{aligned}
\dot{x}(t) &= Ax(t) + Bu(t)\\
y(t) &= Cx(t)
\end{aligned}\right\} \tag{8.01}$$

where $x \in R^n$, $y \in R^m$, and $u \in R^p$. It will be assumed that this system is both controllable and observable, i.e., it is a minimum realization.

The objective of model reduction is to obtain the low-order model

$$\left.\begin{array}{l} \dot{z}(t) = Fz(t) + Gu(t) \\ \hat{y}(t) = Hz(t) \end{array}\right\} \qquad (8.02)$$

where $z \in R^r$ and $r < n$, such that $\hat{y}(t) \in R^m$ is a close approximation to $y(t)$ for all inputs $u(t)$.

It may be noted that here we have specified the problem in the time domain. It is also possible to formulate it in the frequency domain. In this case, given the transfer function matrix of the system, it is desired to obtain a lower order transfer function matrix matching the frequency response over a specified range of frequencies.

8.3 AGGREGATION METHOD

Since the aggregation method proposed by Aoki (1968) has been shown as the most general projective reduction method we shall be discussing this method in detail. The methods of Davison (1966), and Mitra (1967) have been shown to be special cases of aggregation, and will not be considered further.

This method is based on the intuitively appealing relationship

$$z(t) = Kx(t) \qquad (8.03)$$

where K is an $r \times n$ constant projection matrix, and is called the aggregation matrix. Hence, equation (8.03) is also called the aggregation law.

Differentiating both sides of equation (8.03), and substituting for $\dot{x}(t)$ from equation (8.01), we have

$$\dot{z}(t) = KAx(t) + KBu(t) \qquad (8.04)$$

Comparison with equation (8.02) gives

$$\left.\begin{array}{l} KA = FK \\ G = KB \\ C \simeq HK \end{array}\right\} \qquad (8.05)$$

and

where the last is an approximate equality only. Since K is a rectangular matrix, one may obtain F and H from the following equations if K is known

$$\left.\begin{array}{l} F = KAK^* \\ H = CK^{**} \end{array}\right\} \qquad (8.06)$$

where K^* and K^{**} are right inverses of K. Due to the nonuniqueness of the right inverse there are many possible solutions for any given K. One solution is to utilize the pseudoinverse of K, defined as

$$K^+ = K^T(KK^T)^{-1} \tag{8.07}$$

instead of K^* and K^{**}. In this case, we have

$$\left.\begin{array}{l} F = KAK^+ \\ G = KB \\ H = CK^+ \end{array}\right\} \tag{8.08}$$

Although equations (8.08) provide a simple means for determining F, G, and H, we must know the aggregation matrix K.

One method for obtaining K will now be discussed that is particularly useful if the state equations are in the column companion form (Sinha and Rózsa 1976). The controllability matrix of the system is given by

$$U = [B \quad AB \quad A^2B \cdots A^{n-1}B] \tag{8.09}$$

Premultiplying by K, and noting that $KB = G$, and $KA = FK$, we have (Hickin and Sinha (1975a)

$$KU = [G \quad FG \quad F^2G \cdots F^{n-1}G] \tag{8.10}$$

Since the right-hand side of equation (8.09) is known if F and G are also in the column-companion form, and since n columns of U are unit vectors, it is now quite straight-forward to determine K. In particular, for a single-input single-output system, U is the identity matrix for the column-companion form. Hence K is obtained directly.

Another method for obtaining the aggregation matrix will now be described. It was shown by Hickin and Sinha (1976b) that a nontrivial aggregation law exists if and only if the eigenvalues of F are a subset of the eigenvalues of A, and then K is easily obtained from the equation

$$K = T[I_r \mid 0] V^{-1} \tag{8.11}$$

where T is any nonsingular $r \times r$ matrix and V is the modal matrix of A, i.e., the columns of V consist of the eigenvectors (generalized eigenvectors in case of multiple eigenvalues) of A. In the particular case when T is an identity matrix, F will be obtained in the diagonal or Jordan canonical form. The eigenvalues of F correspond to the eigenvectors in the first column of V.

Although equation (8.11) indicates matrix inversion, this is not really necessary. As pointed out by Michailesco et al. (1975), we need only find the eigenvectors of the transpose of A, corresponding to the eigenvalues which are to be retained in F. These eigenvectors give the transpose of K if T is made the identity matrix.

EXAMPLE 8.1

Consider a single-input single-output system described by the transfer function

$$G(s) = \frac{Y(s)}{U(s)} = \frac{s+4}{(s+1)(s+2)(s+3)} \tag{8.12}$$

The state equations for this system in the column companion form are obtained as

$$\dot{x} = \begin{bmatrix} 0 & 0 & -6 \\ 1 & 0 & -11 \\ 0 & 1 & -6 \end{bmatrix} x + \begin{bmatrix} 1 \\ 0 \\ 0 \end{bmatrix} u$$

$$y = \begin{bmatrix} 0 & 1 & -2 \end{bmatrix} x \tag{8.13}$$

We shall now obtain an aggregated model retaining the eigenvalues at -1 and -2. First we shall consider obtaining the model in the column companion form. This gives us, immediately,

$$(s - \lambda_1)(s - \lambda_2) = s^2 + 3s + 2 \tag{8.14}$$

and

$$F = \begin{bmatrix} 0 & -2 \\ 1 & -3 \end{bmatrix}, \quad G = \begin{bmatrix} 1 \\ 0 \end{bmatrix} \tag{8.15}$$

We shall determine the aggregation matrix using the relationship which follows from (8.09) since for this case U is an identity matrix. Hence, for n = 3, we get

$$K = [G \quad FG \quad F^2G]$$

Substituting for F and G from equation (8.15), we have

$$K = \begin{bmatrix} 1 & 0 & -2 \\ 0 & 1 & -3 \end{bmatrix} \tag{8.16}$$

It may be verified that KA = FK and G = KB.

Finally, to obtain H, we note that one possible solution is

$$K^* = \begin{bmatrix} 1 & 0 \\ 0 & 1 \\ 0 & 0 \end{bmatrix} \tag{8.17}$$

which gives

$$H = CK^* = [0 \quad 1] \tag{8.18}$$

The resulting low-order model has the transfer function

$$G_r(s) = \frac{1}{s^2 + 3s + 2} \tag{8.19}$$

Alternatively, if we use the pseudoinverse, we get

$$K^+ = K^T(KK^T)^{-1} = \frac{1}{14} \begin{bmatrix} 10 & -6 \\ -6 & 5 \\ -2 & -3 \end{bmatrix} \tag{8.20}$$

and

$$H' = CK^+ = \frac{1}{14} [-2 \quad 11] \tag{8.21}$$

This gives the transfer function of the reduced-order model as

$$G'_r(s) = \frac{-1/7s + 11/14}{s^2 + 3s + 2} \tag{8.22}$$

Note that the two models are different due to the fact that two different right inverses of K have been used to determine H.

The second model may also be obtained by using equation (8.11). The eigenvectors of A^T given in equation (8.13), corresponding to the eigenvalues at -1 and -2 are obtained simply as

$$V_1 = \begin{bmatrix} 1 \\ -1 \\ 1 \end{bmatrix} \quad \text{and} \quad v_2 = \begin{bmatrix} 1 \\ -2 \\ 4 \end{bmatrix} \tag{8.23}$$

due to the canonical form of A^T. Hence, for $T = I$,

$$\bar{K} = \begin{bmatrix} 1 & -1 & 1 \\ 1 & -2 & 4 \end{bmatrix} \tag{8.24}$$

and

$$\bar{K}^+ = \bar{K}^T(\bar{K}\bar{K}^T)^{-1} = \begin{bmatrix} 1 & -2/7 \\ -1/2 & 1/14 \\ -1/2 & 5/14 \end{bmatrix} \tag{8.25}$$

The reduced-order model is now obtained in the diagonal form as below

$$\bar{F} = \bar{K}A\bar{K}^+ = \begin{bmatrix} -1 & 0 \\ 0 & -2 \end{bmatrix}$$

$$\bar{G} = \bar{K}B = \begin{bmatrix} 1 \\ 1 \end{bmatrix} \tag{8.26}$$

$$\bar{H} = C\bar{K}^+ = [1/2 \quad -9/14]$$

The transfer function of this model is identical with that obtained in equation (8.22). This was expected, since this model is obtained by a linear transformation of the model represented by equations (8.15) and (8.21).

A comparison of the responses of the original system and the two aggregated models to a unit step is shown in Figure 8.1.

Table 8.1 shows the values of the responses at selected instants of time.

Table 8.1

t	0	0.2	0.4	0.6	0.8	1.0	1.5	2.0
$y(t)$	0	0.0174	0.0603	0.1171	0.1795	0.2419	0.3799	0.4816
$y_r(t)$	0	0.0164	0.0543	0.1108	0.1516	0.1998	0.3018	0.3738
$y_r'(t)$	0	−0.0153	−0.0122	0.0010	0.0188	0.0381	0.0830	0.1168

t	2.5	3.0	4.0	5.0
$y(t)$	0.5502	0.5944	0.6395	0.6606
$y_r(t)$	0.4213	0.4515	0.4819	0.4959
$y_r'(t)$	0.1399	0.1545	0.1695	0.1765

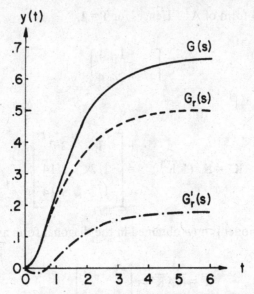

Figure 8.1.   Comparison of the step responses of G(s), $G_r(s)$, and $G'_r(s)$.

It will be seen that responses of the reduced-order models do not quite match that of the original system. Furthermore, two different values of the matrix H give quite different responses. The fact that the steady-state values of the step responses differ considerably is another serious shortcoming of the aggregation method. To overcome this difficulty, we must find some other way to determine the H matrix such that the d.c. steady-state gains of the two transfer functions are identical. A method for doing this will be discussed in section 8.5.

8.4   MATCHING TIME MOMENTS

Another approach to model reduction is based on matching certain time moments of the impulse response of the original system with those of the reduced-order model. Since the continued fraction expansion method of Chen and Shieh (1968) can be considered as such a method, we shall consider this general approach, which will also be applicable to multivariable systems. For the system represented in the state space by equation (8.01), the transfer function matrix is obtained as

$$G(s) = C(sI - A)^{-1} B \qquad (8.27)$$

If we formally expand G(s) in a Laurent series, we get

$$G(s) = \sum_{i=0}^{\infty} J_i s^{-(i+1)} \qquad (8.28)$$

where

$$J_i \triangleq CA^iB \tag{8.29}$$

are called the Markov parameters of the system, and are invariant under linear transformation of the state.

If $G(s)$ has no poles at the origin of the s-plane then we can obtain the following Taylor series expansion

$$G(s) = -\sum_{i=0}^{\infty} T_i s^i \tag{8.30}$$

where

$$T_i \triangleq CA^{-(i+1)}B \tag{8.31}$$

It may be noted that if $g(t)$ is the inverse Laplace transform of $G(s)$, then

$$\int_0^\infty g(t)\, dt = \left[\int_0^\infty g(t)\, e^{-st}\, dt\right]_{s=0} = G(0) = -T_0 \tag{8.32}$$

$$\int_0^\infty t g(t)\, dt = \left[\sum_0^\infty t g(t)\, e^{-st}\, dt\right]_{s=0} = \left[-\frac{dG(s)}{ds}\right]_{s=0} = T_1 \tag{8.33}$$

$$\int_0^\infty t^2 g(t)\, dt = \left[\frac{d^2 G(s)}{ds^2}\right]_{s=0} = -2T_2 \tag{8.34}$$

and

$$\int_0^\infty t^i g(t)\, dt = (-1)^{i+1} (i!)\, T_i, \tag{8.35}$$

where i is an integer.

In other words, T_i are related to the time-moments of the impulse response matrix through a multiplicative constant.

Comparing equations (8.29) and (8.31), it is now noted that

$$J_{-i} = T_{i-1} \qquad \text{for } i \geqslant 1 \tag{8.36}$$

and therefore the term "generalized Markov parameters" will be used to include T_i.

To determine a low-order approximation to the system, then, one should obtain the matrices F, G, and H so that a number of the generalized Markov parameters of the two systems are identical. In particular, it may be noted that by matching the time-moments we shall be equating the steady-state responses to inputs in the form of power series (steps, ramps, parabolic functions, etc.). On the other hand, matching the Markov parameters will improve the approximation in the transient portion of the response.

It is well known that given the Markov parameters of a system, a minimum realization in the form of the matrices A, B, and C can be obtained. A simple procedure due to Rózsa and Sinha (1974) is described in Appendix I, where one starts with a block Hankel matrix consisting of the Markov parameters. This procedure can be generalized to include the time moments in the block Hankel matrix, which is defined as

$$
H_{ij}(k) \triangleq
\begin{bmatrix}
J_{-k} & J_{-k+1} & \cdots & J_{-k+j-1} \\
J_{-k+1} & J_{-k+2} & \cdots & J_{-k+j} \\
\vdots & \vdots & & \vdots \\
J_{-k+i-1} & J_{-k+i} & \cdots & J_{-k+i+j-2}
\end{bmatrix}
\tag{8.37}
$$

If $i \geqslant \alpha$ and $j \geqslant \beta$, where α and β are the observability and controllability indices of the system, respectively, then the rank of $H_{ij}(k)$ is n, and a minimal realization of order n is easily obtained following the reduction to the Hermite normal form (Rózsa and Sinha 1974). If this process is stopped after $r < n$ steps, a partial realization is obtained which matches some of the generalized Markov parameters, instead of all, as would be the case with minimal realization. Hence, partial realization may be viewed as the generalization of Padé approximation to the multivariable case.

EXAMPLE 8.2

Consider again, the single-input single-output system described by the transfer function (8.12) in example 8.1. By simple long division we may write

$$
G(s) = 0s^{-1} + s^{-2} - 2s^{-3} + s^{-4} + \cdots
\tag{8.38}
$$

Alternatively, we may obtain the power series expansion

$$
G(s) = \frac{2}{3} - \frac{19}{18} s + \frac{137}{108} s^2 - \frac{895}{648} s^3 + \cdots
\tag{8.39}
$$

again, by long division.

From equations (8.38) and (8.39), we have

$$\left.\begin{array}{c} j_0 = 0 \\ j_1 = 1 \\ j_2 = -2 \\ j_{-1} = -2/3 \\ j_{-2} = 19/18 \end{array}\right\} \quad (8.40)$$

Selecting a Hankel matrix to match j_{-1}, j_0, j_1, and j_2, we have

$$H_{23}(-1) = \begin{bmatrix} j_{-1} & j_0 & j_1 \\ j_0 & j_1 & j_2 \end{bmatrix} = \begin{bmatrix} -2/3 & 0 & 1 \\ 0 & 1 & -2 \end{bmatrix} \quad (8.41)$$

Transformation to the Hermite normal form gives

$$H_{23}^{(1)}(-1) = \begin{bmatrix} 1 & 0 & -3/2 \\ 0 & 1 & -2 \end{bmatrix} \quad (8.42)$$

and F, G, and H are obtained as

$$F = \begin{bmatrix} 0 & -3/2 \\ 0 & -2 \end{bmatrix}$$

$$G = \begin{bmatrix} 0 \\ 1 \end{bmatrix} \quad (8.43)$$

$$H = [-2/3 \quad 0]$$

It may be easily verified that

$$\left.\begin{array}{c} HF^{-1}G = -2/3 = j_{-1} \\ HG = 0 = j_0 \\ HFG = 1 = j_1 \\ HF^2G = -2 = j_2 \end{array}\right\} \quad (8.44)$$

The resulting transfer function is obtained as

$$G_r(s) = H(sI - F)^{-1}G = \frac{1}{s^2 + 2s + 1.5} \quad (8.45)$$

Table 8.2.   Comparison of Responses $y(t)$ and $y_r(t)$

t	0	0.2	0.4	0.6	0.8	1.0	1.5	2.0
$y(t)$	0	0.0174	0.0603	0.1171	0.1795	0.2419	0.3799	0.4816
$y_r(t)$	0	0.1189	0.2163	0.2970	0.3629	0.4172	0.5140	0.5733

t		2.5	3.0	4.0	5.0	6.0
$y(t)$		0.5502	0.5944	0.6395	0.6606	0.663
$y_r(t)$		0.6096	0.6318	0.6536	0.6618	0.6648

The step responses of this transfer function, and the original system are given in Table 8.2 and a plot of these is shown in Figure 8.2.

It will be seen that there is a good match between the two responses for $t > 3$, as expected.

One problem with models obtained by matching time moments is that the stability of the low-order model is not guaranteed even if the original system is stable.   One way to overcome this difficulty is to combine aggregation with partial realization, as discussed in the next section.

Another approach is the Routh approximation method (Hutton and Friedland 1975) which was originally proposed for single-input single-output systems. The multivariable version (Sinha, El-Nahas, and Alden 1980) will be described

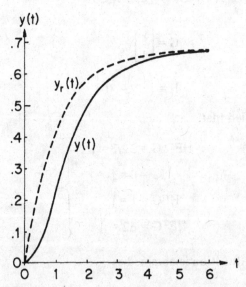

Figure 8.2.   Comparison of responses $y(t)$ and $y_r(t)$.

briefly. A continued fraction expansion of the ratio of the even and odd parts of the characteristic polynomial of A about the poles at the origin is truncated suitably to obtain the characteristic polynomial of F. With F and G in the column comparison form, the parameters of H are then obtained to match as many time moments as possible. The main attraction of this approach is that the eigenvalues and eigenvectors of A need not be calculated.

8.5 AGGREGATION WITH PARTIAL REALIZATION

Since an aggregated model retains the dominant eigenvalues of the original system, its stability is guaranteed if the system is stable. But it has been noted before that the steady-state response of the aggregated model does not normally match with the steady-state response of the original system. This can be remedied by selecting an aggregated model which will match the time moments. Not only will this give a better approximation to the response while retaining stability, we shall also have the projective relationship between the states of the system and the reduced-order model which is particularly useful if the latter is to be utilized for the design of state-variable feedback.

The procedure for obtaining an aggregated model matching some of the time moments will now be described. Since the matrix F in the Jordan form is determined entirely by the eigenvalues to be retained in the low-order model, this leads directly to the aggregation matrix K as well as the matrix $G = KB$. The elements of the matrix H may now be selected to match as many time moments as possible. The column companion form discussed in section 8.3 may also be used in a similar manner. The procedure will now be illustrated by means of an example.

EXAMPLE 8.3

Consider again the system described by equation (8.12). If we want to retain the eigenvalues at -1 and -2, we have, as in example 1,

$$\bar{F} = \begin{bmatrix} -1 & 0 \\ 0 & -2 \end{bmatrix}$$

$$\bar{K} = \begin{bmatrix} 1 & -1 & 1 \\ 1 & -2 & 4 \end{bmatrix} \tag{8.46}$$

$$\bar{G} = \bar{K}B = \begin{bmatrix} 1 \\ 1 \end{bmatrix}$$

Now, in order to match j_0 and j_{-1}, we make

$$\overline{H} = [4/3 \quad -4/3] \tag{8.47}$$

The resulting transfer function is obtained as

$$\overline{G}_r(s) = \frac{4/3}{s^2 + 3s + 2} \tag{8.48}$$

On the other hand, if for the same eigenvalues we want to match j_{-1} and j_{-2}, the low-order is given by

$$F = \begin{bmatrix} -1 & 0 \\ 0 & -2 \end{bmatrix}$$

$$G = \begin{bmatrix} 1 \\ 1 \end{bmatrix} \tag{8.49}$$

$$\overline{H}' = [13/9 \quad -14/9]$$

and the resulting transfer function is obtained as

$$\overline{G}'_r(s) = \frac{-1.9s + 4/3}{s^2 + 3s + 2} \tag{8.50}$$

A comparison of the step responses of the models (8.48) and (8.50) with that of the original system is given in Table 8.3, and a plot of these is shown in Figure 8.3.

Table 8.3

t	0	0.2	0.4	0.6	0.8	1.0	1.5	2.0
$y(t)$	0	0.0174	0.0603	0.1171	0.1795	0.2419	0.3799	0.4816
$y_r(t)$	0	0.0219	0.0725	0.1357	0.2022	0.2664	0.4024	0.4984
$y'_r(t)$	0	0.0384	0.0970	0.1632	0.2297	0.2922	0.4216	0.5114

t	2.5	3.0	4.0	5.0	6.0
$y(t)$	0.5502	0.5944	0.6395	0.6606	0.6630
$y_r(t)$	0.5617	0.6019	0.6425	0.6577	0.6634
$y'_r(t)$	0.5701	0.6072	0.6445	0.6583	0.6636

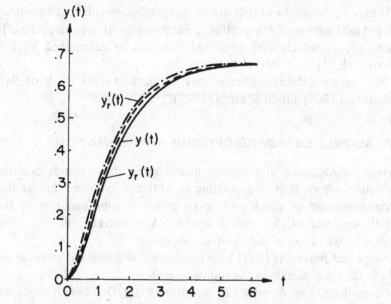

Figure 8.3.   Comparison of responses for Example 8.3.

It will be seen that the step response of the aggregated model matching j_0 and j_{-1} provides a very good approximation to the step-response of the original system.

8.6   THE SINGULAR PERTURBATION METHOD

The singular perturbation is a very useful approach for reducing a system having the two time-scale property, i.e., the eigenvalues can be separated into two groups, called the "fast" modes and the "slow" modes. The system is temporarily decoupled into two lower-order subsystems representing the "slow" and the "fast" parts of the system. Partitioning the state vector of the system represented by equation (8.01), we get

$$\left.\begin{aligned}
\dot{x}_1 &= A_{11}x_1 + A_{12}x_2 + B_1 u \\
\mu\dot{x}_2 &= A_{21}x_1 + A_{22}x_2 + B_2 u
\end{aligned}\right\} \tag{8.51}$$

where $\mu > 0$ is a scalar, $x_1 \in R^r$ and $x_2 \in R^{n-r}$. An rth order low-frequency model is obtained by setting $\mu = 0$, and eliminating x_2 from equation (8.51). This gives

$$\dot{x}_1 = (A_{11} - A_{12}A_{22}^{-1}A_{21})x_1 + (B_1 - A_{12}A_{22}^{-1}B_2)u \tag{8.52}$$

It may be pointed out that unlike aggregation, singular perturbation preserves the physical nature of the problem. Furthermore, if necessary, the effect of the "fast" modes, which were neglected, can also be determined by returning to equation (8.51) since all is not lost.

For further details, reference may be made to the work of Sannuti and Kokotovic (1969) and of Sannuti (1977).

8.7 MODELS OBTAINING OPTIMUM APPROXIMATION

Instead of obtaining a low-order model using the methods described in the previous sections it is also possible to obtain a low-order model the step- or impulse-response of which will be an optimum approximation to the step- or impulse-response of the original system. Alternatively, one may attempt optimum approximation of the frequency response.

Sinha and Bereznai (1971) have considered obtaining an optimum approximation in the time domain in the following manner.

Given the system described by equation (8.01), first obtain its response to the specified input, and consider a discrete set of values of $y(t)$ over a suitable interval of time $t = [0, T]$

$$Y \triangleq \{y_0, y_1, \ldots, y_i, \ldots, y_I\} \tag{8.53}$$

where

$$y_i \triangleq y(t_i) \tag{8.54}$$

The objective is to find another output set Y^*, associated with a model of order r such that for the same input, a scalar objective function J is minimized, where

$$J = f[w_i^T(y_i - y_i^*)] \tag{8.55}$$

which is some suitable function of the errors $y_i - y_i^*$ with a vector weight w_i attached at each sampling instant.

A number of different criteria have been suggested, but the most common are the following

$$J = \sum_{i=0}^{I} w_i \| y_i - y_i^* \|^p, \quad \text{where p is an} \tag{8.56}$$
$$\text{even number}$$

or

$$J = \max_{i = 0, I} \{w_i \| y_i - y_i^* \|\} \tag{8.57}$$

The parameters of the transfer function matrix or the corresponding canonical state equations of the reduced-order model may now be determined so as to minimize J. Sinha and Bereznai (1971) have suggested using the pattern search method of Hooke and Jeeves (1961), whereas Bandler, Markettos and Sinha (1973) have proposed using gradient methods, which require less computation time but now the gradient of the objective function has to be evaluated. Since the dominant part of the expression for the gradient consists of the partial derivatives of the response of the low-order model with respect to its parameters, the additional work required is not excessive. Moreover, this expression is the same for any high-order system and any error criterion.

EXAMPLE 8.4

As an example of application of this method, various second-order models were obtained for a seventh-order system described by the transfer function

$$G(s) = \frac{375000(s + 0.08333)}{s^7 + 83.63s^6 + 4097s^5 + 70342s^4 + 853703s^3 + 2814271s^2 + 3310875s + 281250} \tag{8.58}$$

This transfer function represents the control system for the pitch rate of a supersonic transport aircraft.

The response of this system to a unit step was computed from 0 to 20 sec and 500 samples of this response (at intervals of 0.04 sec) were used for the determination of optimum second-order models by the pattern-search method minimizing the following objective functions:

(a) maximum perpendicular error;
(b) sum of the absolute values of the sample error;
(c) sum of the squares of the sample errors;
(d) maximum perpendicular error with no error in steady-state response to step input;
(e) sum of the absolute values of the sample error with no error in steady-state response to step input;
(f) sum of the squares of the sample errors with no error in steady-state response to step input.

The six resulting models are shown in Table 8.4.

The errors produced by the various models are shown in Table 8.5.

As expected, each model has the smallest error for the criterion it has been minimized with respect to, and the error is smaller if the steady-state constraint is not imposed.

An extension of this method to the multivariable case is also possible, but the amount of computation will be considerably increased.

Table 8.4

Model Objective Function	Transfer Function	Pole Locations	Steady-State Response
(a) Minimax perpendicular error	$\dfrac{0.0254s + 0.2967}{s^2 + 2.4257s + 2.5581}$	$-1.213 \pm j1.043$	0.1160
(b) $\Sigma\lvert e\rvert$	$\dfrac{0.1536s - 0.01329}{s^2 + 1.3456s + 0.1196}$	$-0.0957, -1.250$	0.1112
(c) $\Sigma\, e^2$	$\dfrac{0.3960}{s^2 + 2.6569s + 3.4191}$	$-1.328 \pm j1.286$	0.1158
(d) Minimax perpendicular error with steady-state constraint	$\dfrac{0.0960s + 0.04545}{s^2 + 1.0432s + 0.4091}$	$-0.522 \pm j0.370$	0.1111
(e) $\Sigma\lvert e\rvert$ with steady-state constraint	$\dfrac{0.1536s + 0.01329}{s^2 + 1.343s + 0.1196}$	$-0.0959, -1.247$	0.1111
(f) $\Sigma\, e^2$ with steady-state constraint	$\dfrac{0.1019s + 0.05359}{s^2 + 1.0718s + 0.4823}$	$-0.536 \pm j0.442$	0.1111

Table 8.5

Model No.	Maximum Sample Error	Maximum Perpendicular Error	$\Sigma\lvert e\rvert$	$\Sigma\, e^2$
(a)	0.00934	0.00293	1.086	0.003898
(b)	0.02954	0.01079	0.769	0.01268
(c)	0.00445	0.00373	0.836	0.001915
(d)	0.0172	0.00691	1.942	0.01174
(e)	0.02955	0.01079	0.783	0.01265
(f)	0.01879	0.00735	1.963	0.01075

8.8   COMPARISON OF DIFFERENT METHODS OF MODEL REDUCTION FOR A MULTIVARIABLE SYSTEM

A comparison of four different methods of model reduction will be made for the case of a multivariable system. The methods considered are (a) aggregation, (b) partial realization, (c) combined aggregation and moment matching, and (d) singular perturbations.

We shall consider the example of a synchronous machine connected to an infinite busbar (Elrazaz and Sinha 1979). The system with two inputs and two outputs can be adequately modeled using seven states, and the matrices A, B, and C are given below.

$$
A = \begin{bmatrix}
-6.2036 & 15.054 & -9.8726 & -376.58 & 251.32 & -162.24 & 66.827 \\
0.53002 & -2.0176 & 1.4363 & 0 & 0 & 0 & 0 \\
16.846 & 25.079 & -43.555 & 0 & 0 & 0 & 0 \\
377.4 & -89.449 & -162.83 & 57.988 & -65.514 & 68.579 & 157.57 \\
0 & 0 & 0 & 107.25 & -118.05 & 0 & 0 \\
0.36992 & -0.1445 & -0.26303 & -0.64719 & 0.49947 & -0.21133 & 0 \\
0 & 0 & 0 & 0 & 0 & 376.99 & 0
\end{bmatrix}
$$

$$
B = \begin{bmatrix}
89.353 & 0 \\
376.99 & 0 \\
0 & 0 \\
0 & 0 \\
0 & 0 \\
0 & 0.2113 \\
0 & 0
\end{bmatrix}
\quad \text{and} \quad
C = \begin{bmatrix}
0 & 0 & 0 & 0 & 0 & 1 & 0 \\
0 & 0 & 0 & 0 & 0 & 0 & 1
\end{bmatrix}
\tag{8.59}
$$

The eigenvalues of the system are located at -0.20418, $-0.46526 \pm j9.3538$, $-13.547 \pm j376.34$, -37.482, and -46.339. Retaining the first three eigenvalues, the following aggregation matrix is obtained

$$
K = \begin{bmatrix}
-0.005355 & -1.7121 & -0.088888 & 0.0022745 & 0.0046659 & 4.0937 & -0.0026407 \\
-0.0001483 & 0.58617 & 0.058232 & -0.0032426 & -0.01127 & -1.5353 & 1.0097 \\
-0.053365 & -0.11333 & 0.078472 & -0.37291 & -0.078417 & -40.632 & -0.0054587
\end{bmatrix}
\tag{8.60}
$$

Using equations (8.8) and (8.11), the aggregated model is obtained as below

$$
F = \begin{bmatrix} -0.20418 & 0 & 0 \\ 0 & -0.46526 & -9.3538 \\ 0 & 9.3538 & -0.46526 \end{bmatrix}, \quad G = \begin{bmatrix} -645.93 & 0.86512 \\ 220.97 & -0.32445 \\ -37.957 & -0.0031656 \end{bmatrix}
$$

$$(8.61)$$

Next, partial realization was tried. It was found that the reduced-order model matching the Markov parameters J_0 and J_1 was unstable. The model is given below

$$
F = \begin{bmatrix} 0 & 0 & 1 \\ 376.99 & 0 & 0 \\ 23153 & -0.019201 & 41.17 \end{bmatrix}, \quad G = \begin{bmatrix} 0 & 0.21133 \\ 0 & 0 \\ -21.421 & 8.7468 \end{bmatrix},
$$

$$
H = \begin{bmatrix} 1 & 0 & 0 \\ 0 & 0 & 1 \end{bmatrix}
$$

$$(8.62)$$

The singularly perturbed model, transformed to the block diagonal form, is given below

$$
\dot{z} = \begin{bmatrix} -0.20418 & 0 & 0 \\ 0 & -0.46526 & -9.3538 \\ 0 & 9.3538 & -0.46526 \end{bmatrix} z + \begin{bmatrix} 645.93 & -0.86512 \\ 220.97 & -0.32445 \\ -37.957 & -8.5869 \end{bmatrix} u
$$

$$
\hat{y} = \begin{bmatrix} 0.19193 \times 10^{-3} & -0.12341 \times 10^{-2} & -0.024812 \\ -0.35438 & 1 & 0 \end{bmatrix} z
$$

$$(8.63)$$

$$
+ \begin{bmatrix} -0.021046 & -0.47405 \times 10^{-4} \\ 0.21128 & 0.43666 \times 10^{-4} \end{bmatrix} u
$$

The aggregated model matching J_{-1} is given below

$$
F = \begin{bmatrix} -0.20418 & 0 & 0 \\ 0 & -0.46526 & -9.3538 \\ 0 & 9.3538 & -0.46526 \end{bmatrix}, \quad G = \begin{bmatrix} 645.93 & -0.86512 \\ 220.97 & -0.32445 \\ -37.957 & -8.5869 \end{bmatrix}
$$

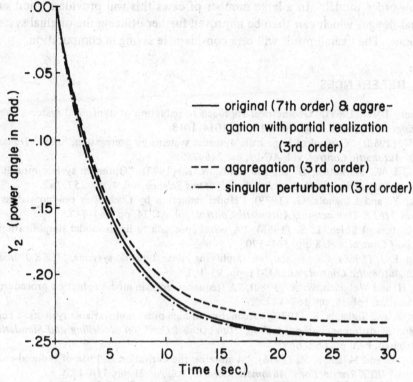

Figure 8.4.   Comparison of responses for different models.

$$H = \begin{bmatrix} 0.18368 \times 10^{-3} & -0.0013039 & -0.02458 \\ 0.35428 & 1.00077 & -0.0021203 \end{bmatrix} \tag{8.64}$$

The response y_2 calculated for the case when $u = \begin{bmatrix} 1 \\ 0 \end{bmatrix}$ for $t > 0$, for the original system, as well as for each reduced-order model, is shown in Figure 8.4. It is seen that the best approximation is obtained by the aggregated model matching the time moments T_0 (or J_{-1}), whereas the model obtained using singular perturbation is almost as good.

8.9   CONCLUDING REMARKS

We have considered a number of different methods for obtaining low-order models for high-order systems. From the point of view of practical applications, the singular perturbation method and the method combining aggregation with partial realization appear to be the most promising. The concept of aggregation used in the latter method is most useful when designing state feedback using the low-order model. In a large number of cases this will provide a good suboptimal design, which can then be improved further utilizing the original system equations. The overall result will be a considerable saving in computation.

8.10 REFERENCES

Anderson, J. H. (1967), "Geometrical approach to reduction of dynamical systems," *Proceedings Inst. of Elec. Eng.*, vol. 114, pp. 1014–1018.

Aoki, M. (1968), "Control of large scale dynamic systems by aggregation," *IEEE Transactions. Automatic Control*, vol. AC-13, pp. 246–253.

Bandler, J. W., Markettos, N. D., and Sinha, N. K. (1973), "Optimum system modelling using recent gradient methods," *Int. J. of Systems Science*, vol. 4, pp. 257–262.

Bistritz, Y. and Langholz, G. (1979), "Model reduction by Chebyshev polynomial techniques," *IEEE Transactions. Automatic Control*, vol. AC-24, pp. 741–747.

Chen, C. F. and Shieh, L. S. (1968), "A novel approach to linear model simplification," *Int. J. of Control*, vol. 8, pp. 561–570.

Davison, E. J. (1966), "A method for simplifying linear dynamic systems," *IEEE Transactions. Automatic Control*, vol. AC-11, pp. 93–101.

Elliott, H. and Wolovich, W. A. (1980), "A frequency-domain model reduction procedure," *Automatica*, vol. 16, pp. 167–177.

Elrazaz, Z. and Sinha, N. K. (1979), "Reduction of high-order multivariable systems: a comparison of different methods," *Proc. 10th Annual Conf. on Modelling and Simulation* (Pittsburgh, PA), pp. 663–667.

Genesio, R. and Milanese, M. (1976), "A note on the derivation and use of reduced-order models," *IEEE Transactions. Automatic Control*, vol. AC-21, pp. 118–122.

Gibarillo, L. G. and Lees, F. P. (1969), "The reduction of complex transfer function models to simple models using the method of moments," *Chem. Eng. Sci.*, vol. 24, pp. 85–93.

Hickin, J. (1978), "A unified theory of model reduction for linear time invariant dynamical systems," Ph.D. Thesis, McMaster University (also available as *Report SOC-195*, Group on Simulation, Optimization and Control, McMaster University).

Hickin, J. and Sinha, N. K. (1975a), "Aggregation matrices for a class of low-order models for large-scale systems," *Electronics Letters*, vol. 10, pp. 318–319.

Hickin, J. and Sinha, N. K. (1975b), "Optimally aggregated models of high-order systems," *Electronics Letters*, vol. 11, pp. 632–633.

Hickin, J. and Sinha, N. K. (1976a), "On near-optimal control using reduced-order models," *Electronics Letters*, vol. 12, pp. 259–260.

Hickin, J. and Sinha, N. K. (1976b), "A new method for reducing multivariable systems," *Proc. 7th Annual Conference on Modelling and Simulation* (Pittsburgh, PA), pp. 259–263.

Hickin, J. and Sinha, N. K. (1977), "An efficient algorithm for transformation of state equations to canonical forms," *IEEE Transactions. Automatic Control*, vol. AC-22, pp. 652–653.

Hickin, J. and Sinha, N. K. (1978), "Canonical forms for aggregated models," *Int. J. of Control*, vol. 27, pp. 473–485.

Hickin, J. and Sinha, N. K. (1979), "On the transformation of linear multivariable systems to canonical forms," *Int. J. Systems Science*, vol. 10, pp. 783–796.

Hickin, J. and Sinha, N. K. (1980), "Model reduction for linear multivariable systems," *IEEE Transactions. Automatic Control*, vol. AC-25, pp. 1121–1127.

Hooke, R. and Jeeves, T. A. (1961), "'Direct search' solution of numerical and statistical problems," *J. Assoc. Comp. Mach.*, vol. 8, pp. 212–229.

Hutton, M. F. (1977), "Routh approximations in state space," *Proc. 8th Annual Conf. on Modelling and Simulation* (Pittsburgh, PA), pp. 311–315.

Hutton, M. F. and Friedland, B. (1975), "Routh approximations for reducing order of linear time-invariant systems," *IEEE Transactions. Automatic Control*, vol. AC-20, pp. 329–337.

Lamba, S. S. and Vittal Rao, S. (1972), "Derivation of aggregation matrices for simplified models of linear dynamic systems and their application for optimal control," *Proc. JACC*, pp. 498–503.

Langholz, G. and Bistritz, Y. (1978), "Model reduction of dynamic systems over a frequency interval," *Proc. 16th Annual Allerton Conf. on Communication, Control, and Computing* (Monticello, IL), pp. 903–912.

Marshall, S. A. (1966), "An approximate method for reducing the order of a large system," *Control Engineering*, vol. 10, pp. 642–648.

Michailesco, G., Siret, J. M., and Bertrand, P. (1975), "Aggregation matrices for high-order systems," *Electronics Letters*, vol. 11, pp. 398–399.

Mitra, D. (1967), "On the reduction of complexity of linear dynamic models," *Report AEEW-R520*, U.K. Atomic Energy Authority.

Rózsa, P. and Sinha, N. K. (1974), "Efficient algorithm for irreducible realization of a rational matrix," *Int. J. of Control*, vol. 21, pp. 273–284.

Sannuti, P. and Kokotovic, P. V. (1969), "Near optimum design of linear systems using singular perturbation method," *IEEE Transactions. Automatic Control*, vol. AC-14, pp. 15–21.

Sannuti, P. (1977), "On the controllability of singularly perturbed on linear systems," *Proc. 8th Annual Conf. on Modelling and Simulation* (Pittsburgh, PA), pp. 317–321.

Shamash, Y. (1974), "Stable reduced order models using Padé-type approximations," *IEEE Transactions. Automatic Control*, vol. AC-19, pp. 615–616.

Shamash, Y. (1975), "Model reduction using minimal realization algorithms," *Electronics Letters*, vol. 11, pp. 385–387.

Shamash, Y. (1975), "Linear system reduction using Padé approximation to allow the retention of dominant modes," *Int. J. of Control*, vol. 21, pp. 257–272.

Sinha, N. K. and Bereznai, G. T. (1971), "Optimum approximation of high-order systems by low-order models," *Int. J. of Control*, vol. 14, pp. 951–959.

Sinha, N. K. and Pille, W. (1971), "A new method for reduction of dynamic systems," *Int. J. of Control*, vol. 14, pp. 111–118.

Sinha, N. K. and Rózsa, P. (1976), "Some canonical forms for linear multivariable systems," *Int. J. of Control*, vol. 23, pp. 865–883.

Sinha, N. K., El-Nahas, I., and Alden, R. T. H. (1980), "Routh-Hurwitz approximation of multivariable systems," *Proc. 18th Annual Allerton Conf. on Communication, Control, and Computing* (Monticello, IL), pp. 285–294.

9
Combined State and Parameter Estimation

9.1 INTRODUCTION

So far we have considered the problem of estimating the parameters of a model from the measurements of the inputs and the outputs. In many control problems, the objective is to feed back the states of the system in order to modify its behavior. Hence, it is also necessary to estimate the states of the system from the measurements which are usually contaminated with noise.

The problem of combined state and parameter estimation was originally posed as a nonlinear state estimation problem by augmenting the state vector with the parameter vector and the extended Kalman filter was used (Farison et al. 1967, Jazwinski 1970). Since this requires a linear approximation of a nonlinear system about the current, estimate divergence may be obtained if the initial estimate is poor. Furthermore, not much is known about the convergence properties of the extended Kalman filter, and the conditions for acceptability of the solution are rather vague. Additional difficulty may be caused by the fact that the amount of computation may be rather excessive due to the linearization required after each iteration of estimation. To overcome these difficulties two new approaches have been proposed recently. The first approach (Nelson and Stear 1976) estimates the system parameters from the input-output data. These estimates are then used for state estimation through a Kalman filter. The entire scheme is based on a particular canonical form for the state-space equations of a linear system which allows the parameters and states to be estimated separately in a suboptimal manner using two linear estimators. It has been shown recently (Padilla et al. 1978) that this canonical form cannot always be obtained in the general case. The second approach (Prasad and Sinha 1977) estimates the parameters and the states of the system in two stages in a bootstrap manner. In the first stage the states are estimated with assumed nominal values of the parameters. In the second stage the parameters of the system are estimated from a pseudoparameter measurement equation which contains the recent estimates of the states from stage one in addition to the input-output data. These two stages are coupled in a bootstrap manner.

In this chapter we shall consider a recently proposed two-stage bootstrap algorithm (El-Sherief and Sinha 1979) for combined state and parameter estimation of linear discrete-time multivariable systems. This algorithm utilizes the idea of the second approach (Prasad and Sinha 1977) with the following improvements:

(a) A canonical form of the state equations is used which allows the parameters of the pseudoparameter measurement equation to be related directly to the parameters of the canonical state space model.
(b) The use of this canonical form simplifies the parameter estimation problem by decomposing the system into m subsystems (where m is the number of outputs) so that the parameters of each subsystem can be estimated independently.
(c) It is shown that using the pseudoparameter measurement equation for estimating the parameters causes the residual errors to be uncorrelated with the forcing function. Hence, unbiased estimates of the system parameters can be obtained using ordinary least-squares without requiring any knowledge of the noise characteristics.

The proposed algorithm starts by transforming the state equations to the row-companion form (Sinha and Rózsa 1976). Then assuming an initial estimate of the states, a recursive least-squares algorithm is used for estimating the parameters of the pseudoparameter measurement equation. From these estimates, the state equations are obtained directly, and these are then utilized for estimating the states of the system by a stochastic approximation algorithm. This procedure is continued in a bootstrap manner.

9.2 FORMULATION OF THE PROBLEM

Consider a system described by the following innovations representation

$$\underline{x}^*(k + 1) = A^*\underline{x}^*(k) + B^*\underline{u}(k) + K^*\underline{e}(k)$$
$$\underline{y}(k) = C^*\underline{x}^*(k) + \underline{e}(k)$$

(9.01)

where $\underline{x}^*(k) \in R^n$, $\underline{u}(k) \in R^p$ and $\underline{y}(k) \in R^m$, are the state input and output vectors, respectively. Also, $\underline{e}(k) \in \overline{R}^m$ is the innovations sequence which is a zero-mean white-noise sequence with covariance Q and K^* is the steady-state Kalman gain matrix.

Assuming that the system is observable, it can be transformed to the row-companion form through the transformation $\underline{x} = P\underline{x}^*$ to obtain

$$\underline{x}(k + 1) = A\underline{x}(k) + B\underline{u}(k) + K\underline{e}(k)$$
$$\underline{y}(k) = C\underline{x}(k) + \underline{e}(k) \tag{9.02}$$

where $A = PA^*P^{-1}$, $B = PB^*$, and $K = PK^*$. Also, A can be written as a block matrix $\{A_{ij}\}$, $i, j = 1, 2, \ldots, m$ where

$$A_{ii} = \begin{bmatrix} 0 & & I_{n_i - 1} \\ \vdots & & \\ a_{ii}(1) & a_{ii}(2) \cdots a_{ii}(n_i) \end{bmatrix}, \quad A_{ij} = \begin{bmatrix} 0 & \cdots & 0 \\ \vdots & & \vdots \\ a_{ij}(1) & \cdots & a_{ij}(n_j) \end{bmatrix} \tag{9.03}$$

The matrix C consists of unit row vectors only, and can be written as

$$C = \begin{bmatrix} \underline{e}^1 \\ \underline{e}^{n_1 + 1} \\ \vdots \\ \underline{e}^{n_1 + n_2 + \cdots + n_{m-1} + 1} \end{bmatrix} \tag{9.04}$$

where $\underline{e}^i$ is the ith unit row vector of dimension n.

The integers $n_1, n_2, \ldots, n_m$ are called the observability subindices of the system and

$$n_1 + n_2 + \cdots + n_m = n \tag{9.05}$$

Our problem is to obtain consistent estimates of the parameters as well as the states of the system (9.02) without knowing the noise covariance matrix Q.

9.3 PARAMETER ESTIMATION

Define

$$B = \begin{bmatrix} \underline{b}^1 \\ \underline{b}^2 \\ \vdots \\ \underline{b}^n \end{bmatrix} \tag{9.06}$$

$$K = \begin{bmatrix} \underline{k}^1 \\ \underline{k}^2 \\ \vdots \\ \underline{k}^n \end{bmatrix} \tag{9.07}$$

and

$$\tilde{A} = \begin{bmatrix} \underline{a}^1 \\ \underline{a}^2 \\ \vdots \\ \underline{a}^m \end{bmatrix} \triangleq \text{the m unknown rows of A} \tag{9.08}$$

where

$$\underline{a}^j = [a_{j1}(1) \cdots a_{j1}(n_1) \quad a_{j2}(1) \cdots a_{jm}(n_m)] \tag{9.09}$$

for $j = 1, 2, \ldots, m$.

Because of the canonical structure of A and C, the jth output of the system may be expressed as

$$y_j(k + n_j) = \underline{Z}_j^T(k + n_j - 1) \, \underline{\theta}_j + \bar{e}_j(k + n_j) \tag{9.10}$$

where

$$\underline{Z}_j(k + n_j - 1) = [\underline{x}^T(k) \quad \underline{u}^T(k) \quad \underline{u}^T(k + 1) \cdots \underline{u}^T(k + n_j - 1)]^T \tag{9.11}$$

$$\underline{\theta}_j = [\underline{a}^j \quad \underline{b}^{n_1 + \cdots + n_j} \cdots \underline{b}^{n_1 + \cdots + n_{j-1} + 1}]^T \tag{9.12}$$

and

$$\bar{e}_j(k + n_j) = e_j(k + n_j) + \sum_{i=1}^{n_j} k^{n_1 + \cdots + n_{j-1} + i} e(k + n_j - i) \tag{9.13}$$

It is easily seen from equation (9.10) that Z_j is uncorrelated with the residual error e_j and from (9.13), $E[\bar{e}_j] = 0$. Hence, an unbiased estimate of the parameter vector $\underline{\theta}_j$ can be obtained by using an ordinary linear least-squares algorithm as in Chapter 4. Moreover, equation (9.10) indicates that the parameter vector for each subsystem can be estimated independently of other subsystems. The following recursive algorithm may be used for parameter estimation.

$$\hat{\underline{\theta}}_j(k+1) = \hat{\underline{\theta}}_j(k) + \frac{P_j(k)\,\underline{Z}_j(k+n_j-1)\,[y_j(k+n_j) - \underline{Z}_j^T(k+n_j-1)\,\hat{\underline{\theta}}_j(k)]}{1 + \underline{Z}_j^T(k+n_j-1)\,P_j(k)\,\underline{Z}_j(k+n_j-1)}$$

$$\tag{9.14}$$

$$P_j(k+1) = P_j(k) - \frac{P_j(k)\,\underline{Z}_j(k+n_j-1)\,[P_j(k)\,\underline{Z}_j(k+n_j-1)]^T}{1 + \underline{Z}_j^T(k+n_j-1)\,P_j(k)\,\underline{Z}_j(k+n_j-1)}$$

where $\hat{\underline{\theta}}_j(k)$ is defined as the estimate of $\underline{\theta}_j$ at the kth iteration.

9.4 STATE ESTIMATION

It may be noted that the vector $\underline{Z}_j$, defined in equation (9.11), includes the states of the system, which are not known. But if we assume an initial estimate of the states then we can estimate the parameter vectors using the algorithm of the previous section. Hence, the system matrices $\hat{A}(k)$ and $\hat{B}(k)$ at the kth iteration are obtained directly.

These may then be used for estimating the states using the following stochastic approximation algorithm

$$\hat{\underline{x}}(k+1|k) = \hat{A}(k)\,\hat{\underline{x}}(k|k) + \hat{B}(k)\,\underline{u}(k)$$

$$\hat{\underline{x}}(k+1|k+1) = \hat{\underline{x}}(k+1|k) + \gamma(k)\,C^T[\underline{y}(k+1) - C\hat{\underline{x}}(k+1|k)]$$

$$\tag{9.15}$$

where $\gamma(k)$ is a scalar sequence satisfying Dvoretzky's theorem (Dvoretzky 1956).

After this state estimate is obtained, the expression for $\underline{x}(k)$ in equation (9.11) may be replaced by $\hat{\underline{x}}(k|k)$ to obtain a new estimate of the parameter vector. The procedure is then repeated between the two stages in a bootstrap manner.

9.5 RESULTS OF SIMULATION

The proposed algorithm was applied to the following 3rd-order two-output one-input system

$$\underline{x}(k+1) = \begin{bmatrix} 0.00 & 1.0 & 0.0 \\ 0.10 & 0.3 & 0.1 \\ 0.95 & 0.1 & 0.7 \end{bmatrix} \underline{x}(k) + \begin{bmatrix} 0.12 \\ 0.36 \\ 0.20 \end{bmatrix} \underline{u}(k)$$

$$\underline{y}(k) = \begin{bmatrix} 1 & 0 & 0 \\ 0 & 0 & 1 \end{bmatrix} \underline{x}(k) + \underline{v}(k)$$

Table 9.1.   Final Estimates of System Parameters After 1000 Iterations

Parameter	$a_{11}(1)$	$a_{11}(2)$	$a_{12}(1)$	$a_{21}(1)$	$a_{21}(2)$	$a_{22}(1)$	$b(1)$	$b(2)$	$b(3)$
True value	0.10	0.30	0.10	0.95	0.10	0.70	0.12	0.36	0.20
Estimated value	0.10	0.29	0.10	0.89	0.12	0.71	0.12	0.36	0.20

where the input was taken as a zero-mean white noise sequence with unit variance. The noise sequences $v_1(k)$ and $v_2(k)$ were taken as uncorrelated zero mean white noise sequences with standard deviations 0.1 and 0.3 respectively.

The proposed algorithm was applied to the above example with zero initial states and assuming zero initial values for the parameters. The final parameter estimates after 1000 iterations are given in Table 9.1.

The rate of convergence of the parameter estimates is shown in Figure 9.1,

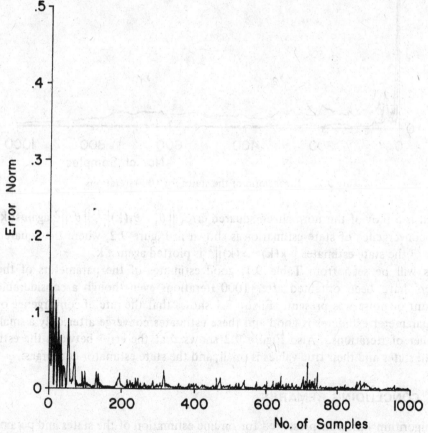

Figure 9.1.   Rate of convergence of the parameter estimates for 1000 observations.

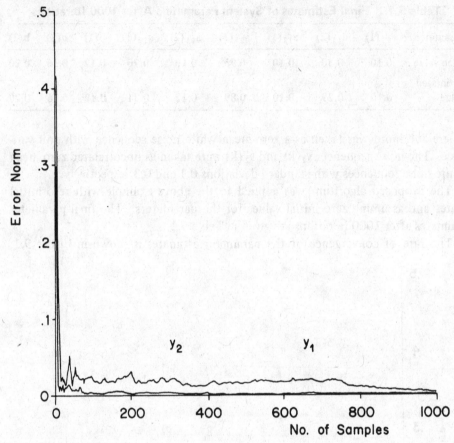

Figure 9.2.   Error norm of the states for 1000 iterations.

which is a plot of the normalized squared error $\|\underline{\theta}_i - \underline{\theta}_i(k)\|^2/\|\underline{\theta}_i\|^2$ against k. The convergence of state estimation is shown in Figure 9.2, where the squared error of the state estimates $\|\underline{x}(k) - \hat{\underline{x}}(k)\|^2$ is plotted against k.

As will be seen from Table 9.1, good estimates of the parameters of the system have been obtained after 1000 iterations even though a considerable amount of noise was present. Figure 9.1 shows that the rate of convergence of the parameter estimates is good and these estimates converge after only a small number of iterations. Also Figure 9.2 shows that the error between the estimated states and their true values is small, and the state estimator converges.

9.6   CONCLUDING REMARKS

An algorithm has been presented for on-line estimation of the states and parameters of linear discrete-time multivariable systems. It is a two-stage bootstrap algorithm, in which a special canonical form of the state equations provides not only a direct relationship between its parameters and those of the resulting pseudoparameter measurement equation, but also causes the residual error sequences of the latter to be uncorrelated with the forcing function. Hence unbiased estimates of the parameters can be obtained by ordinary least-squares method without knowledge of the noise statistics. It is felt that these features of the proposed algorithm provide a definite improvement over an earlier bootstrap algorithm (Prasad and Sinha 1977).

Results of simulation indicate that the proposed algorithm works quite well even with noise-to-signal ratio of 22%.

It may be added that the approach presented here is somewhat similar to the two-stage bootstrap algorithm using instrumental variables presented by Pandya (1974), with the essential difference that we are using state variables as instrumental variables for the multivariable case.

9.7 REFERENCES

Dvoretzky, A. (1956), "On stochastic approximation," *Proc. 3rd Berkeley Symp. on Mathematics, Statistics and Probability*, pp. 35–55.

El-Sherief, H. and Sinha, N. K. (1979), "Bootstrap estimation of parameters and states of linear multivariable systems," *IEEE Transactions. Automatic Control*, vol. AC-24, pp. 340–343.

El-Sherief, H. and Sinha, N. K. (1982), "Suboptimal control of linear stochastic multivariable systems with unknown parameters," *Automatica*, vol. 18, pp. 101–105.

Farison, J. B., Graham, R. E., and Shelton, R. C. (1967), "Identification and control of linear discrete systems," *IEEE Transactions. Automatic Control*, vol. AC-12, pp. 438–442.

Irwin, G. W. and Roberts, A. P. (1976), "The Luenberger canonical form in the state/parameter estimation of linear systems," *Int. J. of Control*, vol. 23, pp. 851–864.

Jazwinski, A. H. (1970), *Stochastic Processes and Filtering Theory*, Academic Press, New York.

Nelson, L. W. and Stear, E. (1976), "The simultaneous on-line estimation of parameters and states in linear systems," *IEEE Transactions. Automatic Control*, vol. AC-21, pp. 94–98.

Padilla, R. A., Padilla, C. S., and Bingulac, S. P. (1978), "Comments on the simultaneous on-line estimation of parameters and states in linear systems," *IEEE Transactions. Automatic Control*, vol. AC-23, pp. 96–97.

Pandya, R. N. (1974), "A class of bootstrap estimators and their relationship to the generalized two stage least squares estimators," *IEEE Transactions. Automatic Control*, vol. AC-19, pp. 831–835.

Prasad, R. M. and Sinha, A. K. (1977), "On bootstrap identification using stochastic approximation," *IEEE Transactions. Automatic Control*, vol. AC-22, pp. 671–672.

Sinha, N. K. and Rózsa, P. (1976), "Some canonical forms for linear multivariable systems," *Int. J. of Control*, vol. 23, pp. 365–383.

10
Distributed Parameter Systems

10.1 INTRODUCTION

Most dynamic models are constructed around a set of differential equations. The initial stage in model building is to assemble equations representing the physical mechanisms that are believed to be applicable to the plant.

Obviously, the equations will vary greatly according to the nature of the plant. Usually the first stage in model building is to assemble equations of mass balance, thermal balance, energy balance, etc., based on physical, chemical, and mechanical laws (Van Dixhoorn and Evans 1974).

These basic equations are supported by other relations including semiempirical formulas.

In each case the modeling of a process requires detailed knowledge of the process and considerable experimentation. In this chapter the common difficulties arising in modeling and simulation of dynamic processes with distributed parameters will be discussed.

The obvious first attempt in solving a complex problem is to cast it in terms of known methods. For distributed parameters models this typically implies use of local linearization and/or lumping procedures. Both approaches are justified when the system is not at a state of bifurcation; i.e., when the system does not change its qualitative nature.

The investigation of bifurcation phenomena is therefore the primary objective of sections 10.2-10.4. In particular, the eigenvalues of the linearized problem take on a very special character when the system is in a state of bifurcation. This will be discussed in sections 10.3 and 10.4.

The existence of bifurcation can be used for identification of parameters included in the eigenvalue problem (Kuszta and Bailey, 1982). In the case when the system does not operate in bifurcation zones one can use the lumping methods and cast the problem in terms of ODE's. Lumping procedures are briefly discussed in section 10.6 and appendix IV. Identification of (nonlinear) lumped parameter systems is discussed in Chapter 2, which can be treated as a continuation of Chapter 10. Bifurcation analysis as a first step in identification of nonlinear distributed parameter systems is specially emphasized. A review of further possible identification procedures can be found in Palis and Goodson (1976).

10.2 MODELS DESCRIBED BY PARTIAL DIFFERENTIAL EQUATIONS

Physical laws for such processes are often stated in terms of nonlinear partial differential equations (PDE). For a general nonlinear differential equation the field is so broad that it is difficult to carry the classification and discussion further.

For our purpose we shall limit ourselves to the set of PDE of parabolic type emphasizing the typical features that designers can come across. Let the system be described by a set of PDE (in vector form)

$$\frac{\partial \underline{u}}{\partial t} + A(a, \underline{u}) + F(b, \underline{u}, t) = 0 \qquad (10.01)$$

where

A—spatial differential operator
F—nonlinear function of arguments
$\underline{u}$—vector of state variables
t—time
a, b—system parameters
$\underline{u} \in \Omega$, which is an n-dimensional Banach space.

Equation (10.01) is considered with the boundary conditions connected with:

(a) elliptic part of (10.01) (the case when $\partial \underline{u}/\partial t = 0$)

(b) $\underline{u}(\Omega)\big|_{t=0}$ \qquad (10.01a)

which makes the problem suitable for further investigation. At the very beginning the question arises whether "all" equations representing the significant effects on the model behavior are included? At the other extreme we have the question whether equations included in the model are not redundant?

Equations include the unknown coefficients which can be only approximately determined from process literature or specially devised tests. From this point of view the problem of solution of (10.01), (10.01a) is not a purely mathematical one; it requires verifications and deep designer inspection.

The model described by (10.01, 10.01a) should be usable in practice. There are two basic types of models taken into consideration in engineering:

(1) models to assist engineering design (in which the phenomenological models are included)
(2) models for use in control system design or for inclusion within control system.

In practice (linear) lumped-parameter models are successfully applied, particularly models of the second type. Therefore the very important problem is to replace the rather complex model of (10.01, 10.01a) type by a much simpler, often linear, one.

This operation can be performed successfully when two conditions are satisfied:

(1) the simplifications (lumping, linearization, lowering of system order) are performed appropriately
(2) the basic set of PDE is well chosen.

This last assumption is hardly verified. The only "proof of this pudding is eating." Nevertheless, there exists some methods which permit evaluation, at least qualitatively, of the model validity during preparation, and avoidance different traps. One of the initial steps in model investigation is steady-state analysis.

10.3   THE STEADY-STATE ANALYSIS

The steady-state is usually the best known behavior of the system. Where an existing plant is being modeled a large amount of steady-state information is usually available. These data can be supported by the knowledge of phenomenological aspects when the process is used in different technological situations.

For plants not yet in existence it may be possible to use data from an existing similar plant (pilot plant, laboratory test). In complex systems, the coupling between variables, for instance, chemical reactions, mass, heat diffusion, etc., can cause various pathological phenomena such as the occurrence of multiple steady-states, some of which are highly unstable.

In the steady-state analysis the following questions present themselves:

(1) Are there equilibrium states of the system?
(2) How many are there?
(3) Are they stable or unstable?
(4) What happens as external parameters are varied?
(5) What kind of instability can occur when system parameters are varied?

The answers to these items can qualitatively evaluate the system of equations (10.01, 10.01a) and bound the region of possible system parameter values.

10.3.1 The Number and Stability of Equilibrium States

In many complicated dynamical systems multiple steady states can occur (Aris 1965, Amundson 1965, Gavalas 1968, Finlayson 1972). Despite their physical reasons the problem of multiple equilibrium states can be discussed as a problem of multiple solutions of nonlinear differential equations describing the physical systems. The mathematical apparatus can be based on topological methods presented by Krasnosielski (1964, 1969, 1975). An excellent review of basic Krasnosielski concepts can be found in the work of Gavalas (1966, 1968).

The investigation of multiple solutions of nonlinear partial differential equations leads to the discussion of the eigenvalue problem of linearized systems.

Let the system of NPDE be given in the form (10.01, 10.01a). By using the Green's function for the given differential operator system (10.01) can be transformed to the equivalent integral equations of the form:

$$\underline{\xi} = H\underline{\xi} \tag{10.02}$$

where H is a nonlinear integral operator.

Every solution of the equation (10.02) is referred to as a fixed point. With each fixed point there is associated a number γ_i called the index.

The investigation for stability makes use of the concept of the index γ_i. Let L be the Frechet derivative of the operator H at the point $\underline{u}$ (see Appendix III). Consider the eigenvalue problem

$$\underline{\phi} = \lambda L\underline{\phi} \tag{10.03}$$

The following lemmas can be proved:

Lemma 1. If $\lambda = 1$ is not an eigenvalue of equation (10.03) then the index is equal to $(-1)^\beta$, where β is the number of eigenvalues in the interval $0 < \lambda < 1$.

Lemma 2. The sum of the indices of all fixed points is equal to 1.

Lemma 3. If $\lambda = 1$ is not an eigenvalue of (10.03), the number of steady-state solutions must be odd.

Lemma 4. If (10.03) has no eigenvalues in the closed interval $[0, 1]$ for any of the steady-states there is only one steady-state.

The investigation of the uniqueness of solution for the system (10.01) can be carried out by examining the local behavior of this system in the neighborhood of some solution, the transformation to the integral equation is not necessary.

EXAMPLE 10.1

Consider the steady state equation of the form

$$\left. \begin{array}{ll} A\underline{u} = f\underline{u} & \text{for} \quad \underline{x} \in \Omega \\ \underline{u} = \underline{u}_0 & \text{for} \quad \underline{x} \in \partial\Omega \end{array} \right\} \tag{10.04}$$

where

A is a differential operator in Ω
dim $\underline{u} = n$ and dim $f = m \times n$

By using the Green's function for the operator A and boundary conditions, equation (10.04) can be transformed to the equivalent integral equation of Hammerstein type:

$$\underline{u}(\underline{x}) = \underline{u}_0(1) + \int_0^1 G(\underline{x}, \underline{x}')\, f[\underline{x}', u(\underline{x}')]\, d\underline{x}' \tag{10.05}$$

where $G(\underline{x}, \underline{x}')$ is the Green's function for (10.04).

For Hammerstein's operator

$$H(\underline{u}(\underline{x})) = \int_\Omega G(\underline{x}, \underline{x}')\, f[\underline{x}', \underline{u}(\underline{x}')]\, d\underline{x}' \tag{10.06}$$

and assuming that $f(\underline{x}', \underline{u})$ and $\partial/\partial u\, f(\underline{x}, \underline{u})$ are continuous, the Frechet derivative has the form:

$$L(\underline{u}(\underline{x})) = \int_\Omega G(\underline{x}, \underline{x}')\, \frac{\partial f[\underline{x}', \underline{u}(\underline{x}'))}{\partial \underline{u}}\, d\underline{x}' \tag{10.07}$$

Returning to the differential equation representation the linearized eigenvalue problem is as follows

$$A\underline{\phi} = \lambda B \underline{\phi} \quad \text{for} \quad \underline{x} \in \Omega$$
$$\underline{\phi} = 0 \quad \text{for} \quad \underline{x} \in \partial\Omega \tag{10.08}$$

where

$$B = [b_{ij}]$$

$$b_{ij} = \frac{\partial f_i}{\partial u_j} \quad \begin{array}{l} i = 1, \ldots, m \\ j = 1, \ldots, n \end{array}$$

The derivatives $\partial f_m / \partial u_n$ are evaluated at some steady states which are assumed as known functions. In practice, only the bounds for the steady states obtained via measurements or theoretical considerations are available.

Remark 1. The linearized eigenvalue problem (10.08) can be reformulated. Equation (10.08) is equivalent to the eigenvalue problem (10.09)

$$A\underline{\phi} - B\underline{\phi} = \mu A \underline{\phi} \tag{10.09}$$

with appropriate boundary conditions.

Due to the relationship

$$\mu = 1 - \frac{1}{\lambda}$$

the interval $(0, 1)$ from lemmas (1)–(4) transforms into interval $(-\infty, 0)$.

10.3.2 Global Stability of Steady States

The crucial consideration about stability of steady states can be made on the basis of lemmas (1)–(4). The value -1 of the index implies instability. Index $+1$ does not itself guarantee the stability of the fixed point. The problem whether a steady state is stable in a global sense requires more subtle consideration in which the maximum principle theorem (Il'lin, Kalashnikov, and Oleiniko 1962) can be useful.

Consider the following partial differential equation

$$\sum_{i,j=1}^{n} a_{ij}(\underline{x}, \tau) \frac{\partial^2 u}{\partial x_i \partial x_j} + \sum_{i=1}^{n} b_i(\underline{x}, \tau) \frac{\partial u}{\partial x_i} + c(\underline{x}, \tau) \underline{u} = \frac{\partial u}{\partial \tau} \tag{10.10}$$

where

a_{ij}, b_i, c are real and finite

$a_{ij} = a_{ji}$ and $u(\underline{x}, \tau)$ continuous in Ω.

Maximum Principle Theorem

If $c(\underline{x}, \tau) < M$ where M is some constant, $u(\underline{x}, 0) \geqslant 0$ and $u(\underline{x}, \tau) \geqslant 0$ for all $\underline{x} \in \partial\Omega$ then the solution of (10.10) for all τ and $\underline{x} \in \Omega$. Analyzing the initial conditions on the boundary $\partial\Omega$ and making use of the maximum principle theorem it has been proved by Luss and Lee (1968), that the unique steady state is stable for the case m = 1.

10.3.3   Approximate Solution of the Eigenvalue Problem

In practice, to solve the eigenvalue problem may be a cumbersome task, particularly in the multidimensional case. Satisfactory results can be obtained using one of the well-known techniques of approximate solutions of the linear differential equations. The comparison of the results obtained via approximation technique is presented in example 10.2.

EXAMPLE 10.2

Let us consider the nonlinear equation often met in chemical reactor systems:

$$\nabla^2 y = \delta^2 y \exp \{\gamma\beta(1 - y)/[1 + \beta(1 - y)]\} = f(y) \qquad (10.11)$$

For some values of the parameters β, γ, δ equation (10.11) admits multiple solution (Parks 1961). Our goal is to estimate the value of the parameter when unique steady-state of the system (10.11) is examined. The solution of equation (10.11) for spherical geometry $\beta = 0.2$, $\gamma = 30$, and $\delta = 1$ is shown in Figure 10.1.

Suppose next that the measurement of y(x) for $x \simeq 0.5$ is available and the value of the Frechet derivative L is calculated at this point. For this value of L, making use of Lemma 4, the following estimates for δ are obtained.

(a) The exact solution.

The linear eigenvalue problem for equation (10.11) takes the form:

$$\frac{d^2\phi}{dx^2} + \frac{2}{x} \frac{d\phi}{dx} + \lambda^*\phi = 0 \qquad (10.12)$$

$$\phi(1) = \phi'(0) = 0 \qquad (10.12a)$$

$$\lambda^* = -\lambda L = -\lambda\delta^2\beta \qquad (10.12b)$$

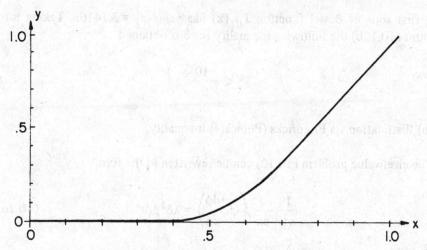

Figure 10.1. The solution of equation 10.11.

Substituting $\xi = \sqrt{\lambda^*}\, x$ into (10.12) we obtain

$$\frac{d^2\phi}{d\xi^2} + \frac{2}{\xi}\,\frac{d\phi}{d\xi} + \phi = 0 \qquad (10.13)$$

which is Bessel's equation

$$u'' + \frac{2}{z}\,u' + \left[1 - \frac{k(k+1)}{z^2}\right] u = 0$$

for $k = 0$.

The general solution of equation (10.13) has the form

$$\phi = C_1 j_0(\sqrt{\lambda^*}\, x) + C_2 n_0(\sqrt{\lambda^*}\, x) \qquad (10.14)$$

where

$$j_0(\sqrt{\lambda^*}\, x) = \frac{\pi}{2\sqrt{\lambda^*}\, x}\, J_{1/2}(\sqrt{\lambda^*}\, x)$$

$$n_0(\omega\overline{\lambda^*}\, x) = \frac{\pi}{2\sqrt{\lambda^*}\, x}\, N_{1/2}(\sqrt{\lambda^*}\, x)$$

Eigenfunction (10.14) satisfies boundary condition (10.12) when λ^* is a root of the Bessel function

$$J_{1/2}(\sqrt{\lambda^*}) = 0 \qquad (10.15)$$

The first root of Bessel function $J_{1/2}(x)$ has value $x_1 = 3.1416$. Taking into account (10.12b) the following inequality for δ is obtained

$$\delta^2 < \frac{-10}{\beta}$$

(b) Estimation via Friedricks (Poincaré) inequality.

The eigenvalue problem (10.12) can be rewritten in the form:

$$\frac{1}{x^2} \frac{d}{dx} \left(x^2 \frac{d\phi}{dx} \right) = \lambda \delta^2 \beta \phi \qquad (10.16)$$

Multiplying by x^2 and integrating both sides of (10.16) one can obtain

$$-\int_0^1 x^2 \left(\frac{d\phi}{dx} \right)^2 dx = \lambda \delta^2 \beta \int_0^1 x^2 \phi \, dx \qquad (10.17)$$

By substitution of the inequality:

$$\int_0^1 x^2 \phi^2 \, dx \leqslant \frac{1}{6} \int_0^1 x^2 \left(\frac{d\phi}{dx} \right)^2 dx$$

into (10.17), we finally obtain

$$\delta^2 < -\frac{6}{\beta} \qquad (10.18)$$

(c) Solution of the eigenvalue problem via weighted residuals method.

The differential equation

$$\nabla^2 \phi - \lambda \delta^2 \beta \phi = 0 \qquad (10.19)$$

can be transformed to the algebraic form using the method of weighted residuals (see Appendix IV).

In this method the Laplacian can be substituted by the matrix M, the elements m_{ij} of which are taken from the tables.

Equation (10.19) in matrix notation has the form

$$\sum_{i=1}^{N+1} m_{ij}\phi_i - \lambda\beta\delta^2\phi_j = 0 \tag{10.20}$$

$$\phi_{N+1} = 0$$

Using only one term approximation (N = 1) we get

$$-10.5\phi_1 + 10.5\phi_2 - \lambda\delta^2\beta\phi_1 = 0 \tag{10.21}$$

$$\phi_2 = 0$$

Finally,

$$\delta^2 < \frac{-10.5}{\beta} \tag{10.22}$$

(d) Finite difference method.

To solve differential equation (10.12) the finite difference scheme can be used (Collatz 1963).

Dividing the interval (0, 1) into N equal parts (say 2) and at the point $x = \frac{1}{2}$ evaluating the first and second derivatives we obtain

$$\frac{\phi_0 - 2\phi_1 + \phi_2}{h^2} + \frac{2}{h}\frac{\phi_2 - \phi_1}{h} = \lambda\delta^2\beta\phi_1 \tag{10.23}$$

where

$$\phi_0 = \phi(0)$$
$$\phi_1 = \phi(\tfrac{1}{2})$$
$$\phi_2 = \phi(1)$$
$$h = \tfrac{1}{2}$$

Taking into account the boundary conditions

$$\phi'(0) \simeq \frac{\phi_1 - \phi_0}{h} = 0$$

$$\phi(1) = \phi(2) = 0$$

and substituting into (10.23), finally the requirement $\lambda > 1$ leads to the inequality

$$\delta^2 < \frac{-12}{\beta} \tag{10.24}$$

Remark 2. The values of the parameter δ obtained from (10.15), (10.18), (10.22) and (10.24) give only the rough estimation of the one side of the region of possibly multiple solutions.

The exact values of δ obtained via computer calculation have been presented by Weisz and Hicks (1965).

10.4   THE BIFURCATION POINTS OF NONLINEAR OPERATORS

In linear systems the eigenvalues and eigenvectors of the linear operators play a very important role. They determine the stability of the whole system, sensitivity to changes in the parameters, etc.

Both analysis and synthesis techniques developed for linear systems require that one of the first steps in the treatment of nonlinear systems be linearization.

The most important question which arises is: Under what conditions is the linearization valid? An intuitive answer is that one can linearize the system when the properties of the original system and its linearized version are the "same" for certain values of parameters, signals, class of disturbances, etc.

The location of the eigenvalues of the linear operator (or alternatively the poles of the transfer function) determine also the classification of the linear system and prompts the choice of control techniques (simplification, the choice of the type of controllers, etc.). One should expect that the eigenvalues and eigenvectors of nonlinear operators have even richer properties than in linear systems. Let us study the problem more carefully.

The vector $\underline{\phi} \in E$ is called an eigenvector of the (nonlinear) operator A, acting in the Banach space E, if there exists a number λ such that

$$A\underline{\phi} = \lambda\underline{\phi} \tag{10.25}$$

The reciprocal of an eigenvalue λ is called a characteristic value μ.

Let us work with the equivalent of equation (10.25) in the form

$$\underline{\phi} = \mu A\underline{\phi} \tag{10.26}$$

For small values of the parameter μ the null solution is unique assuming that $A\underline{\theta} = \underline{\theta}$ ($\underline{\theta}$ is the null solution of the operator A). With the increase of the value of μ, around $\underline{\theta}$ nonzero solution of

$$\underline{\phi} = \mu A \underline{\phi}$$

is obtained.

The number μ_0 is called a bifurcation point if for $\epsilon, \delta > 0$ there exists a number μ, such that

$$|\mu - \mu_0| < \epsilon$$

and for μ there exists at least one eigenfunction ϕ such that $\phi = \mu A \phi$, with norm less than δ.

10.4.1 Krasnosielski Theorem

Let A be a completely continuous operator having a Frechet derivative B at the point θ and satisfying the condition $A\underline{\theta} = \underline{\theta}$. Then each characteristic value μ_0 of odd multiplicity of the linear operator B is a bifurcation point of the operator A, and to this bifurcation point there corresponds a continuous branch of eigenvectors of the operator A.

The Krasnosielski theorem gives the basic tool for examining the nonlinear systems which can be transformed into the integral equation form.

Nonlinear integral operators of Uryson, Hammerstein, and Liapunov type have, under rather wide assumptions, a Frechet derivative B at the origin θ (of the space C or L^P) namely the linear integral operator of the form

$$B\phi(s) = \int K(s, t)\, \phi(t)\, dt \qquad (10.27)$$

It follows from Krasnosielski's theorem that each characteristic value of odd multiplicity of the kernel $K(s, t)$ is a bifurcation point of the corresponding nonlinear operator.

Examples of kernels, all the eigenvalues of which have unit multiplicity (simple eigenvalues) are the Green's function of boundary value problem for the Sturm-Liouville equation.

Bifurcation of the Fixed Point

In description and identification of nonlinear systems a crucial role is played by the concept of weak perturbation on nonlinear operator A. In order to explain the importance of this concept let us return to linear systems.

Let the linear system be described in the matrix form:

$$\left. \begin{array}{l} \dot{\underline{x}} = A\underline{x} + B\underline{u} \\ \underline{x}(0) = 0 \end{array} \right\} \tag{10.28}$$

In the open loop configuration the system is described by the matrix A and during identification the perturbation of its elements (parameters of the system) is evaluated.

The estimation of eigenvalues and their standard deviations leads to the notation

$$A = A^0 + \delta A \tag{10.29}$$

where

A^0 = matrix of the system described by the mean value of parameters of the
   matrix A
δA = perturbation (deviation) of matrix A.

In the models designed for control processes, the input signal u is a linear combination of the state variables, i.e., $\underline{u} = K\underline{x}$ and the whole system can be treated as an autonomous system

$$\dot{\underline{x}} = A\underline{x} + F\underline{x}, \qquad F = BK \tag{10.30}$$

where the matrix F can be treated as a perturbation matrix. In nonlinear systems the following equation has been studied

$$\dot{\phi} = A\phi + \epsilon F\phi \tag{10.31}$$

where

A is a nonlinear operator
F is the smooth operator, and
ϵ is a sufficiently small number.

The goal of mathematical investigations is to determine the numbers and topological types of solution of equation (10.31). This problem corresponds to investigation of bifurcation points of the nonlinear operator A.

In engineering, the problem of finding the bifurcation points of nonlinear operator A is usually linearized: Instead of operator A we consider the linear operator B (the Frechet derivative of the operator A at the point) and find the characteristic values of the linear operator B. If operator B does not have the number 1 as a characteristic value in the neighborhood of a fixed point ψ_0, there exists only one fixed point of (10.31).

If the operator B has the number 1 in its spectrum, different cases should be considered.

The point ψ_0 is called the point of bifurcation of the fixed point (solutions) if for small perturbation ϵF the equation $\underline{\psi} = A\underline{\psi} + \epsilon F\underline{\psi}$ has more than one solution in the neighborhood of $\underline{\psi}_0$.

At the point of bifurcation the topological type of the solution changes. The type of these changes depends on the kind of nonlinearities and the analysis of these changes can give a good judgment about the type of leading nonlinearities.

EXAMPLE 10.3

Let us consider the case where $x_0(\eta)$ is an equilibrium solution for x in an interval $a \leqslant \eta \leqslant b$ of the equation:

$$f(\eta, x_0(\eta)) = 0 \tag{10.32}$$

Suppose that as η crosses η_0, $a < \eta_0 < b$, some of the eigenvalues of $B(\eta) = \partial f_i / \partial x_j (\eta, x_0(\eta))$ cross the imaginary axis. Thus for $\eta < \eta_0$, $x_0(\eta)$ is stable, while $x_0(\eta)$ becomes unstable when $\eta > \eta_0$. (This statement is a version of the Lyapunov theorem.)

This is where the phenomenon of bifurcation occurs. At the point $x_0(\eta_0)$, the change in the topological type of the solution of (10.32) has taken place.

The number and the type of bifurcation solution of (10.31) can be obtained on the basis of analytical considerations but usually it is a very difficult task. In the sequel one typical engineering problem with a nonlinear operator will be analyzed.

Let us consider that the operator A can be rewritten in the following form:

$$A\psi = B\psi + C\psi + D\psi \qquad \psi \in E \tag{10.33}$$

where C and D are completely continuous operators having the following properties:

(a) operator C satisfies the equality

$$C(\lambda\underline{\psi}) = \lambda^\kappa C\psi, \qquad \kappa > 1 \tag{10.34}$$

and is of the Lipschitz type, i.e.,

$$\|C\underline{\psi}_1 - C\underline{\psi}_2\| \leqslant g(\rho)\|\underline{\psi}_1 - \underline{\psi}_2\| \qquad (\|\underline{\psi}_1\|, \|\underline{\psi}_2\| \leqslant \rho) \qquad (10.35)$$

$$\lim_{\rho \to 0} \frac{g(\rho)}{k-1} < \infty \qquad (10.36)$$

(b) operator D satisfies equality

$$\lim_{\|\underline{\psi}\| \to 0} \frac{\|D\psi\|}{\|\underline{\psi}\|^\kappa} = 0 \qquad (10.37)$$

It can be shown (Krasnosielski 1964) that in typical examples operators B, C, and D can be effectively obtained.

EXAMPLE 10.4

For the nonlinear operator of Uhryson type

$$A\psi(s) = \int_\Omega K[s, t, \psi(t)] \, dt \qquad (10.38)$$

under the following assumptions:

$$K_u^{(k)}(s, t, u) \quad \text{exists for s, } t \in \Omega \text{ and } |u| \text{ limited}$$

$$K(s, t, 0) \equiv 0$$

the operators B and C have the following forms:

$$B\psi(s) = \int_\Omega \frac{\partial K(s, t, 0)}{\partial u} \, \psi(t) \, dt \qquad (10.39)$$

and

$$C\psi(s) = \frac{1}{k!} \int_\Omega \frac{\partial^k K(s, t, 0)}{\partial u^k} \, \psi^k(t) \, dt \qquad (10.40)$$

when

$$\frac{\partial^2 K(s, t, 0)}{\partial u^2} \equiv \cdots \equiv \frac{\partial^{k-1} K(s, t, 0)}{\partial u^{k-1}} \equiv 0$$

In the case when $\partial^2 K(s, t, 0)/\partial u^2 \neq 0$, the operator C has the form

$$C\psi(s) = \frac{1}{2} \int_{\Omega} \frac{\partial^2 K(s, t, 0)}{\partial u^2} \psi^2(t) \, dt \qquad (10.41)$$

For the nonlinear operator of Hammerstein type

$$A\psi(s) = \int_{\Omega} K(s, t) f[t, \psi(t)] \, dt \qquad (10.42)$$

under the assumption that the differentiation $\partial^k/\partial u^k \, f(t, u)$ is permissible, the operators B and C have the forms

$$B\psi(s) = \int_{\Omega} K(s, t) \frac{\partial f(t, 0)}{\partial u} \psi(t) \, dt \qquad (10.43)$$

and

$$C\psi(s) = \frac{1}{k!} \int_{\Omega} K(s, t) \frac{\partial^k f(t, 0)}{\partial u^k} \psi^k(t) \, dt \qquad (10.44)$$

when

$$\frac{\partial^2 f(t, 0)}{\partial u^2} \equiv \cdots \equiv \frac{\partial^{k-1} f(t, 0)}{\partial u^{k-1}} \equiv 0 \qquad (s, t) \in \Omega$$

Let us consider the case when the decomposition of the operator A into the form

$$A(\psi, \eta) = B(\psi, \eta) + C_\kappa(\psi, \eta) + D(\psi, \eta) \qquad (10.45)$$

is valid.

In the case when $B(\psi, \eta)$ for all values of the parameters η does not possess 1 as the eigenvalue, the linearization is sufficient for engineering considerations and the utilization of the linear model is legitimate.

In the case when 1 belongs to the spectrum of the operator B, the bifurcation of the fixed point occurs and linearization is no longer valid.

The types of the bifurcation solutions depends on the operators B' and C.

10.4.2 Classification of Bifurcated Solutions

Let for certain values of parameters of unperturbed operator A the eigenvalues of its linear part B be denoted by the vector λ_0. The perturbation of the operator A causes changes of these eigenvalues.

Let the spectrum of perturbed A occupy the interval $\lambda_1 < \lambda_0 < \lambda_2$. For some operator A the small solution (as a result of small perturbation) of the equation.

$$\psi = A(\psi, \eta)$$

may exist both for $\lambda_1 < \lambda_0$ and $\lambda_2 > \lambda_0$.

Another type of operators A (more often met in engineering) can have small solution only for $\lambda_1 < \lambda_0$ or $\lambda_2 > \lambda_0$.

Let us examine the case when only "one-sided" solutions can occur. This problem can be solved on the basis of Liapunov-Schmidt procedure (Liapunov 1906, Schmidt 1908) in which the concept of the fixed point of singular vector field can be incorporated (Krasnosielski 1964).

Let us assume that 1 is an eigenvalue of the operator B

$$B_0 \underline{\psi} = B(\underline{\psi}, \eta_0) \tag{10.46}$$

and with this eigenvalue is connected an eigenvector e_0

$$B_0 \underline{e_0} = \underline{e_0}, \qquad \| \underline{e_0} \| = 1 \tag{10.47}$$

Let g be an eigenvector of the adjoint operator B^*

$$B^* \underline{g_0} = \underline{g_0} \tag{10.48}$$

such that the scalar product $(\underline{e_0}, \underline{g_0}) = 1$.

Suppose that the linear operator can be written in the following form

$$B(\underline{\psi}, \lambda) = B_0 \underline{\psi} + (\lambda - \lambda_0) B_1 \underline{\psi} + 0(\lambda - \lambda_0) \tag{10.49}$$

and the condition

$$\alpha_0 = -(B_1 \underline{e_0}, \underline{g_0}) \neq 0 \tag{10.50}$$

is satisfied.

Suppose next that

$$\alpha_1 = (C_k(\underline{e_0}, \lambda_0), \underline{g_0}) \neq 0 \tag{10.51}$$

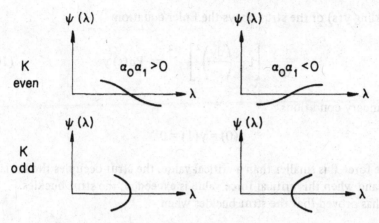

Figure 10.2.   Bifurcation solutions of equation 10.49.

According to theorem 5.3 and 5.4 (Krasnosielski 1964), a "one-sided" solution occurs when

(a) k is odd
(b) $(\lambda - \lambda_0) \alpha_0 \alpha_1 > 0$ (i.e., $(\lambda - \lambda_0) (B_1 e_0, g_0) (C_K e_0, g_0) < 0$)

For k even, small solutions for $\lambda < \lambda_0$ and $\lambda > \lambda_0$ are possible. The above results can be summarized in the following statement.

If during the perturbation of the operator A bifurcation happens only for $\lambda - \lambda_0$ of the given sign, the first nonzero term in the Taylor series expansion of the operator A should be of the odd order.

The possible bifurcations of the function are outlined in Figure 10.2.

EXAMPLE 10.5

Let us consider an elastic strut, fixed at one end and compressed under force P at the other, as shown in Figure 10.3.

Suppose, that strut is of unit length and the modulus of elasticity is

$$\rho(s) = 1/EJ$$

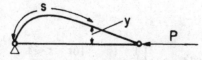

Figure 10.3.   An elastic strut.

The buckling $y(s)$ of the strut obeys the Euler equation

$$\frac{d^2 y}{ds^2} \left[1 - \left(\frac{dy}{ds} \right)^2 \right]^{-1/2} = -P\rho(s)\, y \tag{10.52}$$

with boundary conditions

$$y(0) = y(1) = 0$$

When the force P is smaller than a critical value, the strut occupies the horizontal position and when this critical force value is exceeded, the strut buckles.

Euler has proved that the strut buckles when

$$P = \rho\pi^2$$

Let us analyze this problem from the point of view of the fixed point bifurcation theory (Krasnosielski 1964).

Let

$$y''(s) = -\psi(s) \tag{10.53}$$

and

$$y(0) = y(1) = 0$$

then

$$y(s) = \int_0^1 G(s, t)\, \psi(t)\, dt$$

where $G(s, t)$ is the Green's function

$$G(s, t) = \begin{cases} s(1 - t) & \text{for } s \leqslant t \\ t(1 - s) & \text{for } s > t \end{cases} \tag{10.54}$$

The derivative $y'(s)$ is given by

$$y'(s) = \int_0^1 G_s'(s, t)\, \psi(t)\, dt \tag{10.55}$$

where

$$G_s'(s, t) = \begin{cases} 1 - t & \text{for } s < t \\ -t & \text{for } s > t \end{cases} \tag{10.56}$$

therefore, the differential equation can be substituted by the integral equation:

$$\psi(s) = P\rho(s) \int_0^1 G(s, t)\, \psi(t)\, dt \left\{ 1 - \left[\int_0^1 G(s, t)'\, \psi(t)\, dt \right]^2 \right\}^{1/2}$$

$$= A\psi(s) \tag{10.57}$$

The buckling occurs when the bifurcation of (10.57) for variable P takes place.
The Frechet derivative of the operator A has form

$$B\psi(s) = P\rho(s) \int_0^1 G(s, t)\, \psi(t)\, dt \tag{10.58}$$

and its spectrum is identical with the spectrum generated by Sturm-Liouville
equation:

$$y''(s) + \lambda\rho(s)\, y(s) = y''(s) + \mu y(s) \qquad y(0) = y(1) = 0 \tag{10.59}$$

The eigenvalues of equation (10.58) are

$$\mu_n = n^2 \pi^2 \qquad \text{for} \quad n = 1, 2, \dots \tag{10.60}$$

For $n = 1$ the critical value of the compressing force P_0 is

$$P_0 = \rho \pi^2 \tag{10.61}$$

Equation (10.51) can be rewritten in the following form

$$\psi(s) = P\rho(s) \int_0^1 G(s, t)\, \psi(t)\, dt - PC_3 \psi(s) + O(\|\psi^4\|) \tag{10.62}$$

where

$$C_3 \psi(s) = \tfrac{1}{2}\, \rho(s) \int_0^1 G(s, t)\, \psi(t)\, dt \left[\int_0^1 G_s'(s, t)\, \psi(t)\, dt \right]^2 \tag{10.63}$$

Taking into account, that

$$e_0 = \text{const} \cdot \sin \pi \rho s$$

$$B_1 = B_0$$

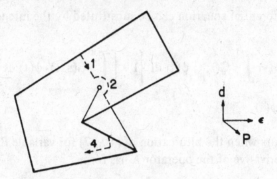

Figure 10.4.　Cusp catastrophe for Euler buckling.

and substituting (10.61) into (10.46)–(10.51) one can obtain

$$\alpha_0 > 0$$
$$\alpha_1 < 0$$

and

$$\alpha_0 \alpha_1 < 0$$

Therefore one should expect the bifurcation of the type presented in the lower-right hand corner of Figure 10.2.

The steady states obtained after bifurcation can also be analyzed by means of catastrophe theory which makes use of a visual topological approach in attempting to explain bifurcation phenomena.

The Euler strut obeys the cusp catastrophe presented in Figure 10.4 (Chillingworth 1974, Zeeman 1975).

In Figure 10.4 the following symbols are used:

P = compressing force
d = deflection of center of beam
ϵ = shift of the force P from the beam axis.

The dotted path shows the arch (1) compressed, (2) buckling upwards, (3) loaded, and (4) snapping downwards.

From Figure 10.4 the following cross-sections can be obtained (Figure 10.5).

More detailed analyses including cases for $\epsilon \neq 0$ are presented in Appendix IV.

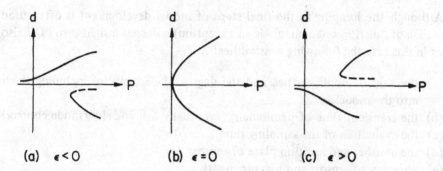

Figure 10.5. The steady states after bifurcation for different imperfections of compressing force position.

10.5 IDENTIFICATION OF DISTRIBUTED PARAMETER SYSTEMS

In general there are two ways to identify systems which are regarded as distributed. One is based on the input-output technique, the second is based on investigation and transformation of the set of partial differential equations that are believed to describe the system.

The input-output technique is basically the same as that used in lumped parameter systems in which delays are added. In a sampled version of input-output identification, the same algorithm is used as in lumped parameter systems—the delays are simultaneously computed with the other values of model parameters. This approach can give successful results even for complicated distributed parameter systems for control purposes (cf. the works of Akaike (1974) concerning the models of a cement rotary kiln).

An alternative to input-output identification is the investigation of partial differential equations which are assumed to describe the system. The advantage of this approach is the possibility of obtaining a model suitable for control purposes. Furthermore, for this model the different possible operating points can be evaluated, and the results of changes in the technology, measurements, kinds of disturbances, and ways of their compensation, etc. can be considered.

The disadvantages are:

(i)   the relatively complicated mathematical apparatus,
(ii) the necessity of individual treatment of each particular process, and
(iii) the "lumping" of the system to get a model for control purposes. This last item is the main objection directed to the identification with PDE technique.

Although the lumping in the final steps of model development is often used (the case of "distributed control" is an exception) a deeper insight into PDE also gives in this case the following possibilities:

(a) the role of nonlinearities and the degree of necessity of including them into the model
(b) the transient time of phenomena (eventually fast and slow mode control)
(c) the evaluation of the sampling time
(d) the number and location place of sensors
(e) accuracy of sensors and measurements.

The transformation of distributed parameter systems into lumped parameter systems (partial differential equations into ordinary differential equations) plays an important role in model utilization for control. This subject is treated below.

10.6   LUMPING OF DISTRIBUTED PARAMETER SYSTEMS

The goal of the procedure called lumping is the transformation of the partial differential equation into a set of ordinary differential equations.

There are three groups of methods for lumping of PDE:

(a) high order difference scheme
(b) Laplace transformation of PDE
(c) Galerkin's method

10.6.1.   In order to use the high order difference scheme one should choose a set of $N + 1$ mesh points $x_0, x_1, \ldots, x_N$ at which the derivatives and the function R of PDE

$$\frac{\partial u}{\partial t} = L(u) + R(x, u), \qquad u(x, t) \in \Omega$$

$$u(0, x) = \psi(x) \qquad \Omega = (0, 1) \times (0, T) \tag{10.64}$$

$$\alpha \frac{\partial u}{\partial x} + \beta u = \gamma = \psi(t) \qquad x \in \partial\Omega$$

can be evaluated (Collins and Khatri 1969, Hlavacek and Kubicek 1971).

The kth derivative at any given point can be approximated by a combination of the values of u at all grid points

$$u^{(k)}(x_i) = u^{(k)} = \sum_{j=0}^{N} C_{ij} u(x_j) = \sum_{j=0}^{N} C_{ij} u_j \tag{10.65}$$

Assuming that the sequence of functions $u = 1$, $u = x$, ..., $u = x^N$ obeys equation (10.65) one can get

$$\sum_{j=0}^{N} C_{ij} = 0$$

$$\sum_{j=0}^{N} C_{ij} x_j = 0$$

$$\overline{\sum_{j=0}^{N} C_{ij} x_j^{k-1} = 0} \qquad (10.66)$$

$$\sum_{j=0}^{N} C_{ij} x_j^{k} = k!$$

$$\overline{\sum_{i=0}^{N} C_{ij} x_j^{N} = \frac{N!}{(N-k)!} x_i^{N-k}}$$

The linear differential operator may then be replaced by a linear combination of the values of the function u at the mesh points. The mesh points can be selected on the basis of spline theory (Shridhar and Balatoni 1973). Equation (10.64) can be rewritten in a lumped form

$$\frac{du_i(t)}{dt} = L_i(u_0, u_1, \ldots, u_N) + R(x_i, u_i) \qquad u_i(0) = \psi(x_i) \quad (10.67)$$

10.6.2 Laplace Transformation of PDE (linear case) (Butkovski 1961, 1975)

The use of the Laplace transformation with respect to t leads to a lumped parameter system.

Equation (10.64) is equivalent to the system of ODE with parameters

$$sU(x, s) = L(x, s) + R(x, s) + \psi(x) \qquad (10.68)$$

Equation (10.68) can be transformed to algebraic equation using Laplace transformation with respect to x

$$sU(p, s) = L(p, s) + R(p, s) + \psi(p) + \psi(s) \qquad (10.69)$$

The disadvantage of this method is the restriction of its use only for linear PDE. Also the inverse Laplace transformation can be cumbersome in many cases.

10.6.3. The Galerkin method is a frequently used tool for solving differential equations. Intuitively applied for engineering problems (since 1915) it has become a useful tool also in pure mathematical works (the general proof of the Galerkin method appeared in 1942).

The general idea of Galerkin's method is that the solution of a differential equation can be presented in the form

$$u(x, t) = \sum_{i=0}^{\infty} a_i(t)\, \psi_i(x) \simeq \sum_{i=0}^{N} a_i(t)\, \psi_i(x) \tag{10.70}$$

assuming that (10.70) is convergent.

The most frequently used set of base functions $\psi_i(x)$ are eigenfunctions of the eigenproblem (Butkovskij 1961):

$$L\psi(x) + \lambda\psi(x) = 0 \tag{10.71}$$

Substitution of (10.70) into (10.64) gives the set of ordinary differential equations.

In many cases the base functions can be found on the basis of analysis of the physical system behavior. Each assumed mode (i.e., $a_i(t)\,\psi_i(x)$) may be regarded as a primitive pattern of behavior and any complicated pattern can be approximated by a superposition of assumed modes (Clymer 1966).

One can find assumed modes that can guarantee more rapid convergence than the modes found on the basis of equation (10.71).

The method of weighted residuals (cf. Appendix III) gives a practical routine of the utilization of Galerkin's method for solving PDE. In this method the base functions are the orthogonal Jacobi (Legendre) polynomials and the mesh points $(x_1, x_2, \ldots, x_n, x_{n+1} = 1)$ are selected as the roots of these polynomials.

Using approximations

$$\frac{\partial u_i}{\partial x_j} = \sum_{j=1}^{n+1} A_{ij} u_j \tag{10.72}$$

and

$$\nabla^2 u_i = \sum_{j=1}^{n+1} B_{ij} u_j \tag{10.73}$$

and substituting (10.72) and (10.73) into (10.74) the problem is rewritten in ODE form.

The general question which arises is under what conditions the resulting system of ODEs is equivalent (and in which sense) to the system of PDEs?

The convergence of Galerkin's method applied to the quasilinear parabolic systems was treated by Vishik (1961).

The equation is of the form in $\Omega \times (0, T)$

$$\frac{\partial u}{\partial t} + L(u) = h(x, t) \qquad (10.74)$$

where:

$$L(u) = \sum_{|\alpha|, |\gamma| \leqslant m} (-1)^{|\alpha|} D_\alpha A_\alpha(x, t, D_\gamma, u)$$

$$D_\alpha = \frac{\partial^{|\alpha|}}{\partial x_{\alpha_1} \cdots \partial x_{\alpha_n}}$$

$$h = [h^1, \ldots, h^M]$$

$$\alpha = [\alpha_1, \ldots, \alpha_n]$$

$$|\alpha| = \alpha_1 + \cdots + \alpha_n$$

The initial and boundary conditions are

$$u(x, 0) = \psi(x)$$

$$u = \phi(x, t), \ldots, D_w u = \phi_w(x, t) \qquad \text{for} \quad x \in \partial\Omega \times (0, T)$$

$$|w| \leqslant m - 1 \qquad (10.75)$$

The solution of the quasilinear problem is a function satisfying the initial and boundary conditions and

$$\int_0^T \left[\left(\frac{\partial u}{\partial t}, v \right) + \sum_{|\alpha|, |\gamma| \leqslant m} (A_\alpha(x, t, D_\gamma u), D_\alpha v) \right] dt = \int_0^T (h, v) \, dt \qquad (10.76)$$

for any function v satisfying the homogeneous boundary conditions with $\psi_j = 0$. The generalized solution is unique when the nonlinear operator is the semiboundness of L(u):

$$\sum_{|\alpha|,|\beta| < m} A_{\alpha\beta}(x, t, D_{\gamma}w D_{\beta}v, D_{\alpha}v)$$

$$\geqslant C^2 \left(\sum_{j,|\alpha|=m} |D_{\alpha}w^j|^{\delta j} D_{\alpha}v^j, Dv^j \right) - K(v,v) \quad (10.77)$$

where

$$A_{\alpha\beta} = \frac{\partial A_{\alpha}}{\partial D_{\beta}}$$

and w, v are arbitrary sufficiently smooth functions satisfying the homogeneous boundary conditions.

The application of the Vishik criterion may be cumbersome. A more convenient criterion valid for operator equations can be found in (Krasnosielski 1964) and can be stated as follows:

Let the point ψ_0 be a solution of the equation

$$\psi = A\psi \quad (10.78)$$

and assume that the operator A has a Frechet derivative B.

Suppose that the Galerkin's presentation of ψ is convergent:

$$\psi = \sum_{i=1}^{\infty} G_i(\psi) g_i \quad (10.79)$$

where

$G_i(\psi), i = 1, 2, \ldots$ are continuous operators.

The following theorems are true:

1. Galerkin's approximation

$$\psi = \sum_{i=1}^{n} G_i(\psi) g_i$$

of equation (10.78) exists for sufficiently large n.

2. If 1 does not belong to the spectrum of the operator B, then the following inequality is valid

$$\left\| \psi_n - \psi_0 \right\| \leqslant (1 + \epsilon_n) \left\| \sum_{i=n+1}^{\infty} G_i(\psi_0) g_i \right\|$$

$$\epsilon_n \to 0 \quad \text{for} \quad n \to \infty \tag{10.80}$$

Galerkin's method can handle problems the solutions of which contain singularities, whereas finite difference methods become unstable as a singularity is approached (boundary layer problem, bifurcation, etc.).

For these reasons Galerkin's method is recommended for lumping of the PDE because the vital physical properties can survive. The basic disadvantage of lumping is that the resulting system of ODE contains a set of dummy coefficients in the place of physical ones. Therefore the identification of DPS thought as an identification of LPS can give only bounds of these coefficients from which the bounds of physical parameters should be deciphered.

10.7   REFERENCES

Akaike, H. (1971), "Autoregressive model fitting for control," *Ann. Inst. Statist. Math.*, vol. 23, pp. 163–180.

Amundson, N. R. (1965), "Some further observations on tubular reactor stability," *The Canadian J. of Chem. Eng.*, vol. 3, pp. 49–55.

Aris, R. (1965), *Introduction to the Analysis of Chemical Reactors*, Prentice-Hall, Inc., Englewood Cliffs, N.J.

Butkovskij, A. G. (1961), "Some approximate methods for solving . . . ," *Automation and Telemechanics*, vol. 22, no. 12, pp. 1565–1575.

Butkovskij, A. G. (1975), "The theory of block structures of distributed parameter systems," in: *Proceedings of VI IFAC Congress*, Boston, paper no. 1.5.

Chillingworth, D. (1974), "The catastrophe of a bucking beam," (*Dynamical Systems—Warwick*), *Lecture Notes in Maths.*, vol. 468, Springer-Verlag, New York.

Clymer, A. B. (1966), "Methods of Simulating Structural Dynamics," *Simulation*, vol. 7, pp. 171–184.

Collatz, L. (1963), *Eigenwertaufgaben mit Technischen Anwendungen*, Geest Portig K. G., Leipzig.

Collins, P. L. and H. C. Khatri (1969), "Identification of distributed parameters using finite differencies," *Trans. ASME, J. Basic Engineering*, vol. 91, ser. D, no. 2, pp. 239–245.

Finlayson, B. A. (1972), *The Method of Weighted Residuals and Variational Principles*, Academic Press, New York.

Gavalas, G. R. (1966), "On the steady states of distributed parameter systems with chemical reactions, heat, and mass transfer," *Chem. Eng. Sci.*, vol. 21, pp. 477–492.

Gavalas, G. R. (1968), *Nonlinear Differential Equations of Chemically Reacting Systems*, Springer-Verlag, New York.

Hlavacek, V., and M. Kubicek (1971), "Transformation of the distributed parameter systems to the lumped parameter systems," *IFAC Symposium on Digital Simulation of Continuous Processes* (Gyor–Hungary).

Il'lin, A. M., A. S. Kalashnikov, and O. A. Oleiniko (1962), *Russ. Math. Survs.*, vol. 17, No. 31.

Krasnosielski, M. A. (1964), *Topological Methods in the Theory of Nonlinear Integral Equations*, Pergamon Press, New York.

Krasnosielski, M. A., et al. (1969), *Approximate Methods for Solving the Operator Equations*, Nauka, Moscow.

Krasnosielski, M. A. and P. P. Zabreiko (1975), *Geometric Methods of Nonlinear Analysis*, Nauka, Moscow.

Kuszta, B. and Bailey, J. E. (1982), "Nonlinear model identification by analysis of feedback-stimulated bifurcation," *IEEE Transactions. on Automatic Control*, vol. AC-27, pp. 227–228.

Liapunov, A. M. (1906), "Sur les figures d'equlibre pen differentes des elli psoides d'une masse liquide homogene dounee d'un mouvement de rotation," *Premier partie. Etude generale du probleme. Notes of Academy of Sciences*, Saint Petersburg, pp. 1–225.

Luss, D., and N. R. Amudson (1965), "Some general observations on tubular reactor stability," *Canadian J. of Chem. Eng.*, vol. 45, pp. 341–346.

Luss, D., and J. C. M. Lee (1968), "On global stability in distributed parameter systems," *Chem. Eng. Sci.*, vol. 23, pp. 1237–1248.

Mikhlin, S. G. and K. L. Smolitskij (1968), *Approximate Methods for Solutions of Differential and Integral Equations*, Elsevier, New York.

Palis, M. P. and Goodson, R. E. (1976), "Parameter identification in distributed systems: A synthesizing overview," *Proceedings IEEE*, vol. 64, No. 1, pp. 45–61.

Parks, J. R. (1961), "Criticality criteria of various configurations of a self-heating chemical as functions of activation energy and temperature of assembly," *J. of Chem. Physics*, vol. 34.

Root, R. B. and R. A. Schmitz (1965), "An experimental study of steady state multiplicity in a loop reactor," *AIChE J.*, vol. 15, pp. 670–679.

Schmidt, E. (1908), "Zur Theorie der linearen und nichlinearen Integralgleichungen," III Teil, *Math. Ann.*, vol. 65, pp. 370–399.

Shridhar, M. and N. P. Balatoni (1973), "Application of cubic splines to system identification," *3rd IFAC Symposium on Identification and System Parameter Estimation*, The Hague, pp. 787–791.

Stewart, W. E., and J. V. Villadsen (1969), "Graphical calculation of multiple steady states and effectiveness factors for porous catalysts," *AIChE J.*, vol. 15, pp. 28–34.

Thoma, J. U. (1974), *Grundlagen und Anwendungen der Bonddiagramme*, Verlag W. Girardet.

van Dixhoorn, J. J. (1974) and P. J. Evans (editors), *Physical Structure in Systems Theory*, Academic Press.

Vishik, M. I. (1961), "Boundary value problems for quasilinear parabolic systems of equations and Cauchy's problem for hyperbolic equations," *Soviet Mathematics (Doklady)*, vol. 2, no. 5, pp. 1292–1295.

Weisz, P. B. and J. S. Hicks (1965), "The behaviour of porous catalyst particles in view of internal mass and heat diffusion effects," *Chem. Eng. Sci.*, 20, pp. 729–736.

Zeeman, E. C. (1975), "Euler bucking," in: *Lectures Notes in Mathematics*, vol. 525, Springer-Verlag, New York.

11
Identification of Nonlinear Systems

11.1 INTRODUCTION

We focus our attention on processes that can be described by means of a set of ordinary nonlinear differential equations (ODE). These equations can be obtained in different ways. The set of ODE:

(a) are believed to describe the lumped nonlinear process
(b) are the result of lumping of nonlinear partial differential equations
(c) are the result of transformation of boundary problems of linear ordinary equations.

The problem of identification of nonlinear systems can be divided into two groups: identification of deterministic systems (noise free situation) and stochastic systems (existence of plant and observation noise). The latter can be solved by means of the Extended Kalman Filter method in which the system is linearized along the reference trajectory, then transformed into a discrete-time equivalent form.

A combined parameter and state estimation procedure is then used, as discussed in Chapter 9. The Extended Kalman Filter method assumes validity of linearization, which makes it similar to Bellman's quasilinearization method (Chen, 1970).

In the case when the system cannot be linearized, a bifurcation technique for model structure and parameter identification is suggested.

Irrespective of their origin a unified approach for the identification of parameters and verification of the models can be used. The basic questions which arise are:

(i) How to evaluate the coefficients of the given set of ODE?

193

(ii)   What kind of data should be collected to carry out such evaluation?

(iii) What limits the accuracy in identification?

(iv) How to evaluate the model fitting the process?

(v)   What should be changed in the model when it is suspected that it is an inadequate representation of the process?

(vi) How to incorporate small imperfections in the model and describe subtle phenomena?

In this chapter we present an attempt to answer all of these questions except question (iv), which will be discussed in Chapter 14. Due to their profoundness we do not pretend to answer them completely, but rather put a little light on some vital questions which arise in nonlinear system identification.

This chapter is organized as follows:

In section 11.2 we describe the identification of the parameters incorporated to a set of ODE. This problem leads to the solution of the Two-Point Boundary Value Problem (TPBVP) discussed in section 11.3, in which the question of the "initial guess," which affects the possibility of obtaining reasonable solution of TPBVP, will also be considered.

Section 11.4 will be devoted to the description of the Riccati Transformation which is used to evaluate the initial conditions for linearized TPBVP. Nonlinear parameter estimation problems via optimization methods will be outlined in sections 11.5 and 11.6.

Problems connected with the last two items of our list of questions will be discussed in section 11.7.

The choice of problems is two fold:

(i)   They are natural continuation of problems discussed in Chapter 10.

(ii) They are introduced in a way in which new mathematical achievements (for example, algebraic topology) can be met.

Many methods used nowadays for nonlinear identification will not be discussed.

References cited by Haber and Kevicky (1976) are a good starting point for further studies.

11.2   PARAMETER IDENTIFICATION IN NONLINEAR SET OF EQUATIONS

Suppose that one is given a set of ODE containing a vector of unknown parameters $\underline{\theta}$:

$$\frac{dy}{dx} = F(\underline{y}, \underline{\theta}, x)$$

$$\underline{y} \in R^N, \qquad x \in [0, 1], \qquad \underline{\theta} \in R^m$$

(11.01)

with

$$y_i(0) = \alpha_i, \qquad y_j(1) = \beta_j,$$

N boundary conditions are obtained from the two end points.

Suppose now that some discrete values of the solution $\underline{y}(x)$ are given, for instance

$$y_i(x_i) = b_i \tag{11.02}$$

Assuming constant values of $\underline{\theta}$, equation (11.01) can be augmented by introducing

$$\dot{\theta} = 0 \tag{11.03}$$

To make a well-posed problem for the augmented set of equations lacking conditions, $\underline{q} = \underline{\theta}(0)$ must be incorporated.

It can be done by minimizing E

$$\frac{dE}{d\underline{\theta}} = 0 \tag{11.04}$$

where

$$E = \sum_{i=1}^{M} (y_i(x_i) - b_i)^2 \tag{11.05}$$

Equations (11.01), (11.03), and (11.04) form a well-posed two-point boundary value problem (TPBVP) which can be solved by the technique of contraction mapping.

11.3   SOLUTION OF NONLINEAR TWO-POINT BOUNDARY VALUE PROBLEMS

Let us consider TPBVP of the form

$$\dot{y} = F(\underline{y}, x)$$
$$g(\underline{y}(0)) + \underline{h}(\underline{y}(1)) = \underline{c} \tag{11.06}$$

where F, $\underline{g}$, $\underline{h}$ are suitable vector-valued functions and $\underline{c}$ is a constant vector.

Solution of (11.06) requires a formal linear TPBVP investigation, thus we devote some attention to linear TPBVP of the form:

$$\dot{y} = V(x) \underline{y}$$
$$M\underline{y}(0) + N\underline{y}(1) = \underline{c}$$

(11.07)

where $V(x)$, M, N are p $\times$ p matrices and $f(x)$ and $\underline{c}$ are p vectors.

A p vector valued function $\psi(x)$ is called a solution of (11.07) if

(i) $\psi(x)$ is absolutely continuous
(ii) $\dot{\psi}(x) = V(x) \psi(x) + f(x)$ for almost all x
(iii) $M\psi(0) + N\psi(1) = \underline{c}$

Let $\phi^V(x, s)$ be the fundamental matrix of the linear system

$$\dot{y} = V(x) \underline{y}$$

The following corollary has been proved by Falb and deJong (1969).

If $\det([M + N\phi^V(1, 0)]) \neq 0$, then (11.07) has a unique solution which can be expressed in the following form

$$\psi(x) = H^{VMN}(x) \underline{c} + \int_0^1 G^{VMN}(x, s) f(s) \, ds$$

(11.08)

where the Green's matrices $H^{VMN}(x)$ and $G^{VMN}(x, s)$ are given by

$$H^{VMN}(x) = \phi^V(x, 0)[M + N\phi^V(1, 0)]^{-1}$$

(11.09)

and

$$G^{VMN}(x, s) = \begin{cases} \phi^V(x, 0)[M + N\phi^V(1, 0)]^{-1}M\phi^V(0, s), & 0 \leqslant s < x \\ -\phi^V(x, 0)[M + N\phi^V(1, 0)]^{-1}N\phi^V(1, s), & x < s \leqslant 1 \end{cases}$$

(11.10)

respectively.

In the sequel, the notion of a boundary compatible set of matrices plays a crucial role (Falb and deJong 1969).

Let $V(x)$, M, N be p $\times$ p matrices. Then the set $\{V(x), M, N\}$ will be called boundary compatible if

(i) $V(x)$ is measurable with $\|V(x)\| \leqslant m(x)$ for an integrable $m(x)$
(ii) $\det[M + N\phi^V(1, 0)] \neq 0$

A necessary and sufficient condition that there be a $V(x)$ with $\{V(x), M, N\}$ boundary compatible is that the $p \times 2p$ matrix $[MN]$ have full rank p.

For nonlinear TPBVP a strong mathematical apparatus has been introduced for integral equation representation (Picard 1929, Kantorovich 1964).

The equivalence between differential equation and integral equation representation of TPBVP is based on the following theorem (Falb and deJong 1969).

Let D be an open set in R_p and let I be an open set in R containing $[0, 1]$. Suppose that

(i) $F(\underline{y}, x)$ is a map of $D \times I$ into D which is measurable in x for each fixed y and continuous in y for each fixed x
(ii) there is an integrable function $m(x)$ such that

$$\|F(\underline{y}, x)\| \leqslant m(x) \quad \text{on} \quad D \times I$$

(iii) $g(\underline{y})$ and $h(\underline{y})$ are maps of D into D, and
(iv) $\underline{y} = \{V(x), \bar{M}, N\}$ is a boundary compatible set of dimension p.

Then the boundary value problem

$$\dot{\underline{y}} = F(\underline{y}, x)$$
$$g(\underline{y}(0)) + h(\underline{y}(1)) = \underline{c} \tag{11.11}$$

has the equivalent representation

$$\underline{y}(x) = H^{VMN}(x) \{\underline{c} - g[\underline{y}(0)] - h[\underline{y}(1)] + M\underline{y}(0) + N\underline{y}(1)\}$$
$$+ \int_0^1 G^{VMN}(x, s) \{F(\underline{y}(s), s) - V(s) \underline{y}(s)\} \, ds = T^J(y) \tag{11.12}$$

where the Green's function $H^{VMN}(x)$ and $G^{VMN}(x, s)$ are given by

$$H^{VMN}(x) = \phi^V(x, 0)[M + N\phi^V(1, 0)]^{-1} \tag{11.13}$$

and

$$G^{VMN}(x, s) = \begin{cases} \phi^V(x, 0)[M + N\phi^V(1, 0)]^{-1}M\phi^V(0, s), & 0 \leqslant s < x \\ -\phi^V(x, 0)[M + N\phi^V(1, 0)]^{-1}N\phi^V(1, s), & x < s \leqslant 1 \end{cases} \tag{11.14}$$

$\phi^V(x, s)$ is the fundamental matrix of the linear system $\dot{y} = V(x) y$.

The conditions that guarantee the convergence of equation (11.12) are difficult to deduce from this theorem. This convergence requires a good initial guess of the solution $\underline{y}(x)$ and appropriate estimates of the norms of (Frechet) derivatives of the integral operator.

Let us consider the convergence problem more precisely. Equation (11.12) is equivalent to the fixed-point problem

$$\underline{y} = T^J(\underline{y}) \tag{11.15}$$

The convergence of the equation (12.15) has been considered by many authors (Kantorovich and Akilov 1964).

In terms of successive sequences, equation (11.12) can be rewritten (Bosorge 1971)

$$u_n(x) + \tau y_0(x) = H^J(x) \{ \tau [\underline{c} - g(y_0(0)) - h(y_0(1)) + My(0) + \underline{c}y(1) \}$$

$$+ \tau \int_0^1 G^J(x, s) \{ F(y_0(s), s) - V(s) y(s) \} \, ds + H^J(x) \tag{11.16}$$

$$\cdot \left\{ \left(M - \frac{\partial g}{\partial y} \Big|_{y_n(0)} \right) u_n(0) + \left(N - \frac{\partial h}{\partial y} \Big|_{y_n(1)} \right) u_n(1) \right\}$$

where

$$u_n = y_{n+1} - y_n$$

$$n = 0, 1, \ldots, N_1$$

$$\tau = \frac{1}{N_1}$$

Equation (11.16) can be rewritten in standard TPBVP form

$$\dot{u}_n = \left[\frac{\partial F}{\partial y} \right] \Big|_{y_n(x)} u_n(x) + \tau_1 [F(y_0(x), x) - \dot{y}_0(x)]$$

$$\left[\frac{\partial F}{\partial y} \right] \Big|_{y_n(0)} u_n(0) + \left[\frac{\partial h}{\partial y} \right] \Big|_{y_n(1)} u_n(1) = \tau_1 [N - g(y_0(0)) - h(y_0(1))], \tag{11.17}$$

$$\text{for} \quad n = 0, 1, \ldots, N_1 - 1$$

and

$$\dot{y}_{n+1} = F(y_n(x), x) + \left[\frac{\partial F}{\partial y}\right]\bigg|_{y_n(x)} (y_{n+1}(x) - y_n(x)),$$

$$g(y_n(0)) + h(y_n(1)) + \left[\frac{\partial g}{\partial y}\right]\bigg|_{y_n(0)} (y_{n+1}(0) - y_n(0)) + \left[\frac{\partial h}{\partial y}\right]\bigg|_{y_n(1)} \qquad (11.18)$$

$$(y_{n+1}(1) - y_n(1)) = \underline{c}$$

As we see the nonlinear TPBVP is decomposed now into two subproblems:

(i) linear TPBVP problem generated by equation (11.17) for $n = 0, 1, \ldots,$
     $N_1 - 1$
(ii) standard quasilinearization equation (11.18) for $n \geqslant N_1$.

In applications it may be easier to compute the Green's function matrices for a boundary compatible set other than J_0. In such cases, the elements of the set

$$\left[\frac{\partial F}{\partial y}\right]\bigg|_{y_0(t)}, \qquad \left[\frac{\partial g}{\partial y}\right]\bigg|_{y_0(0)} \qquad \text{and} \qquad \left[\frac{\partial h}{\partial y}\right]\bigg|_{y_0(1)}$$

are replaced by elements of the new boundary compatible set.

The method described above produces convergent sequences of iterates in cases where the initial iterate (guess), J_0, is "far" from the desired solution.

Nevertheless, a reasonable initial guess should be chosen to ensure the convergence of quasilinearization procedure. In the case, when the Dirichlet type of boundary condition is considered (i.e., given are the values of $y(0)$ and $y(1)$, N at whole) the initial guess from available measurement data can be deduced. Otherwise (mixed Dirichlet-Neuman condition) the initial problem solution obtained via Riccati transformation of linearized equation can be treated as the guess.

11.4 THE GENERALIZED RICCATI TRANSFORMATION
(Rybicki and Usher 1966)

Let us consider the system of linear equations in the matrix form:

$$\left.\begin{array}{l} \dfrac{d\phi_1}{dx} = \Gamma_{11}\phi_1 + \Gamma_{12}\phi_2 + h_1 \\[3mm] \dfrac{d\phi_2}{dx} = \Gamma_{21}\phi_1 + \Gamma_{22}\phi_2 + h_2, \qquad x \in (0, 1) \end{array}\right\} \qquad (11.19)$$

where $\phi_1(x)$ and $h_1(x)$ are column n_1-vectors and $\phi_2(x)$ and $h_2(x)$ are column n_2-vectors. Similarly $\Gamma_{11}(x)$, $\Gamma_{12}(x)$, $\Gamma_{21}(x)$ and $\Gamma_{22}(x)$ are matrices of dimensionality $n_1 \times n_1$, $n_1 \times n_2$, $n_2 \times n_1$, and $n_2 \times n_2$ respectively.

The boundary conditions of equation (11.19) are

$$\phi_1(0) = C_1 \tag{11.20a}$$

$$\phi_2(1) = C_2 \tag{11.20b}$$

Define a column vector $\psi_1(x)$ of dimensionality n_1 by the relation

$$\phi_1(x) = R_{12}(x)\phi_2(x) + \psi_1(x) \tag{11.21}$$

The derivative of equation (11.21) is

$$\phi_1'(x) = R_{12}\phi_2' + R_{12}'\phi_2 + \psi_1' \tag{11.22}$$

By substituting (11.21) in (11.19) and eliminating ϕ_1, ϕ_1', and ϕ_2' one can get

$$\psi_1' = (\Gamma_{11} - R_{12}\Gamma_{21})\,\psi_1 - (R_{12}' + R_{12}\Gamma_{22} - \Gamma_{11}R_{12} + R_{12}\Gamma_{21}R_{12} - \Gamma_{12})$$
$$\cdot\,\phi_2 + (h_1 - R_{12}h_2) \tag{11.23}$$

The variable ϕ_2 vanishes when

$$R_{12}' + R_{12}\Gamma_{22} - \Gamma_{11}R_{12} + R_{12}\Gamma_{21}R_{12} - \Gamma_{12} = 0 \tag{11.24}$$

That is, $R_{12}(x)$ is the solution of a nonlinear matrix Riccati equation with initial value imposed at $x = 0$, i.e., $R_{12}(0) = 0$.

Equation (11.23) simplifies to

$$\psi_1' = (\Gamma_{12} - R_{12}\Gamma_{21})\,\psi_1 + (h_1 - R_{12}h_2)$$
$$\psi_1(0) = C_1 \tag{11.25}$$

Now, the function ψ_1 may be obtained as a solution of the one point boundary value problem.

The boundary condition $\phi_1(1)$ may be obtained by setting $x = 1$ in equation (11.21), i.e.,

$$\phi_1(1) = R_{12}(1)\,C_2 + \psi_1(1) \tag{11.26}$$

Now the original system (11.19) may be integrated from the point $x = 1$ by using one point conditions (11.20b) and (11.26).

11.5 NONLINEAR PARAMETER ESTIMATION PROBLEMS

In this paragraph we shall consider the problem of estimation of unknown parameters involved in nonlinear ODE.

Let us consider a situation when one is given a measured vector y of dimensionality p (p = number of experiments) and y is supposed to be related to variables x according to the equation

$$y = f(x, \theta) \qquad (11.27)$$

For each experiment the error $e_i(\theta)$ can be described as

$$e_i(\theta) = y_i - f(x_i, \theta) \qquad (11.28)$$

Let us define the error matrix $M(\theta)$ as

$$M(\theta) = \sum_{i=1}^{p} e_i(\theta) \, e_i^T(\theta) \qquad (11.29)$$

The problem of estimating the parameter θ can be solved via maximization technique. Usually the objective function involved in this maximization is of the form (Bard 1970)

$$\phi(\theta) = \psi(M(\theta) + \Pi(\theta)) \qquad (11.30)$$

where ψ and Π are functions depending on the particular method used.

  (i)   Least Squares Method
       In this method

$$\left.\begin{aligned} \Pi &= 0 \\ \psi &= -\mathrm{Tr}(M(\theta)) \end{aligned}\right\} \qquad (11.31)$$

  (ii) Least squares, weighted by variables.

$$\left.\begin{aligned} \Pi &= 0 \\ \psi &= -\mathrm{Tr}(WM(\theta)) \end{aligned}\right\} \qquad (11.32)$$

       where W is a given matrix.
  (iii) Maximum Likelihood
       In this method the following assumptions are introduced:
       a) x_i are known precisely

b) measurements y_i are contaminated by zero mean noise with covariance matrix V

c) errors in different experiments are uncorrelated.

In this method the matrices take the form

$$\left.\begin{array}{l} \Pi = 0 \\ \psi = -\frac{1}{2}\ Tr(V^{-1}M(\theta)) \end{array}\right\} \qquad (11.33)$$

(iv) Maximum likelihood with unknown covariance matrix V
Here

$$\left.\begin{array}{l} \Pi = 0 \\ \psi = -n/2 \log \det M(\theta) \end{array}\right\} \qquad (11.34)$$

(v) Bayesian estimation
Here

$$\left.\begin{array}{l} \Pi = \log p_0(\theta) \\ \psi = \log L(\theta) \end{array}\right\} \qquad (11.35)$$

where $p_0(\theta)$ is the prior density function of θ and $L(\theta)$ is the likelihood function.

In all cases the value θ^* of θ is estimated at which $M(\theta)$ attains a maximum under the condition

$$g(\theta^*) \leqslant 0 \qquad (11.36)$$

satisfying certain physical requirements.

This maximizing value of θ is to be found by means of iterative procedure using the formula

$$\theta_{i+1} = \theta_i + \rho_i R_i g_i \qquad (11.37)$$

where

g_i = gradient vector of $\phi(\theta)\big|_{\theta=\theta_i}$

ρ_i = scalar

R_i = positive definite matrix.

The proper choice of ρ_i and R_i can guarantee the convergence and efficiency of iterative methods (Bard 1970, Bandler 1969).

In this case, when the $f(\cdot)$ is an unknown function Galerkin's representation of $f(\cdot)$ can be used.

This representation is of the form

$$f(x) = \sum_1^n \alpha_i \phi_i(x) \qquad (11.38)$$

where $\{\phi_i(x)\}$ is a fixed linearly independent set of base functions.

The n parameters α_i form the set over which optimization is to take place. The problem can be stated as follows:
Minimize

$$E(\alpha) = \|x_\alpha - y\|^2$$

where

$$\|\cdot\|^2 = \int_0^T (\cdot)^2 \, dt \qquad (11.39)$$

and

$$\frac{dx}{dt} = \sum_{i=1}^n \alpha_i \phi_i(x(t)), \qquad x(0) = \alpha_0$$

This problem was solved by Lermit (1975) where the "steepest descent" method and the Newton-Gauss method were used.

The problem (11.39) can be also solved by means of the method discussed by Bandler (1969).

11.6 PARAMETER IDENTIFICATION OF POLYNOMIAL MODELS

In this section, we shall consider the deterministic identification problem of the polynomial models' parameters.

The presented approach matches the methods from Chapter 9 and paragraph 11.3.

Let us consider the system

$$\dot{x} = f_i(x) + u g_i(x), \qquad i = 1, 2, \ldots, n \qquad (11.40)$$

where $x \in R^n$ is the vector of the state variables.

$u \in R^1$ is an input signal

$f(\cdot)$ and $g(\cdot)$ are analytic functions of x in some neighborhood of the free response.

Suppose next that the functions $f(x)$ and $g(x)$ can be developed in a (truncated) Taylor series

$$f_i(x) = \sum_{j=1}^{n} c_{ij} x_j + \sum_{\substack{j,k,\ell,\ldots \\ m+k+\ell \geqslant 2}} \beta_{ijk\ell} x_j x_k x_\ell$$

$$(11.41)$$

$$g_i(x) = \sum_{j=1}^{n} c_{ij} x_j + \sum_{\substack{j,k,\ell \\ j+k+\ell \geqslant 2}} d_{ijk\ell} x_j x_k x_\ell$$

One can use Carleman linearization (Bellman and Richardson 1963) introducing new state variables

$$x^{[2]} \text{ of dim } \binom{n+1}{2} \text{ with elements}$$

$$x_1^{[2]} = x_1^2$$

$$x_2^{[2]} = x_1 x_2 \quad \text{etc.}$$

$$\vdots$$

and in general,

$$x_1^{[p]} = x_1^p$$

$$x_2^{[p]} = x_1^{p-1} x_2$$

$$\vdots$$

$$x_H^{[p]} = x^j x^k x^\ell, \qquad j + k + \ell = p$$

$$(11.42)$$

$$\vdots$$

$$x_{H_p}^{[p]} = x_n^p \qquad H_p = \binom{n+p-1}{p}$$

The Carleman linearization to degree p gives the following representation of the original system (11.40)

$$
\begin{bmatrix} \dot{x}^{[1]} \\ \dot{x}^{[2]} \\ \vdots \\ \dot{x}^{[p]} \end{bmatrix} = A \begin{bmatrix} x^{[1]} \\ x^{[2]} \\ \vdots \\ x^{[p]} \end{bmatrix} + uB \begin{bmatrix} x^{[1]} \\ x^{[2]} \\ \vdots \\ x^{[p]} \end{bmatrix} + Cu \qquad (11.43)
$$

where

$$
\dim x^{[p]} = H_p = \binom{n+p-1}{p}
$$

A, B are $N \times N$ matrices,

$$
N = n + \binom{n+1}{2} + \cdots + \binom{n+p-1}{p}
$$

System (11.43) is a bilinear system which can be rewritten in a form

$$
\left. \begin{aligned} \dot{v} &= Av + uBv + Cu \\ y &= Dv \end{aligned} \right\} \qquad (11.44)
$$

where $v^T = [x^{[1]}, \ldots, x^{[p]}] \in R^N$

$$
y \in R^q, \qquad \forall\, t \in [0, T],
$$

Consider now the case when in model (11.44) a vector $\theta \in R^r$ of unknown parameters appears. Introducing the augmented state

$$
z(t) \triangleq \begin{bmatrix} v(t) \\ \theta \end{bmatrix} \in R^m, \qquad \forall\, t \in [0, T], \quad m = r + N \qquad (11.45)
$$

and taking into account the identity $\dot{\theta} = 0$, a new differential model (without unknown parameters) may be defined, which turns out to be quadratic (Bruni et al. 1973)

$$
\begin{aligned} \dot{z} &= Qzz + Lz + c \\ y &= Gz \end{aligned} \qquad (11.46)
$$

where   Q is an m × m × m matrix which maps the space $R^M \times R^m$ into the
space R^m,

L and c are an m × m matrix and an m × 1 vector, respectively.

In general, Q, L, c are functions of time.

Assuming the knowledge of y(t) without noise in the discrete instants $t_i \in$ [0, T], the identification problem consists of finding the solution of (11.46) with the condition

$$\tilde{y} = \sum_{i=1}^{R} G_i z(t_i) \tag{11.47}$$

where

$$\left. \begin{aligned} \tilde{y}^T &\triangleq [y(t_i), \ldots, y(t_R)] \\ G_i^T &\triangleq [0, \ldots, G, \ldots, 0] \end{aligned} \right\} \tag{11.48}$$

G_i is an m × m matrix, built with R q × m blocks, all of which are zero except the i-th block equal to G.

The identification problem is stated as the quadratic multipoint boundary value problem (MPBVP) with equations (11.46) and (11.47).

As in paragraph 11.3, one can transform MPBVP into an equivalent integral problem (Falls and deJong 1969; Bruni et al. 1973). Denote by $\phi(t, \tau)$ the solution of the equation

$$\left. \begin{aligned} \frac{\partial \phi(t, \tau)}{\partial t} &= W(t)\, \phi(t, \tau) \\ \Phi(\tau, \tau) &= I, \qquad t, \tau \in [0, T] \end{aligned} \right\} \tag{11.49}$$

and introduce m × m matrices M_i, i = 1, 2, . . . , R.

The following matrix P may be defined

$$P \triangleq \sum_{i=1}^{R} M_i \phi(\tau_i, 0) \tag{11.50}$$

Under the assumption that P is nonsingular, the MPBVP defined by equations (11.46) and (11.47) is equivalent to the integral equation

$$z(t) = H^{(W,M_i)}(t)\left[\tilde{y} - \sum_{i=1}^{R} (G_i - M_i) x(t_i)\right] + \int_{0}^{T} S^{(W,M_i)}(t, \tau)$$

$$\cdot \{[Q(\tau) z(\tau) + L(\tau) - W(\tau)] z(\tau) + c(\tau)\} \, d\tau \qquad (11.51)$$

$$\triangleq T(z)(t)$$

where $H^{(W,M_i)}$, $S^{(W,M_i)}(t, \tau)$ are Green's matrices for the MPBVP and are given by

$$H^{(W,M_i)}(t) \triangleq \phi(t, 0) P^{-1} \qquad (11.52)$$

$$S^{(W,M_i)}(t, \tau) \triangleq \phi(t, 0) P^{-1} \sum_{i=1}^{R} G_i \phi(t_i, \tau)[\delta_{-1}(t - \tau) - \delta_{-1}(t_i, \tau)] \qquad (11.53)$$

where δ_{-1} is the unit step function.

The problem (11.51) is equivalent to the fixed-point problem (cf. equation 11.15)

$$z = T(z) \qquad (11.54)$$

If the problem (11.54) is convergent, the sequence $\{z_k\}$ generated by (11.51) from a given z_0 is (Bruni et al., 1973)

$$\dot{z}_{k+1}(t) = [2Q(t) z_k(t) + L(t)] z_{k+1}(t) - Q(t) z_k(t) z_k(t) + c(t) \qquad (11.55)$$

$$\sum_{i=1}^{R} G_i z_{k+1}(t_i) = \tilde{y} \qquad (11.56)$$

which can serve as a base for the identification problem algorithm.

11.7   STRUCTURAL STABILITY AND BIFURCATION IDENTIFICATION

11.7.1   Identification of the nonlinear system parameters is reasonable when the structure of the system of nonlinear differential equations (ODE) describing the process is known. To the given set of ODE

$$\dot{x}_i = X_i(x_1, \ldots, x_n, \theta_1, \ldots, \theta_m) \qquad (11.57)$$

$(\theta_1, \ldots, \theta_m$ are parameters) corresponds a trajectory in n-dimensional phase-space. If the "shape" (structure) of the n-dimensional phase portrait remains the same with changes in the vector θ, the system of ODE is called a "coarse" system.

According to Andronov and Pontriyagin (1937), the dynamic system described by equation (11.57) is coarse, when there exists a positive number δ such that the systems described by

$$\dot{x}_i = X_i(x_1, \ldots, x_n) + \xi_i(x_1, \ldots, x_n) \tag{11.58}$$

where $\xi_i(x_1, \ldots, x_n)$ is sufficiently small for all i and

$$\sum_{i=1}^{n} \left\{ |\xi_i| + \sum_{j=1}^{n} \left| \frac{\partial \xi_i}{\partial x_j} \right| \right\} < \delta \tag{11.59}$$

have the same phase-portrait structure.

In that case the concept of the coarse system may be replaced by the notion of structurally stable systems.

If for a certain parameters value vector θ the phase-portrait changes its structure, the phenomenon of bifurcation occurs. The division of the parameter space into subspaces to which one type of phase-portrait is connected with, can be done by means of Versal Families Theory, introduced by Arnold (1972).

Let us introduce few concepts which are useful for formulation of the Reduction Theorem.

(i) If for two systems

$$\dot{x} = v(x), \qquad x \in X \tag{11.60}$$

and

$$\dot{y} = w(y), \qquad y \in Y \tag{11.61}$$

there exists a transformation h: $X \to Y$ such that phase trajectories (orbits) of the first system are transformed to the orbits of the second, these systems are called topological orbit equivalent.

(ii) Topological orbit equivalence refers to the division of the parameter space into subspaces. This division is called bifurcation diagram of the family.

(iii) The family of differential equations depending on the parameter μ

$$\dot{x} = u(x, \mu) \tag{11.62}$$

is said to be induced by the family

$$\dot{x} = v(x, \epsilon) \tag{11.63}$$

if equation (11.62) is obtained from equation (11.63) by continuous change of parameters, i.e., when there exists continuous mapping $\epsilon = \phi(\mu)$ such that

$$u(x, \mu) = v(x, \phi(\mu)) \tag{11.64}$$

(iv) $\dot{x} = v(x, \epsilon)$ at the point $\epsilon = 0$ is called the deformation of equation $\dot{x} = v(x, 0)$. The deformation (11.64) is called the versal deformation of $\dot{x} = v(x, 0)$ if any other deformation of this equation is equivalent to the deformation induced by (11.63).

The theory of Versal Families leads to the Reduction Theorem (Shoshitaishvili 1972). This theorem can be reformulated as follows:
Let us be given the family of equations

$$\dot{x} = v(x, \theta), \quad x \in R^n, \quad \theta \in R^\ell \tag{11.65}$$

where θ is the vector of parameters.

Let us assume that for $\theta = 0$, the system is in equilibrium at the origin and the operator A of the linear part of v ($A = \partial v/\partial x \, (0, 0)$) has k roots on the imaginary axis. The number of roots with negative and positive real parts are n^- and n^+ respectively. Hence, $k + n^- + n^+ = n$. The local family (11.65) is equivalent to the following family

$$\left. \begin{array}{ll} \dot{p} = w(p, \theta) & p \in R^k, \quad \theta \in R^\ell \\ \dot{g} = -g & g \in R^{n^-} \\ \dot{r} = r & r \in R^{n^+} \end{array} \right\} \tag{11.66}$$

This theorem points out that for a study of bifurcation phenomena it is possible to analyze the reduced system of dimensionality k because the topological type of the singular point in R^n can be characterized by the orbits in a k-dimensional subspace. The Reduction Theorem admits bifurcational analysis of the parameter values by selection of the set of bifurcational parameters.

A parameter value is called bifurcational, if there are values of the parameters close to it at which the corresponding dynamical system has a different qualitative structure (Andronova and Belyustina 1961).

The establishment of effective methods of the qualitative investigation is based on the following idea: If the set of all bifurcational values of the parameters is known, as well as the type of bifurcations at these values, and if the qualitative structure of the dynamical system at some particular value of the parameters is known too, then the qualitative structure can be found by continuity for any point of the parameter space.

The classification of the qualitative structure for all high dimension n and ℓ (dimension ℓ in the system (11.66) is called codimension) is difficult and even impossible (Arnold 1970). For practical purposes the case k = 1, 2 and ℓ = 1 is of special interest. The classification of the singularities of higher dimensionality has been described by Arnold (1972, 1978).

11.7.2 Bifurcation of Singular Points in the System with Codimension 1

The bifurcational analysis is relatively simple in the case when only one parameter changes its value (ℓ = 1). It follows from the Versal Families Theory that if θ_0 is a bifurcational parameter then only one singular point of the system (11.65) exists and for this value θ_0 the linear part of v (equation (11.65)) has either one null eigenvalue (k = 1) or two eigenvalues on imaginary axis (k = 2) (Arnold 1972).

In the case when k = 1, the set of differential equations (11.65) can be transformed to the form

$$\left. \begin{array}{ll} \dot{x} = \pm x^2 + \theta, & X \in R, \quad \theta \in R \\ \dot{y} = -y & y \in R^{n^-} \\ \dot{y} = z & z \in R^{n^+} \end{array} \right\} \tag{11.67}$$

As an example, in Figure 11.1 the orbits for n = 2 (n = k + n$^-$) are presented.

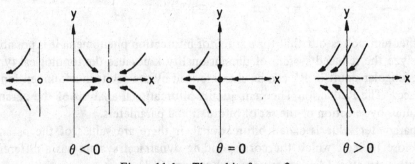

$$\theta < 0 \qquad\qquad \theta = 0 \qquad\qquad \theta > 0$$

Figure 11.1. The orbits for n = 2.

In the case when k = 2, the set (11.65) can be transformed to the form

$$\dot{z} = z(j\omega + \theta \pm cz\bar{z}), \qquad z \in C^1, \quad \theta \in R$$
$$\dot{p} = -p, \qquad\qquad p \in R^{n^-} \qquad\qquad (11.68)$$
$$\dot{r} = r, \qquad\qquad r \in R^{n^+}$$

where

z is a complex coordinate in R^2
z = x + jy
ω, c = real, nonzero constants
θ = real parameter

The bifurcation of nonlinear systems in the case k = 2 plays an important role because in this case the nonlinear oscillations are generated.

The complete analysis of the orbits generated by (11.51) can be found in many monographs (cf. Andronov et al. 1967). As an example we will outline the orbits for different signs of constants c and θ. When c < 0 the following orbits are generated (Figure 11.2).

When the increasing value of θ crosses zero, the system loses the stability. For $\theta = 0$ there is a stable sink but not coarse: The orbit approaches the origin but not exponentially. For $\theta > 0$ there is a circle with the radius $\rho = \sqrt{\theta}$. When the parameter θ changes its value starting from negative to positive a stable periodical cycle is generated and the case of weak bifurcation occurs.

At the other extreme for c > 0 the following orbits can be obtained (Figure 11.3).

In this case, the system pushed out from the origin loses its stability and rapidly obtains another orbit. This kind of bifurcation is called hard bifurcation.

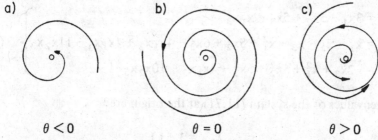

a) $\theta < 0$ b) $\theta = 0$ c) $\theta > 0$

Figure 11.2. The orbits generated for c < 0.

a)   b)   c)

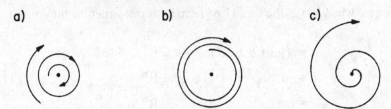

Figure 11.3.   The orbits generated for $c > 0$.

11.7.3   Example

The *structure* of the mathematical model can be verified when the system is forced to bifurcate. An especially attractive case is when as a result of bifurcation persistent oscillations in the system are obtained. One can in such situations transform the model to the standard form (11.68) and compare the computed parameters of the limit cycles with measured ones.

Algebraic manipulations carried out while transforming the model to the Poincaré form are rather cumbersome. In order only to show the procedure and outline the results, let us work with "known" model coefficients.

Consider the model

$$
\left.
\begin{aligned}
\dot{x}_1 &= -5x_2 + 5x_3 + ux_3 - 3u \\
\dot{x}_2 &= x_1 - x_2 - x_3 - x_2x_3 + x_1^2 + 5x^2 - 10x_2x_3 + 4(x_2 - x_3)u \\
\dot{x}_3 &= -2x_3 + x_1^2 + 5x_2^2 + 5x_3^2 - 4x_1x_2 + 4x_1x_3 - 10x_2x_3
\end{aligned}
\right\} \quad (11.69)
$$

The system (11.69) is stable at the origin.

Introducing feedback

$$u = -x_1 \qquad (11.70)$$

model (11.69) takes form

$$
\left.
\begin{aligned}
\dot{x}_1 &= 3x_1 - 5x_2 + 5x_3 - x_1x_3 \\
\dot{x}_2 &= x_1 - x_2 - x_3 + x_1^2 + 5x_2^2 + 6x_3^2 - 4x_1x_2 + 4x_1x_3 - 11x_2x_3 \\
\dot{x}_3 &= -2x_3 + x_1^2 + 5x_2^2 + 5x_3^2 - 4x_1x_3 - 10x_2x_3
\end{aligned}
\right\} \quad (11.71)
$$

The eigenvalues of the system (11.71) at the origin are:

$$
\left.
\begin{aligned}
\lambda_{1,2} &= 1 \pm j \\
\lambda_3 &= -2
\end{aligned}
\right\} \qquad (11.72)
$$

Introduced feedback (11.70) forces the system to oscillate. The qualitative behavior of oscillations can be examined when the system (11.71) is transformed
to the Poincaré form (11.68).

Such transformations can be performed in the following steps.

i) Transformation to the normal form.

The linear part of the system (11.71) is described by a matrix A

$$A = \begin{bmatrix} 3 & -5 & 5 \\ 1 & -1 & -1 \\ 0 & 0 & -2 \end{bmatrix} \tag{11.73}$$

Let P be a nonsingular matrix such, that

$$P^{-1}AP = J \tag{11.74}$$

where

$$J = \begin{bmatrix} 1 & -1 & 0 \\ 1 & 1 & 0 \\ 0 & 0 & -2 \end{bmatrix}$$

is the Jordan form of A.

Introducing new variables y

$$y = P^{-1}x \tag{11.75}$$

where

$$P = \begin{bmatrix} 1 & 2 & 0 \\ 0 & 1 & 1 \\ 0 & 0 & 1 \end{bmatrix} \tag{11.76}$$

the normal form of system (11.71) is

$$\left. \begin{array}{l} \dot{y}_1 = y_1 - y_2 - y_1 y_3 \\ \dot{y}_2 = y_1 + y_2 - y_2 y_3 \\ \dot{y}_3 = -2y_3 + y_1^2 + y_2^2 \end{array} \right\} \tag{11.77}$$

ii) Transformation to Poincaré form.

In order to obtain the form given by equation (11.68), let us introduce new (complex) variable z

$$z = y_1 + jy_2 \tag{11.78}$$

Multiplying the second equation in (11.77) by j and adding to the first, we obtain

$$\left.\begin{array}{l} \dot{z} = \lambda z - zy_3 \\ \dot{y}_3 = -2y_3 + z\bar{z} \end{array}\right\} \tag{11.79}$$

where $\lambda = 1 + j$

$$\bar{z} = y_1 - jy_2$$

One can express y_3 as a function of z and $\bar{z}$ (Hassard and Wan 1978)

$$y_3 = \sum_{i+j>2} \frac{\alpha_{ij}}{i!j!} z^i \bar{z}^j \tag{11.80}$$

By equating coefficients, we obtain

$$y_3 = \tfrac{1}{4} z\bar{z} + \tfrac{1}{48} z^2 \bar{z}^2 + \cdots \tag{11.81}$$

Substituting (11.81) into (11.79), we get

$$\dot{z} = \lambda z - \tfrac{1}{4} z^2 \bar{z} - \tfrac{1}{48} z^3 \bar{z}^2 + \cdots \tag{11.82}$$

The parameters of the limit cycle generated by the system (11.82) can be obtained by substituting in (11.82)

$$z = \rho e^{j\psi} \tag{11.83}$$

We get

$$\dot{\rho} + \rho j\dot{\psi} = (1 + j)\rho - \tfrac{1}{4}\rho^3 - \tfrac{1}{48}\rho^5 + \cdots \tag{11.84}$$

or equivalently,

$$\dot{\rho} = \rho - \tfrac{1}{4}\rho^3 - \tfrac{1}{48}\rho^5 + \cdots \tag{11.85}$$

$$\dot{\psi} = 1 = \omega$$

The parameters of the limit cycle are obtained from (11.85) for $\dot{\rho} = 0$ and $\psi = \omega t$..
We get

$$z = \bar{\rho} e^{jt} \qquad (11.86)$$

where $\bar{\rho} \approx 1.779$.

From (11.78) and (11.81), we have

$$\left.\begin{array}{l} y_1 = \bar{\rho} \cos t \\ y_2 = \bar{\rho} \sin t \\ y_3 = 1 \end{array}\right\} \qquad (11.87)$$

The original state variables are obtained from

$$x = Py \qquad (11.88)$$

We get

$$\left.\begin{array}{l} x_1 = \bar{\rho} \cos t + 2\bar{\rho} \sin t \\ x_2 = \bar{\rho} \sin t + 1 \\ x_3 = 1 \end{array}\right\} \qquad (11.89)$$

Time plot of the state variables from equation (11.71) is presented in Fig. 11.4.

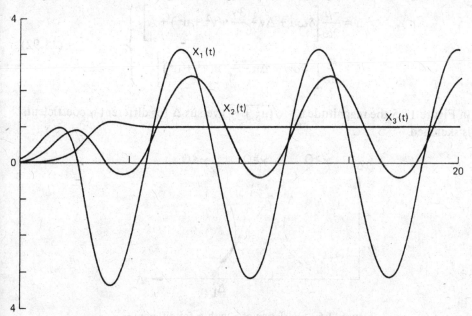

Figure 11.4. Time plot of state variables.

11.7.4   Example

Let us consider the nonlinear oscillator excited by harmonic input signal with frequency near resonance frequency. The differential equation describing such a system has the form

$$\ddot{x} + \omega_0^2 x = \mu\{-\delta\dot{x} - \gamma x^3 + A \sin \omega_1 t\}$$

$$= \mu\{-\delta\dot{x} + \Delta x - \gamma x^3 + A \sin \omega_0 t\} \qquad (11.90)$$

where

μ = small parameter
δ = damping coefficient
Δ = parameter proportional to $(\omega_0 - \omega_1)$
A = magnitude of the input signal.

Introducing new variables u and v such that

$$\left. \begin{array}{l} x = u \cos \omega_0 t + v \sin \omega_0 t \\ \dot{x} = -\omega_0 \sin \omega_0 t + \omega_0 v \cos \omega_0 t \end{array} \right\} \qquad (11.91)$$

and using the Method of Averaging (Neimark 1963, Bogolubov et al. 1955) one can obtain

$$\left. \begin{array}{l} \dot{u} = \dfrac{-\mu}{2\omega}\left[\delta\omega u + \Delta v - \dfrac{3\gamma}{4} v(v^2 + u^2) + A\right] \\[3mm] \dot{v} = \dfrac{\mu}{2\omega}\left[-\delta\omega v + \Delta u - \dfrac{3\gamma}{4} u(v^2 + u^2)\right] \end{array} \right\} \qquad (11.92)$$

In Figure 11.5 the magnitude $a = \sqrt{(u_0^2 + v_0^2)}$ versus Δ for different γ coefficients is sketched.

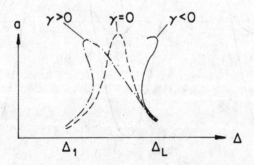

Figure 11.5.   Variation of α with Δ for different γ.

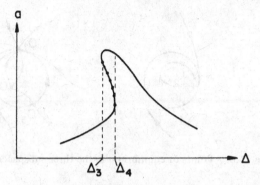

Figure 11.6.   Jump resonance.

In Figure 11.5 parts of resonance curves marked by crosses refer to the stability of saddle type, the parts of curves marked by dots refer to the stability points in which periodical oscillation with magnitude $a = \sqrt{(u_0^2 + v_0^2)}$ and frequency ω_0 takes place.

Let us analyze the case $\gamma > 0$ more carefully (Figure 11.6).

For $\Delta < \Delta_3$ and $\Delta < \Delta_4$ there exist sole stability points. Limited jumps occur for $\Delta = \Delta_3$ and $\Delta = \Delta_4$ depending on the way of changing the input signal frequency. The existence and kind of these jumps point out the existence and kind ($\gamma > 0$ or $\gamma < 0$) of nonlinear term.

The R^2 space (plane) of the parameters Δ, A can be divided into 3 subspaces D_1, D_2 and D_3 (Andronov 1956), as shown in Figure 11.7.

In D_1 there exist only sole points O_1 stable in global sense (Figure 11.8). In D_2 the point O_1 transforms to the unstable point O_2 and at the same time the limit cycle C arises (Figure 11.8b). In the area D_3 there are 3 points of equilib-

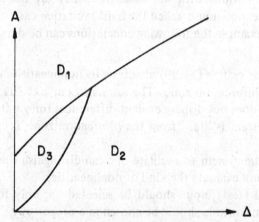

Figure 11.7.   Subspaces of the parameter plane.

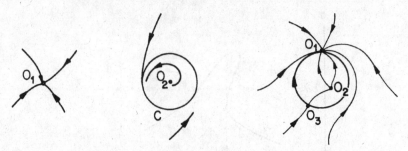

Figure 11.8.   Points of equilibrium in the three subspaces.

rium, one stable O_1, one unstable O_2 (stable for $t \to \infty$) and one saddle point O_3 (Figure 11.8c).

When the border line between D_2 and D_3 is crossed, the points O_1 and O_3 join and disappear and when the line between D_3 and D_1 is crossed, points O_2 and O_3 join and disappear. Therefore for the parameter value taken from D_1 and D_3 the only stable oscillations are oscillations with the frequency ω_1 (external input frequency).

For the parameter values taken from D_2 quasiperiodical (double-periodical) oscillation occurs. One of the frequencies is equal to ω_1, the second varies in the wide range (near ω_0 in the neighborhood of the D_1 area and axis, near O value in the interior of D_2).

In the case when the parameter value varies from D_1 to D_2 the oscillation frequency changes smoothly from m_0 to double periodical oscillation (the weak excitation case). In this case the forced internal oscillations with frequency ω_1 are modulated by small magnitude oscillation with frequency near ω_0. When the bifurcation border D_3-D_2 is crossed, the forced oscillation with frequency ω_1 changes to beat oscillations with the basic frequency ω_1 but slowly changing magnitude. This phenomenon is called the hard excitation case.

From the above example the following conclusions can be drawn:

(i)   The nonlinear system (11.90) manifests its nonlinearities in the neighborhood of the bifurcation zone. The resonance curve evaluation for $\Delta < \Delta_1$ and $\Delta > \Delta_2$ does not display evident differences for $\gamma = 0$ and $\gamma \neq 0$.

(ii)   When the system is "far" from the bifurcation zone, it can be treated as linear.

(iii)   By forcing the system to oscillate one can distinguish the hard and weak excitations and evaluate the kind of nonlinearities.

(iv)   The external (test) input should be selected not only for its spectrum, but also its magnitude should be chosen in a proper way.

11.7.5   In the preceding paragraph the analysis of a special type of nonlinear equation (codim 1) was outlined.   The varieties of nonlinear system are extremely rich and some obvious questions arise:

(i)   Is the example presented in section 11.7.4 a typical one?

(ii)   To what group of the system are the conclusions in 11.7.4 valid?

(iii)   How to evaluate the existence of nonlinearities and their "kind" if the system does not work in the bifurcation zone that appears dangerous for normal system operation?

In this section an attempt to answer the above questions is made.   The basic idea is to transform a wide group of nonlinear systems to one subclass which can be analyzed and identified in the same manner.

The Reduction Theorem points out that qualitative examination of nonlinear systems is equivalent to the analysis of the reduced subsystem in the lower dimension.   This subsystem contains the eigenvalues on the imaginary axis exclusively.   In other words the behavior of the system can be described by its oscillation.   This approach was successfully used as one method of the controller adjustments (Ziegler-Nicholc 1942).   On the other hand, nonlinear systems have, in general, such a very rich nature that any generalization can be rather illusory.

Nevertheless, of a variety of different bifurcation diagrams cited in Arnold's works one type of bifurcation seems to be of a paramount interest.   This is the case when one pair of conjugate eigenvalues crosses the imaginary axis.   This case has been intensively investigated by both mathematicians and engineers as a base of nonlinear oscillation descriptions.

Usually it is assumed that the nonlinear part of the equations is multiplied by a small coefficient ϵ.   This approach leads to the nonlinear equations of the following (Poincaré) types:

(i)   nonautonomous perturbations

$$\dot{x} = Ax + \epsilon f(t, x, \epsilon) \qquad (11.93)$$

(ii)   autonomous perturbations

$$\dot{x} = Ax + \epsilon f(x, \epsilon) \qquad (11.94)$$

In the case (i), A is a matrix with constant entries, such that the integer ω^2 is an eigenvalue and $f(t, x, \epsilon)$ is a 2π periodical function with respect to t.

In the case (ii), A is a matrix with constant entries, and f and $\partial f/\partial x$ are continuous functions with respect to x and ϵ (within the certain region for sufficiently small $|\epsilon|$).

Equations (11.93) and (11.94) have been analyzed in different parts of mathematics and engineering under the headings: perturbation theory, small parameter method, bifurcation theory of almost periodical oscillation, and nonlinear oscillations.

Let us now focus our attention on the validation of transforming the systems to a perturbed form. It is very risky to judge about the order of the system, the validity of linearization, or leading nonlinearities for the system not being operated.

Systems that operate in closed loop change their dynamics and react more "quickly." It can be interpreted that their eigenvalues shift towards the imaginary axis (or equivalently, the fast modes of the closed-loop system are excited by the error signal of the higher frequency). Besides, there is a tendency to make the regulator "responsible" for the dynamics of the whole system and release the designer from the lack of "deep" knowledge of the plant. Bode's approach (1942) containing the case of an infinitely large gain coefficient is an example.

Let us consider the nonlinear system of the form

$$x^{(n)} = f(t, x) + g(t, x) u, \qquad g(t, x) > 0 \tag{11.95}$$

Suppose, now that we want to transform the system (11.95) to (or close to) the bifurcation zone. Let the form of a transformed system, convenient for identification, be as follows

$$x^{(n)} = F(x, x^0) \tag{11.96}$$

We can design the control signal u to satisfy

$$u = K[F(x, x^0) - x^{(n)}] \tag{11.97}$$

Substituting (11.97) into (11.95) one can get

$$x^{(n)} = F(x, x^0) + \mu(t, x)[f(t, x) - F(x, x^0)] \tag{11.98}$$

where

$$\mu(t, x) = [1 + g(t, x) K]^{-1} \tag{11.99}$$

For K sufficiently large, equation (11.60) will be transformed to a Poincaré form.

11.7.6   The particular but very important form of equation (11.98) is the following

$$\ddot{x}_\kappa + \omega_\kappa^2 x_\kappa = \mu X_\kappa(t, x_\kappa, \dot{x}_\kappa), \qquad \kappa = 1, 2, \ldots, n \qquad (11.100)$$

Using the Method of Averaging (Bogolubov and Mitropolski 1955) equation (11.100) can be transformed to the normal form

$$\dot{x}_\kappa = \mu X_\kappa(t, x_1, \ldots, x_n), \qquad \kappa = 1, 2, \ldots, n \qquad (11.101)$$

where

$$X_\kappa(t, x_1, \ldots, x_n) = \sum_\nu e^{j\nu t} X_\nu(x_1, \ldots, x_n) \qquad (11.102)$$

or in the vector form

$$\dot{x} = \mu X(t, x) = \mu \sum_\nu e^{j\nu t} X_\nu(x) \qquad (11.103)$$

For the sake of simplicity, let the right side of equation (11.103) be periodical with the period τ.

Introducing operators

$$\underset{\tau}{E}[X(t, x)] = X_0(x) \qquad (11.104)$$

$$\tilde{X}(t, x) = \sum_{\nu \neq 0} \frac{e^{j\nu t}}{j\nu} X_\nu(x) \qquad (11.105)$$

$$\tilde{\tilde{X}}(t, x) = \sum_{\nu \neq 0} \frac{e^{j\nu t}}{(j\nu)^2} X_\nu(x) \qquad (11.106)$$

having the following properties

$$\frac{\partial \tilde{\tilde{X}}}{\partial t} = \tilde{X}, \qquad \frac{\partial \tilde{X}}{\partial t} = X - \underset{\tau}{E}(X) = X - X_0 \qquad (11.107)$$

the equation (11.100) can be transformed to the normal autonomous form.

11.7.7 Example

Let us consider the following equation

$$\ddot{x} + \omega^2 x = \mu\{-\delta\dot{x} + \Delta x - \gamma x^3 + A \sin \omega t\} \tag{11.108}$$

It is convenient to work with new variables u and v connected with x and $\dot{x}$ in the following way

$$x = u \cos \omega t + v \sin \omega t \tag{11.109a}$$

$$\dot{x} = -\omega u \sin \omega t + \omega v \cos \omega t \tag{11.109b}$$

differentiating (11.109a) and comparing with (11.109b) we get

$$\dot{u} \cos \omega t + \dot{v} \sin \omega t = 0 \tag{11.110}$$

Substituting (11.109a), (11.109b), and (11.110) into (11.108), we get

$$-\omega\dot{u}(\sin^2 \omega t + \cos^2 \omega t)$$
$$= \mu\{\delta\omega u \sin^2 \omega t - \delta\omega v \cos \omega t \sin \omega t + \Delta u \cos \omega t \sin \omega t + \Delta v \sin \omega t$$
$$- \gamma[u^3 \cos^3 \omega t \sin \omega t + 3u^2 v \cos^2 \omega t \sin^2 \omega t + 3uv^2 \cos \omega t \sin^3 \omega t$$
$$+ v^3 \sin^4 \omega t] + A \sin^2 \omega t\} \tag{11.111a}$$

and

$$\omega\dot{v}(\sin^2 \omega t + \cos^2 \omega t)$$
$$= \mu\{\delta\omega u \sin \omega t \cos \omega t - \delta\omega v \cos^2 \omega t + \Delta u \cos^2 \omega t + \Delta v \sin \omega t \cos \omega t$$
$$- \gamma[u^3 \cos^4 \omega t + 3u^2 v \cos^3 \omega t \sin \omega t + 3uv^2 \cos^2 \omega t \sin^2 \omega t$$
$$+ v^3 \sin^3 \omega t \cos \omega t] + A \sin \omega t \cos \omega t\} \tag{11.111b}$$

Averaging both sides of (11.111a) and (11.111b) using the operator

$$E(\cdot) = \underset{\omega t}{E}(\cdot) = \frac{1}{2\pi} \int_0^{2\pi} (\cdot) \, dt$$

and taking into account that

$$E[\sin^2 \omega t] = E[\cos^2 \omega t] = \tfrac{1}{2}$$

$$E[\sin^4 \omega t] = E[\cos^4 \omega t] = \tfrac{3}{8}$$

$$E[\sin \omega t \cos \omega t] = E[\cos^3 \omega t \sin \omega t] = E[\cos \omega t \sin^3 \omega t] = 0$$

we get the final form

$$\dot{u} = -\frac{\mu}{2\omega}\left[\delta\omega u + \Delta v - \frac{3\gamma}{4} v(v^2 + u^2) + A\right] \tag{11.112a}$$

$$\dot{v} = \frac{\mu}{2\omega}\left[-\delta\omega v + \Delta u - \frac{3\gamma}{4} u(u^2 + v^2)\right] \tag{11.112b}$$

Notice that equation (11.112) does not contain the variable $t(\omega t)$ explicitly.

11.7.8   In equation (11.97) describing the control law the estimate of nth state derivative is involved. In practice the derivative $x^{(n)}$ is not available and only its estimate can be taken into consideration.

To satisfy the condition of physical realizability, the filter which permits the estimation of $x^{(n)}$ should contain small time constant, i.e., its transfer function is of the form (Gerashtchenko 1975).

$$G_f^i(\mu s) = \frac{s^i}{M(\mu s)} = \frac{y^{(i)}(s)}{X(s)} \tag{11.113}$$

where

$$M(\mu s) = \sum_{i=0}^{n} d_i \mu^i s^i, \qquad d_n = d_0 = 1$$

μ is a small number. The filter differential equation is

$$y^{(n)} = \mu^{-n}(x - y) - \sum_{i=1}^{n-1} d_i \mu^{-n+i} y^{(i)} \tag{11.114}$$

Combining (11.73) with (11.77) we get

$$x^{(n)} = f(x, t) + g(t, x) K[F(y, x^0) - y^{(n)}] \tag{11.115}$$

$$\mu^n y^{(n)} = (x - y) - \sum_{i=1}^{n-1} d_i \mu^i y^{(i)}$$

The system (11.115) points out the existence of slow and fast motion and the nature of stiffness.* Therefore, the transformation of the system (11.95) into

---

*The analysis of system

$$\dot{x} = f(x, y)$$

$$\epsilon \dot{y} = g(x, y) \text{ where } \epsilon \text{ is a small number}$$

can be read under the headings: stiff differential equation, boundary layer phenomena, and singularly perturbed systems.

the Poincaré form should include the dynamics of the closed loop which permit this transformation.

11.7.9 In section 11.5.5 the possibility of transforming of nonlinear system with separable control (11.95) to the form in which the phenomenon of bifurcation can take place was discussed. This transformation is possible when the feedback loop with the high gain coefficient is introduced. In practice, a limited value of K (of order 20 to 50) is sufficient to obtain the desired form of the whole system (Ryabov 1961).

In order to observe the system behavior near the bifurcation region an external harmonic input should be introduced. This input should satisfy the requirements:

(i) the magnitude of a harmonic wave should be small.*
(ii) the frequency of the input ω_i should be chosen to obtain the resulting frequency difference $\omega_i - \omega_0$ (ω_0 is the natural system frequency) close to the bifurcation region (Figure 11.5).

The experimental evaluation of the structure of ODE is therefore more complicated than in the case of linear system. The main features of this experiment are as follows:

(i)   the system should be examined in a closed loop situation
(ii) the feedback should guarantee the possibility of obtaining the bifurcation region
(iii) an extra input $\epsilon A \sin \omega_i t$ should be introduced in the system for "static" evaluation of system behavior in the bifurcation region.

In order to obtain a uniform approach the transformation of the system equation to the normal form is suggested. It can be done when the high gain coefficient in the feedback loop is introduced. In this case, a boundary layer phe-

---

*In the case when the magnitude of the external input is not small, in equation

$$\ddot{x} + \omega^2 x = \mu f(x, \dot{x}) + A \sin \omega_i t$$

the change of variable

$$x = y + [A/(\omega^2 - \omega_i)] \sin \omega_i t$$

removes the term

$$A \sin \omega_i t$$

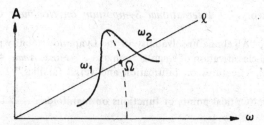

Figure 11.9.   Relationship between the frequencies of the points of intersections between lines ℓ = const · ω and the natural frequencies.

nomenon should be analyzed and the small (parasitic) filter time constants should be taken under consideration.

In practice, the requirement of the work in the bifurcation zone is often not acceptable. In this case, an attempt to transform the system "close" to the bifurcation zone is very tempting. One of the methods of system nonlinear term evaluation is presented in the following example.

11.7.10 Example

Suppose the system in a certain range of the input signal spectrum has a resonance character and can be described by the following equation

$$\ddot{x} + 2\delta\dot{x} + \Omega^2 f(x) = \rho\omega^2 \sin \omega t \qquad (11.117)$$

The input signal magnitude explicitly depends on the input signal frequency in a quadratic way. It can be proved (Novak 1961) that for a general equation of the resonance curve a simple relation

$$\Omega = \sqrt{\omega_1 \omega_2} \qquad (11.118)$$

exists between the frequencies of the points of intersection of the lines ℓ = const · ω with that of natural frequencies (Fig. 11.9).

Having described curve Ω one can evaluate the kind and degree of nonlinear term $f(x)$.

11.8 REFERENCES

Andronov, A. A. (1956), *Selected Works*, Publ. ANUSSR.

Andronov, A. A. and Pontriyagin, L. S. (1937), "Coarse system," *Dokl. Akad. Nauk*, 14.

Andronov, A. et al. (1967), *The theory of bifurcation on the plane*, Nauka, Moscow.

Andronova, E. A. and Belyustina, L. N. (1961), "The theory of bifurcation of second order dynamical systems and its application to the investigation of the nonlinear problems of the oscillation theory," *I International Symposium on Nonlinear Oscillations*, Kiev, U.S.S.R.

Arnold, V. I. (1970), "Algebraic unsolvability of the Lyapunov stability problem and problems of topological classification of singular points . . . ," *Funk. Anal.*, 4:3, pp. 1–9.

Arnold, V. I. (1972), "Lectures on bifurcation and versal families," *Uspieh Mat. Nauk.*, XXVII.

Arnold, V. I. (1978), "Critical points of functions on manifolds . . . ," *Uspieh Mat. Nauk.*, 203, No. 5.

Bandler, J. W. (1969), "Optimization methods for computer-aided design," *IEEE Trans. MTT*, 17, No. 8.

Bard, Y. (1970), "Comparison of gradient methods for the solution of nonlinear parameter estimation problems," *SIAM J. Numer. Anal.*, vol. 7, No. 1.

Bellman, R. and Richardson, J. M. (1973), "On some questions arising in the approximate solution of nonlinear differential equations," *Quart. Appl. Math.*, vol. 20, pp. 333–339.

Bogolubov, H. H. and Mitropolski, Yu. A. (1955), *Asymptotic methods in nonlinear oscillation theory*, Fizmatgiz, Moscow.

Bosorge Jr., W. E. (1971), "Interative continuation and the solution of nonlinear two-point boundary value problem," *Numer. Math.*, 17.

Bruni, C., Di Pillo, G., and Koch, G. (1973), "Mathematical models and identification of bilinear systems," in: *Geometric Methods in System Theory*, D. Q. Mayne and R. W. Buckett, eds., D. Reidell Publishing Company, Boston.

Bunich, A. L. and Rajbman, N. S. (1973), "A dispersion equation of nonlinear plant identification," *Problems of Control and Information Theory*, vol. 1, pp. 29–36.

Chen, R. T. N. (1970), "A recursive relationship for parameter estimation via method of quasilinearization and its connection with Kalman filtering," *AIAA J.*, vol. 8, pp. 1696–1698.

Eisenpress, H. and Greenstadt, J. (1966), "The estimation of nonlinear econometric systems," *Econometrica*, 34.

Falb, P. L. and deJong, J. L. (1969), "Some successive approximation methods in control and oscillation theory," Academic Press, New York.

Gerashtchenko, E. I. and Gerashtchenko, S. M. (1975), *The method of splitting motion and nonlinear system optimization*, Nauka.

Haber, R. and Kevicky, L. (1976), "Identification of nonlinear dynamic systems," *Proc. IV IFAC Symposium on Identification and System Parameter Estimation* (Tbilisi, U.S.S.R.).

Hassard, B. and Wan, Y. H. (1978), "Bifurcation formulae derived from center manifold theory," *Journal Math. Anal. Applications*, vol. 63, pp. 297–312.

Kantorovich, L. V. "The method of successive approximations for functional equations," *Acta Math.*, 71, pp. 63–97.

Kantorovich, L. V. and Akilov, G. P. (1964), *Functional Analysis in Normal Spaces*, Macmillan, New York.

Lermit, R. J. (1975), "Numerical methods for the identification of differential equations," *SIAM J. Numer. Anal.*, vol. 12, No. 3.

Neimark, Yu. I. (1963), "Method of averaging from the point of view of the point-wise transformation method," *Radiophysics*, 6.

Nowak, M. (1961), "Analysis of experimental nonlinear resonance curves," *Preprints of the I International Symposium on Nonlinear Oscillation*, Kiyev.

Picard, E. (1929), *Traite d'Analyse*, 3rd ed., vol. III, Gauthiers-Villars, Paris.

Roth, R. S. (1981), "Techniques in the identification of deterministic systems," *IEEE Transactions. on Automatic Control*, vol. AC-26, pp. 1169–1176.

Ryabov, Yu. A. (1961), "On the evaluation of the applicability limits for the small parameter method in the theory of nonlinear oscillation," *Preprint of the I International Symposium on Nonlinear Oscillation*, Kiyev.

Rybicki, G. B. and Usher, P. D. (1966), "The generalized Riccati transformation as a simple alternative to invariant imbedding," *Astrophysics*, vol. 146 no. 3.

Shoshitaishvili, A. N. (1972), "On the bifurcation of topological type of a vector field near a singular point," *Functional Anal. i Prilozheniye*, 6:2, pp. 97–98.

12
Design of Optimal Input Signal

12.1 INTRODUCTION

A large class of physical and biological systems can be identified by observing their response to a suitable input signal. In the identification and model verification problem, we are interested in certain specific system behavior, therefore, appropriate input signals should be selected so that from the resulting response the "most accurate" model may be identified. Consider, as an example, an electronic amplifier. Its mathematical model (equivalent circuit) depends on the frequency range of the expected input signal. The amplifier gain parameter can be estimated when the "middle" frequency signal is applied, whereas for estimation of the parasitic capacitance, a "high" frequency signal is necessary.

A priori knowledge of experimental conditions on the basis of which the optimal input signal for parameter identification can be chosen, should contain:

a) a priori knowledge of the object being identified. This can be specified by assumed:
   (i)   structure of the system (distributed, nonlinear, linearized, closed-loop, open-loop)
   (ii) order of the system
   (iii) range of parameter values
b) noise conditions (noise free experiment, experiment including process noise and/or measurement noise).

Of a variety of possible combinations of assumptions the most exhaustive literature is available on linear systems.

Since 1960, a number of papers on test signal design have appeared and different criteria for a measure of the parameter estimation "goodness" have been discussed. Mehra (1974), Mehra and Lainiotis (1976), and Goodwin and Payne (1976) list a large number of references.

Assuming that during an experiment an efficient estimator is used in the sense that the Cramer-Rao lower bound on the parameter covariance matrix (given by the inverse of Fisher's information matrix, M) is achieved, the most popular method is the use of a scalar function ϕ of M as a suitable measure J of the "goodness" of the experiment

$$J = \phi(M) \tag{12.01}$$

The possible choices for the function ϕ are (Goodwin and Payne 1976):

(i)   Trace (M)
(ii) $\text{Det}(M^{-1})$ (equivalently, $\text{Det}(M)$ or $\text{Log Det}(M)$)
(iii) Trace (WM^{-1}) where W is a nonnegative definite matrix.

The standard expression for the information matrix is

$$M = E_{Y|\theta} \left\{ \left[\frac{\partial \log p(Y|\theta)}{\partial \theta} \right] \left[\frac{\partial \log p(Y|\theta)}{\partial \theta} \right]^T \right\} \tag{12.02}$$

where Y is a random variable corresponding to the observations $Y_1, \ldots, Y_N$, and θ is the vector of parameters in the system

$$d\underline{x} = A\underline{x}\, dt + B\underline{u}\, dt + d\eta$$
$$d\underline{y} = C\underline{x}\, dt + d\xi \tag{12.03}$$
$$\underline{x} \in R^n, \qquad \underline{u} \in R^m, \qquad \underline{y} \in R^p$$

$d\eta$, $d\xi$ are Wiener Processes with appropriate incremental covariance. In equation. (12.02) $p(Y|\theta)$ is the likelihood function for the parameters and $E_{Y|\theta}$ denotes expectation over the distribution of Y for given θ.

For assumed Gaussian noise process, the conditional distribution can be expressed as

$$p(Y|\theta) = \left((2\pi)^{rN} \prod_{k=1}^{N} \det S_k \right)^{-1/2}$$

$$\cdot \exp \left\{ -\tfrac{1}{2} \sum_{k=1}^{N} (y_k - \bar{y}_k)^T S_k^{-1} (y_k - \bar{y}_k) \right\} \tag{12.04}$$

which when substituted to (12.02) yields

$$M_{ij} = \sum_{k=1}^{N} \left(\frac{\partial \bar{y}_k}{\partial \theta_i} \right)^T S_k^{-1} \left(\frac{\partial \bar{y}_k}{\partial \theta_j} \right)$$

$$+ \frac{1}{2} \sum_{k=1}^{N} \text{Trace} \left\{ S_k^{-1} \frac{\partial S_k}{\partial \theta_i} \right\} \text{Trace} \left\{ S_k^{-1} \frac{\partial S_k}{\partial \theta_j} \right\} \qquad (12.05)$$

In equations (12.04) and (12.05) $y_1, \ldots, y_N$ are the observations

$\bar{y}_k$ is the conditional mean
S_k is the conditional covariance

Equation (12.05) points out that the information matrix M can be treated as a matrix the elements of which are appropriate sensitivity quantities

$$\frac{\partial \bar{y}_k}{\partial \theta_i} \quad \text{and} \quad \frac{\partial S_k}{\partial \theta_i}.$$

Therefore, the objective function to be maximized can also be a sensitivity matrix obtained from given system model (Kalaba and Spingarn 1973). Another approach can use the concept presented by Gagliardi (1967), which permits input signal design for assumed bounds of parameter values of the system.

Each technique can be used for time-domain and frequency-domain signal synthesis, both for continuous and discrete parameter systems and also for distributed parameter and (weakly) nonlinear systems. Therefore a reasonable criterion for discrimination of possible methods is the objective function to be optimized.

For practical purposes, signal synthesis in the frequency domain appears more attractive. The process of design can be decomposed into two steps:

(i) designing the optimal power spectrum
(ii) designing the signal having the desirable (obtained in step (i)) power spectrum, subject to certain constraints (signal form, sampling period, etc.)

In this chapter, three methods (having basically the same root) will be discussed:

a) method based on properties of Fisher's information matrix
b) method based on system sensitivity function optimization
c) method based on Gagliardi theorem—the "direct" method

This Chapter is organized as follows:

In section 12.2, an optimal input synthesis method for linear system parameter estimation on the basis of information matrix theory and a simple example of a second order system identification will be discussed. In section 12.3, an optimal input design based on the sensitivity criterion will be outlined. A direct method of optimal input design will be discussed in section 12.4. This is divided into four subsections. In section 12.4.1, the basic assumptions and the main result are stated. Two examples supporting the optimal signal design procedure are included. In section 12.4.2, an assumption of system discrete parameter value is released and practical procedure for obtaining "extreme" parameter values is outlined. Section 12.4.3 describes method of input signal realization for long time observation. Short time duration signals and procedure for their designing are discussed in section 12.4. In section 12.5, an optimal input synthesis for a distributed parameter system is presented.

In this chapter, a signal design for open-loop experiments is described. Certain features of signal synthesis for closed-loop system identification were presented at the end of Chapter 7.

12.2 OPTIMAL INPUT SYNTHESIS FOR LINEAR SYSTEM PARAMETER ESTIMATION ON THE BASE OF INFORMATION MATRIX THEORY (FREQUENCY-DOMAIN SYNTHESIS)

The most popular (and deeply theoretically developed) approach of input signal synthesis is based on the property of Fisher's information matrix. This technique will be outlined using the example of a constant coefficient linear dynamic system (Mehra 1976), described by

$$\left. \begin{array}{c} \underline{x}(k + 1) = F\underline{x}(k) + Gu(k) \\ \underline{y}(k) = H\underline{x}(k) + \underline{v}(k) \\ k = 0, 1, \ldots, N \end{array} \right\} \qquad (12.06)$$

where

$\underline{x}(k) = n \times 1$ state vector
$u(k) = $ scalar input
$\underline{y}(k) = p \times 1$ output vector
$\underline{v}(k) = p \times 1$ measurement noise vector.

$u(k)$ and $\underline{y}(k)$ are measured at $k = 1, 2, \ldots, N$ and are to be used for estimating a set of unknown parameters $\underline{\theta}$ in F, G, and H. It is also assumed that the system is completely controllable and observable, all eigenvalues of F lie inside the unit circle, and u(k) and $\underline{v}$(k) are stationary independent normal second-order processes with zero mean and correlation functions $R_{uu}(k - s)$ and $R_{vv}(k - s)$ respectively.

Let $T(z, \underline{\theta})$ be the system transfer function

$$T(z, \underline{\theta}) = H[zI - F]^{-1}G \tag{12.07}$$

where $\underline{\theta}$ is a vector of m unknown parameters in H, F, and G. Assuming appropriate differentiability one can expand $T(z, \theta)$ in a Taylor series about the a priori known value $\underline{\theta}_0$

$$T(z, \underline{\theta}) = T(z, \underline{\theta}_0) + \sum_{i=1}^{m} \frac{\partial T(z, \underline{\theta})}{\partial \theta_i} \Delta\theta_i + 0(\|\Delta\underline{\theta}\|^2) \tag{12.08}$$

where

$$\Delta\underline{\theta} = \underline{\theta} - \underline{\theta}_0 = \begin{bmatrix} \Delta\theta_1 \\ \vdots \\ \Delta\theta_m \end{bmatrix}$$

The output signal $\underline{y}$(k) can be expressed as

$$\underline{y}(k) = T(z, \underline{\theta}) \underline{u}(k) + \underline{v}(k)$$

$$= T(z, \underline{\theta}_0) \underline{u}(k) + \sum_{i=1}^{m} \frac{\partial T(z, \underline{\theta})}{\partial \theta_i} \Delta\theta_i \underline{u}(k) + \underline{v}(k) \tag{12.09}$$

Defining the p × 1 vectors $\underline{f}_i$(k) as

$$\underline{f}_i(k) \triangleq \frac{\partial T(z, \underline{\theta})}{\partial \theta_i} \underline{u}(k), \tag{12.10}$$

the p × m matrix f(k) as

$$f(k) \triangleq [\underline{f}_1(k), \underline{f}_2(k), \ldots, \underline{f}_m(k)] \tag{12.11}$$

and

$$\Delta\underline{y}(k) \triangleq \underline{y}(k) - \frac{\partial T(z, \underline{\theta})}{\partial \underline{\theta}} \underline{u}(k) \tag{12.12}$$

Equation (12.09) can be rewritten as

$$\Delta \underline{y}(k) = f(k) \Delta \underline{\theta} + \underline{v}(k) \qquad (12.13)$$

$$k = -\frac{N}{2}, \ldots, \frac{N}{2} - 1 \quad (N-\text{even})$$

The solution to $\Delta \underline{\theta}$ in equation (12.13) can be regarded as a regression problem in m unknowns and N equations.

It can be shown (Mehra 1976), that for $N \to \infty$

$$\text{cov} [\Delta \hat{\underline{\theta}}] = M^{-1} \qquad (12.14)$$

and

$$M = \frac{1}{2\pi} \int_{-\pi}^{\pi} \frac{\partial T^*(e^{j\omega}, \underline{\theta}_0)}{\partial \underline{\theta}} S_{vv}^{-1}(\omega) \frac{\partial T(e^{j\omega}, \underline{\theta}_0)}{\partial \underline{\theta}} dF_{uu}(\omega) \quad (12.15)$$

where

$T(e^{j\omega}, \underline{\theta}_0)$ is obtained by substituting $z = e^{j\omega}$ in equation (12.08)

T^* is the complex conjugate of T

$S_{vv}(\omega)$ is a spectral distribution function of $\underline{v}(k)$, absolutely continuous and nonsingular

$F_{uu}(\omega)$ is a spectral distribution function of u(k)

Now the problem of optimal input signal design can be stated as follows:

Find a signal u(k) (with spectral distribution function $F_{uu}(\omega)$) such that the suitable norms of the information matrix M reach extrema. The norms of M given in the terms of matrix M itself or its inverse D, known as the Dispersion Matrix, are the ones cited by Mehra (1974, 1976).

One of the possible input design algorithms can be based on following lemmas (Mehra, 1976):

a) the optimum design F (spectral distribution function) maximizes

$$\text{Tr} \{S_{vv}^{-1}(\omega) d(\omega, F)\} \qquad \omega \in (-\pi, \pi) \qquad (12.16)$$

where

$$d(\omega, F) = \frac{\partial T(\omega)}{\partial \underline{\theta}} M^{-1} \frac{\partial T^*(\omega)}{\partial \underline{\theta}} \qquad (12.17)$$

b) a mixed input (stochastic and deterministic) can always be replaced by a deterministic input with less than $[m(m + 1)/2 + 1]$ frequencies. Therefore, while designing optimal inputs one can confine the search to sinusoidal inputs with a finite number of frequencies.

A practical algorithm of numerical computation of optimal input signal is suggested (Mehra 1976) below:

(i)   Choose a nondegenerate design $F_0(\omega)$ consisting of more than $[m/2p]$ points. For example, F_0 may consist of r equally spaced frequencies where

$$\left[\frac{m}{2p} \right] \leqslant r \leqslant m(m + 1)/2$$

(ii) Compute the function $\text{Tr} \{S_{\underline{vv}}^{-1}(\omega) \, d(\omega, F_0)\}$ and find its maximum, say at ω_0, i.e.

$$\text{Tr} \{S_{\underline{vv}}^{-1}(\omega_0) \, d(\omega_0, F_0)\} = \max_{\omega \in (-\pi, \pi)} \text{Tr} \{S_{\underline{vv}}^{-1}(\omega) \, d(\omega, F_0)\}$$

(iii) Update the design to

$$F_1 = (1 - \alpha_0) \, F_0 + \alpha F(\omega_0)$$

and

$$M(F_1) = (1 - \alpha_0) \, M(F_0) + \alpha_0 M(F(\omega_0)), \qquad 0 \leqslant \alpha_0 \leqslant 1$$

(iv) Repeat steps (ii)-(iv) until the change in the criterion function or gradient is below a threshold value.

EXAMPLE (12.1) (Gupta, et al., 1976)

Consider a second-order system in which we wish to estimate the squared frequency parameter, θ. Let θ_0 be the a priori value of θ, and the state equations be

$$\underline{\dot{x}} = \begin{bmatrix} 0 & 1 \\ -\theta & -1 \end{bmatrix} \underline{x} + \begin{bmatrix} 0 \\ 1 \end{bmatrix} u \tag{12.18}$$

$$y = x_1 + v \tag{12.19}$$

$$\underline{x} = \begin{bmatrix} x_1 \\ x_2 \end{bmatrix} \tag{12.20}$$

The discrete time equivalent of this system is (for small time step Δ)

$$\underline{x}(k+1) = \begin{bmatrix} 1 & \Delta \\ -\Delta\theta & 1-\Delta \end{bmatrix} \underline{x}(k) + \begin{bmatrix} 0 \\ \Delta \end{bmatrix} u(k) \qquad (12.21)$$

Assuming that $v(k)$ is white with known power spectral density S_{vv}

$$T(\omega, \theta) = \begin{bmatrix} 1 & 0 \end{bmatrix} \begin{bmatrix} e^{-j\omega} - 1 & -\Delta \\ \Delta\theta & \Delta + e^{-j\omega} - 1 \end{bmatrix}^{-1} \begin{bmatrix} 0 \\ \Delta \end{bmatrix}$$

$$= \frac{\Delta^2}{(e^{-j\omega} - 1)(e^{-j\omega} - 1 + \Delta) + \Delta^2\theta} \qquad (12.22)$$

$$\frac{\partial T^*}{\partial \theta}\bigg|_{\theta_0} = -\frac{\Delta}{\{(e^{j\omega} - 1)(e^{j\omega} - 1 + \Delta) + \Delta^2\theta\}^2} \qquad (12.23)$$

$$M(\omega)\big|_{\theta_0} = \frac{\Delta^2 S_{vv}^{-1}}{\{(e^{j\omega} - 1)(e^{j\omega} - 1 + \Delta) + \Delta^2\theta\}^2 \{(e^{-j\omega} - 1)(e^{-j\omega} - 1 + \Delta) + \Delta^2\theta_0\}^2}$$

$$(12.24)$$

By simple calculation, one can show that for small Δ, M is maximized at

$$\begin{aligned} \omega &= \sqrt{\theta_0 - \tfrac{1}{2}} \qquad \text{for} \quad \theta_0 > \tfrac{1}{2} \\ \omega &= 0 \qquad \text{for} \quad \tfrac{1}{2} \geqslant \theta_0 \geqslant \tfrac{1}{4} \end{aligned} \qquad (12.25)$$

Equation (12.25) shows that for high damping it is best to use a constant input. With low damping, an oscillatory input at the damped natural frequency is the optimal input.

12.3 OPTIMAL INPUT DESIGN BASED ON SENSITIVITY CRITERION

As was mentioned in section 12.1 for optimal input signal design a criterion based on sensitivity of the system output to the unknown parameters can be used. The optimal input signal is the signal which maximizes this sensitivity under the assumption that the input signal is either energy or power constrained (Mehra 1974a, Goodwin and Payne 1976).

For the linear time-invariant dynamic system

$$\left. \begin{aligned} \dot{\underline{x}} &= F\underline{x} + G\underline{u} \\ \underline{y} &= H\underline{x} + \underline{v} \end{aligned} \right\} \qquad (12.26)$$

where

$$\underline{x} \in R^n,$$
$$\underline{y} \in R^p,$$
$$\underline{u} \in R^m, \underline{v} \in R^p$$

and

$$E\{\underline{v}\} = 0, E\{\underline{v}(t)\, \underline{v}^T(\tau)\} = R\delta(t - \tau)$$

the optimization problem can be stated as follows:

Maximize the sensitivity function $\nabla_\theta \underline{x}$ subject to the input energy constraint

$$\int_0^\infty \underline{u}^T \underline{u} \, dt = \text{const} \tag{12.27}$$

The sensitivity function can be obtained by applying the operator

$$\nabla_\theta = \left(\frac{\partial}{\partial \underline{\theta}_1}, \frac{\partial}{\partial \theta_2}, \ldots, \frac{\partial}{\partial \theta_m} \right)$$

to the system (12.26).

Consider the case in which $\underline{\theta}$ is an unknown parameter in F (Mehra 1974a). The sensitivity equation is

$$\nabla_\theta \dot{\underline{x}} = F\nabla_\theta \underline{x} + (\nabla_\theta F)\, \underline{x} \tag{12.28}$$

Since the sensitivity function contain two variables ($\nabla_\theta \underline{x}$ and $\underline{x}$) the following system should be considered:

$$\dot{\tilde{\underline{x}}} = \tilde{F}\tilde{\underline{x}} + \tilde{G}\underline{u} \tag{12.29}$$

where

$$\tilde{\underline{x}}^T = [\underline{x}^T \quad \nabla_\theta \underline{x}^T] \tag{12.30}$$

$$\tilde{F} = \begin{bmatrix} F & 0 \\ \nabla F & F \end{bmatrix} \tag{12.31}$$

$$\tilde{G}^T = [G^T \;\vdots\; 0] \tag{12.32}$$

The performance index J is

$$J = \frac{1}{2} \int_0^T \left[-\tilde{\underline{x}}^T \tilde{H}^T R^{-1} \tilde{H}\tilde{\underline{x}} + \mu\left(\underline{u}^T \underline{u} - \frac{\text{const}}{\lambda} \right) \right] dt \tag{12.33}$$

where

$$\tilde{H} = [0 \mid I] \tag{12.34}$$

Optimization of J leads to the two-point boundary value problem:

$$\begin{bmatrix} \dot{\tilde{x}} \\ \dot{\lambda} \end{bmatrix} = \begin{bmatrix} \tilde{F} & -1/\mu \tilde{G} \tilde{G}^T \\ \tilde{H}^T R^{-1} \tilde{H} & -\tilde{F} \end{bmatrix} \begin{bmatrix} \tilde{x} \\ \lambda \end{bmatrix} \tag{12.35}$$

$$-\underline{u} = -\frac{1}{\mu} \tilde{G}^T \underline{\lambda} \tag{12.36}$$

$$\tilde{\underline{x}}(0) = \begin{bmatrix} x(0) \\ 0 \end{bmatrix} \tag{12.37}$$

$$\lambda(T) = 0 \tag{12.38}$$

This two-point boundary value problem can be solved by means of the methods outlined by Mehra and Lainiotis (1976, Chapter 11).

12.4 DIRECT METHOD OF OPTIMAL INPUT DESIGN

12.4.1 Design for Discrete Set of Parameters

The direct method of optimal input design is based on Gagliardi's work (1967). He has shown that for a finite set of parameters the input vectors that map into the output set with the largest perimeter in the vector space maximize the probability of identifying the correct parameters.

The problem of input design can be stated as follows. Let the transfer function of the given system be denoted by $G(\theta_i, s)$, where θ_i, i = 1, 2, ..., m represents a discrete set of possible values for the parameter θ, which are assumed to be equally likely a priori. Our problem is to select the best input for determining which of the finite set $\{\theta_i\}$ i = 1, 2, ..., m is the true value of θ. The best input signal is the signal whose output set has the largest perimeter when plotted in the vector space. It will be assumed that the observations of the output are contaminated with zero-mean white Gaussian noise, and the variance of this noise will be normalized to unity, without any loss in generality.

Consider the case where m = 2 (it can be easily extended to the more general case m > 2). The requirement of the largest perimeter of the output signal can be expressed in the following form (Kuszta and Sinha 1976):

$$J = \max_{u(t)} \int_0^\infty [y_1(t) - y_2(t)]^2 \, dt \tag{12.39}$$

where

$$y_1(t) = \text{output of the system } G(\theta_1, s) \text{ with input } u(t)$$
$$= L^{-1}[G(\theta_1, s) U(s)] \qquad (12.40)$$

$$y_2(t) = \text{output of the system } G(\theta_2, s) \text{ with input } u(t)$$
$$= L^{-1}[G(\theta_2, s) U(s)] \qquad (12.41)$$

In equations (12.40) and (12.41), L^{-1} represents inverse Laplace transformation and $U(s)$ is the Laplace transform of $u(t)$.

By a direct application of Parsevals' formula, equation (12.39) may be replaced by the maximization of

$$J' = \max_{u(s)} \int_0^\infty |\Delta G(j\omega)|^2 \phi_u(\omega) \, d\omega \qquad (12.42)$$

where $\phi_u(\omega)$ is the power spectral density of the input signal and

$$\Delta G(j\omega) = G(\theta_1, j\omega) - G(\theta_2, j\omega) \qquad (12.43)$$

Hence, the optimal input signal design problem is reduced to finding the signal with the spectral density $\phi_u(\omega)$ which will maximize J in equation (12.42).

The actual solution to this problem will depend upon the nature of constraints which the input signal must satisfy. For instance, if the input signal is constrained to have a certain maximum area under the spectral density curve (equivalent to a maximum power in the input), it is obvious that the solution is an impulse in the spectral density at the peak of $|\Delta G(j\omega)|$. This corresponds to applying a sine wave input at the frequency at which the transfer function $\Delta G(j\omega)$ has the maximum amplitude.

On the other hand, if we apply the constraint that

$$\int_0^\infty \phi_u^2(\omega) \, d\omega = \text{constant} \qquad (12.44)$$

thereby ruling out impulsive spectral density functions, it is easily shown (using calculus of variations) that J is maximized if

$$\phi(\omega) = K |\Delta G(j\omega)|^2 \qquad (12.45)$$

where K is a constant.

EXAMPLE 12.2

Let us consider the same system as in example 12.1. The system is described by the equation

$$\left.\begin{array}{c} \ddot{x} + \dot{x} + \theta x = u \\[2mm] y = x + v \end{array}\right\} \tag{12.46}$$

Suppose that $\theta = 2.5 \pm 0.5$, then

$$G_1(s) = \frac{1}{s^2 + s + 3} \quad \text{and} \quad G_2(s) = \frac{1}{s^2 + s + 2}$$

A plot of $|\Delta G(j\omega)|^2$ is shown in Figure 12.1, and is seen to have the peak at $\omega = \sqrt{2}$. On the other hand, if $\theta = \frac{3}{8} \pm \frac{1}{8}$, the resulting $|\Delta G(j\omega)|^2$, shown in Figure 12.2 has a peak at $\omega = 0$.

EXAMPLE 12.3

Direct approach to input synthesis can also be applied in time-domain design. Consider the discrete, time-invariant system described by equation (12.47)

$$y_{n+1} = \sum_{j=1}^{K} \theta_j y_{n-j+1} + u_n, \quad n = 0, 1, \ldots \tag{12.47}$$

or in a matrix form

$$\underline{y} = G\underline{u} \tag{12.48}$$

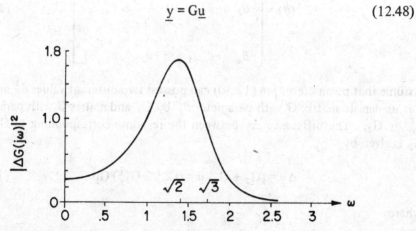

Figure 12.1.   Plot of $|G(j\omega)|^2$ against ω for $\theta = 2.5 \pm 0.5$.

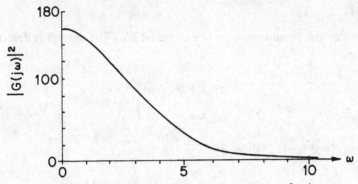

Figure 12.2.   Plot of $|G(j\omega)|$ against ω for $\theta = \frac{3}{8} \pm \frac{1}{8}$.

or, equivalently, (Aoki and Stanley 1970)

$$\underline{u} = G^{-1} \underline{y} \tag{12.49}$$

where

$$\underline{y}^T = [y_1, y_2, \ldots, y_n]^T$$
$$\underline{u}^T = [u_0, u_1, \ldots, u_{n-1}]^T$$

From equation (12.49), it is easily seen that

$$G^{-1}(\theta) = \begin{bmatrix} 1 & & & & & 0 \\ -\theta_1 & 1 & & & & \\ -\theta_2 & -\theta_1 & 1 & & & \\ \vdots & & & \ddots & & \\ \vdots & & & & \ddots & \\ -\theta_\kappa & -\theta_{\kappa-1} & \cdots & -\theta_2 & -\theta_1 & 1 \end{bmatrix} \tag{12.50}$$

Assume that parameters θ_j in (12.50) can possess two different values θ_j^1 and θ_j^2. Let us denote matrix G with parameter θ_j^1 by G_1 and matrix G with parameter θ_j^2 by G_2. The difference $\Delta\underline{y}$ between the response corresponding to G_1 and G_2 is given by

$$\Delta\underline{y} = (G_2 - G_1)\,\underline{u} = (G_1^{-1} - G_2^{-1})\,\tilde{G}\underline{u} \tag{12.51}$$

where

$$\tilde{G} = G_1 G_2 = G_2 G_1$$

Define

$$H(\theta) = \tilde{G}^T (G_1^{-1} - G_2^{-1})^T (G_1^{-1} - G_2^{-1}) \tilde{G} \tag{12.52}$$

Since H is a positive definite matrix the objective function takes the following form

$$J = \Delta \underline{y}^T \cdot \Delta \underline{y} = \underline{u}^T H \underline{u} \tag{12.53}$$

Introducing

$$Q = G_1^{-1} - G_2^{-1} \tag{12.54}$$

and

$$x = \tilde{G} u \tag{12.55}$$

and substituting into (12.53) we obtain

$$\underline{y} = \underline{x}^T Q^T Q \underline{x} \tag{12.56}$$

In (12.56) matrix Q has a form

$$Q = \begin{bmatrix} 0 & & & 0 \\ \delta_1 & 0 & & \\ \vdots & \vdots & & \\ \delta_i & & \ddots & \\ \delta_\kappa & \delta_i & & 0 \end{bmatrix} \tag{12.57}$$

where

$$\delta_i = \theta_i^2 - \theta_i^1 \tag{12.58}$$

The optimal input signal $\underline{u}$ can be obtained from (12.55)

$$\underline{u} = \tilde{G}^{-1} \underline{\tilde{x}} \tag{12.59}$$

where $\underline{\tilde{x}}$ is obtained as the solution that maximizes the quadratic form

$$Q^T Q \underline{\tilde{x}} = \lambda_{\max} \underline{\tilde{x}}, \qquad \| \underline{\tilde{x}} \| = 1 \tag{12.60}$$

In (12.60) λ_{max} is the maximum eigenvalue of the matrix $Q^T Q$. In the case when $n \to \infty$ (dim $Q \to \infty$) an approximate value of λ_{max} can be obtained as follows.

Matrix $Q^T Q$ can be rewritten in the form

$$Q^T Q = C - DD^T \tag{12.61}$$

where C is an $n \times n$ Toeplitz matrix with entries $c_{ij} = c_{|i-j|}$ given by equalities

$$c_0 = \sum_{i=1}^{\kappa} \delta_i^2$$

$$c_1 = \delta_1 \delta_2 + \cdots + \delta_{\kappa-1} \delta_\kappa$$

$$c_2 = \delta_2 \delta_3 + \cdots + \delta_{\kappa-2} \delta_\kappa$$

$$\overline{c_i = \delta_i \delta_{i+1} + \cdots + \delta_{\kappa-i} \delta_\kappa}$$

Matrix D has a form

$$D = \begin{bmatrix} & 0 & & 0 \\ \hline \delta_\kappa & 0 & & \\ \vdots & & & 0 \\ \delta_2 & & & \\ \delta_1 & \delta_2 \cdots \delta_\kappa & & \end{bmatrix} \tag{12.62}$$

Matrix DD^T is a square matrix having the form

$$DD^T = \begin{bmatrix} 0 & 0 \\ \hline 0 & \begin{array}{c} \text{nonzero} \\ \text{elements} \end{array} \end{bmatrix} \tag{12.63}$$

Aoki and Stanley (1970) have shown that for $n \gg \kappa$

$$\lim_{n \to \infty} \frac{x^T Q^T Q x}{\|x\|^2} = \frac{x^T C x}{\|x\|^2} \tag{12.64}$$

The maximum eigenvalue of matrix C is given by

$$\lambda_{max} = c_0 + 2 \sum_{j=1}^{K} c_j \cos j \frac{\pi}{n} \tag{12.65}$$

The value of λ_{max} substituted to (12.60) permits for obtaining $\tilde{x}$ and hence an optimal input sequence from (12.59).

12.4.2   Case of a Continuous Set of Parameters

An important limitation of Gagliardi's approach is that it restricts the unknown parameter to belong to a finite discrete set. In most practical situations the parameter belongs to a continuous set, and only a mean value and approximate probability distribution can be assumed.

These difficulties can be removed in two ways:

(i) by evaluating the limits of the possible values of the parameters and thereby finding the "extremes" of the transfer function for use in equation (12.43)

(ii) by replacing the continuous probability distribution $p(\theta)$ by a discrete set $p_i = pr\,(\theta = \theta_i)$, $i = 1, 2, \ldots, m$, where θ_i and p_i are chosen by solving the reduced moment problem (Spang 1966).

Suppose that the values of the parameter θ are limited by

$$\theta_0 - \beta \leqslant \theta \leqslant \theta_0 + \beta \tag{12.66}$$

and the probability function satisfies the differential equation

$$\frac{dp(\theta)}{d\theta} = \frac{Q(\theta)}{R(\theta)} \, p(\theta) \tag{12.67}$$

where

$$Q(\theta) = \sum_{i=1}^{\ell} q_i \theta^i \tag{12.68}$$

and

$$R(\theta) = \sum_{i=1}^{n} r_i \theta^i \tag{12.69}$$

The moments of $p(\theta)$ satisfy the linear difference equation

$$\sum_{i=0}^{\ell} q_i \mu_{k+i} + \sum_{i=0}^{n_*} (k+i) r_i \mu_{k+i-1} = \sum_{i=0}^{n} r_i \delta_i \qquad (12.70)$$

where

$$p(\theta) = \sum_{i=1}^{\rho} p_i \delta(\theta - \theta_i)$$

$$\mu_j = \sum_{i=1}^{\rho} p_i(\theta_i)^j \qquad (12.71)$$

$$\delta_i = 2\theta_0 \delta_{i-1} - (\theta_0^2 - \beta^2)\, \delta_{i-2}$$

ρ is the number of moments to be matched, θ_i are roots of the nth order orthogonal polynomials $f_n(\theta)$ such that

$$\int f_i(\theta)\, f_n(\theta)\, p(\theta)\, d\theta = 0, \qquad i = 0, \ldots, n-1$$

and the initial conditions are

$$\mu_0 = 1$$
$$\delta_0 = p(\theta_0 + \beta) - p(\theta_0 - \beta)$$
$$\delta_1 = (\theta_0 + \beta)\, p(\theta_0 + \beta) - (\theta_0 - \beta)\, p(\theta_0 - \beta)$$

For example, the difference equation for truncated Gaussian distribution

$$p(\theta) = \frac{1}{\lambda} \exp\left[-\frac{1}{2\sigma^2}(\theta - \bar{\theta})^2\right]; \qquad \theta_0 - \beta \leqslant \theta \leqslant \theta_0 + \beta \qquad (12.72)$$

is

$$\mu_{n+1} = \bar{\theta}\mu_n + n\sigma^2 \mu_{n-1} - \delta_n$$

with

$$\mu_0 = 1 \quad \text{and} \quad \mu_1 = \bar{\theta} - \delta_0$$

For uniform probability distribution the difference equation is

$$\mu_{n+1} = \frac{\delta_{n+1}}{n+1} \tag{12.73}$$

Substitution of the distribution function by a discrete probability function makes it possible to apply the approach considered in section 12.4.1.

Another approach for finding the "extreme" values of parameters θ incorporated in the input design problem (12.42) (12.43) is a straightforward use of optimization. Combining equation (12.42) and equation (12.45) we obtain

$$y(\theta) = \max_{\theta_1, \theta_2} \int_0^\infty \left| G(\theta_1, j\omega) - G(\theta_2, j\omega) \right|^4 d\omega \tag{12.74}$$

where

$$\theta = [\theta_1, \theta_2], \qquad \theta_1, \theta_2 \in \Xi$$

The 'extreme' parameter values θ_1 and θ_2 are those values of θ which maximize the functional (12.74).

The optimization problem may be stated as follows:

Maximize $y(\theta)$ subject to $h(\theta) = 0$ and $a \leqslant \theta \leqslant b$ where θ, a, and b are vectors of coefficients appearing in $G(j\omega)$ in equation (12.74), $h(\theta)$ is an m-dimensional constraint, in general, nonlinear, which represents a possible set of relationships between the coefficients, and $y(\theta)$ is a real scalar-valued objective function.

Both the objective function and the equality constraint are assumed continuously differentiable over [a, b]. The maximization of y can be obtained by utilization of any optimization procedure known in the literature.

12.4.3   Input Signal Realization

From the extreme value of parameters θ_1 and θ_2, the power spectrum of the desired input signal can be obtained on the basis of equation (12.45). The signal power spectrum has the form

$$\phi_u^*(\omega) = \frac{a_0 + a_1\omega^2 + a_2\omega^4 + \cdots + a_{n-1}\omega^{2(n-1)}}{b_0 + b_1\omega^2 + b_2\omega^4 + \cdots + b_n\omega^{2n}} \tag{12.75}$$

The input signal that has the power spectral density given by equation (12.75) is, in fact, a stochastic signal. In many applications, a staircase pseudorandom signal is more desirable. If there is no restriction on the duration of the input signal, the following algorithm may be used (Wellstead, 1975):

(i) Select an equally spaced sequence of $\frac{1}{2}$ N frequencies at $\omega = \omega_0 k$, $k = 0$, $1, 2, \ldots, N/2$.

(ii) Obtain the discrete power spectrum at $\omega = k\omega_0$, $k = 1, 2, \ldots, N/2$, bounded by the envelope given by equation (12.75).

(iii) Construct the discrete Fourier transform F(k) of the required pseudo-noise sequence as follows:
Let

$$F(k) = \alpha(k) + j\beta(k) \tag{12.76}$$

Define

$$\alpha(k) = [\phi(k\omega_0)]^{1/2} \, r_k m_k \tag{12.77}$$

$$\beta(k) = [\phi(k\omega_0)]^{1/2} \, r_k (1 - m_k) \tag{12.78}$$

$$k = 1, 2, \ldots, N/2 - 1$$

where

r_k takes values ± 1 as a random function of k, and
m_k takes values $0, 1$ as a random function of k independently of r_k.

(iv) Construct the remaining discrete Fourier transform components according to the relations

$$\left.\begin{array}{l} \alpha(0) = \phi(0) \\ \alpha(N/2) = \phi(\omega_0 N/2), \\ \beta(0) = 0 \\ \beta(N/2) = 0 \end{array}\right\} \tag{12.79}$$

Also,

$$\left.\begin{array}{l} \alpha(N - k) = \alpha(k), \qquad k = 1, 2, \ldots, N/2 - 1 \\ \beta(N - k) = \beta(k) \end{array}\right\} \tag{12.80}$$

(v) Calculate the required pseudorandom sequence, $u(n)$, $n = 0, 1, \ldots, N$ by taking the inverse discrete Fourier transform of $F(k)$ as below

$$u(n) = \sum_{k=0}^{N-1} F(k) \exp(j2\pi kn/N) \qquad (12.81)$$

Although N, the length of the sequence, may be selected arbitrarily, it must be made sufficiently large so that a close approximation to the envelope given by equation (12.75) is obtained.

It may be noted that the substitution of the continuous power spectrum by a discrete spectrum with equidistant lines gives an input signal which is suboptimal in the sense of equation (12.42).

The results of the theory of optimum design of regression experiments can be utilized in designing the optimal input signal with a discrete power spectrum (Fedorov 1969). The main objective in the design may be stated as the determination of a discrete spectrum $\phi(\omega_i)$ of the input signal which will be equiva-. lent to the continuous spectrum $\phi_u^*(\omega)$ given in equation (12.75).

The spectral density given by equation (12.75) can be expanded into the following power series

$$\phi_u^*(\omega) = \sum_{i=0}^{\infty} \alpha_i \omega^{2i} \qquad (12.82)$$

where the coefficients α_i are obtained simply by long division. They may also be obtained using the following recurrence relationship

$$\alpha_k = \frac{1}{b_0} a_k - \sum_{i=1}^{k} b_i \alpha_{k-i} \qquad (12.83)$$

The infinite series in (12.82) may be approximated by a finite series in a weighted least squares sense, i.e.,

$$\phi^*(\omega) \simeq \sum_{i=0}^{m-1} \hat{\alpha}_i \omega^{2i} = \underline{\hat{\alpha}}^T \underline{f}(\omega) \qquad (12.84)$$

where

$$\underline{\hat{\alpha}} = [\hat{\alpha}_0 \quad \hat{\alpha}_1 \cdots \hat{\alpha}_{m-1}]^T \qquad (12.85)$$

$$\underline{f}(\omega) = [1 \quad \omega^2 \quad \omega^4 \cdots \omega^{2(m-1)}]^T \qquad (12.86)$$

This approximation problem is the determination of $\hat{\underline{\alpha}}$ such that

$$\sum_{i=0}^{m-1} w_i [\phi^*(\omega_i) - \hat{\underline{\alpha}}^T \underline{f}(\omega_i)]^2 = S(\hat{\alpha}) \tag{12.87}$$

is minimized.

This problem can be solved through the following theorem.

Theorem 1. The best estimate of unknown parameters in a weighted least-squares sense is

$$\hat{\alpha} = M^{-1} \underline{Y} \tag{12.88}$$

where the nonsingular matrix M is given by

$$M = \sum_{i=0}^{m-1} w_i \underline{f}(\omega_i) \, \underline{f}^T(\omega_i) \tag{12.89}$$

and

$$Y = \sum_{i=0}^{m-1} w_i \phi^*(\omega_i) \, \underline{f}(\omega_i) \tag{12.90}$$

The proof is given in the paper by Kuszta and Sinha (1979).

The main task in our problem, then, is to determine a set of points ω_i which maximize M. De la Garza (1954) has considered the estimation of a polynomial of degree m and showed that for any arbitrary distribution of the points of observation there is a distribution at only m + 1 points for which M is the same.

Let the end points ω_0 and ω_m be -1 and $+1$, respectively. It may be noted that in practice, a transformation from the domain $[-1, 1]$ to $[0, \omega_b]$, i.e., the desired bandwidth, will be necessary. One may now, take advantage of theorem 2.

Theorem 2. The points of measurement for minimax variance are to be located at -1, $+1$, and the roots of $(1 - \omega^2) P'_{m-1}(\omega)$, where $P'_{m-1}(\omega)$ is the derivative of the Legendre polynomial $P_m(\omega)$ of degree m. The proof is given in the paper by Kuszta and Sinha (1979).

When the observations are spaced at equal intervals, the maxima and minima of variance are points given by

$$\sum_{j=0}^{m} (2j + 1) P_j(\omega) P'_j(\omega) = 0 \tag{12.91}$$

which, from the recurrence relation for Legendre polynomials, reduces to (Guest 1958)

$$P'_{m-1}(\omega)\, P'_m(\omega) = 0 \qquad (12.92)$$

The points of maximum variance are then the roots of $P'_{m-1}(\omega)$ and the points of minimum variance are the roots of $P'_m(\omega)$. A comparison between the minimum variance V_1 and the maximum variance V_2 in the uniform spacing method shows that over most of the region $[-1, 1]$

$$V_1 = \frac{2}{\pi}\, V_2 \qquad (12.93)$$

The design of the optimal input signal can be divided into the following steps:

(i) Determine the envelope of the power spectral density of the input following equations (12.43) and (12.74).

(ii) If this envelope is flat, the optimal signal is given by

$$u(t) = \sum_{j=1}^{m} V_j \sin \omega_j t \qquad (12.94)$$

where ω_j are chosen on the basis of theorem 2, and V_j are chosen from the envelope (12.75) at points ω_j.

(iii) In the case when the envelope has one or more maxima, the uniform spacing method can be used. Once the discrete spectrum is obtained, one may calculate the required pseudorandom sequence by obtaining the inverse discrete Fourier transform according to equation (12.81). Signals obtained from the weighted m-sequence generator can also be used (Kuszta and Sinha, 1977).

12.4.4 Input Signals of Short Duration

The derivations of the previous section apply to the case when the period of observation is sufficiently large. We shall now consider the minimum value of the time of experiment, T, that is necessary to obtain a good approximation to the desired power spectrum. As is well known from Heisenberg's uncertainty principle, there is a reciprocal relationship between the frequency spectrum of a signal and its duration in time. Hence it is not possible to find a time function of finite duration which will correspond exactly to a prescribed frequency-limited signal. We can, therefore, attempt to obtain only a reasonable approximation in practical problems.

As proposed by Landau and Pollack (1961), the 'time-spread,' T, of f(t) may be defined by the equation

$$T^2 = \frac{\int_{-\infty}^{\infty} (t - t_0)^2 \, |f(t)|^2 \, dt}{\int_{-\infty}^{\infty} |f(t)|^2 \, dt} \tag{12.95}$$

and, correspondingly, the 'frequency-spread,' Ω, of $F(\omega)$ may be expressed by the equation

$$\Omega^2 = \frac{\int_{-\infty}^{\infty} (\omega - \omega_0)^2 \, |F(\omega)|^2 \, d\omega}{\int_{-\infty}^{\infty} |F(\omega)|^2 \, d\omega} \tag{12.96}$$

Then, for any choice of t_0 and ω_0, it follows that

$$\Omega T \geqslant \tfrac{1}{2} \tag{12.97}$$

Since equation (12.97) provides only a rough approximation, the following has been proposed by MacCall in an unpublished paper (Landau and Pollack 1961)

$$\Omega T > 2\pi \alpha^2 \beta^2 \tag{12.98}$$

where

$$\alpha = \frac{\int_{t_0}^{t_0 + T} |f(t)|^2 \, dt}{\int_{-\infty}^{\infty} |f(t)|^2 \, dt} \tag{12.99}$$

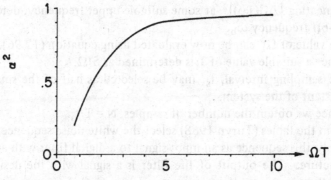

Figure 12.3. Plot of σ^2 against ΩT for $\beta^2 \simeq 1$.

and

$$\beta = \frac{\displaystyle\int_{\omega_0}^{\omega_0 + \Omega} |F(\omega)|^2 \, d\omega}{\displaystyle\int_{-\infty}^{\infty} |F(\omega)|^2 \, d\omega} \tag{12.100}$$

For the case when $\beta^2 \simeq 1$, the relationship between α^2 and ΩT has been calculated by Landau and Pollack (1961) and is shown in Fig. 12.3. It will be seen that, although initially α^2 increases linearly with ΩT, the curves indicate 'saturation' with larger values of ΩT. Hence, it will be of very little practical value to make ΩT larger than, say, 5.

This, therefore, provides a simple rule for estimating the minimum reasonable duration of the experiment.

A short time duration signal with prescribed power density spectrum can be obtained as a result of applying a discrete-time, short-duration white-noise signal to a digital filter.

The problem of selection of pulse sequences that have power spectra closely approximating white noise has been studied in detail by Barder (1953) and Huffman (1962). Turyn (1968) has presented tables of sequences with small autocorrelation except at the origin. Moreover, Turyn and others have shown that there are no other codes with this property.

For time-limited type experiments the procedure of input signal design is as follows:

(i)   Evaluate the function $|\Delta G(j\omega)|^2 = \phi(\omega)$ from (12.74).

(ii)   Truncating $|\Delta G(j\omega)|^2$ at some suitable upper frequency, determine the cut-off frequency ω_b.

(iii) The value of Ω^2 can be now evaluated using equation (12.96).

(iv)   Hence a suitable value of T is determined as $5/\Omega$.

(v)   The sampling interval, t_s, may be selected as half of the smallest time constant of the system.

(vi)   Hence we obtain the number of samples, $N = T/t_s$.

(vii) From the tables (Turyn 1968) select the white-noise sequence.

(viii) Apply this sequence as an input signal to a digital filter with appropriate structure. The output of the filter is a signal with the desired power spectrum.

EXAMPLE 12.4

Suppose that the binary sequence 2251111211 (plot presented in Fig. 12.4) was selected as a white-noise sequence. The normalized autocorrelation function of this signal is presented in Fig. 12.5.

Suppose now that desired signal power spectrum $\phi(\omega)$ has a peak coinciding with ω_ℓ, given by

$$\omega_\ell = \frac{1}{2\ell t_s} \tag{12.101}$$

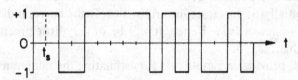

Figure 12.4.   Plot of the binary sequence 2251111211.

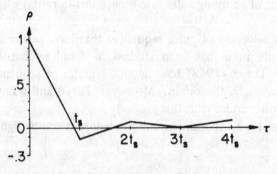

Figure 12.5.   Normalized autocorrelation function for the binary sequence 2251111211.

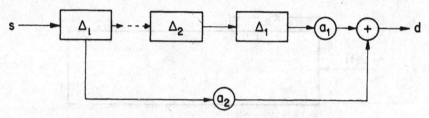

Figure 12.6. Block diagram for generating the desired signal.

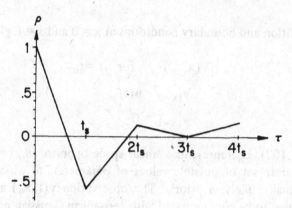

Figure 12.7. Normalized autocorrelation function of the signal generated.

A block diagram of a shift register with weighted outputs which can form such signal is presented in Fig. 12.6.

In Fig. 12.6, s is the white-noise sequence, d is the desirable output signal, and a_1, a_ϱ are shift-register weights.

In Fig. 12.7 the normalized autocorrelation function of the signal d for the case $\varrho = 2$, $a_1 = 1$, $a_2 = -1$ (ternary sequence) is presented.

12.4.5 Optimal Input Synthesis for Distributed Parameter Systems

A direct approach can be used for design of an optimal signal for a distributed parameter system. Consider such a system shown in Fig. 12.8.

The system can be described on $R = (0, L) \times (0, T)$ by the partial differential equation

$$\frac{\partial y(t, x)}{\partial t} = L_x \{\theta_i, y(t, x)\} \tag{12.102}$$

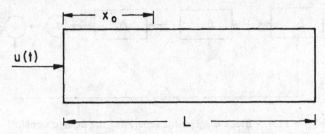

Figure 12.8. A distributed-parameter system.

with initial condition and boundary conditions at x = 0 and x = L given by

$$y_0 = y(x, t_0) \qquad \text{for} \quad t = t_0$$
$$y\big|_{x=0} = u(t) \tag{12.103}$$
$$y\big|_{x=L} = 0$$

In equation (12.102), L_x represents a linear space operator; θ_i, $i = 1, 2, \ldots, m$ represents a discrete set of possible values of parameters θ, which will be assumed to be equally likely, a priori. The observation $y(t, x_0)$ at the chosen point x_0 is assumed to be contaminated with zero-mean Gaussian noise.

Applying the basic equation (12.39), the optimization problem can be expressed in the following form:

$$J = \max_{u \in U} \int_0^\infty \big| y_1(t, x_0) - y_2(t, x_0) \big|^2 \, dt \tag{12.104}$$

where $y_i(t, x_0)$ is the value of $y(t, x_0)$ in equation (12.102) for "extreme" values θ_i, $i = 1, 2$, and some $u(t)$.

The solution of equation (12.102), with the initial and boundary conditions specified in equation (12.103), is obtained, following Tichonow and Samarski (1951), as below:

$$y(\theta_i, t, x_0) = \int_0^L G(\theta_i, t, t_0, x_0, \xi) \, (y(\xi, t_0)) \, d\xi$$

$$+ \int_0^t G'(\theta_i, \tau, t_0, x_0) \, u(\tau) \, d\tau$$

$$= y'(\theta_i, t, x_0) + y''(\theta_i, t, x_0) \tag{12.105}$$

where

$G(\cdot)$ is the Green's function for the system defined by equation (12.101),
$G'(\cdot)$ is the "boundary" Green's function,
$y'(\cdot)$ is the output signal component related to nonzero initial conditions, and
$y''(\cdot)$ is the output signal component related to external boundary input signal.

Since, during the test for identification, only the component $y''(\cdot)$ can be affected by the input signal, the criterion for the design of the optimum input should be rewritten in the following form:

$$J = \max_{u \in U} \int_0^\infty \left| y_1''(t, x_0) - y_2''(t, x_0) \right|^2 \, dt \qquad (12.106)$$

Combining equations (12.105) and (12.106) and recalling Parseval's formula, we have

$$J = \int_0^\infty \left| G'(\theta_1, t_0, x_0, j\omega) - G'(\theta_2, t_0, x_0, j\omega) \right|^2 \, \phi(\omega) \, d\omega$$

$$= \int_0^\infty \left| \Delta H(t_0, x_0, j\omega) \right|^2 \, \phi(\omega) \, d\omega \qquad (12.107)$$

where

$$H_i(t_0, x_0, j\omega) = \int_0^\infty G'(\theta_i, t_0, x_0, \tau) \exp(-j\omega\tau) \, d\tau \qquad (12.108)$$

$$\Delta H(t_0, x_0, j\omega) = H_1(t_0, x_0, j\omega) - H_2(t_0, x_0, j\omega) \qquad (12.109)$$

and $\phi(\omega)$ is the power spectral density of the bounded input signal $u(t)$. The functional J is maximized if

$$\phi(\omega) = K \left| \Delta H(t_0, j\omega) \right|^2 \qquad (12.110)$$

where K is a constant, and it is assumed that $u(t)$ is square integrable.

EXAMPLE 12.5

To illustrate the approach to the design of the optimal input signal described above, consider the example of a one-dimensional heat-conduction system described by the partial differential equation

$$\frac{\partial y(x, t)}{\partial t} = a^2 \frac{\partial^2 y(x, t)}{\partial x^2} \qquad (12.111)$$

with boundary and initial conditions

$$\left.\begin{array}{l} y(x, 0) = 0 \\ y(0, t) = u(t) \\ u(L, t) = 0 \end{array}\right\} \qquad (12.112)$$

The Green's function for the system described by equations (12.111) and (12.112) has the following form (Tichonow and Samarski 1951)

$$G(a, t, \tau; x, \xi) = \frac{2}{L} \sum_{n=1}^{\infty} \sin\left(\frac{n\pi x}{L}\right) \sin\left(\frac{n\pi\xi}{L}\right) \exp\left[-\frac{n^2\pi^2}{L^2} a^2(t - \tau)\right] \qquad (12.113)$$

Since equation (12.113) is time-invariant, the substitution of

$$\lambda = t - \tau \qquad (12.114)$$

gives the following Green's function

$$G(a, \lambda, x, \xi) = \frac{2}{L} \sum_{n=1}^{\infty} \sin\left(\frac{n\pi x}{L}\right) \sin\left(\frac{n\pi\xi}{L}\right) \exp\left(-\frac{n^2\pi^2 a^2}{L^2} \lambda\right) \qquad (12.115)$$

The boundary Green's function is obtained as

$$G'(a, \lambda, x) = a^2 \left.\frac{\partial G(a, \lambda, x, \xi)}{\partial \xi}\right|_{\xi=0} \qquad (12.116)$$

The explicit form of the boundary Green's function is given by

$$G'(a, \lambda, x) = \frac{2\pi a^2}{L^2} \sum_{n=1}^{\infty} n \exp\left(-\frac{n^2\pi^2 a^2}{L^2} \lambda\right) \sin\left(\frac{n\pi x}{L}\right) \qquad (12.117)$$

Finally, we have

$$y''(a, x, t) = y(a, x, t) = \frac{2\pi a^2}{L^2} \int_0^t \sum_{n=1}^{\infty} n \exp\left(-\frac{n^2\pi^2 a^2}{L^2}(t-\tau)\right)$$

$$\cdot \sin\left(\frac{n\pi}{L} x\right) u(\tau) \, d\tau \qquad (12.118)$$

Taking into account only one term ($n = 1$) of the boundary Green's function, the power spectral density of the input signal is obtained as below:

$$\phi(\omega) = K |\Delta H(j\omega)|^2 = \left| \int_0^{\infty} a^2 \, \Delta \left. \frac{\partial G(a, t, x_0, \xi)}{\partial \xi} \right|_{\xi=0} \exp(-j\omega t) \, dt \right|^2$$

$$= \frac{2\pi^2}{L^2} \sin\left(\frac{\pi x_0}{L}\right) \left\{ \frac{1}{\frac{\pi^2 a_1^2}{L^2} + j\omega} - \frac{1}{\frac{\pi^2 a_2^2}{L^2} + j\omega} \right\}^2 \qquad (12.119)$$

For $L = \pi$, $x_0 = L/2$, $a_1 = 1.1$, and $a_2 = 0.9$, the power spectral density simplifies to

$$\phi(\omega) = K \frac{\omega^2}{(0.98 - \omega^2)^2 + 2.02\omega^2} \qquad (12.120)$$

One of the many possible input signals can be selected as

$$u(t) = F^{-1}[\psi(j\omega)] \qquad (12.121)$$

where F^{-1} represents inverse Fourier transformation, and

$$\psi(j\omega) \, \psi(-j\omega) = \phi(\omega) \qquad (12.122)$$

For the given examples from equations (12.120), (12.121), and (12.122)

$$u(t) = 3.025 \exp(-1.21 t) - 2.025 \exp(-0.8 t) \qquad (12.123)$$

In the case when the input signal should be generated as a staircase function it is also possible to approximate $u(t)$ by a Walsh function series (Corrington 1973).

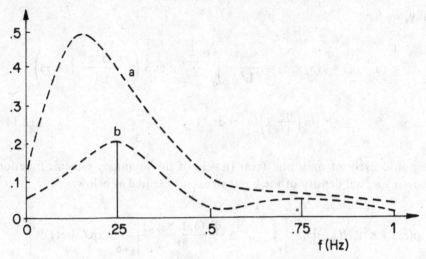

Figure 12.9.   Power spectrum of input signal: (a) desired (b) Walsh function approximation.

For example, an eight-term approximation to u(t) in equation (12.123) has the form

$$\hat{u}(t) = -0.197\psi_0 + 0.613\psi_1 + 0.298\psi_{10} - 0.004\psi_{11} + 0.149\psi_{100}$$
$$-0.01\psi_{101} - 0.001\psi_{110} + 0.011\psi_{111} \qquad (12.124)$$

The power spectral density of the approximate function, obtained through equation (12.124) is shown in Fig. 12.9.

REFERENCES

Aoli, M. and Stanley, R. M. (1970), "On input signal synthesis in parameter identification," *Automatica*, vol. 6, pp. 431–440.

Barker, R. H. (1953), "Group synchronizing of binary digital systems," in *Communication Theory*, W. Jackson, ed., Butterworths Scientific Publications, London, England, pp. 273–287.

Corrington, M. S. (1973), "Solution of differential and integral equations with Walsh functions," *IEEE Trans. Circuit Theory*, 20, pp. 470–476.

de La Garza, A. (1954), "Spacing the information in polynomial regression," *Ann. Math. Stat.*, 25, pp. 123–130.

Fedorov, W. W. (1969), *The Theory of Optimal Experiments* (in Russian), Nauka, Moscow.

Gagliardi, R. M. (1967), "Input selection for parameter identification in discrete systems," *IEEE Transactions. Automatic Control*, AC-12, pp. 597–599.

Goodwin, G. C. and Payne, R. L. (1976), "Choice of sampling intervals," in: *System Identification*, R. K. Mehra and D. G. Laniotis, eds., Academic Press, New York, pp. 251–282.

Goodwin, G. C. and Payne, R. L. (1977), "Dynamic system identification. Experiment design and data analysis," Academic Press, New York, San Francisco, London.

Guest, P. G. (1958), "The spacing observations in polynomial regression," *Annals of Math. Stat*, *29*, pp. 294–299.

Gupta, N. K. et al., (1976), "Application of optimal input synthesis to aircraft parameter identification," *Trans. ASME, Journal of Dynamic Systems, Measurement and Control*, pp. 139–145.

Huffman, D. H. (1962), "The generation of impulse-equivalent pulse trains," *I.R.E. Trans. Inf. Theory*, *8*, pp. 5–10.

Kalaba, R. E. and Spingarn, I. (1973), "Optimal inputs and sensitivities for parameter estimation," *JOTA*, vol. 11, no. 1, pp. 56–67.

Kalaba, R. E. and Spingarn, K. (1975), "Optimal inputs system identification . . . ," *JOTA*, vol. 16, nos. 5/6, pp. 487–496.

Kalaba, R. E. and Spingarn, K. (1976), "Optimal input system identification for nonlinear dynamic systems," *JOTA*, vol. 21, no. 1, pp. 91–101.

Kuszta, B. and Sinha, N. K. (1976), "Optimum input signals for parameter identification," *Int. J. Systems Sci.*, vol. 7, pp. 935–941.

Kuszta, B. and Sinha, N. K. (1977), "Optimal m-squence input signal for system identification," *Int. J. Systems Sci.*, vol. 8, pp. 1097–1103.

Kuszta, B. and Sinha, N. K. (1979), "Synthesis of optimal input signals for system identification," *Int. J. Systems Sci.*, vol. 10, pp. 251–258.

Landau, H. Y. and Pollack, H. O. (1961), "Prolate spheriodal wave functions . . . ," *Bell Syst. Tech. J.*, vol. 40, pp. 43–84.

Mehra, R. H. (1974a), "Optimal inputs for linear system identification," *IEEE Transactions. Automatic Control*, vol. 19, no. 3, pp. 192–200.

Mehra, R. K. (1974b), "Optimal input signal for parameter estimation in dynamic system—survey and new results," *IEEE Transactions. Automatic Control*, AC-19, pp. 753–768.

Mehra, R. K. (1976), "Frequency domain synthesis of optimal inputs for linear system parameter estimation," *Transactions of ASME, JDMC*, vol. 98, ser. G, no. 2, pp. 130–138.

Mehra, R. K. and Lainiotis, D. G. (eds.) (1976), *System Identification—Advances and Case Studies*, Academic Press, New York, pp. 211–249.

Spang, H. A. (1966), "The effect of estimation error on the control of an unknown linear plant," *Proc. 3rd IFAC Congress*, London.

Tichonow, A. H. and Samarski, A. A. (1951), *Equations of Mathematical Physics* (in Russian), G.I.T.T.L., Moscow.

Turyn, R. (1968), in: *Error Correcting Codes*, H. B. Mann, ed., J. Wiley & Sons, New York.

Wellstead, P. E. (1975), "Pseudonoise test signals and fast Fourier transform," *Electronics Letters*, *11*, p. 202.

Zarrop, M. B. (1979), "Optimal experiment design for dynamic system identification," Lecture Notes in Control and Information Sciences, volume 21, Springer-Verlag, Berlin, Heidelberg, New York.

13

Determination of the Order and Structure

13.1 INTRODUCTION

In the previous chapters we have considered many algorithms for estimating the parameters of a model of known order from noise-contaminated input-output data. In practice, the order is not known a priori. Moreover, for multivariable systems, we require a knowledge of the structural parameters in addition to the order. Hence, in this chapter we shall study the various methods available for estimating the order of single-input single-output systems and the structural parameters of multivariable systems from the data.

In section 13.2, we shall start with the determination of the order from the impulse response sequence of a single-input single-output system. A number of methods for estimating the order will be discussed. In section 13.3, we shall consider the estimation of the order of a single-input single-output system from the samples of the input-output data. Section 13.4 will be devoted to the determination of the structural parameters of a special canonical form for linear multivariable systems. In section 13.5, we shall discuss the determination of the order and the number of integrations required for time-series models.

13.2 ESTIMATION OF THE ORDER OF A DISCRETE-TIME MODEL FROM ITS IMPULSE RESPONSE SEQUENCE

As discussed in chapters 2, 3, and 5, a number of methods for system identification start with estimating the samples of the impulse response. These methods are called nonparametric since one does not have to make any assumption about the order of the system or any of its parameters. Since it is seldom practical to use such a sequence for design purposes, the next step is to obtain the parameters of a suitable linear model from this impulse response sequence. Such a procedure was described in Chapter 2, where it was assumed that the order of

the system was already known. Hence, we shall now discuss methods for estimating the order of the model from the samples of the impulse response.

13.2.1 Use of the Hankel Matrix

Given the impulse response sequence, $w_0, w_1, w_2, \ldots, w_N$, we can determine
the order from the rank of the Hankel matrix, defined as

$$H(\ell, k) = \begin{bmatrix} w_k & w_{k+1} & w_{k+2} & \cdots & w_{k+\ell-1} \\ w_{k+1} & w_{k+2} & w_{k+3} & \cdots & w_{k+\ell} \\ \vdots & \vdots & \vdots & & \vdots \\ w_{k+\ell-1} & w_{k+\ell} & w_{k+\ell+1} & \cdots & w_{k+2\ell-2} \end{bmatrix} \qquad (13.01)$$

since it is well-known that if ℓ is greater than n then the rank of the Hankel
matrix is equal to the order of the system n (Lee 1964). Hence, one can determine n by evaluating the determinant of $H_{(\ell, k)}$ for each k and different values
of ℓ since the determinant will vanish for all k when $\ell = n + 1$.

In practice, these determinants will not vanish identically because of noise
contained in the data. Hence, some criterion must be introduced to establish
the level of significance. One approach is to calculate the average value of the
determinant of $H(\ell, k)$ for each ℓ, and plot the ratio D_ℓ against ℓ, where

$$D_\ell \triangleq \left| \frac{\text{average value of determinant of } H(\ell, k)}{\text{average value of determinant of } H(\ell + 1, k)} \right| \qquad (13.02)$$

From this plot, the order n is obtained as that value of ℓ for which D_ℓ is a
maximum.

Another approach is to first obtain an estimate of the autocorrelation sequence from the data using the relationship

$$\phi_i = \frac{1}{N - i + 1} \sum_{k=0}^{N-i} w_k w_{k+i} \qquad (13.03)$$

and then determine the rank of the Hankel matrix the elements of which are the
estimated autocorrelation coefficients, ρ_i, defined as

$$\rho_i = \frac{\phi_i}{\phi_0}, \qquad i = 0, 1, 2, \ldots \qquad (13.04)$$

Again, the determinant may not exactly vanish, and we may use the determinant ratio test described by equation (13.02).

EXAMPLE 13.1

As an example we shall consider the following 48 samples of the impulse response sequence of a biological process.

k	0	1	2	3	4	5	6	7	8	9	10	11	12
w_k	1.0	0.8	0.65	0.54	0.46	0.39	0.35	0.31	0.28	0.26	0.24	0.23	0.22

k	13	14	15	16	17	18	19	20	21	22	23	24
w_k	0.21	0.20	0.19	0.19	0.18	0.18	0.18	0.17	0.17	0.17	0.16	0.16

k	25	26	27	28	29	30	31	32	33	34	35	36
w_k	0.15	0.15	0.15	0.15	0.14	0.14	0.14	0.13	0.13	0.13	0.13	0.12

k	37	38	39	40	41	42	43	44	45	46	47	48
w_k	0.12	0.12	0.12	0.12	0.11	0.11	0.11	0.11	0.10	0.10	0.10	0.10

$$\text{Average value of det. } H(2, k) = 0.00087872$$

$$\text{Average value of det. } H(3, k) = -0.00029311$$

$$\text{Average value of dét. } H(4, k) = -3.214 \times 10^{-7}$$

$$\text{Average value of det. } H(5, k) = -5.709 \times 10^{-9}$$

$$D_2 = 2.998, \quad D_3 = 911.9, \quad D_4 = 56.296$$

From the above, it would appear that probably the order of the model is three.

Let us now consider the correlation coefficients. The estimated values of these, calculated according to equations (13.03) and (13.04), are given below:

$$\rho_0 = 1, \quad \rho_1 = 0.88052126, \quad \rho_2 = 0.79025506, \quad \rho_3 = 0.72231277,$$

$$\rho_4 = 0.67060564, \quad \rho_5 = 0.62999127, \quad \rho_6 = 0.60107303,$$

$$\rho_9 = 0.57697552$$

From these correlation coefficients the determinants of Hankel matrices of different orders were calculated. These are given below.

$$H(2, 0) = 0.01493737$$

$$H(3, 0) = -0.00001235$$

$$H(4, 0) = 0$$

This confirms that the order of the model should be three, although a model of order two would provide a good "fit."

13.2.2   Akaikes' Information Criterion

This criterion can be obtained with the aid of an information theoretic interpretation of the method of maximum likelihood. In practice, it requires estimating the parameters of models of different order using the maximum likelihood method and then selecting the model which minimizes the following (Akaike 1974):

$$AIC = -2 \log_e L + 2m \tag{13.05}$$

where L = likelihood function as defined in Chapter 3 (section 3.3), and m is the number of independently adjustable parameters in the model.

It may be noted that this approach emphasizes the principle of parsimony in model building, since if two models are equally likely, the one with fewer parameters is selected.

The use of this criterion requires obtaining the maximum likelihood estimates of the parameters for different assumed values of the order of the model, following the procedure described in section 3.3. The logarithmic likelihood function is then calculated and the AIC determined for each case. Hence, the order which gives the minimum AIC estimate is determined.

Although this is a very powerful and practical approach, it requires an excessive amount of computation. For this reason, it has been applied mostly to the problem of stochastic modeling of time series.

13.3   ESTIMATION OF THE ORDER OF A SINGLE-INPUT SINGLE-OUTPUT SYSTEM FROM INPUT-OUTPUT OBSERVATIONS

We shall now consider the more general case when we have available sets of observations of the samples of the input and output of a single-input single-output system. Methods for estimating the parameters of a model of given order have been discussed in Chapter 3. These methods are based on the assumption that the input is sufficiently rich so that it persistently excites all the modes of the system. In the sequel we shall assume that this condition is satisfied.

Following Woodside (1971), let $\{u_k\}$ and $\{y_k\}$ be the noise-contaminated observations of the samples of the input and output, respectively, and let

$$
\underline{a}_k \triangleq \begin{bmatrix} u_0 \\ y_0 \\ u_1 \\ y_1 \\ \vdots \\ u_{k-1} \\ y_{k-1} \end{bmatrix}
\tag{13.06}
$$

Define the product moment matrix as

$$
Q_k = E[\underline{a}_k \underline{a}_k^T]
\tag{13.07}
$$

It will be seen that it is the covariance matrix of $\underline{a}_k$. Normally, this expectation can be approximated by taking correlation in the time domain assuming stationarity and ergodicity.

It can be shown that for the noise-free case, Q is singular if k is greater than n, and

$$
\text{rank } Q_k = k + n
\tag{13.08}
$$

provided that the input sequence satisfies the assumption of persistently exciting all the modes of the system.

In the presence of noise, however, Q_k will almost always be of full rank. Woodside has shown that if starting from a given value of k, one plots the ratio

$$
D_k \triangleq \frac{\det Q_k}{\det Q_{k+1}}
\tag{13.09}
$$

against k, then a jump is exhibited in D_k at k = n. This jump is very pronounced for low values of the noise-to-signal ratio, but as the noise-level is increased, it is hard to distinguish. For a fourth-order system example it was found that this method did not prove useful for noise-to-signal ratios of more than 3 percent. A better result was obtained (Woodside 1971) by using the enhanced product moment matrix $\hat{Q}_k$, defined as

$$\hat{Q}_k = Q_k + \sigma^2 R \tag{13.10}$$

where $\sigma^2 R$ is the covariance matrix of the measurement noise. Applying the determinant ratio test to $\hat{Q}_k$, the jump was unmistakable up to a noise-to-signal ratio of 10 percent for the example considered.

Woodside (1971) has shown that further improvement is obtained by using the ratio

$$D_k^* = \frac{\det \hat{P}_k}{\det \hat{Q}_k^*} \tag{13.11}$$

where $\hat{P}_k$ is the lower right $(2k + 1) \times (2k + 1)$ corner of $\hat{Q}_k$ and $\hat{Q}_k^*$ is the lower $2k \times 2k$ corner of $\hat{Q}_k$. For the example considered by him, the jump was clearly indicated for noise-to-signal ratios of up to 30%.

An alternative to the enhancement of the product moment matrix is the use of an instrumental product moment matrix (Wellstead 1976, 1978), where an instrumental variable approach is used. In this, the matrix Q_k is replaced by

$$\Gamma_k \triangleq E[\underline{a}_k \underline{b}_k^T] \tag{13.12}$$

where

$$\underline{b}_k = \begin{bmatrix} u_0 \\ z_0 \\ u_1 \\ z_1 \\ \vdots \\ u_{k-1} \\ z_{k-1} \end{bmatrix} \tag{13.13}$$

where $\{z_i\}$ are the instrumental variables, generated as the output sequence of a stable system of order k or greater, and subject to the same input sequence. If it is assumed that the instrumental variables generated in this manner are statistically orthogonal to the observation noise, then the rank of the instrumental product moment matrix is given by

$$\text{rank } \Gamma_k = \min [k + n + 1, 2k + 1] \tag{13.14}$$

Wellstead (1978) has reported that applying the determinant ratio test to the instrumental moment product matrix, a distinct jump was noticeable even for high noise-to-signal ratios. The main difficulty, as with the instrumental variable method for parameter estimation, is the choice of the auxiliary model used for generating the instrumental variables. For further discussion of this method, reference may be made to the recent paper by Young et al. (1980).

13.4 DETERMINATION OF THE STRUCTURE OF MULTIVARIABLE SYSTEMS

As discussed in Chapter 5, the identification of the parameters of multivariable systems requires prior knowledge of its structural parameters. Moreover, the structural parameters are different for the various representations of the system. In this section we shall consider the determination of the structural parameters of the canonical state-space model described in section 5.3. These structural parameters, are the observability subindices, n_i, of the system. Moreover, the order of the system is obtained as

$$n = \sum_{i=1}^{p} n_i \qquad (13.15)$$

where p is the number of outputs.

From equation (5.76), the output of the jth subsystem can be written as

$$y_j(k + n_j) = \sum_{i=1}^{p} \sum_{l=1}^{n_{ji}} a_{ji}(l) \, y_i(k + 1 - 1)$$

$$+ \sum_{i=1}^{m} \sum_{l=1}^{n_j} \beta_{(n_1 + \cdots + n_{j-1} + l), i} u_i(k + 1 - 1) \qquad (13.16)$$

where $\beta_{i,j}$ are obtained through the transformation given by equation (5.73).

We shall first consider the determination of the structural parameters for the noise-free case utilizing the residual error method (Suen and Liu 1978). This will then be extended to the case of noisy observations (El-Sherief and Sinha 1979).

13.4.1 The Residual-Error Method for the Noise-Free Case

Suppose that we have been given a set of n vectors $\underline{x}_1, \underline{x}_2, \ldots, \underline{x}_n$, and we want to determine whether or not a vector $\underline{y}$ is a linear combination of the set. Let

$$X = [\underline{x}_1, \underline{x}_2, \ldots, \underline{x}_n] \qquad (13.17)$$

Then $\underline{y}$ is a linear combination of the given set if and only if we can find a non-zero vector $\underline{\theta}$ such that

$$\underline{y} = X\underline{\theta} \tag{13.18}$$

However, such a vector $\underline{\theta}$ is usually difficult to find. Alternatively consider the vector

$$\underline{\theta}^0 \triangleq X^+\underline{y} \tag{13.19}$$

where X^+ is the pseudoinverse of X as defined in Appendix I. Also, define

$$e(\underline{\theta}^0) \triangleq (\underline{y} - XX^+\underline{y})^T (\underline{y} - XX^+\underline{y})$$
$$= \underline{y}^T(I - XX^+)\,\underline{y} \tag{13.20}$$

as the residual error for $\underline{\theta}^0$.

It can be shown (Wiberg 1971) that $e(\underline{\theta}^0) \leqslant e(\underline{\theta})$ for all $\underline{\theta}$.

Lemma 1.   The vector $\underline{y}$ is a linear combination of $\{\underline{x}_1, \underline{x}_2, \ldots, \underline{x}_n\}$ if and only if $e(\underline{\theta}^0) = 0$.

Note that the above lemma does not require the linear independence of the set of vectors $\{\underline{x}_1, \underline{x}_2, \ldots, \underline{x}_n\}$.

We shall now apply this result to determine the structural parameters from noise-free data. For the ith subsystem, equation (13.16), collecting K input-output sequences, and assuming that the order of this subsystem is ℓ_i, we get

$$Y_i(K) = H_i(\ell_i, K)\,\underline{\theta}_i(\ell_i) \tag{13.21}$$

where

$$Y_i(K) = [y_i(k+1)\, y_i(k+2) \cdots y_i(k+K)] \tag{13.22}$$

$$H_i(l_i, K) = \begin{bmatrix} y_1(k) & \cdots y_1(k-\ell_i) & y_2(k) & \cdots y_i(k-1) & \cdots \\ y_1(k+1) & \cdots y_1(k-\ell_i+1) & y_2(k+1) & \cdots y_i(k) & \cdots \\ \vdots & \vdots & \vdots & \vdots & \\ y_1(k+K-1) & \cdots y_1(k+K-1-\ell_i) & y_2(k+K-1) & \cdots y_i(k+K-2) & \cdots \end{bmatrix}$$

$$\begin{bmatrix} y_i(k-\ell_i) & \cdots y_{i+j}(k-1) & \cdots u_1(k-1) & \cdots u_m(k-\ell_i) \\ y_i(k-\ell_i+1) & \cdots y_{i+j}(k) & \cdots u_1(k) & \cdots u_m(k-\ell_i+1) \\ \vdots & \vdots & \vdots & \vdots \\ y_i(k+K-\ell_i-1) & \cdots y_{i+j}(k+K-2) & \cdots u_1(k+K-2) & \cdots u_m(k+K-\ell_i-1) \end{bmatrix} \tag{13.23}$$

and $\underline{\theta}_i(\ell_i)$ is a vector of parameters characterizing the ith subsystem.

It follows that the vector $\underline{Y}_i(K)$ is a linear combination of the vectors of $H_i(\ell_i, K)$ if $\ell_i \geqslant n_i$, and it is not if $\ell_i < n_i$.

From equations (13.20) and (13.21) we get

$$e_i^0(\ell_i) = \underline{Y}_i^T(K)\, [I - H_i(\ell_i, K)\, H_i^+(\ell_i, K)]\, \underline{Y}_i(K) \triangleq \Delta_i(\ell_i) \quad (13.24)$$

Following lemma 1, we get

$$e_i^0(\ell_i) = 0 \quad \text{if} \quad \ell_i \geqslant n_i$$
$$= \Delta_i(\ell_i) > 0 \quad \text{if} \quad \ell_i < n_i \quad\quad (13.25)$$

Hence, we get the following rule:

Estimation Rule 1. For the ith subsystem, the residual $e_i^0(\ell_i)$ is plotted against ℓ_i. From this plot, n_i is obtained as the smallest integer ℓ_i for which $e_i^0(\ell_i) = 0$.

13.4.2 The Residual-Error Method for the Noisy Case

Consider the case of the noise-contaminated vector $\underline{y}^*$, given by

$$\underline{y}^* = \underline{y} + \underline{v} \quad\quad (13.26)$$

where $\underline{v}$ is a zero-mean noise vector.

In view of equation (13.18), we may write

$$\underline{y}^* = X\underline{\theta} + \underline{v} \qu\quad (13.27)$$

The residual error is thus obtained as

$$e^0 = \underline{y}^{*T}(I - XX^+)\, \underline{y}^*$$
$$= \underline{y}^T(I - XX^+)\, \underline{y} + 2\underline{y}^T(I - XX^+)\, \underline{v} + \underline{v}^T(I - XX^+)\, \underline{v} \quad (13.28)$$

Taking the expectation of both sides of equation (13.28) and assuming that $\underline{v}$ is uncorrelated with $\underline{y}$, we have

$$E[e^0] = \underline{y}^T(I - XX^+)\, \underline{y} + E[\underline{v}^T(I - XX^+)\, \underline{v}] \quad (13.29)$$

This leads us to the following lemma.

Lemma 2. Assuming that $\underline{v}$ is a zero mean vector uncorrelated with $\underline{y}$, then if $\underline{y}$ is a linear combination of $\{\underline{x}_1, \underline{x}_2, \ldots, x_n\}$ we have

$$E[e^0] = E[\underline{v}^T(I - XX^+)\underline{v}] \tag{13.30}$$

and otherwise

$$E[e^0] = \underline{y}^T(I - XX^+)\underline{y} + E[\underline{v}^T(I - XX^+)\underline{v}] \tag{13.31}$$

It can be observed that the right-hand side of equation (13.31) is strictly greater than that of equation (13.30).

We shall now apply these results to determine the structural parameters from noisy data, i.e., from

$$y_i^*(k) = y_i(k) + v_i(k), \qquad i = 1, 2, \ldots, p \tag{13.32}$$

where $y_i^*(k)$ is the ith noisy output and $v_i(k)$ is the noise at the ith output which is a zero-mean white noise sequence. Then substituting for $y_i(k)$ from equation (13.32) into equation (13.16), we get

$$y_i^*(k + n_i) = \sum_{j=1}^{p} \sum_{\ell=1}^{n_{ij}} a_{ij}(\ell)\, y_j^*(k + \ell - 1)$$

$$+ \sum_{j=1}^{m} \sum_{\ell=1}^{n_i} B_{(n_1 + \cdots + n_{i-1} + \ell),\, j}\, u_j(k + \ell - 1) + w_i(k + n_i) \tag{13.33}$$

where

$$w_i(k + n_i) = -\sum_{j=1}^{b} \sum_{\ell=1}^{n_{ij}} a_{ij}(\ell)\, v_j(k + \ell - 1) + v_i(k + n) \tag{13.34}$$

It is evident that $w_i(k)$ is also a zero-mean noise sequence.

Using K input-output sequences and assuming that the order of the ith subsystem is ℓ_i, we obtain the following expression similar to equation (13.21)

$$Y_i^*(K) = H_i^*(\ell_i, K)\, \underline{\theta}_i(\ell_i) + W_i(K) \tag{13.35}$$

where

$$W_i(K) \triangleq [w_i(k + 1)\, w_i(k + 2) \cdots w_i(k + K)] \tag{13.36}$$

and $Y_i^*(K)$ and $H_i^*(\ell_i, K)$ are as defined in equations (13.22) and (13.23) but with $y_i(k)$ replaced by $y_i^*(k)$.

Define

$$Z_i(K) \triangleq Y_i^*(k) - W_i(k) \qquad (13.37)$$

Then, we can observe that the vector $Z_i(K)$ is a linear combination of the vectors of $H_i^*(\ell_i, K)$ if $\ell_i \geqslant n_i$ and not if $\ell_i < n_i$. From lemma 2, we obtain the following results

$$E[e_i^0(\ell_i) | H_i^*(\ell_i, K)] = g_i(\ell_i) \quad \text{if} \quad \ell_i \geqslant n_i \qquad (13.38)$$

$$= g_i(\ell_i) + \Delta_i(\ell_i) \quad \text{if} \quad \ell_i < n_i \qquad (13.39)$$

where

$$e_i^0(\ell_i) \triangleq Y_i^{*T}(K) [I - H_i^*(\ell_i, K) H_i^{*+}(\ell_i, K)] Y_i^*(K) \qquad (13.40)$$

$$g_i(\ell_i) \triangleq E[W_i^T(K) \{I - H_i^*(\ell_i, K) H_i^{*+}(\ell_i, K)\} W_i(K)] \qquad (13.41)$$

and

$$\Delta_i(\ell_i) \triangleq Z_i^T(K) [I - H_i^*(\ell_i, K) H_i^{*+}(\ell_i, K)] Z_i(K) \qquad (13.42)$$

Let $\hat{e}_i^0(\ell_i)$ be the estimate of $E[e_i^0(\ell_i) | H_i^*(\ell_i, K)]$ where $e_i^0(\ell_i)$ is evaluated by equation (13.40) from the given input-output sequences. Then equations (13.38) and (13.39) can be rewritten as

$$\hat{e}_i^0(\ell_i) = f_i(\ell_i) + g_i(\ell_i) \qquad (13.43)$$

where

$$f_i(\ell_i) = 0 \quad \text{if} \quad \ell_i \geqslant n_i \qquad (13.44)$$

$$= \hat{\Delta}_i(\ell_i) > 0 \quad \text{if} \quad \ell_i < n_i \qquad (13.45)$$

From equation (13.41) we can see that $g_i(\ell_i)$ is nearly constant if K is sufficiently large. Therefore, the plot of the residual $\hat{e}_i^0(\ell_i)$ against ℓ_i for the noisy case has the same shape as the residual plot for the noise-free case, with the difference that it is raised by a nearly constant value. Hence, we get the following estimation rule:

Estimation Rule 2. From the ith output the residual error $e_i^0(\ell_i)$ is plotted against ℓ_i. From this plot n_i is obtained as the smallest integer ℓ_i for which the part of the residual plot for $\ell_i \leqslant n_i$ is almost flat.

In practice, it is better to plot the difference in the residual error $e_i^{0*}(\ell_i)$ against ℓ_i, where

$$e_i^{0*}(\ell_i) \triangleq e_i^0(\ell_i) - e_i^0(\ell_i - 1) \tag{13.46}$$

13.4.3 Structural Identification Using the Correlation Method (Tse and Wienert 1975, El-Sherief 1980)

Another approach to structural identification is the correlation method, which is based on the rank of a Hankel matrix. Let R be the correlation matrix of the output sequence, defined as

$$R(\sigma) = E[\underline{y}(k + \sigma)\,\underline{y}^T(k)] \tag{13.47}$$

where the expectation is approximated as a time-average, assuming stationarity and ergodicity. Define $r_{ij}(\sigma)$ as the entry in the ith row and jth column of $R(\sigma)$.

We now define the Hankel matrix $H\ell_i(K)$, where ℓ_i is the assumed order of the ith subsystem and K is a large number denoting the length of the output sequence, as

$$H_{\ell i}(K) = \begin{bmatrix} r_{1j}(1) \cdots r_{1j}(n_1) & \cdots r_{ij}(1) \cdots r_{ij}(\ell_i) \\ \vdots & \vdots & \vdots & \vdots \\ r_{1j}(K) \cdots r_{1j}(K + n - 1) & \cdots r_{ij}(K) \cdots r_{ij}(K + \ell - 1) \end{bmatrix} \tag{13.48}$$

Define

$$S(\ell_i) = H_{\ell_i}^T(K)\,H_{\ell_i}(K) \tag{13.49}$$

It is easily seen that (El-Sherief 1980)

$$\det S(\ell_i) = 0 \quad \text{if} \quad \ell_i > n_i \tag{13.50}$$

Hence, the true value of n_i, $i = 1, 2, \ldots, p$, can be estimated for each value of i as follows.

Estimation Rule 3. Construct the matrix $S(\ell_i)$ of dimension ℓ_i where ℓ_i is the assumed value of n_i. For different values of ℓ_i, plot $\det S(\ell_i)$ against ℓ_i until the determinant becomes zero for $\ell_i = \ell_i^*$. Then $n_i = \ell_i^* - 1$.

13.5 ORDER AND THE NUMBER OF INTEGRATIONS IN TIME-SERIES MODELS

In Chapter 6, we discussed determination of the parameters of various types of time-series models of assumed orders. In this section, we shall look into the problem of obtaining the orders of stationary autoregressive and moving-average models, as well as the number of integrations required for nonstationary time series.

13.5.1 Determination of the Order of a Stationary Purely Autoregressive Model

In section 6.3.3, we considered the determination of the parameters of the nth-order autoregressive model. It is pointed out that for such a process the autocorrelation coefficients satisfy the difference equation

$$\rho_k = \phi_1 \rho_{k-1} + \phi_2 \rho_{k-2} + \cdots + \phi_n \rho_{k-n}; \qquad k > 0. \qquad (13.51)$$

where ρ_i are the autocorrelation coefficients, and ϕ_i are the autoregressive parameters.

Equation (13.51) implies that only the first n correlation coefficients are linearly independent. Hence, a Hankel matrix formed from the correlation coefficients will be of rank n. However, since we only have the estimated values of the correlation coefficients, one may again use the determinant ratio test, as suggested in section 13.2.

13.5.2 Determination of the Order of a Stationary Moving Average Model

In section 6.3.6, we considered the determination of the parameters of the nth-order moving-average model for a given value of n. It was also pointed out that for such a model, it is necessary that the correlation coefficients ρ_i be zero for i greater than n.

From the above, we may conclude that if we want to fit a moving-average model to a time series, its estimated correlation coefficients must be negligibly small after a certain lag. Thus, the order is n if

$$\gamma_i \simeq 0 \qquad \text{for} \quad i > n \qquad (13.52)$$

In practice, one may use a ratio test, similar to the determinant ratio test, to estimate the value of n if the correlation coefficients decrease rapidly.

13.5.3   Order and the Number of Integrations for Nonstationary Time-Series

As may be recalled from section 6.4, the determination of a nonstationary time-series model is based on the assumption that some suitable difference of the series is stationary. The number of times that one must take differences of the given time-series is also the number of integrations required of a stationary time-series to obtain the given time series.

Hence, modeling a nonstationary time-series consists of two steps. The first step is to determine the number of integrations. The second step is then modeling the resulting stationary time-series. The order of this model can be determined using the methods described in sections 13.5.1 and 13.5.2. Hence, here we shall focus our attention to obtaining the number of integrations.

Since a time-series is said to be stationary if it has a stationary mean, it is evident that one should examine the running average of such a series. If this running average is approximately constant the process may be considered stationary. On the other hand, if the running average is not constant, it may be modeled as a power series. The order of this power series is then the number of times this process must be differentiated in order to obtain a stationary process. This, therefore, provides a simple rule for determining the number of integrations.

An important question which remains unanswered is the amount of data over which the running average should be calculated. Some computational experience (Sinha and Abul-Haggag Ibrahim 1980) indicates that best results are obtained when the averaging is done over approximately 90% of the available data.

13.6   CONCLUDING REMARKS

In this chapter we have considered the determination of the order of a suitable model to fit a given impulse response sequence, input-output data, or time-series. Most of the methods described depend upon the determination of the rank of a matrix. Due to the presence of observation noise and other errors, the corresponding determinants do not exactly vanish. Hence, a determinant ratio test is generally used to estimate the rank of the related matrix.

Another approach to the problem is to estimate the parameters of models of different orders and compare these for accuracy. One such method is the AIC criterion which combines the log likelihood with the number of parameters to be estimated to obtain a practical comparison between models of different order. Other methods for diagnostic tests and comparison of different models will be studied in the next chapter.

13.7 REFERENCES

Akaike, H. (1974), "A new look at the stochastic model identification," *IEEE Transactions. Automatic Control*, vol. AC-19, pp. 716-623.

Chew, C. J. C. (1972), "On estimating the order of an autoregressive moving average process with uncertain observations," *IEEE Transactions. Automatic Control*, vol. AC-17, pp. 707-709.

El-Sherief, H. and Sinha, N. K. (1979), "Determination of the structure of a canonical model for the identification of linear multivariable systems," *Proc. 5th IFAC Symp. on Identification and System Parameter Estimation* (Darmstadt, Federal Republic of Germany), pp. 569-576.

El-Sherief, H. (1980), "Structure and parameter identification of linear multivariable systems using the correlation method," *Proc. 23rd Midwest Symposium on Circuits and Systems* (Toledo, Ohio).

Lee, R. C. K. (1964), *Optimal Estimation, Identification, and Control*, M.I.T. Press, Cambridge, Mass.

Sinha, N. K. and Ibrahim, O. Abul-Haggag (1980), "On the choice of the number of integrations in ARIMA models for time series," *Proc. International Conference on Applied Systems Research and Cybernetics* (Acapulco, Mexico), pp. 2688-2693.

Suen, L. C. and Liu, R. (1978), "Determination of the structure of multivariable stochastic systems," *IEEE Transactions. Automatic Control*, vol. AC-23, pp. 458-464.

Tse, E. and Wienert, H. L. (1975), "Structure determination and parameter identification of multivariable stochastic linear systems," *IEEE Transactions. Automatic Control*, vol. AC-20, pp. 603-613.

Van Den Boom, A. J. W. and Van Den Enden, A. W. M. (1974), "The determination of the order of process and noise dynamics," *Automatica*, vol. 10, pp. 245-256.

Wellstead, P. E. (1976), "Model identification using an auxiliary system," *Proc. I.E.E.*, vol. 123, pp. 1373-1379.

Wellstead, P. E. (1978), "An instrumental product moment test for model order estimation," *Automatica*, vol. 14, pp. 89-71.

Woodside, C. M. (1971), "Estimation of the order of linear systems," *Automatica*, vol. 7, pp. 727-733.

Young, P., Jakeman, A., and McMurtree, R. (1980), "An instrumental variable method for model order identification," *Automatica*, vol. 16, pp. 281-294.

13.8 PROBLEMS

1. For the time series of the annual flow of the Nile river at Aswan dam, given in the table in Chapter 6, determine the order of a suitable autoregressive model using the method described in section 13.5.1.

2. Estimate the order of a suitable model for the input-output data in Tables 1 and 2 in Chapter 3.

14
Diagnostic Tests and Model Validation

14.1 INTRODUCTION

After a model has been obtained, it is always necessary to test it for suitability. Diagnostic tests are also required for selecting the best among several rival models for the same process. These tests are based on comparing the response of the process with that of the model for a number of test inputs. The model is considered suitable if the two responses are "sufficiently close." This closeness is quantified in terms of the sequence of residuals, defined as the difference between the actual output sequence and the predicted output for the model. A model is considered satisfactory if the residuals form a white-noise sequence with zero mean, and as small a variance as possible. It may be recalled that a similar criterion was also used in Chapters 3 and 4 to test if the estimates of the parameters are unbiased and consistent. If the sequence of residuals satisfies the tests for whiteness, then we select the model for which this sequence has the minimum variance.

In section 14.2, we shall discuss methods for testing a finite sequence of numbers for whiteness. These tests will be applied to two examples of linear models in section 14.3. One of these is the set of stochastic models for annual flow of the Nile river developed in Chapter six. The other example is that of the impulse response sequence of a biological process considered in example 13.1 in Chapter 13. In this case we shall compare a second-order and a third-order model obtained using the least-squares method. In section 14.4, we shall be concerned with the verification of linear models for nonlinear plant by using dispersion functions.

14.2 TESTS FOR WHITENESS

Given a random sequence $\{r_k\}$, $k = 1, 2, \ldots, N$, its autocorrelation sequence is defined as

$$\rho_i = \frac{\gamma_i}{\gamma_0} \tag{14.01}$$

where

$$\gamma_i = \lim_{N \to \infty} \frac{1}{N-i} \sum_{k=1}^{N-i} r_k r_{k+i} \tag{14.02}$$

The process $\{r_i\}$ is said to be white if and only if the correlation coefficients

$$\rho_i = 0 \qquad \text{for all} \quad i > 0 \tag{14.03}$$

In practice, however, only a finite number of elements of $\{r_k\}$ are available. Hence, it is not possible to obtain γ_i exactly, as indicated in equation (14.02). As a result, with finite N, we have only estimates of the correlation coefficients, and equation (14.03) will not be satisfied exactly even if $\{r_k\}$ is part of a white noise sequence.

As pointed out by Box and Jenkins (1970), one may consider the sequence $\{r_k\}$ as white within 95 percent confidence limits if

$$|\rho_i| \leqslant \frac{1.98}{\sqrt{N}} \qquad \text{for all} \quad i \geqslant 1 \tag{14.04}$$

In practice, it is sufficient to test this inequality for i = 1 to 20.

Another approach is to apply the Portmanteau test (Box and Jenkins 1970). If the sequence is white then it has a chi-square distribution with m degrees of freedom, and for large m

$$N \sum_{i=1}^{m} \rho_i^2 \leqslant n(m, 2n) \tag{14.05}$$

with a risk of about 5 percent.

Equation (14.05) requires referring to the chi-square table. This is sometimes inconvenient. As shown by Stoica (1977), one can make the following approximation with a risk of 5 percent if m is sufficiently large

$$N \sum_{i=1}^{m} \rho_i^2 \leqslant (m + 1.65\sqrt{2m}) \tag{14.06}$$

Again a value of m = 20 is usually satisfactory in practice.

14.3 EXAMPLE OF DIAGNOSTIC TESTS FOR LINEAR MODELS

We shall apply these tests to two examples. One of these is a stochastic model; the other is a deterministic model obtained from the impulse response sequence of a biological process.

14.3.1 Model of the Annual Flow of the Nile River at Aswan

In section 6.5, twelve different stochastic models of the annual flow of the Nile River at Aswan were obtained from the data for the period 1903 to 1944. Out of these twelve, it was found that the fourth-order autoregressive model gave the minimum mean-square error. Hence, we shall test this model for adequacy.

The correlation coefficients of the sequence of residuals for lags up to ten are given below:

$$\rho_1 = 0.138, \quad \rho_2 = -0.034, \quad \rho_3 = -0.005, \quad \rho_4 = 0.012, \quad \rho_5 = -0.130$$

$$\rho_6 = 0.015, \quad \rho_7 = -0.272, \quad \rho_8 = 0.112, \quad \rho_9 = -0.171, \quad \rho_{10} = -0.032$$

Note that only ten correlation coefficients are used because of the short length of the data.

Since $1.98/\sqrt{N} = 0.316$, the first test is satisfied, and the sequence is white within 95 percent confidence limits.

Also,

$$N \sum_{i=1}^{10} \rho_i^2 = 5.868$$

and

$$m + 1.65\sqrt{2m} = 17.38 \quad \text{for} \quad m = 10 \tag{14.07}$$

Thus, the second test is also satisfied, and we may conclude that the fourth-order autoregressive model is satisfactory within 95 percent confidence limits.

14.3.2 Modeling a Biological Process from its Impulse Response Sequence

In Chapter 13 we had considered the example of a biological process. From its impulse response sequence, it was decided that the model should be of order three, but probably a second-order model could be adequate. Here we shall test the two models.

Following the procedure described in section 2.5.1, a least-squares estimate of the second-order model is obtained as

$$H_2(z) = \frac{z^2 - 0.8404087z - 0.00844085}{z^2 - 1.6404087z + 0.65388613} \tag{14.08}$$

and the third-order model is obtained as

$$H_3(z) = \frac{z^3 - 0.27771z^2 - 0.5315z - 0.0055914}{z^3 - 1.07771z^2 - 0.319325z + 0.410382} \tag{14.09}$$

For the second-order model, the sequence of residuals has a mean value of 0.000619, and standard deviation of 0.00621. While these values do not look bad, the correlation coefficients give a different picture. These are

$$\rho_1 = -0.56458, \quad \rho_2 = 0.09653, \quad \rho_3 = 0.13508, \quad \rho_4 = 0.11014$$

$$\rho_5 = 0.31377, \quad \rho_6 = -0.41380, \quad \rho_7 = 0.38314, \quad \rho_8 = 0.19211$$

These values are much larger than $1.98/\sqrt{N} = 0.2929$, and indicate that the residuals are highly correlated. Hence, the second-order model is inadequate.

For the third-order model, the residual sequence has mean value 0.0002998 and standard deviation 0.0005408. The first ten correlation coefficients are given below:

$$\rho_1 = -0.25837, \quad \rho_2 = 0.36306, \quad \rho_3 = 0.19174, \quad \rho_4 = 0.12296$$

$$\rho_5 = 0.10717, \quad \rho_6 = -0.28881, \quad \rho_7 = 0.16158, \quad \rho_8 = -0.03092$$

$$\rho_9 = 0.08611, \quad \rho_{10} = 0.04443$$

Only one of these values, ρ_2, is larger than $1.98/\sqrt{N} = 0.29516$, hence it is quite probable that the residual sequence is white. Also,

$$N \sum_{i=1}^{10} \rho_i^2 = 17.418 \tag{14.10}$$

which is slightly higher than $m + 1.65\sqrt{2m} = 17.379$.

Hence, this third-order model is marginally acceptable.

14.4 THE VERIFICATION OF LINEAR MODELS FOR NONLINEAR PLANT

Although most physical plant is nonlinear, we usually obtain a linear model for convenience in analysis and design. The quantitative assessment of adequacy between such model and plant may be made by means of dispersion function techniques introduced by Rajbman and coworkers (1965, 1966, 1972, 1975).

For two real random functions y(t), $t \in T_y$ and x(t), $t \in T_x$, the cross-dispersion function is defined as

$$\theta_{yx}(t, \tau) \triangleq E\{[E\{y(t)|x(\tau)\} - E\{y(t)\}]^2\} \qquad (14.11)$$

where E is the expectation operator, and $E\{y(t)|x(\tau)\}$ is the conditional mean of the random function y(t) with respect to the random function x(τ).

If in equation (14.11) we assume that y(t) = x(τ) for all t and τ, then we have the definition for the dispersion (autodispersion) function of the random variable x(t).

$$\theta_{xx}(t, \tau) \triangleq E\{[E\{x(t)|x(\tau)\} - E\{x(t)\}]^2\} \qquad (14.12)$$

The normalized dispersion function is defined as the positive square root of the ratio of the dispersion function to the variance of the random function. For example, the normalized cross-dispersion function of y(t) with respect to x(τ) is

$$\zeta_{yx}(t, \tau) \triangleq \sqrt{\frac{\theta_{yx}(t, \tau)}{D\{y(t)\}}} \qquad (14.13)$$

and the normalized dispersion function of x(t) is

$$\zeta_{xx}(t, \tau) \triangleq \sqrt{\frac{\theta_{xx}(t, \tau)}{D\{x(t)\}}} \qquad (14.14)$$

where $D\{x(t)\}$ is the variance of x(t) and $D\{y(t)\}$ is the variance of y(t).

If y(t) and x(τ) are independent, or $E\{y(t)|x(\tau)\} = E\{y(t)\}$, then by virtue of the definition (14.11)

$$\theta_{yx}(t, \tau) = E\{[E\{y(t)\} - E\{y(t)\}]^2\} \qquad (14.15)$$

and

$$\zeta_{yx}(t, \tau) = 0 \qquad \text{if} \quad D\{y(t)\} \neq 0 \qquad (14.16)$$

In the case where the random functions y(t) and x(τ) are related by the exact functional relationship

$$y(t) = f\{x(\tau)\} \qquad (14.17)$$

the cross-dispersion function is equal to the variance of the random variable $y(t)$, since

$$\theta_{yx}(t, \tau) = E\{[f\{y(\tau)\} - E\{f\{x(\tau)\}\}]^2\} = D\{y(t)\} \qquad (14.18)$$

and the normalized cross-dispersion function

$$\zeta_{yx}(t, \tau) = 1 \qquad (14.19)$$

From the above definitions, it follows that the normalized dispersion functions are nonnegative, with lower and upper limits of 0 and 1, respectively. It may also be shown that the normalized cross-dispersion function is not less than the modulus of the normalized cross-correlation function (Rajbman and Chadeev 1975), i.e.,

$$\zeta_{yx}(t, \tau) \geqslant |\rho_{yx}(t, \tau)| \qquad (14.20)$$

In the case of linear dependence of $y(t)$ on $x(\tau)$,

$$E\{y(t)|x(\tau)\} = a_1(t, \tau) + b_1(t, \tau) x(\tau) \qquad (14.21)$$

and of linear dependence of $x(\tau)$ on $y(t)$,

$$E\{x(\tau)|y(t)\} = a_2(\tau, t) + b_2(\tau, t) y(t) \qquad (14.22)$$

the normalized dispersion function is equal to the modulus of the corresponding normalized correlation function, i.e.,

$$\zeta_{yx}(t, \tau) = |\rho_{yx}(t, \tau)| \qquad (14.23)$$

and

$$\zeta_{xy}(\tau, t) = |\rho_{xy}(\tau, t)| \qquad (14.24)$$

and only in this case are the dispersion functions symmetrical, i.e.,

$$\zeta_{yx}(t, \tau) = \zeta_{xy}(\tau, t) \qquad (14.25)$$

We may now define the degree of nonlinearity of a single-input single-output system with input $x(\tau)$ and output $y(t)$ as

$$Q_{yx}(t, \tau) \triangleq \min_{a(t, \tau), b(t, \tau)} \left[\frac{E\{[E\{y(t)|x(\tau)\} - \{a(t, \tau) + b(t, \tau) x(\tau)\}]^2\}}{D\{y(t)\}} \right]^{1/2}$$

$$(14.26)$$

The minimum of the quantity under the symbol of mathematical expectation is obtained when

$$a(t, \tau) = E\{y(t) - \rho_{yx}(t, \tau)\left[\frac{D\{y(t)\}}{D\{x(\tau)\}}\right]^{1/2} E\{x(\tau)\} \tag{14.27}$$

$$b(t, \tau) = \rho_{yx}(t, \tau)\left[\frac{D\{y(t)\}}{D\{x(\tau)\}}\right]^{1/2} \tag{14.28}$$

Then, by the definition of the cross-dispersion and correlation functions, we get the relationship

$$Q_{yx}^2(t, \tau) = \zeta_{yx}^2(t, \tau) - \rho_{yx}^2(t, \tau) \tag{14.29}$$

This is a very simple relationship and tells us that by evaluating the normalized dispersion and correlation functions we can judge the suitability of a model for a nonlinear system. If the system is linear, the average value of Q_{yx} will be zero. On the other hand, if this quantity is much smaller than 1, a linear model may be adequate.

The basis for evaluation of degree of nonlinearity is the time average $\overline{Q}_{yx}$ of the function $Q_{yx}(t, \tau)$.

$$\overline{Q}_{yx} = \lim_{T \to \infty} \frac{1}{T^2} \int_0^T \int_0^T Q_{yx}(t, \tau)\, d\tau\, dt = \frac{1}{2}\tilde{Q}_{yx} + \frac{1}{2}\tilde{\tilde{Q}}_{yx} \tag{14.30}$$

where

$$\tilde{Q}_{yx} = \lim_{T \to \infty} \frac{2}{T^2} \int_0^T \int_0^T Q_{yx}(t, \tau)\, d\tau\, dt; \quad t \geqslant \tau \tag{14.31}$$

$$\tilde{\tilde{Q}}_{yx} = \lim_{T \to \infty} \frac{2}{T^2} \int_0^T \int_t^T Q_{yx}(t, \tau)\, d\tau\, dt; \quad t < \tau \tag{14.32}$$

The scalar (14.30) depends on the type of nonlinearity (with an accuracy of up to constant multipliers and additive constants) and on the type of input signal.

14.4.1 Example Calculation of the Degree of Cubic Nonlinearity for a Gaussian Input Signal (Rajbman and Terechin, 1965).

The main task in calculations of degree of nonlinearity is obtaining the function $Q_{yx}(t, \tau)$.

For the cubic static device we have

$$y(t) = x^3(t) \tag{14.33}$$

where

x(t) is an input signal
y(t) is an output signal

For a Gaussian process with zero mean value we have (Davenport and Root, 1958):

$$E\{x^n(t)\} = 1 \cdot 3 \cdot 5 \cdots (n-1) [D\{x(t)\}]^{n/2}, \qquad n \text{ even} \tag{14.34}$$

$$E\{X_1 X_2 X_3 X_4\} = E\{X_1 X_2\} E\{X_3 X_4\} + E\{X_1 X_3\} E\{X_2 X_4\}$$
$$+ E\{X_1 X_4\} E\{X_2 X_3\} \tag{14.35}$$

From equation (14.11)

$$\theta_{yx}(t, \tau) = \theta_{x^3 x}(t, \tau) = 3D^3\{x(t)\} [3\rho_{xx}^2(t, \tau) + 2\rho_{xx}^6(t, \tau)] \tag{14.36}$$

Taking advantage of equations (14.33) and (14.34) we have

$$D\{y(t)\} = E\{y^2(t)\} = E\{x^6(t)\} = 15D^3\{x(t)\} \tag{14.37}$$

The normalized cross-dispersion function is

$$\varsigma_{yx}(t, \tau) = \sqrt{\frac{\theta_{yx}(t, \tau)}{Dy(t)}} = \left[\frac{1}{5}(3\rho_{xx}^2(t, \tau) + 2\rho_{xx}^6(t, \tau))\right]^{1/2} \tag{14.38}$$

The second term in equation (14.29) is a cross-correlation function:

$$\rho_{yx}(t, \tau) = \frac{R_{yx}(t, \tau)}{\sqrt{D\{y(t)\}}}$$

From equations (14.33) and (14.35) we have

$$R_{yx}(t, \tau) = E\{y(t) x(\tau)\} = E\{x^3(t) x(\tau)\}$$
$$= 3E\{x^2(t)\} E\{x(t) x(\tau)\} = 3D\{x(t)\} R_{xx}(t, \tau) \tag{14.39}$$

The normalized cross-correlation function is:

$$\rho_{yx}(t, \tau) = \frac{R_{yx}(t, \tau)}{[D\{y(t)\}]^{1/2}} = \frac{3D\{x(t)\} R_{xx}(t, \tau)}{[15D^3\{x(t)\}]^{1/2}} = \frac{3}{\sqrt{15}} \rho_{xx}(t, \tau)$$

(14.40)

From equation (14.29)

$$Q_{yx}^2(t, \tau) = \tfrac{3}{5} \rho_{xx}^2(t, \tau) + \tfrac{2}{5} \rho_{xx}^6(t, \tau) - \tfrac{9}{15}\rho_{xx}^2(t, \tau) = \tfrac{2}{5} \rho_{xx}^6(t, \tau) \quad (14.41)$$

Eventually:

$$Q_{yx}(t, \tau) = \sqrt{\tfrac{2}{5}} \left|\rho_{xx}(t, \tau)\right|^3$$

(14.42)

Similar calculations carried out for quadratic nonlinearity give (Rajbman and Terechin, 1965)

$$Q_{yx}(t, \tau) = \left|\rho_{xx}(t, \tau)\right|^2$$

(14.43)

The degree of nonlinearity for quadratic device is greater than for cubic characteristic, as expected.

14.5 REFERENCES

Box, G. E. P. and Jenkins, G. M. (1970), *Time Series Analysis—Forecasting and Control*, Holden Day, San Francisco.

Bunich, A. L. and Rajbman, N. S. (1972), "A dispersion equation for nonlinear plant identification," *Problems of Control and Information Theory*, vol. 1, pp. 29–36.

Davenport, W. B. and Roots, W. L. (1958), *Random Signals and Noise*. McGraw-Hill, Inc., New York.

Rajbman, N. S. and Terechin, A. T. (1965), "Dispersion functions for random variables and their application for examining nonlinear plant," *Automation and Remote Control*, vol. 26, pp. 496–506.

Rajbman, N. S. (1966), "Nonlinear plant identification with the aid of dispersion functions," *Proc. 3rd IFAC Congress* (London).

Rajbman, N. S. and Chadeev, V. N. (1975), *Identification of Industrial Processes* (in Russian), Energiya, Moscow.

Rajbman, N. S. (1977), "Dispersion function of random functions and some of their applications," *Trans. of the 7th Prague Conference on Information Theory, Statistical Decision Functions, Random Processes and of the 1974 European Meeting of Statisticians*, vol. A., Academic Publishing House of the Czechoslovak Academy of Sciences.

Stoica, P. (1977), "A test for whiteness," *IEEE Transactions Automatic Control*, vol. AC-22, pp. 992–993.

14.6 PROBLEMS

1. Obtain the maximum likelihood estimate of the third-order model of the impulse response of the biological process described in example 13.1, and perform diagnostic tests for adequacy.
2. Determine the degree of nonlinearity of the process in example 1 by obtaining the dispersion function of its impulse response.

15
Concluding Remarks

The material presented in this book could be divided into three parts which are closely related. The first part (Chapters 2 to 9) is concerned with linear models only. For a large number of practical cases, although the plant is nonlinear, the operating point is selected carefully on the basis of past experiences, and a linear model is generally adequate for normal conditions. However, the results of changes in the operating point must be investigated carefully. Furthermore, for plants under construction there may not be sufficient prior knowledge or experience to enable the determination of a proper operating point, as well as the safe regions of operation. The material in Chapters 10 and 11 provides some answers, and should be treated as the starting point for further investigations. There is some overlap in the material in these two chapters, and the interested reader is also invited to read the work of Arnold (1973). This overlap was introduced deliberately for two reasons: (i) not to use too many new notions with which engineers are not familiar, and (ii) not to emphasize the problems which have not been completely solved by mathematicians. Nevertheless, such branches of mathematics as algebraic topology, nonlinear differential equations, and perturbation analysis have developed quite rapidly, and it is worth while to keep track of the achievements in these fields and introduce new results to modeling and identification. The classification of nonlinear models by means of Soshitaishivili's theorem (cf. Chapter 11) is still far from completeness and farther from becoming a routine procedure. An attempt to verify general nonlinear models on the basis of n-dimensional trajectories has so far been unsuccessful for n greater than two. It is due to such extraordinary complication of phase-portraits that even a stochastic treatment is often suggested for their consideration (Batalova et al. 1972, Curry et al. 1978).

In Chapter 11, we suggest the investigation of nonlinear systems transformed to the Poincaré form. This may be realized when a feedback loop with high gain coefficient can be introduced and the system can be excited by periodical input signal. The justification of such an approach is as follows.

For systems of order greater than 2 there are no methods describing the global behavior of nonlinear systems. The systems of Poincaré form are the only type of equations with complete description, and some kind of perturbation technique is used to discuss the behavior of solutions. By using these perturbation techniques one can build up a catalogue of phenomena which may occur in higher-order systems in the hope that one can use this experience as a guide to the eventual development of topological techniques which are applicable to high-order systems.

The reason for investigation of nonlinear phenomena is two-fold. Although models for automatic control are stated in linear terms one should test the validity of linearization and "coarseness" of the system. The other reason is to investigate the possibility of the operating point location being "closer" to the bifurcation zone. It can be observed that for such operating points the system reacts more "quickly" and displays "readiness" for changes. Also the physical (chemical) phenomena are more significant (efficient) when the operating point is close to the oscillation zone (Bailey 1978, Pikos et al. 1977).

The basic information for such investigations can be derived by examining the behavior of the system transformed to the Poincaré form. The global investigation of a nonlinear system requires more sophisticated methods, and more complete model verification should be carried out on the basis of topological investigations (Mehra et al. 1977).

The third part of the book deals with the determination of the order and the structure of the linear model, as well as the validation of the model, linear or nonlinear. From practical considerations, it is important to determine the adequacy of the model under the types of inputs the process is likely to encounter. In all of these cases, the design of the test input is very closely related to the design of the input for the verification of the model.

The problems which have not been completely solved are listed below:

1. Problems related to linear models.
   (a) In the case of linear multivariable systems, as was pointed out in Chapter 5, there is a need to develop a procedure for identification for the case of interacting noise, i.e., when the noise at each output affects the other outputs.
   (b) The convergence of the bootstrap algorithm for combined state and parameter estimation, discussed in Chapter 9, has not been proved, although the algorithms for state estimation and parameter estimation are known to converge separately. This needs further investigation.
2. Problems relating to linearization.
   (a) Can a particular system be treated as linear? What are the limits of

such linearization (i.e., the range of external signals for which this is valid)?

(b) In what way does the introduction of feedback affect the properties of such system? In particular, does the system become less (or more) sensitive to external signals?

(c) What knowledge is required to obtain prescribed behavior of the system under certain uncertainties (Horowitz et al. 1975, Richalet et al. 1978)?

3. Problems relating to quasilinearization.

(a) What kind of quasilinear models (Hammerstein, Wiener, etc.) can be used for approximating a given system?

(b) How many terms of the Volterra series are sufficient for such an approximation? The question of the possibility of parameter estimation should be carefully considered.

(c) How to transform the system so that it may be described by the Poincaré form? What experiments should be performed for the identification of the model in this form?

(d) Preparation of a "catalogue" of different possible behaviors in the case of nonlinear systems of higher dimensions in the Poincaré form.

4. Global nonlinear problems.

(a) Does the dynamic system obey Smale's assumptions? (Smale 1961 a, b, 1965, 1966, also Appendix VI).

(b) Preparation of a "catalogue" of the behaviors of such a system.

(c) How to obtain information from chaotic trajectories about the nature of the system?

From the above, it will be evident that the art of modeling and identification is still at the stage of infancy. It should also convince beginners in the field that a large number of problems in this branch of engineering are practically unsolved.

REFERENCES

Arnold, V. I. (1973), *Differential Equations*, M.I.T. Press, Cambridge, MA.

Bailey, V. E. (1978), in: *Periodic Phenomena in Chemical Reactor Theory: A Review*, N. R. Amudson and L. Lapidus, eds., Prentice-Hall, Englewood Cliffs, NJ.

Batalova, I. C. and Neymark, V. I. (1972), "On the dynamic system with homoclinic structure," *Radiophysics* (in Russian), vol. 11.

Curry, J. H. and Yorke, J. A. (1978), *A transition from Hopf bifurcation to chaos—computer experiments with maps on R^2,*" Springer-Verlag Lecture Notes in Mathematics, vol. 668, pp. 48–66, Springer-Verlag, New York.

Horowitz, I. et al. (1975), "A synthesis theory for nonlinear systems with plant uncertainty," *Proc. VI IFAC World Congress* (Boston), paper 372.

Mehra, R. K., Kessel, W. C., and Carroll, J. V. (1977), "Global stability and control analysis of aircraft at high angles of attack," *Report ONR-CR215-248-1*, Office of Naval Research, Arlington, Va.

Pikos, C. A. and Luss, D. (1977), "Isothermal concentration oscillations on catalytic surfaces," *Chem. Eng. Science*, vol. 32, pp. 191-194.

Richalet, J. et al. (1978), "Model predictive heuristic control: Applications to industrial processes," *Automatica*, vol. 14, p. 413.

Smale, S. (1961a), "On gradient dynamical systems," *Ann. of Math.*, vol. 14, pp. 199-206.

Smale, S. (1961b), "On dynamical systems," *Symp. Int. on Ordinary Differential Equations*, La Univers. Nec. di Mexico.

Smale, S. (1965), "Diffeomorphisms with many periodic points," *Differential and Combinatorial Topology*, Princeton University Press, Princeton, NJ.

Appendix I
The Matrix Pseudoinverse

AI.1 BASIC DEFINITIONS

Every real $k \times p$ matrix A possesses a unique real pseudoinverse A^+ satisfying the following four equations:

$$A^+AA^+ = A^+ \tag{AI.01}$$

$$AA^+A = A \tag{AI.02}$$

$$[AA^+]^T = AA^+ \tag{AI.03}$$

$$[A^+A]^T = A^+A \tag{AI.04}$$

These are the necessary and sufficient conditions for defining the unique pseudoinverse (Penrose 1955). It may be noted from these equations that both AA^+ and A^+A are symmetric matrices, and that at least one of them is the identity matrix. Some other properties of the pseudoinverse are summarized below:

(i) $[A^+]^+ = A$ (AI.05)

(ii) $[A^T]^+ = [A^+]^T$ (AI.06)

(iii) If $\det A \neq 0$, then $A^+ = A^{-1}$ (AI.07)

(iv) $[\lambda A]^+ = \lambda^+A^+$ (AI.08)

where λ is scalar, and $\lambda^+ = 1/\lambda$ if $\lambda \neq 0$, $\lambda^+ = 0$ if $\lambda = 0$.

(v) $[A^TA]^+ = A^+A^{+T}$ (AI.09)

$[AA^T]^+ = A^{+T}A^+$ (AI.10)

Note that in general, $[AB]^+ \neq B^+A^+$.

(vi) The ranks of A, A^TA, A^+ and A^+A are equal to the trace of A^+A.

In general, the pseudoinverse of any $k \times p$ matrix A of rank r is given by (Greville 1959)

$$A^+ = C^T[CC^T]^{-1}[B^TB]^{-1}B^T \text{ if } A \neq 0$$
$$= 0 \text{ if } A = 0 \tag{AI.11}$$

where B is a $k \times r$ matrix, C an $r \times p$ matrix, both of rank r, such that

$$A = BC \tag{AI.12}$$

Equation (AI.11) reduces to two important subclasses under certain conditions.

(i) When $r = k, (k < p)$

$$A^+ = A^T[AA^T]^{-1} \tag{AI.13}$$

and is the right pseudoinverse of A since

$$AA^+ = I \tag{AI.14}$$

This is the only right inverse of A having columns in the column space of A^T.

EXAMPLE AI.1

Consider

$$A = [1 \quad 2]$$

Then

$$A^+ = A^T[AA^T]^{-1} = \begin{bmatrix} 1 \\ 2 \end{bmatrix} \left[[1 \quad 2] \begin{bmatrix} 1 \\ 2 \end{bmatrix} \right]^{-1} = \begin{bmatrix} 0.2 \\ 0.4 \end{bmatrix}$$

and

$$AA^+ = [1 \quad 2] \begin{bmatrix} 0.2 \\ 0.4 \end{bmatrix} = 1$$

also

$$AA^+ = \begin{bmatrix} 0.2 \\ 0.4 \end{bmatrix} [1 \quad 2] = \begin{bmatrix} 0.2 & 0.4 \\ 0.4 & 0.8 \end{bmatrix}$$

and trace $A^+A = 1$.

(ii) When $r = p$, $(k > p)$

$$A^+ = [A^T A]^{-1} A^T \qquad (AI.15)$$

which is the left pseudoinverse of A since

$$A^+ A = I \qquad (AI.16)$$

This is the only left inverse of A having rows in the row space of A.

EXAMPLE AI.2

Consider

$$A = \begin{bmatrix} 1 & 0 \\ 0 & 1 \\ 1 & 1 \end{bmatrix}$$

$$A^+ = [A^T A]^{-1} A^T = \left[\begin{bmatrix} 1 & 0 & 1 \\ 0 & 1 & 1 \end{bmatrix} \begin{bmatrix} 1 & 0 \\ 0 & 1 \\ 1 & 1 \end{bmatrix} \right]^{-1} \begin{bmatrix} 1 & 0 & 1 \\ 0 & 1 & 1 \end{bmatrix}$$

$$= \begin{bmatrix} 2 & 1 \\ 1 & 2 \end{bmatrix}^{-1} \begin{bmatrix} 1 & 0 & 1 \\ 0 & 1 & 1 \end{bmatrix} = \tfrac{1}{3} \begin{bmatrix} 2 & -1 \\ -1 & 2 \end{bmatrix} \begin{bmatrix} 1 & 0 & 1 \\ 0 & 1 & 1 \end{bmatrix}$$

$$= \tfrac{1}{3} \begin{bmatrix} 2 & -1 & 1 \\ -1 & 2 & 1 \end{bmatrix}$$

and

$$A^+ A = \begin{bmatrix} 1 & 0 \\ 0 & 1 \end{bmatrix}$$

Note that if $p = k = r$, the left and right pseudoinverses are both equal to A^{-1}.

AI.2 SYSTEM OF LINEAR EQUATIONS

Consider the system of equations

$$A\underline{x} = \underline{y} \qquad (AI.17)$$

where A is a general $p \times k$ matrix, $\underline{x} \in R^p$ and $\underline{y} \in R^k$.

One of the following three mutually exclusive and collectively exhaustive situations may occur.

(i)   There are fewer equations than unknowns, i.e., $k < p$. In this case, equation (AI.17) has an infinite number of solutions. We shall later see that in this situation, we can utilize the pseudoinverse to obtain the minimum-norm solution, i.e., that solution which is closest to the origin.

(ii) There are as many independent equations as unknowns, i.e., $k = p$ and det $A \neq 0$. In this case, equation (AI.17) has a unique solution

$$\underline{x} = A^{-1}\underline{y} \tag{AI.18}$$

(iii) There are more equations than unknowns ($k > p$) and the equations are inconsistent. In this case, we can utilize the pseudoinverse to obtain the least-squares solution $\hat{\underline{x}}$, such that $\|\underline{y} - A\hat{\underline{x}}\|^2$ is minimized where $\|\cdot\|$ represents the Euclidean norm.

AI.2.1   Minimum Norm Solution ($k < p$) and the Right Pseudoinverse

For the first case, a general solution is given by

$$\underline{x} = A^+\underline{y} + \underline{z} \tag{AI.19}$$

where

$$\underline{z} = [I - A^+A]\,\underline{w} \tag{AI.20}$$

We shall now consider a geometric interpretation of equation (AI.19). The solution vector $\underline{x}$ has been decomposed into two unique vectors (following the decomposition theorem of the theory of linear vector space) as follows

$$\underline{x} = \hat{\underline{x}} + \underline{z} \tag{AI.21}$$

where $\hat{\underline{x}}$ is the projection of $\underline{x}$ on the column space of A^T and $\underline{z}$ is the projection on the orthogonal complement of the column space. Hence, it follows that

$$\hat{\underline{x}} = A^+\underline{y} = A^+A\underline{x} = I_R\underline{x} \tag{AI.22}$$

where $I_R = A^+A$ is a projector for the column space of A^T, and

$$Q = I - I_R = I - A^+A \tag{AI.23}$$

is a projector of the complementary subspace.

It should be noted that if the rank of A equals p (i.e., $k = p$), then the column space of A^T is R^p, and its orthogonal complement is zero. Thus, we get a unique solution. This is the situation in case 2.

A unique solution for case 1 may be obtained if we require that the solution may have the minimum (Euclidean) norm. Since from (AI.21)

$$\|\hat{x}\|^2 \leqslant \|x\|^2 \qquad (AI.24)$$

it follows that the minimum-norm solution is given by

$$\hat{x} = A^+ y = A^+(AA^T)^{-1} y \qquad (AI.25)$$

if A has full rank (i.e., $r = k < p$), and A^+ is the right pseudoinverse defined by equation (AI.13).

AI.2.2 Least Squares Solution ($k > p$) and the Left Pseudoinverse

For case 3 ($k > p$), equation (AI.17) does not have an exact solution since y is not in the column space of A. However,

$$\hat{x} = A^+ y = [A^T A]^{-1} A^T y \qquad (AI.26)$$

is the best solution in the least-squares sense. Note that A^+ in equation (AI.26) is the left pseudoinverse of A.

The fact that $\hat{x}$ in (AI.26) is the least-squares solution for (AI.27) follows if we note that $A\hat{x}$ is the projection of y on the column space of A.

In general, if a vector y is premultiplied by $I_L = AA^+$, the resulting vector $v = I_L y$ is the projection of y on the column space of A, while $(I - I_L) y$ is the projection of y on the orthogonal complement of this space. In other words, of all the vectors in the column space of A, the one closest to y is v, i.e., $\|y - v\|$ is a minimum.

It may also be shown that $(y - A\hat{x})$ is orthogonal to the column-space of A, since

$$A^T A\hat{x} = A^T y$$

or

$$A^T(y - A\hat{x}) = 0 \qquad (AI.27)$$

Thus, $A\hat{x}$ is the orthogonal projection of y on this space.

Also, the minimal squared error is given by

$$E = \|y - A\hat{x}\|^2 = \|y - AA^+y\|^2$$
$$= y^T(I - AA^+) y \qquad (AI.28)$$

AI.3   DERIVATION OF RECURSIVE ALGORITHMS

The recursive algorithms for the pseudoinverse of a matrix with an additional row were first obtained by Wells (1967) as an extension of the work of Greville (1959) and Albert and Sittler (1966). The same results will be derived here in a slightly different manner (Sinha and Pille 1971).

To the four basic equations defining the matrix pseudoinverse (AI.01 to AI.04) we shall first add the following two:

$$A^T AA^+ = A^T \tag{AI.29}$$

$$A^+ AA^T = A^T \tag{AI.30}$$

These equations are obtained by transposing (AI.02) and combining with either (AI.03) or (AI.04). With the help of these six equations, we shall now derive the recursive algorithms. For convenience of notation we shall denote the $k \times p$ matrix A by A_k, since we shall be increasing the value of k from 1 to N, where $N > p$. In particular, let

$$A_{k+1} = \begin{bmatrix} A_k \\ \underline{a}_{k+1}^T \end{bmatrix} \tag{AI.31}$$

where

$$\underline{a}_{k+1}^T \text{ is the last row of } A_{k+1}.$$

Assuming that A_k is of full rank, the pseudoinverse of A_{k+1} may be written as

$$A_{k+1}^+ = [C_k^T : \underline{c}_{k+1}] \tag{AI.32}$$

Lemma 1

$$C_k^T A_k A_k^+ = C_k^T \tag{AI.33}$$

Proof.   For $k \le p$, $A_k A_k^+ = I$, hence equation (AI.33) is obviously correct.

For $k > p$, C_k^T has columns in the column space of A_k^T, and may therefore be written as

$$C_k^T = (A_k J)^T = J^T A_k^T$$

where

$$J = (A_k^T A_k)^{-1}$$

Hence,

$$\begin{aligned}
C_k^T A_k A_k^+ &= (J^T A^T) A_k A_k^+ \\
&= J^T J_k^T, \text{ using equation (AI.29)} \\
&= C_k^T
\end{aligned}$$

Lemma 2

$$A_{k+1}^+ A_{k+1} A_k^+ = A_k^+ \tag{AI.34}$$

Proof.   For $k > p - 1$, $A_{k+1}^+ A_{k+1} A_{k+1} = I$, hence equation (AI.34) is obvious.
   For $k < p - 1$, we have $A_k^+ = A_k^T J$, where $J = [A_k A_k^T]^{-1}$.
   Also, we may write $A_k = H A_{k+1}$, where the rows of H are the first k unit row vectors of dimension $k + 1$, in their natural order. Then,

$$A_k^T = A_{k+1}^T H^T$$

and multiplying both sides by J, we get

$$A_k^+ = A_{k+1}^T H^T J$$

Using equation (AI.30),

$$A_{k+1}^+ A_{k+1} A_{k+1}^T H^T J = A_{k+1}^T H^T J = A_k^+$$

Hence,

$$A_{k+1}^+ A_{k+1} A_k^+ = A_k^+$$

With the help of these two lemmas, we shall now proceed with our derivation. From equations (AI.31) and (AI.32)

$$A_{k+1}^+ A_{k+1} = C_k^T A_k + \underline{c}_{k+1} \underline{a}_{k+1}^T \tag{AI.35}$$

Postmultiplying equation (AI.35) by A_k^+ we have

$$A_{k+1}^+ A_{k+1} A_k^+ = C_k^T A_k A_k^+ + \underline{c}_{k+1} \underline{a}_{k+1}^T A_k^+ \tag{AI.36}$$

Utilizing equations (AI.33) and (AI.34), equation (AI.36) may be written as

$$C_k^T = A_k^+ - \underline{c}_{k+1} \underline{a}_{k+1}^T A_k^+ \tag{AI.37}$$

Therefore, equation (AI.32) may now be written as

$$A_{k+1}^+ = [A_k^+ - \underline{c}_{k+1} \underline{a}_{k+1}^T A_k^+ : \underline{c}_{k+1}] \tag{AI.38}$$

Thus to determine A_{k+1}^+, we need only know A_k^+, $\underline{a}_{k+1}^T$ and $\underline{c}_{k+1}$. We shall now see how to evaluate $\underline{c}_{k+1}$. Substituting equation (AI.37) into (AI.35),

$$A_{k+1}^+ A_{k+1} = A_k^+ A_k + \underline{c}_{k+1} \underline{a}_{k+1}^T (I - A_k^+ A_k) \tag{AI.39}$$

Define

$$Q_k \triangleq I - A_k^+ A_k \tag{AI.40}$$

and

$$\underline{\alpha}_{k+1} \triangleq \underline{a}_{k+1}^T Q_k \tag{AI.41}$$

Note that $Q_k \cdot Q_k = Q_k$, i.e., Q_k is an idempotent matrix. This can easily be verified by multiplication and using equation (AI.01). Moreover, $A_k Q_k = 0$, from equation (AI.02).

The determination of $\underline{c}_{k+1}$ depends upon whether $k < p$ or $k > p$. Let us first consider the case when $k < p$.

Case 1. For $k < p$, $\underline{a}_{k+1}^T$ is not in the row-space of A_k. Hence,

$$\underline{\alpha}_{k+1} \cdot \underline{\alpha}_{k+1}^+ = 1 \tag{AI.42}$$

and

$$A_k \underline{\alpha}_{k+1}^+ = A_k Q_k [\underline{a}_{k+1}^T]^+ = 0 \tag{AI.43}$$

Postmultiplying equation (AI.39) by $\underline{\alpha}_{k+1}^+$ thus gives

$$A_{k+1}^+ A_{k+1} \underline{\alpha}_{k+1}^+ = \underline{c}_{k+1} \tag{AI.44}$$

Premultiplying both sides of equation (AI.44) by $A_{k+1}^+ A_{k+1}$ and using equation (AI.02), we obtain

$$\underline{\alpha}_{k+1}^+ = \underline{c}_{k+1} = [\underline{a}_{k+1}^T Q_k]^+ \tag{AI.45}$$

Since $\underline{c}_{k+1}$ has maximal rank, applying the definition of the right pseudoinverse and recalling that Q_k is idempotent, we get

$$\underline{c}_{k+1} = Q_k \underline{a}_{k+1} [\underline{a}_{k+1}^T Q_k \underline{a}_{k+1}]^{-1} \tag{AI.46}$$

Using equations (AI.39), (AI.40), and (AI.46), we have

$$Q_{k+1} = I - A_{k+1}^+ A_{k+1}$$

$$= I - A_k^+ A_k - Q_k \underline{a}_{k+1} [\underline{a}_{k+1}^T Q_k \underline{a}_{k+1}]^{-1} \underline{a}_k^T Q_k$$

$$= Q_k - \frac{(Q_k \underline{a}_{k+1})(Q_k \underline{a}_{k+1})^T}{\underline{a}_{k+1}^T Q_k \underline{a}_{k+1}} \tag{AI.47}$$

since Q_k as a symmetric matrix.

Equations (AI.38), (AI.46), and (AI.47) form a recursive algorithm which can be utilized for obtaining the pseudoinverse as k as increased from 1 to p. To start the algorithm, we make $Q_0 = I$ and $A_0^+ = 0$.

Case 2.   For $k > p$, $\underline{a}_{k+1}^T$ is in the row-space of A_k. Here $Q_k = 0$ and the previous algorithm does not apply.

Combining equations (AI.01) and (AI.03), we have

$$A_{k+1}^+ A_{k+1}^+ A_{k+1}^T = A_{k+1}^+ \tag{AI.48}$$

Substituting (AI.31) and (AI.38) into (AI.48), postmultiplying the first resulting equation by $A_k^{+T} \underline{a}_{k+1}$ and substituting the result into the second equation yields

$$\underline{c}_{k+1}(1 + \underline{a}_{k+1}^T A_k^+ A_k^{+T} \underline{a}_{k+1}) = A_k^+ A_k^{+T} \underline{a}_{k+1} \tag{AI.49}$$

Hence,

$$\underline{c}_{k+1} = (1 + \underline{a}_{k+1}^T A_k^+ A_k^{+T} \underline{a}_{k+1})^{-1} A_k^+ A_k^{+T} \underline{a}_{k+1} \tag{AI.50}$$

Define

$$P_k \triangleq A_k^+ A_k^{+T} \tag{AI.51}$$

Then

$$\underline{c}_{k+1} = (1 + \underline{a}_{k+1}^T P_k \underline{a}_{k+1})^{-1} P_k \underline{a}_{k+1} \tag{AI.52}$$

Also,

$$P_{k+1} = A_{k+1}^+ A_{k+1}^{+T} A_{k+1}^{+T} \tag{AI.53}$$

Substituting (AI.31), (AI.38), and (AI.52) into (AI.53), and utilizing the fact that $\underline{a}_{k+1}^T P_k \underline{a}_{k+1}$ is a scalar yields

$$P_{k+1} = P_k - (p_k \underline{a}_{k+1})(P_k \underline{a}_{k+1})^T (1 + \underline{a}_{k+1}^T P_k \underline{a}_{k+1}) \tag{AI.54}$$

Thus, a recursive algorithm for $k > p$ is obtained by using equations (AI.38), (AI.52), and (AI.54). To start the algorithm one must convert the matrix A_p (for $k = p$) and also obtain

$$P_p = A_p^+ A_p^{+T} = [A_p^T A_p]^{-1} \tag{AI.54}$$

since

$$A_p^+ = A_p^{-1}$$

The matrix inversion required for the determination of P_p may be avoided by computing P_k iteratively from $k = 1$. In this case, substituting (AI.31), (AI.38), and (AI.46) into (AI.54) and utilizing the fact that $\underline{a}_{k+1}^T Q_k \underline{a}_{k+1}$ and $\underline{a}_{k+1}^T P_k \underline{a}_{k+1}$ are scalars results in

$$P_{k+1} = P_k - \frac{(P_k \underline{a}_{k+1})(Q_k \underline{a}_{k+1})^T + (Q_k \underline{a}_{k+1})(P_k \underline{a}_{k+1})^T}{\underline{a}_{k+1}^T Q_k \underline{a}_{k+1}}$$
$$+ \frac{(Q_k \underline{a}_{k+1})(Q_k \underline{a}_{k+1})^T (1 + \underline{a}_{k+1}^T P_k \underline{a}_{k+1})}{(\underline{a}_{k+1}^T Q_k \underline{a}_{k+1})^2} \tag{AI.55}$$

AI.4 RECURSIVE ALGORITHM FOR SYSTEM IDENTIFICATION

The algorithms derived in the previous section can be applied to the problem of parameter estimation of a single-input single-output system of known order in a straightforward manner. Following the notation of Chapters 3 and 4, the input-output relationship may be expressed as

$$\underline{\phi}_k^T \underline{\theta} = y_k \tag{AI.56}$$

where

$$\underline{\phi}_k \triangleq [u_k \quad u_{k+1} \cdots u_{k-m} \quad -y_{k-1} \quad -y_{k-2} \cdots -y_{k-n}]^T \tag{AI.57}$$

$\underline{\theta} \triangleq$ parameter vector of dimension $(m + n + 1)$

$$= [a_0 \quad a_1 \quad a_2 \cdots a_m \quad b_1 \quad b_2 \cdots b_n]^T \tag{AI.58}$$

Then, starting with $\hat{\underline{\theta}}_0 = 0$, $P_0 = 0$ and $Q_0 = I$, we use the following algorithms:
For $k \leqslant (m + n + 1)$,

$$\hat{\underline{\theta}}_{k+1} = \hat{\underline{\theta}}_k + \frac{Q_k \underline{\phi}_k (y_k - \underline{\phi}_k^T \hat{\underline{\theta}}_k)}{\underline{\phi}_k^T Q_k \underline{\phi}_k} \tag{AI.59}$$

$$Q_{k+1} = Q_k - \frac{(Q_k \underline{\phi}_k)(Q_k \underline{\phi}_k)^T}{\underline{\phi}_k^T Q_k \underline{\phi}_k} \qquad (AI.60)$$

$$P_{k+1} = P_k - \frac{(P_k \underline{\phi}_k)(Q_k \underline{\phi}_k)^T + (Q_k \underline{\phi}_k)(P_k \underline{\phi}_k)^T}{\underline{\phi}_k^T Q_k \underline{\phi}_k}$$

$$+ \frac{(Q_k \underline{\phi}_k)(Q_k \underline{\phi}_k)^T (1 + \underline{\phi}_k^T P_k \underline{\phi}_k)}{(\underline{\phi}_k^T Q_k \underline{\phi}_k)^2} \qquad (AI.61)$$

For $k > (m + n + 1)$

$$\underline{\hat{\theta}}_{k+1} = \underline{\hat{\theta}}_k + \frac{P_k \underline{\phi}_k (y_k - \underline{\phi}_k^T \underline{\hat{\theta}}_k)}{1 + \underline{\phi}_k^T P_k \underline{\phi}_k} \qquad (AI.62)$$

$$P_{k+1} = P_k - \frac{(P_k \underline{\phi}_k)(P_k \underline{\phi}_k^T)}{1 + \underline{\phi}_k^T P_k \underline{\phi}_k} \qquad (AI.63)$$

AI.5 REFERENCES

Albert, A. and Sittler, R. (1965), "A method for computing least squares estimators that keep up with the data," *SIAM J., Control*, vol. 3, pp. 394–417.

Greville, T. N. (1959), "The pseudoinverse of a rectangular matrix and its applications of the solutions of systems of linear equations," *SIAM Rev.*, vol. 1, pp. 38–43.

Greville, T. N. (1960), "Some applications of the pseudoinverse of a matrix," *SIAM Rev.*, vol. 2, pp. 15–22.

Penrose, R. (1955), "A generalized inverse for matrices," *Proc. Cambridge Philos. Soc.*, vol. 51, pp. 406–413.

Penrose, R. (1956), "On best approximate solutions of linear equations," *Proc. Cambridge Philos. Soc.*, vol. 52, pp. 17–19.

Sinha, N. K. and Pille W. (1971), "On-line parameter estimation using matrix pseudoinverse," *Proc. IEEE*, vol. 118, pp. 1041–1046.

Wells, C. H. (1967), "Minimum norm control of discrete systems," *IEEE Internat. Conv. Rec.*, vol. 15(3), pp. 55–64.

Appendix II
Transformation of a Matrix
to the Hermite Normal Form

AII. 1   INTRODUCTION

A square matrix is said to be in the Hermite normal form if the following conditions are satisfied:

(i)   It is of the upper triangular form with the elements on the main diagonal being either 1 or 0,

(ii) if a certain diagonal element is equal to 1, then all other elements in the corresponding column are 0, and

(iii) if a certain diagonal element is equal to 0, then all elements in the corresponding row are 0.

It is evident that the rank of a matrix in the Hermite normal form is equal to the number of 1's on the main diagonal.

Now the procedure for transformation of any rectangular matrix to this form will be described. Consider a matrix S with n rows and m columns, i.e.,

$$S = \begin{bmatrix} s_{11} & s_{21} & \cdots & s_{1m} \\ s_{21} & s_{22} & \cdots & s_{2m} \\ \vdots & \vdots & & \vdots \\ s_{n1} & s_{n2} & \cdots & s_{nm} \end{bmatrix}, \qquad m \geqslant n \qquad (AII.02)$$

We first select any nonzero element, say $s_{i_1 1}$, in the first column (it is computationally advantageous to select the element with the largest absolute value), and then obtain the matrix

$$S^{(1)} = S - \frac{1}{s_{i_1 1}} (Se_1 - e_{i_1})(e^{i_1} S) \qquad (AII.02)$$

where e_{i_1} is the i_1th unit column vector of dimension n and e^{i_1} is the i_1th unit row vector of dimension m.

Note that we may also write

$$S^{(1)} = T_1 S \qquad (AII.03)$$

where

$$T_1 = I - \frac{1}{s_{i_1 1}} (Se_1 - e_{i_1}) e^{i_1} \qquad (AII.04)$$

and

$$\det T_1 = \frac{1}{s_{i_1 1}} \qquad (AII.05)$$

Hence, $S^{(1)}$ is a nonsingular transformation of S. Also, the resulting matrix $S^{(1)}$ has the property that its first column is the unit vector e_i.

The next step in the transformation is to select a nonzero element in the second column of $S^{(1)}$, say $s_{i_2}^{(1)}$, with $i_2 \neq i_1$ and obtain

$$S^{(2)} = S^{(1)} - \frac{1}{s_{i_2 2}} (S^{(1)} e_2 - e_{i_2}) (e^{i_2} S^{(1)}) \qquad (AII.06)$$

It follows that

$$S^{(2)} = T_2 S^{(1)} = T_2 T_1 S \qquad (AII.07)$$

where T_2 is also nonsingular, and the first two columns of $S^{(2)}$ are e_{i_1} and e_{i_2}, respectively.

Continuing in this manner, after a maximum of m steps, we get a matrix $S^{(m)}$ which can be brought to the Hermite normal form by an appropriate permutation of its rows, i.e., by premultiplication with a nonsingular permutation matrix P. Hence, we have

$$H = PS^{(m)} = PT_m T_{m-1} \cdots T_1 S \qquad (AII.08)$$

It follows that the rank of S is equal to the number of independent unit column vectors in $S^{(m)}$.

AII.2   MINIMAL REALIZATION OF A TRANSFER FUNCTION MATRIX

Let G(s) be an $m \times r$ system transfer function matrix, each element of which is a strictly proper rational function of s. Then the minimal realization problem is to obtain the triple (A, B, C) where A, B, and C are $n \times n$, $n \times r$, and $m \times n$

constant matrices, for minimum n, such that

$$G(s) = C(sI - A)^{-1} B \qquad (AII.09)$$

Because of the strictly proper nature of G(s), it can be expanded as

$$G(s) = J_0 s^{-1} + J_1 s^{-2} + J_2 s^{-3} + \cdots \qquad (AII.10)$$

where

$$J_i = CA^i B, \qquad i = 0, 1, 2, \ldots \qquad (AII.11)$$

are called the Markov parameters of the system.

Following Ho and Halman (1965) define the block Hankel matrix S_{ij} as

$$S_{ij} = \begin{bmatrix} J_0 & J_1 \cdots J_{j-1} \\ J_1 & J_2 \cdots J_j \\ \vdots & \\ J_{i-1} & J_i \cdots J_{i+j-2} \end{bmatrix} \qquad (AII.12)$$

Then the rank of S_{ij} is n, provided that $i \geqslant \beta$ and $j \geqslant \alpha$, where α is the controllability index of the system and β its observability index. From (AII.11) and (AII.12), it follows that

$$S_{ij} = \begin{bmatrix} C \\ CA \\ \vdots \\ CA^{i-1} \end{bmatrix} [B \quad AB \cdots A^{j-1} B] = V_i U_j \qquad (AII.13)$$

where U_i and V_j are called the controllability and observability matrices, respectively, each with rank equal to n, and n is the order of the minimal realization.

It is evident that the factorization indicated in equation (AII.13) is not unique. It can, therefore, be simplified by requiring that the r columns of B be columns of the n X n identity matrix, I_n. This will be justified when the rank of B is equal to r, as will be the case with all systems having r independent inputs.

The algorithm for determining A, B, and C in this canonical form will now be described. From the given G(s), first the Markov parameters are calculated by long division of the numerator of each element of G(s) by the corresponding denominator. Forming the Hankel matrix S_{ij}, it is transformed into the Hermite normal form, H. Since the rank of H is n, any additional rows, consisting of only zero elements, are deleted from H. The first r columns of the resulting matrix will be $e_1, e_2, \ldots, e_r$, and these constitute the matrix B, whereas the next n columns will give the matrix A. The columns of C are obtained from the first m rows of the matrix S_{ij} corresponding to the locations of the n unit column vectors of H. Further details of the procedure are given by Rozsa and Sinha (1974).

It may be added that in a recent comparison (Sinha 1975) between different methods for obtaining the minimal realization of a transfer function matrix, it was shown that the method described above was computationally the most efficient.

AII.3   TRANSFORMATION OF STATE EQUATIONS TO CANONICAL FORMS

Often in the design of feedback control systems, it is required to transform the state equations of multivariable systems to their canonical form. Such transformations were first described by Luenberger (1967) who also proposed two special canonical forms known as (i) the column-companion form and (ii) the controllable canonical form. Luenberger's method requires the determination of a set of n linearly independent vectors from the controllability matrix of the system, selected in a particular order. The transformation matrix, consisting of these vectors, has then to be inverted to obtain A, B, and C in the column-companion form. The transformation to the controllable canonical form requires the inversion of two $n \times n$ matrices in addition to determining a set of linearly independent vectors selected in a special order from the controllability matrix.

The application of the algorithm described in section 1 makes it possible to obtain the canonical form without any matrix inversion. For example, consider first the transformation to the column-companion form. In this case, one first starts with the columns of the controllability matrix rearranged in the following form

$$S = [b_1 \quad Ab_1 \cdots A^n b_1 \quad b_2 \quad Ab_2 \cdots A^{n-1} b_2 \cdots b_r \quad Ab_r \cdots A^{n-r-1} b_r]$$

$$(AII.14)$$

where b_i is the ith column of B.

Transformation of S to the Hermite normal form gives

$$H = [e_1 e_2 \cdots e_{n_1} \alpha_1 \, ** \, e_{n_1+1} \cdots \alpha_2 \, ** \cdots e_n \alpha_r \, ** \cdots]$$ (AII.15)

where the columns marked with asterisk are of no particular significance.

The columns of the canonical form matrices are now readily obtained as follows

$$\bar{B} = [e_1 \quad e_{n_1+1} \quad e_{n_1+n_2+1} \cdots e_{n-n_r+1}]$$ (AII.16)

$$\bar{A} = [e_2 \quad e_3 \cdots e_{n_1} \quad \alpha_1 \quad e_{n_1+1} \cdots \alpha_2 \cdots e_n \quad \alpha_r]$$ (AII.17)

and

$$\bar{C} = C[b_1 \quad Ab_1 \cdots A^{n_1-1} b_1 \cdots b_r \cdots A^{n_r-1} b_r] = CP$$ (AII.18)

It may be noted that the columns of the transformation matrix P are obtained as the columns of S in equation (AII.14) corresponding to the independent unit column vectors in H.

The transformation to the controllable canonical form can be obtained in a similar manner, without requiring any matrix inversion. In this case, two reductions to the Hermite normal form are required, first on a column basis and then on a row basis. Details of the algorithm are given in Hickin and Sinha (1979).

AII.4 REDUCTION OF HIGH-ORDER SYSTEMS BY PARTIAL REALIZATION

Another important problem in the design of control systems is the determination of a low-order model which approximates a given high-order system. Consider a system described by the equations

$$\dot{x} = Ax + Bu \qquad (AII.19)$$

$$y = Cx \qquad (AII.20)$$

where $x \in R^n$, $u \in R^m$, and $y \in R^p$, with $n \gg m, p$. The problem of reduction is the determination of the equations

$$\dot{z} = Fz + Gu \qquad (AII.21)$$

$$\hat{y} = Hz \qquad (AII.22)$$

where $z \in R^r$, and $r \ll n$, such that $\hat{y}(t)$ is a close approximation of $y(t)$ for all $u(t)$ and all t.

As in section AII.2, the transfer function matrix of the high-order system is given by

$$G(s) = C(sI - A)^{-1}B = J_0 s^{-1} + J_1 s^{-2} + J_2 s^{-3} + \cdots \qquad (AII.23)$$

where

$$J_i = CA^i B, \qquad i = 0, 1, 2, \ldots \qquad (AII.24)$$

If the matrix A is nonsingular, one may also expand G(s) in the following Laurent series

$$G(s) = -\sum_{i=0}^{\infty} T_i s^i \qquad (AII.25)$$

where

$$T_i = CA^{-(i+1)}B, \qquad i = 0, 1, 2, \ldots \qquad (AII.26)$$

It may be recognized that $\{-1/iT_i\}$ is the set of time moments of the inverse Laplace transform of $G(s)$. It may also be noted that

$$J_{-i} = T_{i-1} \quad \text{for} \quad i \geqslant 1 \tag{AII.27}$$

Next, define a Hankel matrix of order (i, j) and index k as

$$S_{ij}^{(k)} = \begin{bmatrix} CA^kB & CA^{k+1}B \cdots CA^{k+j-2}B \\ CA^{k+1}B & CA^{k+2}B \cdots CA^{k+j}B \\ \vdots & \vdots \qquad \vdots \\ CA^{k+i-1}B & CA^{k+i}B \cdots CA^{k+i+j-2}B \end{bmatrix} \tag{AII.28}$$

One may now factor the Hankel matrix as below

$$S_{ij}^{(k)} = V_i^{(\delta)} U_j^{(\epsilon)} = \begin{bmatrix} CA^\delta \\ CA^{\delta+1} \\ \vdots \\ CA^{\delta+i-1} \end{bmatrix} [A^\epsilon B \quad A^{\epsilon+1}B \cdots A^{\epsilon+j-1}B] \tag{AII.29}$$

where δ and ϵ are integers, and $\delta + \epsilon = k$.

It is easily shown that transformation of the Hankel matrix leads to a minimal realization of the system, as in section 2. However, if the process is stopped after r steps then a partial realization is obtained, which matches some of the generalized Markov parameters instead of all, as would be the case with minimal realization. This may be regarded as the generalization of the Pade approximation to the reduction of multivariable systems (Hickin and Sinha 1976).

An advantage of the method is its iterative nature. If the reduced model of order r does not provide a satisfactory match with $G(s)$, we may try one of order r + 1 by transforming S one more time. It is conceptually easy and ideally suited for either hand calculation or implementation on a digital computer.

AII.5   DETERMINATION OF CONTROLLABILITY AND OBSERVABILITY OF LARGE-SCALE COMPOSITE SYSTEMS

The investigation of the controllability and observability of large-scale composite linear time-invariant systems by direct application of the conventional criteria is generally very cumbersome since it requires the determination of the ranks of matrices containing terms of the form A^iB and CA^j where the matrix A is usually of a high order. In fact, there may often be problems due to truncation errors caused by repeated multiplications by a large matrix. An important contribution to the field was made by Davison and Wang (1975) in a recent paper in which they avoid the need to obtain the product terms of the form A^iB and CA^j. However, their approach involves computations of both eigenvalues and rank. In a recent paper, Porter (1976) has presented a method which also does not require the product terms, only the computation of the rank of a larger matrix is necessary. For a system of order n, with m imputs and p outputs, this method requires the determination of the rank of an $n^2 \times n(n + m - 1)$ matrix for controllability and the rank of an $n(n + p - 1) \times n^2$ matrix for observability. Porter has applied this method for determining the controllability and observability of feedback and series-parallel connections. Extension to the cascade interconnection is fairly straightforward (Sinha and El-Sherief 1978).

Although Porter's approach is a great step forward from the approach of Davison and Wang, the main difficulty with this method has been summarized by Porter as follows, "the only computational constraint in the use of this method is the availability of an effective algorithm for the computation of the rank of a large matrix."

An effective algorithm of this type can be obtained easily by a simple modification of the algorithm for transformation to the Hermite normal form discussed in section 1. As was mentioned there, the rank of the matrix is simply the number of independent unit vectors obtained after transformation to the Hermite normal form. The total number of arithmetic operations (additions, multiplications, and divisions) required for the general case of an $n \times m$ matrix of rank r is given by

$$N = r(2n + 1)(2m - r + 1) \tag{AII.30}$$

In practice, the actual number of arithmetic operations will be much less if the matrix is sparse, with a large number of zero entries, and advantage is taken of this fact in programming.

The procedure can be further improved if it is recognized that to determine the rank of a given matrix, it is sufficient to make each column, starting with the first, have zero elements below the pivot element which is transformed into one. The resulting matrix, by a simple permutation of rows, takes the form of an upper triangular matrix, and hence its rank is determined immediately. It may be added that this permutation is not necessary for our purpose.

The proposed modification for determining the rank of an $n \times m$ matrix S will now be described in detail for the case when $m \geq n$ (Sinha and El-Sherief 1978). For the case when $m < n$, the same procedure can be carried out starting with the transpose of S. After selecting a suitable nonzero element s_{i-1} in the first column of S as the pivot, the following matrix is obtained

$$S^{(1)} = S - \frac{1}{s_{c_1 1}} \begin{bmatrix} 0 \\ 0 \\ \vdots \\ s_{i_1, 1} - 1 \\ s_{i_1 + 1, 1} \\ \vdots \\ s_{n1} \end{bmatrix} [s_{i_1 1}, s_{i_1 2}, \ldots, s_{i_1 m}] \tag{AII.32}$$

$S^{(1)}$ is seen to be a nonsingular transformation of S, since the determinant of the transformation matrix is again $1/s_{i_1}$.

It may be noted that the transformation in equation (AII.31), differs from that in equation (AII.02) in that all elements above s_{i_1} are made zero in the outer product, with the result that the rows above i_1 are unchanged by the transformation.

Continuing this process, in r steps a matrix $S^{(r)}$ is obtained, where $r \leqslant n$, after a nonzero pivot has been utilized from each row. Then the rank of S is equal to r.

The total number of arithmetic operations required for this improved algorithm is given by

$$M = (2n + 1)\,mr + \frac{1}{2}\,r(r - 1)\,(2r - 1) - \frac{1}{2}\,r(r - 1)\,(2m + 2n + 1) \qquad \text{(AII.32)}$$

In general, M will be much smaller than N given by equation (AII.30). For example, if $n = 121$ and $m = 132$, assuming that $r = 121$, we have

$$N = 2,117,016 \qquad \text{(AII.33)}$$

and

$$M = 1,350,844 \qquad \text{(AII.34)}$$

which indicates a reduction of about 36%.

Further reduction in the number of arithmetic operations can be obtained by taking advantage of the sparsity of the matrix. This simply requires testing each element in the row vector in the outer product and changing only those columns for which this element is nonzero.

In an example given by Sinha and El-Sherief (1978), the total time required for determining the rank on a CDC 6400 computer was 105 seconds using the algorithm described in section 1. With the modification suggested in this section, the computation time was reduced to 63.16 seconds without taking advantage of the sparsity of the matrix. When additional modification to utilize the advantage of sparsity was introduced, the computation time was reduced to only 2.87 seconds.

AII.7   SOME COMMENTS ON THE COMPUTATIONAL PROCEDURE

The computational procedure for the transformation of a matrix to the Hermite normal form can be further improved by following the procedure described below. It is assumed that the matrix has more columns than rows, i.e., $m \geqslant n$.

(i)   Starting with the first column of the matrix search for the element in this column which has the largest absolute value. This element will be used as the pivot.

(ii)   Interchange the first row of the matrix with this row, and then set up the column vector as well as the row vector for the outer product as the first column and the first row of the matrix, with 1 subtracted from the pivot element, p, in the column vector. Let the elements of the column vector be denoted by b_i, $i = 1, 2, \ldots, n$ and those of the row vector be e_j, $j = 1, 2, \ldots, m$.

(iii) Replace each element s_{ij}, of the matrix S by $s_{ij}^{(1)}$ of the matrix S as below

$$S_{ij}^{(1)} = \frac{ps_{ij} - b_i c_j}{p}$$

Note that it is better to calculate $s_{ij}^{(1)}$ as above than as $s_{ij} - (b_i C_j)/p$ because of the truncation error which may be introduced if the division is performed before subtraction.

It is convenient to perform this computation one column at a time. In particular, if $c_j = 0$, then the jth column of $S^{(1)}$ is the same as the jth column of S. This fact can be utilized to avoid unnecessary computation.

(iv) After the above has been completed, examine the second column of $S^{(1)}$, starting from the second row to search for the next pivot in the same was as in step (i). Interchange rows if necessary, as in (ii) and proceed as in (iii).

(v) The process can be continued until all columns and rows are exhausted. The exception is the case when in a particular column a nonzero-pivot cannot be found. In this case, simply proceed to the next column.

AII.8 REFERENCES

Davison, E. J. and Wang, S. W. (1975), "New results on the controllability and observability of general composite systems," *IEEE Transactions. Automatic Control*, vol. AC-20, pp. 123–128.

Egervary, E. (1935), "Uber die Faktorisation von Matrizen and ihre Anwendung auf die Losung von linearen Gleichungssystemen," *Zeitschrift für Angewandte Mathematik und Mechanik*, vol. 35, pp. 111–118.

Hickin, J. and Sinha, N. K. (1976), "A new method for reducing multivariable systems," *Proc. 7th Annual Conf. on Modeling and Simulation* (Pittsburgh, PA), pp. 259–263.

Hickin, J. and Sinha, N. K. (1979), "An efficient algorithm for transformation of linear multivariable systems to canonical forms," *Problems of Control and Information Theory*, vol. 8(3), pp. 193–211.

Ho, B. L. and Kalman, R. E. (1965), "Effective construction of linear state-variable models from input-output functions," *Proc. 3rd Allerton Conf. on Circuit and System Theory* (Urbana, Ill.), pp. 449–459.

Luenberger, D. G. (1967), "Canonical forms for linear multivariable systems," *IEEE Transactions. Automatic Control*, vol. AC-12, pp. 290–293.

MacDuffee, C. C. (1943), *Vectors and Matrices*, The Mathematical Association of America, Buffalo, NY.

Porter, B. (1976), "Necessary and sufficient conditions for the controllability and observability of general composite systems," *Proc. IFAC Symp. Large Scale Systems Theory and Applications* (Udine, Italy), pp. 265–269.

Rozsa, P. (1974), "Linearis Algebraes Alkalmazasai," Muszaki Konyvkiado, Budapest.

Rozsa, P. and Sinha, N. K. (1974), "Efficient algorithm for irreducible realization of a rational matrix," *Int. J. Control*, vol. 20, pp. 739–751.

Sinha, N. K. (1975), "Minimal realization of transfer function matrices: a comparative study of different methods," *Int. J. Control*, vol. 22, pp. 627–640.

Sinha, N. K. and El-Sherief, H. (1978), "Efficient algorithm for determining controllability and observability of large-scale composite systems," *Int. J. of Systems Science*, vol. 9, pp. 1295–1302.

Appendix III
Fixed Point of Nonlinear Integral Equation

This appendix is based on the work of Krasnosielski (1964, 1969, 1975) along lines given in Chapter 11. All considerations presented in section 1 of Chapter 11 are around the concept of the fixed point of the nonlinear integral equation

$$u = Hu \qquad (AIII.01)$$

considered in Banach space B with the norm

$$\|u\| = \sum_{n=1}^{N} \max |u_n(x)| \qquad (AIII.02)$$

Definition AIII.1. An operator H with domain and range in a Banach space is called completely continuous if it is continuous and if for every bounded sequence $u^{(n)} \in B$, the sequence $\{Hu^{(n)}\}$ contains a convergent subsequence.

Definition AIII.2. The set of vectors u-Hu is called the vector field associated with the operator H and is denoted by $\overline{H} = I - H$ where I is the identity operator. In the sequel the vector field $\overline{H}$ will be considered as an operator with domain on a closed, bounded, and connected region $\Omega \in B$ with a boundary $\partial\Omega$.

Definition AIII.3. A point $u \in \Omega$ such that u = 0 (or u = Hu) is called a fixed point of the operator H.

Definition AIII.4. For each isolated fixed point u of the operator H there exists an integer γ_n (positive, zero, or negative) which is called the index of the fixed point. If H has a number of isolated fixed points in the interior Ω and no fixed point on the boundary $\partial\Omega$ then the sum of indices is called the rotation γ_H of H on $\partial\Omega$.

Definition AIII.5.   Two completely continuous operators H and H_0 are called homotopic if they have no fixed points on the boundary $\partial\Omega$ of the region Ω and if there exists a completely continuous operator $H_1(s)$ depending on a parameter s such that

(a) H_1 has no fixed points on $\partial\Omega$ for any $0 \leqslant s \leqslant 1$
(b) $H_1(0) = H_0, H_1(1) = H$

The following choice of H_1 is suggested (Krasnosielski 1964)

$$H_1(s) = sH + (1 - s) H_0 \qquad (AIII.03)$$

Theorem 1 (Hopf). 'The rotations of a completely continuous homotopic operator are identical.

Corollary (Krasnosielski 1964).   The null operator

$$H_0 u = 0 \qquad (AIII.04)$$

has rotation 1 over any sphere $\|u\| = $ const.
   To prove the existence of the fixed point of the differential equations the following procedure is suggested (Gavalas 1966):

(a)   transform the differential equations to integral equation (AIII.01)
(b)   discuss the existence of the fixed point on $\partial\Omega$ of the integral equation

$$H_1 u = s u_s + s \int_\Omega G(x, x') f(u(x') dx' \qquad (AIII.05)$$

for $0 \leqslant s < 1$

where $G(x, x')$ is Green's function for the differential operator of differential equation.
   If equation (AIII.05) has no fixed point on $\partial\Omega$ then equation (AIII.01) has at least one fixed point.
   In practical considerations, the linearized eigenvalue problem plays a very important role. The uniqueness of the fixed point as well as existence of multiple solutions can be derived from the discussion of the eigenproblem

$$\psi = \lambda L \psi \qquad (AIII.06)$$

where L is Frechet derivative of the operator H at point u.

Definition AIII.6. A completely continuous operator H is called (Frechet) differentiable at the point u if

$$H(u + v) - Hu = Lv + \omega(u, v)$$

where L is linear and

$$\lim_{\|v\| \to 0} \frac{\|\omega(u, v)\|}{\|v\|} = 0$$

For typical nonlinear integral operators the Frechet derivative is of the form:

(a) For the Uhryson operator

$$Hu(x) = \int_{\Omega} K[x, \xi, u(\xi)] \, d\xi$$

If the function $K[x, \xi, u]$ is continuous for all variables and differentiable on u for all x, $\xi \in \Omega$ and $\|u\| < r$ (real number) and $K(x, \xi, 0) \equiv 0$, then

$$Lu(x) = \int_{\Omega} \frac{\partial K(x, \xi, 0)}{\partial u} u(\xi) \, d\xi \tag{AIII.07}$$

(b) For the Hammerstein operator

$$Hu(x) = \int_{\Omega} K(x, \xi) f[\xi, u(\xi)] \, d\xi$$

the Frechet derivative is

$$Lu(x) = \int_{\Omega} K(x, \xi) \frac{\partial f(\xi, 0)}{\partial u} u(\xi) \, d\xi \tag{AIII.08}$$

The basis for the uniqueness criteria is the following theorem.

Theorem 2 (Schauder). Let u be a fixed point of the completely continuous operator H and L the Frechet derivative of H at u. Suppose that $\lambda = 1$ is not an eigenvalue of

$$\psi = \lambda L \psi \tag{AIII.09}$$

Then u is an isolated fixed point of H and the index of this fixed point is equal to $(-1)^\beta$ where β is the sum of the orders of the eigenvalues of (AIII.09) which lie in the interval (0, 1).

CONCLUSION

If λ does not lie in the interval (0, 1) then $\beta = 0$ and the index of fixed point is 1. If it is true for any fixed point u then the fixed point is unique since the rotation is 1.

Therefore, since the index of each fixed point is +1 and the rotation (i.e., the sum of these indices) is 1, the number of fixed points is odd.

Appendix IV
The Method of Weighted
Residuals (MWR)

The method of weighted residuals is used for approximation of the solution of differential equations.

Let us consider an unknown function $y(u)$ which satisfies the nonlinear differential equation

$$L^V(y) = 0 \text{ in } V \qquad (AIV.01)$$

with boundary conditions

$$L^S(y) = 0 \text{ on } S \qquad (AIV.02)$$

where $S = \partial V$.

Accurate solution $y(u)$ of equation (AIV.01) is approximated by the polynomial expansion of degree N in a form

$$y_N(u) = \sum_{i=1}^{N} a_i F_i(u) \qquad (AIV.03)$$

where

$F_i(u)$ = the trial (base) function
a_i = the unknown coefficients.

The quality of the approximation can be evaluated by the linear measure

$$E_N(u) = y(u) - y_N(u) \qquad (AIV.04)$$

In practice the accurate solution $y(u)$ is unknown, therefore the role of the quality measure is played by the residual

314

$$L^V(y_N) = R_N[y_N(u); a_i] \text{ in } V \qquad (AIV.05)$$

The constants a_i are chosen in such a way that the residual is forced to be zero in an average sense with the weight $w(u)$

$$\int_V R[y_N(u), a_i] \cdot w(u) \, du = 0 \qquad (AIV.06)$$

The values of N unknown coefficients a_i are obtained as a solution of equation (AIV.06) at N chosen points (nodes)

$$\int_V R_N(a_j, u) \cdot w_j(u) \, dV = 0 \qquad j = 1, 2, \ldots, N \qquad (AIV.07)$$

The choice of the trial functions, weighting function, and nodes is arbitrary and depends on the variant of the method.

The choice $w_j(u) = u^{j-1}$, $j = 1, 2, \ldots, N$ leads to the method of moments in which

$$\int_V R_N(a, u) \, u^{j-1} \, dV = 0 \qquad (AIV.08)$$

whereas the choice of $w_j(u) = \partial y_N / \partial a_j$ leads to Galerkin's method. The discrete version of Galerkin's method is called the collocation method, in which

$$w_j(u) = \delta(u - u_j) \qquad j = 1, 2, \ldots, N \qquad (AIV.09)$$

or equivalently,

$$\int_V R[a_i, y(u)] \cdot w(u) \, dV = R_N[a_i, y(u_j)] = 0 \qquad (AIV.10)$$

In the collocation method the choice of trial functions and nodes, although arbitrary, influences the convergence and accuracy.

The choice as the trial functions of the orthogonal polynomials in a form

$$P_{i-1}(u) = \sum_{j=0}^{i-1} c_j u^j \qquad (AIV.11)$$

defined by

$$\int_V u^\beta (1 - u)^\alpha \, P_j(u) \, P_N(u) \, du = 0 \qquad j = 0, 1, \ldots, N - 1 \quad (AIV.12)$$

can guarantee sufficient convergence and accuracy. The Jacobi polynomials defined by equation (AIV.12) in the case $\alpha = \beta = 0$ give the more popular Legendre polynomials. The choice of Jacobi polynomials leads to the orthogonal collocation method in which the coefficients c_j can be obtained via equation (AIV.12) or on the basis of the methods presented in various monographs (e.g., Villadsen and Michelsen 1978). For the one dimensional case, equation (AIV.12) can be rewritten in a form

$$\int_{b_1}^{b_2} x^{\beta}(1 - x)^{\alpha} P_j(x) P_N(x) x^{a-1} \, dx = 0 \qquad j = 0, 1, \ldots, N - 1 \qquad \text{(AIV.13)}$$

Substitution

$$dV = x^{a-1} \, dx \qquad \text{(AIV.14)}$$

is valid for different geometries:

  a = 1: planar geometry
  a = 2: cylindrical geometry
  a = 3: spherical geometry

On the basis of equation (AIV.13) one can get the values of c_j and on the basis of equation (AIV.10) easily get coefficients a_i. This is sufficient to obtain the solution in the form

$$y_N(u) = y_N(u, t) = \sum_{i=1}^{N+1} a_i(t) F_i(u) \qquad \text{(AIV.15)}$$

It is also possible to write the solution $y_N(u)$ having evaluated the solution at the collocation points $y_N(u_j)$.

The first and second derivatives of $y(j)$ at collocation points are:

$$\left. \frac{dy}{du} \right|_{u_j} = \sum_{i=1}^{N+1} \left. \frac{du^{i-1}}{du} \right|_{u_j} \cdot d_i \qquad \text{(AIV.16)}$$

$$\left. \nabla^2 y \right|_{u_j} = \sum_{i=1}^{N+1} \left. \nabla^2(u^{i-1}) \right|_{u_j} \cdot d_i \qquad \text{(AIV.17)}$$

or in a matrix form

$$y = Qd \qquad \text{(AIV.18)}$$

$$\frac{d}{du} y = Fd \tag{AIV.19}$$

$$\nabla^2 y = Vd \tag{AIV.20}$$

By elimination of d, one can get

$$\frac{d}{du} y = A \cdot y \tag{AIV.21}$$

$$\nabla^2 y = B \cdot y \tag{AIV.22}$$

where

$$A = FQ^{-1} \tag{AIV.23}$$

$$B = VQ^{-1} \tag{AIV.24}$$

The integration formulae can be obtained in the same manner in the form

$$\int_0^1 f(u) \, u^{a-1} \, du = \sum_{j=1}^{N+1} w_j f(u_j) \tag{AIV.25}$$

where the parameter a depends on the kind of geometry considered and

$$W = fQ^{-1} \tag{AIV.26}$$

The entries $Q_{j,i}$, $F_{j,i}$, $V_{j,i}$, and f_i do not depend on time and therefore can be prepared a priori for typical cases.

i) The case of symmetry.

In the case when a symmetrical solution is expected, the following convenient properties can be used:

the solution can be evaluated only in the half of the domain considered,
the boundary condition $(\partial y_N / \partial x)|_{x=0} = 0$ can be assumed,
the solution can be expressed in terms of even powers of x.

The approximation of the solution can be written in a form

$$y_N(x^2) = y_N(u) = c_1 + (1 - u) \sum_{i=1}^{N} b_i P_{i-1}(u) \tag{AIV.27}$$

where $P_{i-1}(u)$ are orthogonal polynomials defined by the equation

$$\int_V u^\beta (1 - u)^\alpha P_j(u) P_N(u) \, dV = 0 \qquad j = 0, 1, \ldots, N - 1 \quad \text{(AIV.28)}$$

The elements of the matrices f, Q, F, and V can be written in the following form:

$$f_i = \frac{1}{2i - 2 + a} \qquad\qquad \text{(AIV.29)}$$

$$Q_{ji} = x_j^{2i-2} \qquad\qquad \text{(AIV.30)}$$

$$F_{ji} = 2(i - 1) \, x_j^{2i-3} \qquad\qquad \text{(AIV.31)}$$

$$V_{ji} = 2(i - 1)(2i - 3) \, x_j^{2i-4} \qquad\qquad \text{(AIV.32)}$$

For the normed interval of variables (i.e., for $x \in [0, 1]$), different types of geometry and for the cases $\alpha = \beta = 0$ and $\alpha = 1, \beta = 0$, the roots of orthogonal polynomials and matrices A, B, W for different number of collocation points are presented in the literature (Finlayson 1972, Villadsen and Sorensen 1969, Villadsen and Steward 1967).

ii) Asymmetrical Case

This case should be considered when either the boundary conditions or given geometry suggest the asymmetrical solution.

The approximation of the solution can be written in a form

$$y_N(x) = c_1 + c_2 x + x(1 - x) \sum_{i=1}^{N-1} a_i P_{i-1}(x) \qquad\qquad \text{(AIV.33)}$$

satisfying the boundary conditions

$$y_N(0) = c_1 \qquad \text{for} \quad x = 0$$

$$y_N(1) = c_1 + c_2 \qquad \text{for} \quad x = 1$$

The polynomials $P_{i-1}(x)$ are shifted Legendre polynomials. The elements of matrices f, Q, F, V are

$$f_i = i^{-1} \qquad\qquad \text{(AIV.34)}$$

$$Q_{ji} = x_j^{i-n} \qquad\qquad \text{(AIV.35)}$$

$$F_{ji} = (i - 1) \, x_j^{i-2} \qquad\qquad \text{(AIV.36)}$$

$$V_{ji} = (i - 1)(i - 2) \, x_j^{i-3} \qquad\qquad \text{(AIV.37)}$$

For $x \in [0, 1]$, $a = 1$, and $\alpha = \beta = 0$, the values of the roots of orthogonal polynomials and matrices A, B, W are presented by Finlayson (Finlayson 1972).

Analogous tables are constructed for the forthcoming example and presented at the end of this Appendix.

Having obtained solutions at collocation points one can get the approximation of the solutions at other points of $u \in [0, 1]$ using the Lagrange polynomial

$$y_N(u) = \sum_{i=1}^{N=1} y(u_i) \cdot L_i(u) \tag{AIV.38}$$

where

$$L_i(u) = \prod_{\substack{j=1 \\ j \neq i}}^{N+1} \frac{u - u_j}{u_i - u_j} \tag{AIV.39}$$

Remark.   Extensions of the orthogonal collocation method are the spline collocation method (Villadsen and Michelsen 1978) and the orthogonal collocation method on finite elements (Carey and Finlayson 1975). These methods are convenient in the case of multilayer geometry and nonlinear multiphase processes.

EXAMPLE AIV.1

Let us consider the temperature distribution at the equilibrium state in a wall of pipe reactor. Assume the linear, one-dimensional case with the following boundary conditions.

$$T(b_0) = 1$$

$$T(b_1) = 0$$

$$\frac{b_0}{b_1} = 0.5, \quad b_1 = 1$$

The equation describing the temperature distribution is

$$\frac{d^2 T(r)}{dr^2} + \frac{1}{r} \frac{dT(r)}{dr} = 0 \tag{AIV.40}$$

The analytical solution is available

$$T(r) = \frac{\ln \dfrac{b_1}{r}}{\ln \dfrac{b_1}{b_0}} \tag{AIV.41}$$

and will serve for the error evaluation of the suggested orthogonal collocation method.

Using the matrices A and B of the derivatives, equation (AIV.40) can be rewritten in the form

$$\sum_{i=1}^{N} B_{ji} T_i + \frac{1}{r} \sum_{i=1}^{N} A_{ji} T_i = 0 \qquad j = 2, \ldots, N-1 \qquad (AIV.42)$$

where

$$r = b_0 + (b_1 - b_0) u_j, \qquad u_j \in [0, 1].$$

The solution is known at the boundary points. For the remaining $N - 2$ points the solution can be obtained from the set of $N - 2$ algebraic equations with respect to T_j, $j = 2, \ldots, N-1$.

Transforming equation (AIV.42) to the form

$$\sum_{i=1}^{N} C_{ji} T_i = 0 \qquad j = 2, \ldots, N-1 \qquad (AIV.43)$$

where

$$C_{ji} = B_{ji} + \frac{1}{b_0 + (b_1 - b_0) u_j} A \qquad (AIV.44)$$

one can use the tables constructed for $b_0/b_1 = 0.5$ and different numbers of collocation points.

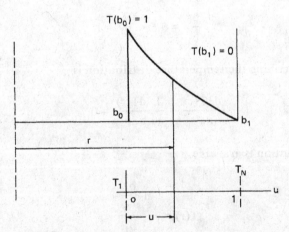

Figure AIV.1. Temperature distribution in a wall of a pipe reactor (at equilibrium).

The solution at the collocation points is obtained from the set of equations

$$d \cdot T = e \qquad\qquad \text{(AIV.45)}$$

where

$T^T = [T_2, \ldots, T_{N-1}]$ is the vector of solution at the internal collocation points

$$d = \begin{bmatrix} C_{22} & \cdots & C_{2,N-1} \\ \vdots & & \\ C_{N-1,2} & \cdots & C_{N-1,N-1} \end{bmatrix} \text{ is the matrix of coefficients}$$

$$e = \begin{bmatrix} -C_{2,1}T_1 & - C_{2,N}T_N \\ & \vdots & \\ -C_{N-1,1}T_1 & - C_{N-1,N}T_N \end{bmatrix} \begin{array}{l} \text{is a vector containing the boundary} \\ \text{(known) values } T_1, T_N \end{array}$$

*) First approximation, $N = 3$ (one interval collocation point). On the basis of equation (AIV.43) and Table AIV.2 we have

$$\sum_{\substack{i=1 \\ i \neq j = 2}}^{3} C_{j,i} \cdot T = \Delta_{j,1}T_1 - C_{j,3}T_3$$

for

$$j = 2, \quad T_3 = 0$$

$$C_{2,2}T_2 = -C_{2,1}T_1 - C_{2,3} \cdot T_3$$

$$T_2 = -\frac{C_{2,1}}{C_{22}}T_1 = -\frac{3,33333}{-8} - 0.416662$$

$$T(r_2) = T(0.75) = 0.416662$$

One can get the solution at an arbitrary point of the domain [0, 1] using interpolation given by equation (AIV.38)

$$T(u) = \sum_{i=1}^{N} T(u_i) \cdot L_i(u)$$

where $L_i(n)$ is defined by equation (AIV.39).
   For our case,

$$u_1 = 0 \qquad T(u_1) = 1$$

$$u_2 = 0.5 \qquad T(u_2) = 0.416662$$

$$u_3 = 1 \qquad T(u_3) = 0$$

and

$$L_1(u) = \frac{u - u_2}{u_1 - u_2} \frac{u - u_3}{u_1 - u_3} = 2u^2 - 3u + 1$$

$$L_2(u) = \frac{u - u_1}{u_2 - u_1} \frac{u - u_3}{u_2 - u_3} = -4u^2 + 4u$$

$$L_1(u) = \frac{u - u_1}{u_3 - u_1} \frac{u - u_2}{u_3 - u_2} = 2u^2 - u$$

Hence

$$T(u) = 0,3333336\,u^2 - 1,3333336\,u + 1$$

**) Second approximation, N = 5 (3 internal collocation points). On the basis of enclosed tables, the elements of the matrices d and e are:

$$d = \begin{bmatrix} -69.85263 & 28.52304 & -14.49357 \\ 14.51501 & -21.33333 & 18.81832 \\ -12.64929 & 25.57220 & -75.38546 \end{bmatrix}$$

$$e = \begin{bmatrix} -48.45334 \\ 5 \\ -6.4038 \end{bmatrix}$$

The solution of equation

$$d \cdot T = e$$

Table AIV.1.

u	Exact Solution	N = 3		N = 5	
		Appr. Solution	Error %	Appr. Solution	Error %
0.112701	0.845933	0.853965	0.95	0.845703	−0.027
0.5	0.415037	0.416666	0.39	0.414953	−0.019
0.887298	0.083677	0.079368	−5.1	0.083804	0.15

Table AIV.2.   Hollow Cylindrical Geometry Number of Internal Collocation Points, N = 1 Shifted Legendre Polynomials

R = 1   R2 = 0.5

Matrix A

X(1) = 0.00000	3.00000	4.000000	-1.00000
X(2) = 0.50000	-1.00000	0.00000	1.00000
X(3) = 1.00000	1.00000	-4.00000	3.00000

Matrix C

W(1) = 0.166667	1.00000	-4.0000	3.00000
W(2) = 0.666667	3.33333	-8.00000	4.66667
W(3) = 0.166667	4.50000	-10.00000	5.50000

Number of Internal Collocation Points N = 2

Matrix A

X(1) = 0.0000000000	-7.00000	8.19615	-2.19615	1.00000
X(2) = 0.2113248654	-2.73205	1.73205	1.73205	-0.73205
X(3) = 0.7886751346	0.73205	-1.73205	-1.73205	2.73205
X(4) = 1.0000000000	-1.00000	2.19615	-8.19615	7.00000

Matrix C

X(1) = -0.000000	17.00000	-28.98076	22.98076	-11.00000
X(2) = 0.500000	14.13688	-22.57012	13.42988	-4.99664
X(3) = 0.500000	-3.98303	11.03166	-24.96834	17.91972
X(4) = -0.000000	-12.50000	26.27499	-41.27499	27.50000

Number of Internal Collocation Points N = 3

Matrix A

X(1) = 0.0000000000	-13.00000	14.78831	-2.66667	1.87836	-1.00000
X(2) = 0.1127016654	-5.32379	3.87298	2.06559	-1.29099	0.67621
X(3) = 0.5000000000	1.50000	-3.22748	-0.00000	3.22749	-1.50000
X(4) = 0.8872983346	-0.67621	1.29099	-2.06559	-3.87298	5.32379
X(5) = 1.0000000000	1.00000	-1.87836	2.66667	-15.78831	13.00000

Matrix B

W(1) = 0.000000	71.00000	-107.27486	56.00000	-42.72514	23.00000
W(2) = 0.277778	48.45334	-69.85264	28.52304	-14.49357	7.39682
W(3) = 0.444444	-5.00000	14.51501	-21.33333	18.81832	-7.00000
W(4) = 0.277778	6.40380	-12.64929	25.57220	-75.38546	56.05875
W(5) = 0.000000	24.50000	-45.54268	60.00000	-129.45732	90.50000

is

$$u_2 = 0.112706654 \qquad T(u_2) = 0.8457032$$

$$u_3 = 0.5 \qquad T(u_3) = 0.4149591$$

$$u_4 = 0.88 + 2983346 \qquad T(u_4) = 0.083804845$$

The comparison of the solution obtained for N = 3 and N = 5 gives the following Table AIV.1.

REFERENCES

Carey, G. F. and Finlayson, B. A. (1975), "Orthogonal collocation on finite elements," *Chem. Eng. Sci.*, vol. 30.

Finlayson, B. A. (1972), *The Method of Weighted Residuals and Variational Principles*, Academic Press, New York.

Hansen, K. W. (1971), "Analysis of transient models for catalytic turbular reactors by orthogonal collocation," *Chem. Eng. Sci.*, vol. 26, p. 1555.

Villadsen, J. V. and Steward, W. E. (1967), "Solution of boundary-value problems of orthogal collocation," *Chem. Eng. Sci.*, vol. 22, pp. 1493--1501.

Villadsen, J. V. and Steward, W. E. (1969), "Solution of parabolic partial differential equation by a double collocation method," *Chem. Eng. Sci.*, vol. 243, pp. 1337--1349.

Villadsen, J. V. and Michelsen, M. L. (1978), "Solution of differential equation models by polynomial approximation," Prentice-Hall, Englewood Cliffs, New Jersey.

Appendix V
Bifurcation Solution of
Nonlinear Operator

The bifurcated solution of the nonlinear operator equation can be analyzed by means of weak perturbation theory. Consider the operator equation

$$x = \lambda Ax$$
$$A(\theta) = \theta \tag{AV.01}$$

and assume the small change of operator A

$$x = \lambda Ax + \epsilon fx \tag{AV.02}$$

where

  f = fixed element
  ϵ = small parameter.

Suppose next that the following representation is valid

$$Ax = Bx + C_k x + Dx \tag{AV.03}$$

where

    B = linear, continuous operator (Frechet derivatives)
    C_k = homogeneous form of the order k, and the operator S satisfies

$$\lim_{\|x\| \to 0} \frac{\|Dx\|}{\|x\|^k} = 0 \tag{AV.04}$$

Let

  λ_0^{-1} = dominant eigenvalue of the operator B
  e_0 = eigenvector of the operator B referring to λ_0^{-1}

$$\lambda_0 B e_0 = e_0$$
$$\| e_0 \| = 1$$

(AV.05)

Let ℓ satisfy equation

$$\lambda_0 B^* \ell = \ell$$

(AV.06)

where

$B^* = $ linear operator adjoint with B.

The functional ℓ is chosen to satisfy the scalar product relationship

$$(\ell, e_0) = 1$$

(AV.07)

According to the Krasnoselski Theorem, bifurcation of equation (AV.01) occurs when the spectrum of the operator B contains the value 1. Let E be an invariant space generated by the eigenvectors of B and E_1 the subspace generated by the eigenvector corresponding to the eigenvalue 1. According to Riesz (Krasnoselski et al. 1969), the space E can be presented as a direct sum of two invariant subspaces

$$E = E_1 + E^1$$

(AV.08)

The representation of the function $x \in E$ in the form

$$\left. \begin{array}{l} x = u + \phi \\ u \in E_1 \\ \phi \in E^1 \end{array} \right\}$$

(AV.09)

defines the projection operators P_1 and P^1:

$$P_1 x = u$$

(AV.10)

$$P^1 x = \phi$$

(AV.11)

which commute with operator B. Perturbation of the operator A causes the change of the eigenvalues λ. For small perturbation, the representation

$$\lambda = \lambda_0 + \nu$$

(AV.12)

is valid.

Taking into account equations (AV.03), (AV.08), and (AV.12), equation (AV.01) can be rewritten in the form

$$0 = \nu u + (\lambda_0 + \nu)\, P_1 [C_k(u + \phi) + D(u + \phi)] + \epsilon P_1 f \qquad \text{(AV.13)}$$

$$= (\lambda_0 + \nu)\, B\phi + (\lambda_0 + \nu)\, P^1 [C_k(u + \phi) + D(u + \phi)] + \epsilon P^1 f \quad \text{(AV.14)}$$

It is convenient to assume that

$$P_1 f = e_0 \qquad \text{(AV.15)}$$

(Otherwise the parameter ϵ can be rescaled $\epsilon_1 = \epsilon \ell(f)$.)
Substituting (AV.15) into (AV.13) one can obtain

$$\epsilon = -\nu \ell(u) - (\lambda_0 + \nu)\, \ell[C_K(u + \phi) + D(u + \phi)] \qquad \text{(AV.16)}$$

Combining (AV.16) with (AV.14) one can get an equation expressing ϕ as a result of the operator equation

$$\phi = (\lambda_0 + \nu)\, B\phi + R(u, \phi, \nu) \qquad \text{(AV.17)}$$

In the subspace E^1 the operator B does not have 1 as the eigenvalue and the operator

$$(I - (\lambda_0 + \nu)\, B)^{-1}$$

is defined. The function can be expressed in the form

$$\phi = (I - (\lambda_0 + \nu)\, B)^{-1}\, R(u, \phi, \nu) \qquad \text{(AV.18)}$$

It can be proved (Krasnoselski et al. 1965), that equation (AV.18) satisfies the assumption valid for the Newton-Kantorovic successive approximation method and therefore the solution of

$$\phi = Q(\nu, u) \qquad \text{(AV.19)}$$

is available.
Substituting (AV.19) and (AV.15) into (AV.13) one can get the equation

$$0 = \nu u + (\lambda_0 + \nu)\, P_1 \{C_k[u + Q(\nu, u)] + D[u + Q(\nu, u)]\} + \epsilon e_0 \quad \text{(AV.20)}$$

from which u can be obtained.
Equation (AV.20) operator in E_1 subspace which non-emptiness implies the phenomenon of bifurcation. Therefore the number and quality of the solution of equation (AV.20) define the solutions of (AV.02). Let us examine equation (AV.20).

Table AV.1.   Types of Functions $\nu(\xi)$ for ϵ and χ_0 as Parameters

	$\epsilon = 0$	$\epsilon > 0$	$\epsilon < 0$
$k = 2$ $\lambda_0 \chi_0 < 0$			
$k = 2$ $\lambda_0 \chi_0 > 0$			
$k > 2$ k even $\lambda_0 \chi_0 < 0$			
$k > 2$ k even $\lambda_0 \chi_0 > 0$			
$k > 2$ k odd $\lambda_0 \chi_0 < 0$			
$k > 2$ k odd $\lambda_0 \chi_0 > 0$			

Let

$$u = \xi e_0 \tag{AV.21}$$

or equivalently

$$\xi = \ell(u) \tag{AV.22}$$

and substitute to equation (AV.20) one can get

$$0 = \nu\xi + (\lambda_0 + \nu)\ \ell\{C_k[\xi e_0 + Q(\nu, \xi e_0)] + D[\xi e_0 + Q(\nu, \xi e_0)]\} + \epsilon \tag{AV.23}$$

Introducing the parameter χ_0

$$\chi_0 = \ell(C_K, e_0) \tag{AV.24}$$

and substituting into (AV.23) the following is obtained

$$0 = \nu\xi + \lambda_0\chi_0\xi^\kappa[1 + \psi(\nu, \xi)] + \epsilon \tag{AV.25}$$

where

$$\lim_{\nu, \xi \to 0} \psi(\nu, \xi) = 0$$

In practice, the simplified equation is considered

$$\nu(\xi) = -\frac{\epsilon}{\xi} - \lambda_0\chi_0\xi^{k-1} \tag{AV.26}$$

which is obtained from (AV.25) assuming ν, ξ sufficiently small. Equation (AV.26) expresses the change of the eigenvalues due to perturbation of the operator A. It should be emphasized that the shift of the eigenvalues depends on the leading nonlinearity, i.e., the first term in Taylor's expansion of the operator A following the linear term B. In Table A.V.I. the types of functions $\nu(\xi)$ for ϵ, χ_0 as parameters are summarized by Krasnoselski et al.

REFERENCES

Kontorovic and Akilov, G. P. (1977), *Functional Analysis*, Nauka, Moscow.
Krasnoselski, M. A., Vainikko, G. M., Zabreiko, P. P., Rutickii, Ya. B., Stecenko, V. Ya., (1969), *Approximate Solution of the Operator Equations*, Nauka, Moscow.

Appendix VI
Attractors for Differential
Equations

The Reduction Theorem cited in Chapter 11 permits the qualitative analysis of the local behavior of nonlinear systems. This theorem emphasizes the role of the eigenvalues located on the imaginary axis, i.e., the case when bifurcation can occur.

The question arises as to what types of system behavior, following a bifurcation, one can expect. Two-dimensional systems can bifurcate only to a new singular point or a periodic orbit. Such structures are known as attractors. A more precise definition follows.

An attractor for a differential equation is a compact set Λ such that all points sufficiently close to Λ tend to Λ when the time tends to $\pm\infty$. The set of different equations obeys "Axiom A" when Λ is connected (finite numbers of attractors).

For n dimensions $(n > 2)$ strange attractors may exist. An attractor is called strange if it does not reduce to a fixed point or a periodic orbit. An example of a strange attractor is the Lorentz attractor. Consider the system of equations

$$\left.\begin{array}{l} \dot{x} = -\sigma x + \sigma y \\ \dot{y} = -xz + rx - y \\ \dot{z} = xy - bz \end{array}\right\} \qquad \text{(AVI.01)}$$

The right-hand side of equation (AVI.01) vanishes at the point (0, 0, 0) which is thus a steady state solution. For $r < 1$ this is the only steady state solution and it is attracting because the matrix of partial derivatives of the right-hand side of equation (AVI.01) at point 0, given by

$$\frac{\partial x_i}{\partial x_j} = \begin{bmatrix} -\sigma - \lambda & +\sigma & 0 \\ -z + r & -1 - \lambda & -x \\ y & x & -b - \lambda \end{bmatrix} \qquad \text{(AVI.02)}$$

has only real negative eigenvalues.

For $r > 1$ the origin loses its attracting character and 2 near steady-states appear

$$
\left.
\begin{aligned}
S_1 &= (\sqrt{b(r-1)},\ \sqrt{b(r-1)},\ r-1) \\
S_2 &= (-\sqrt{b(r-1)},\ -\sqrt{b(r-1)},\ r-1)
\end{aligned}
\right\}
\qquad \text{(AVI.03)}
$$

For S_1 and S_2 eigenvalues obtained from (AVI.02) have negative real part. However, if

$$
r > 6(\sigma + b + 3)(6 - b - 1)^{-1} > 0 \qquad \text{(AVI.04)}
$$

then the complex pair has a positive real part.

As a result we have 3 steady-state solutions, none of them attracting. Lorentz studied equation (AVI.01) for the following values: $\sigma = 10$, $b = \frac{8}{3}$, $r = 28$. For these values the phase-portraits display chaotic nature such that after a large number of computations they occupy the whole volume.

The Lorentz attractor is not unique. Another example of a strange attractor is the Rikitake dynamo, i.e., the system of equations

$$
\left.
\begin{aligned}
\dot{x} &= -\mu x + zy \\
\dot{y} &= -\mu y - \alpha x + xz \\
\dot{z} &= 1 - xy
\end{aligned}
\right\}
\qquad \text{(AVI.05)}
$$

Dynamic systems that have the property of a strange attractor are met quite often. The turbulence of the flows, generation of vibrations in a laser, oscillation of reduced pyridine nucleotide in a cell, non-isothermal chemical reactions, etc., can be treated as strange attractors.

The ergodic properties of the motion in zones of instability are so far unknown (1981). The old dispute between Einstein and Bohr about the deterministic or stochastic nature of phenomena is still open.

Index